Women and Education in Latin America

Women and Change in the Developing World

Series Editor
Mary H. Moran, Colgate University

Women and Education in Latin America

Knowledge, Power, and Change

edited by
Nelly P. Stromquist

Lynne Rienner Publishers · Boulder & London

To Gail Kelly (USA) and Julieta Kirkwood (Chile),
whose analyses of gender in education and society
gave us lasting insight

Published in the United States of America in 1992 by
Lynne Rienner Publishers, Inc.
1800 30th Street, Boulder, Colorado 80301

and in the United Kingdom by
Lynne Rienner Publishers, Inc.
3 Henrietta Street, Covent Garden, London WC2E 8LU

Library of Congress Cataloging-in-Publication Data
Women and education in Latin America : knowledge, power,
  and change / edited by Nelly P. Stromquist.
    (Women and change in the developing world)
    Includes bibliographical references and index.
    ISBN 1-55587-777-X (pbk. : alk. paper)
    1. Women—Education—Latin America. 2. Education and state—Latin
America. 3. Education—Economic aspects—Latin America.
I. Stromquist, Nelly P. II. Series.
LC1912.W66 191
376'.98—dc20   91-22989
                                                                      CIP

British Cataloguing in Publication Data
A Cataloguing in Publication record for this book
is available from the British Library.

Printed and bound in the United States of America

The paper used in this publication meets the requirements
of the American National Standard for Permanence of
Paper for Printed Library Materials Z39.48-1984.

▲
Contents

Part 1 ▲ Education, the State, and the Economy

Part 2 ▲ Women and the Formal Education System

9   Women and Popular Education in Latin America
    Marcy Fink   171
10 Vocational Training and Job Opportunities for Women in
    Northeast Brazil
    Elena Viveros   195

Part 4 ▲ Making Changes

11 Altering Sexual Stereotypes Through Teacher Training
    Gloria Bonder   229
12 Women and the Microsocial Democratization of Everyday
    Life
    Beatriz Schmukler   251
13 The Women's Rural School: An Empowering Educational
    Experience
    Ximena Valdes   277

    Contributors   303
    Index   305
    About the Book   310

▲

Tables

vii

▲

Preface

This book is offered in an attempt to fill a gap with regard to gender issues in Latin America. While there are strong feminist currents in that region, studies of the economic and social conditions of women still represent a small proportion of the body of social science research. Moreover, the attention to gender issues has tended to focus primarily on economic issues, such as the condition of women in the formal and informal sectors of the labor market, their participation in domestic and subsistence production, and the sex segregation that occurs in occupations and professions. Some attention has been given to the problems of family and marital violence and, more recently, to the role of women in the survival of the family under conditions of economic crisis. Much less attention has been given to the role of education in socialization and how women experience the educational system. Thus, a major agency in the production of ideologies that serve to reproduce—or that could possibly serve to question—gender relations has been relatively unexamined.

We need not only to examine education as it relates to women, but to see it as a gendered experience with its own dynamics and consequences. In the chapters that follow, there are important commonalities and differences. The shared themes are those of the persistent subordination of women in various levels and aspects of the educational system, and in the consequences of education for life chances. The differences are highlighted through the various disciplinary voices that come forth in the chapters. These voices reflect women's multiple perceptions of their lives, experiences, and needs as seen through the lenses of such disciplines as sociology, economics, political science, psychology, and popular education. These voices are also new in North American academia because the work of many of the contributors—all well known in their respective countries and even in the region—appears here for the first time in English. Edited books can be weak if their contributions are too discordant. On the other hand, their strength derives from their ability to produce a choir of voices, all vocalizing the same theme but each adding its own distinct yet complementary perspective. In this regard, this anthology weaves disciplinary diversity into the twin themes of social justice for women and the need to alter social relations.

Nelly P. Stromquist

▲

Introduction

Nelly P. Stromquist

▲ The Latin American region shows a greater degree of social and economic development than many other developing areas. Diverse indicators, such as the GNP per capita, life expectancy, access to potable water, and literacy levels, are better in Latin America than in Africa, South Asia, and the Middle East.

The post–World War II years brought a substantial expansion in education in Latin America. The growth in primary and secondary education was extensive and sustained in the 1950s and 1960s. In the subsequent decade, a dramatic growth in higher education ensued and has kept stable over time. Statistics for the region today show that in the majority of Latin American countries primary school enrollment is almost universal, even though a few cases of insufficient student coverage exist (primarily in Central America). Secondary school enrollments also show progress, as 9 out of 19 Latin American countries register student enrollments of at least 50 percent of the corresponding age group. In higher education, the proportion of those ages 20–25 attending college is 17 percent, a figure that compares very favorably with those of other developing areas (that of Africa being 2 percent; Asia, 7 percent; and the Arab states, 12 percent [UNESCO, 1988, pp. 2–33]).

The educational statistics presented in Table 1 show that formal schooling in Latin America has a tendency toward gender parity: The differential between men's and women's enrollments is minimal at the primary school level and small at the secondary school level. The gender gap is slightly more sizable at the university level; on the other hand, in 4 of 12 cases, the participation of women exceeds that of men at this level (in Argentina, Cuba, Nicaragua, and Panama).

We can get only limited comfort, however, from the above statistics. Gross enrollment rates are not indicators of system performance because they reveal only the initial conditions in any one academic year. They do not identify the number of children who completed their grade or cycle of studies, much less whether the students were successful in the acquisition of

1

Table 1. Gross School Enrollment Rates in Latin America by Gender, 1986

	Primary Education		Secondary Education		University Education	
	Women	Men	Women	Men	Women	Men
Argentina	109	109	79	68	42	36
Bolivia	75	83	24	28	—	—
Brazil	99	108	—	—	11	11
Chile	109	110	73	67	14	18
Colombia	74	72	56	55	13	14
Costa Rica	88	87	44	41	—	—
Cuba	94	95	89	84	25	20
Dominican Rep.	126	121	61	68	—	—
Ecuador	117	117	53	51	26	39
El Salvador	62	61	16	12	12	16
Guatemala	70	82	—	—	—	—
Honduras	101	102	36	31	8	11
Mexico	113	115	54	56	12	19
Nicaragua	77	72	57	27	10	8
Panama	89	90	51	44	30	22
Paraguay	84	86	24	25	—	—
Peru	120	125	61	68	—	—
Uruguay	109	111	—	—	—	—
Venezuela	110	110	50	41	22	31

Source: UNESCO (1988), cited in Birgin and Kisilevsky (1989).
Note: Dashes indicate data not available.

knowledge. Indicators that more closely approximate educational performance are the repetition and dropout rates. Data on primary school repetition indicate that women repeat by the same proportion as or slightly less than men (UNESCO, 1988). On the other hand, girls tend to drop out of school in larger numbers, which accounts for their generally lower levels of educational attainment and the considerably higher levels of illiteracy among adult women.

Even though women's participation shows a trend toward gender parity at the university level, the concentration of women in a few fields, defined as conventional for their gender, continues. Most of the female students are in the humanities and social sciences. Engineering and agronomy continue to be masculine fields. The selection of fields at the university level is conditioned by previous high school studies. Within vocational education at that level, women are represented mostly in commercial fields, and only a small number are enrolled in technical schools. Data from Argentina for 1986, for instance, show that 50 percent of the women in vocational education were in commercial schools and only 22 percent in technical schools (Birgin and Kisilevsky, 1989, quoting Gallart).

As in many other parts of the world, the experience girls have in schools is significantly different from that of boys. The messages they receive through the curricula, teacher practices and attitudes, and textbooks gradually incorporate men and women into traditional gender structures and social relations—in which women are defined as having first and foremost a maternal role to play while men are characterized as those to whom the public world and decisionmaking belong.

▲ Education of Women as a Subject of Study in Latin America

Because an educational system has been in existence in Latin America longer than in the other developing areas, certain events and conditions in Latin American countries reveal scenarios other developing countries are likely to encounter further down the road. Thus the examination of educational issues and problems in this region offers lessons to ponder.

With the help of the social sciences, educational analyses have outgrown much of the initial naivete that characterized them until the 1960s and have incorporated the notions of power and ideology into the understanding of the production and transmission of knowledge. Significant scholarly attention has been paid to the role of education in producing a dominant ideology and in exerting social control. (Pertinent examples are Bourdieu and Passeron, 1977; Baudelot and Establet, 1975; Althusser, 1971; Gramsci, 1971; and those of their U.S. interpreters, such as Bowles and Gintis, 1976; Carnoy, 1982; Carnoy and Levin, 1982.) Several observers have concluded in fact that organized education is a highly political affair (Hargreaves, 1985; Carnoy, 1990; Torres, 1990).

In studies of education in Latin America, attention has also centered on the role of state policies in shaping educational processes and life outcomes of citizens. Those concerned with social and economic inequalities have focused attention on the relationship between education and life chances inasmuch as education affects workers, particularly proletarian laborers (Morales-Gomez and Torres, 1990; Torres, 1990). On the other hand, there has been limited consideration of the processes by which the state shapes the content of women's education and how women experience educational messages and processes on a daily basis. Given the recognition of education as a major transmitter of consolidated values and norms in society, the issue of women and education has received significantly less attention than it merits. There have been a number of studies dealing with sexual stereotypes in textbooks, but other dimensions of education, such as the education/work relationship, parental attitudes toward the education of children, and students' development of attitudes and values, are extremely limited. One study that involved a detailed examination of educational investigations in Chile (a country whose research environment is unquestionably one of the most developed in the region) concluded that "the educational condition of women in Chile has not been researched in a systematic and comprehensive manner" (Rossetti, p. 97).

Recent additions to the field of adult education (in particular, Torres, 1990) have brought to the fore the social control role of education and have even recognized it as the principal ideological apparatus of the state (Carnoy, 1990). Yet these researchers have remained oblivious to the education women receive, and to how women experience and perceive this education.

Why has so very little attention been given to gender as a major social marker? Several reasons come to mind. The awareness of gender problems as a social question did not emerge until the 1970s. Within the feminist movement—which has been dynamic and increasingly strong in Latin America—there was also an awareness that education increases the individual's capacity to act. At the same time, however, there was a still firmer belief that the priority for social change lay in the modification of inequitable structures such as those regulating the labor market (and reflected in the level of income and type of jobs women had) and in women's control over their bodies (affecting in turn women's ability to shape freely their sexuality and the number of children they desired). A third factor is that formal education in Latin America is still seen as essentially pedagogical; the contributions of the social sciences to education are relatively new. Therefore, the political, social, and cultural features of education have not usually been subject to examination and questioning in that part of the world.

It also must be remembered that the mechanisms the educational system uses for the reproduction of gender relations are subtle. Although rates of participation in the various educational levels and disciplines reveal gender inequalities, they are the end products of a long chain of subtle and relatively small processes that occur through the daily interaction among teachers, administrators, students, and parents. The school's curriculum objectives usually refer to personality development, participation in social change, and participation in work without explicitly mentioning gender issues. In fact, the overt curriculum may say very little about gender, as Rossetti (1988) found in her review of programs and plans of study enacted between 1968 and 1981 in Chile.[1] The subtlety of the gender-producing mechanisms of the educational system makes time-intensive, observational methodologies necessary. In countries where research funds are limited, this type of investigation calling for field research is infrequent.

French feminists have identified the silence and the absence of women in key areas of society as the major forms of women's oppression (Marks and de Courtivron, 1980). This premise is valid when applied within the educational system. In education the most effective method of transmission of gender relations is not through explicit reference to the prescribed conditions for men and women but through the avoidance of these issues, while in practice— through everyday discourse and ordinary events—building gender asymmetries. In other words, by making the curriculum officially gender-neutral while genderizing the social practices of the school (e.g., through the presence of sexual stereotypes in textbooks, the presence of men in authority positions, and the higher occupational expectations toward boys that teachers often hold), the school conveys the message that gender does make a difference and that this social marker is to be accepted as a given. By being a nonissue, the question of gender is taken for granted and thus neither examined nor changed.

Education outside the formal system, commonly labeled nonformal education (NFE), is very active in Latin America. Known in the region mainly as *popular education*, this type of education generally addresses marginal adults who failed in the formal system or who did not have an opportunity to attend it. This education is characterized by forms of knowledge that are of an emancipatory nature—knowledge that questions the status quo and seeks its transformation. In the case of women, many popular education programs cover basic needs such as health and infrastructural services (water, sewage, electricity). These issues appear at first sight intimately linked with the definition of women as mothers and housekeepers, but if done correctly, they can serve as a bridge between the state institutions and the women's private world. To this extent, the mobilization of women through participation in popular education programs constitutes an effort toward democratization that deserves further study.

▲ Education's Role in Hegemony

Education as a social institution fulfills a critical role in the transmission of representations and beliefs about the "appropriate" and "natural" social order. Acceptance of and respect for the multiple institutions of society (from family to state) are solidified through the school experience. Education builds consensus, which in turn sustains the hegemonic thinking of society. Education plays a key role in the process of social reproduction and control. For women, it plays the role of conveying traditional messages about women's reproductive functions in household and family and about productive functions in "feminine" occupations.

The consensus created by the school system is functional for the established order. It is dysfunctional only for those who play a subordinate role and may subsequently wish to change it. One of the reasons education has been designed so that it produces a negative effect upon women is that not every social actor participates in consensus creation. Most women are persuaded by the educational system and come to accept its overriding message.

Some women, as they are exposed to influences outside the educational system and through the experience of their adult lives in the world of work and the family, are able to create ruptures from the impacts of conventional education and to assume a critical position toward it. Ruptures tend to occur at higher levels of education (university) or outside the formal education system (popular education). But because relatively few women succeed in this rupture and engage in alternative understandings of social relations, patterns of domination and resistance coexist.

The subordination of women is anchored in both ideological and material conditions. It is plausible that ideological conditions emerged first, as an early consequence of biological differences and the state of technologies dealing with them at that time. Although technological developments have since contributed to liberate women from some physical and biological constraints (the use of physical force in work activities and the constraints of menstruation come to mind), the ideology that developed around the notions of femininity and masculinity persists today. It is also clear that ideological and material conditions have evolved so that they reinforce each other, producing a comfortable position for both capitalist and working men. The reality of gender is such that people do not simply play roles but are made to live identities—a more pervasive and unavoidable social feature.

There is wide recognition that the state expands the educational system primarily to create more appropriate citizens and more efficient workers rather than individuals who question current social arrangements. To some extent undeservedly, the expansion of schooling increases the belief that education does offer social mobility and hence increases the social belief in its role in meritocracy. The role of the state in the education of women operates mostly to reproduce the dominant thought and discourse. It seldom engages in efforts to call attention to instances of discrimination and inequality.

The state plays a key role in the education of women via its monopoly of the school system. Through its monopoly of formal education, it shapes the "supply" of schooling—the quantity and content of schooling, the types of personnel working in schools, and the overall learning experience. And through the manipulation of the supply of schooling, the state further affects the demand for schooling. The more that knowledge becomes codified, the more that formal education will be needed to provide and certify this knowledge. Predictably, under these conditions the state will continue its hold over education.

Today, the existence of gender inequalities in education in general and the subordinate position of women in particular are not the result of deliberate policies of exclusion but rather the persistence of unchallenged social norms regarding the social roles of men and women. The state affects women's education by acts of omission: by endorsing a curriculum content that takes the social system for granted, by allowing the sex segregation of teaching staff to go unchallenged, and by failing to disturb the authority structures that are male dominated. Although some countries have altered the presence of sex stereotypes in school textbooks, these countries are a minority. In Latin America, only Mexico has reportedly taken steps on this matter. For most countries, little in the curriculum fosters what Livingston and Luxton (1989) label "oppositional gender consciousness"—the awareness that gender identities of masculinity and femininity have been arbitrary and constraining for both men and women, and that gender relations have involved domination and oppression of women by men.

Yet, as noted by others, the role of the state is fraught with tension. As Carnoy (1990) explains, the state faces opposing demands: a call for democratization, which requires mass education and increasingly higher levels of education, and a call for reproduction of the economic and social status quo, which requires the maintenance of inequalities in access to school and the unquestioned content of educational programs. In the case of women, the state resolves this tension by providing access to education (although opportunity is more limited at university levels) while maintaining a gender-biased content at all levels of education. The state deploys patriarchal ideologies to keep women restricted in time and circumstance. It endorses and uses the sexual division of labor to hold women responsible for the private sphere and to limit their participation to selected public roles. Public education conveys what Carnoy (1990) terms "state-defined knowledge" (p. x). This knowledge provides learning for women—but it is in fact "old learning" inasmuch as it does not incorporate emancipatory knowledge to envisage, much less produce, a new social equilibrium.

Education can be seen as a dependent variable, itself the product of norms and expectations by other institutions in society. But it can also be an independent variable, creating individual changes that, when aggregated, may foster macrolevel changes.

A question that comes to mind, then, is this: When are spaces or opportunities created in the educational system for the introduction of emancipatory gender ideas? Limited cases do occur, mostly through curriculum change and elimination of stereotypical sexual behaviors. They occur also through new classroom practices of individual teachers who are feminists or profeminists. Gender-related changes, not surprisingly, occur more often outside the school system, and frequently at the adult level, through popular education programs run by women's groups themselves.

Changes in the social environment with implications for the treatment of women in educational systems are those that open up the participation of women in the economy and increase their presence in public office and public agencies. The need for liberal states to be legitimate makes them offer spaces, albeit not the most desirable, for women. Unfortunately, several regions of the world, and particularly Latin America, face conditions that will activate other forms of state response. The need to maintain economic competitiveness and to pay the external debt will force many countries to give priority to economic survival and to consider social improvements at a later time.

▲ Methodological Approach

In a discussion about the condition of women's education, it is necessary to look at all levels, because each level and each type of education contributes its own socializing message and experience. Likewise, it is necessary to consider diverse perspectives. That said, however, a qualification is in order: The reader will quickly realize that all of the contributors to this book are women. This did not happen by a willful exclusion of men, but rather because the researchers known to the editor to be working on problematic aspects of women's education happened to be women.[2]

The research that follows is the product of both conventional and feminist researchers. The latter term is meant to refer to researchers who examine women's educational experiences through in-depth interviews and an understanding of their subjective accounts. Feminist researchers are also those who question sexist assumptions and stereotypes, and whose purpose is to redress the balance by placing more emphasis upon women's lives and by opening the debate about women's experience (Scott, 1985, p. 72).

The chapters present a wide range of data-gathering and analytical approaches. They include the use of structured instruments, observations, and open-ended interviews. They include also quantitative analysis such as bivariate and multiple regression analysis and qualitative/interpretive studies such as life histories and case studies. This all shows that in the search for a greater understanding of the experience of women in society, methods are really secondary and that although there are preferred methods, they should suit the research questions, not the converse.

This book covers both formal and nonformal education (NFE). Attention to formal education is crucial because it represents a sanctioned and massive form of coverage. Although ostensibly committed to norms of equality and merit, schools maintain asymmetries in social relations based on gender, a condition that needs further documentation. Nonformal education covers far fewer individuals, but from a social change perspective NFE is extremely important because it works with adult women who are currently acting out roles of mothers and wives; as they undergo the consciousness-raising process, they will be able to carry out important socialization functions with a substantial multiplier effect. In Latin America today, NFE in its popular education version offers the most liberating and vindicatory forms of education.

The book begins with a discussion of illiteracy by Stromquist. It shows how in Latin America, where parity has almost been attained by girls and boys in elementary education, illiteracy affects more women than men. Although illiteracy is linked to poverty and lack of political and economic power by certain ethnic and racial groups, the sexual division of labor poses an additional burden for women. State policies on literacy reveal a lack of concern regarding the educational conditions of marginal groups and a tendency to offer women literacy programs whose content is designed to perpetuate their roles in the private sphere as mothers and household caretakers.

Very little has been documented about women's educational experiences within schools in developing countries. Contributors Sara-Lafosse and Viveros use different methodological approaches—one quantitative and the other qualitative—to provide a close look at the experiences girls and boys undergo in educational systems and the consequences of these experiences upon their attitudes toward one another, toward family relations, and toward the role of women in the labor force and other arenas of social life.

The relation between education and work is explored qualitatively by Viveros. It should be noted that various theories exist for the selection of jobs by women. One of these theories, expounded by Strober (1984), asserts that white men have entered into a social contract that assures them the best jobs. If such is the case, women learn that certain opportunities are off-limits and prepare themselves for the leftover choices. This pattern receives confirmation in Viveros's in-depth study of three women and one man preparing for occupations in computer programming. The study by Viveros examines a technical school and how it structures both its personnel and training offerings so that, unintentionally and perhaps unconsciously, gender differences are reproduced. The discourse of the four students in the technical school clearly shows how social preconceptions about men's and women's social and family responsibilities affect the students' selection of technical fields and their subsequent search for jobs.

The relationship between education and work is also explored by Catanzarite. She examines this relationship by first demonstrating that official statistics hide women's contribution as well as disadvantaged conditions in agricultural and informal-sector work. Analyzing macrolevel data, including censuses and household surveys, she shows that the linear linkage between education and work is less stable for women than for men because it reflects social disparities in the recognition of men's and women's work.

The chapter by Mendiola examines the impact of the expansion of higher education in Costa Rica on field-of-study choices and income. She finds that the expansion has not significantly decreased gender differences in university enrollment; she finds also that gender differentiation has emerged among universities, a situation derived not so much from the statuses of the universities but rather from the fields of study they provide. Interestingly, although expansion has increased the participation of women in previously male-dominated fields, social stratification of women by field of study has also increased. Tracing the impact of education on income, Mendiola discovers not only that women tend to earn less than men, but that graduates from universities that serve large numbers of women tend to earn less than those from other universities. These findings, precise and recent, cast doubts upon the supposed equalizing power of educational institutions.

Stromquist's chapter on the politics of the university in Peru further contributes to our understanding of gender relationships in Latin American universities. By examining the extent to which radical student politics have considered gender issues, Stromquist reveals that the discourse of the Left— even though concerned with social change and social democracy—has been gender blind and thus unable to define the problem in correct terms.

The issue of coeducation has not been explored in Latin America. It has been examined in other countries, particularly Britain and the United States, where doubts have been expressed about the wisdom of always placing women in coeducational situations. A few studies concerning developing countries have appeared, notably those produced by Lockheed and associates, that analyze the relationship of coeducational/single-sex environments and academic performance, particularly in math (Jimenez and Lockheed, 1989; Lee and Lockheed, 1990). These studies show that in general women do better when they are in a single-sex environment (presumably because they feel less inhibited than when with men), can devote more time to academic efforts, and receive more attention from teachers. These studies, however, take a narrow look at the effects of placing female and male students in single-sex settings. Aspects such as notions about sexuality, the development of affective behaviors, friendships across sex, and beliefs regarding "suitable" roles for men and women are not examined by these studies and deserve investigation, particularly in the context of developing societies, where the status of women tends to be low and where single-sex schools are often associated with the preservation of class elitism. Sara-Lafosse's chapter remedies this situation by comparing a series of outcomes produced separately by coeducational and single-sex schools. She identifies a number of positive consequences for both girls and boys from their attending coeducational schools, particularly in areas pertaining to the development of social friendships, the reduction of stereotypes regarding intellectual attributes of men and women, and the acceptance of more egalitarian roles between men and women in society. Sara-Lafosse's findings suggest that the question of coeducational education must be examined in its societal context, and that in societies where there are strong macho norms, the joint presence of boys and girls in classroom situations may serve to dispel notions of male superiority.

Braslavsky's chapter ties macrolevel data to individual information regarding beliefs and choices about educational and social opportunities. The cumulative impacts of structural and individual factors are woven to formulate an explanation of how young women decide on life projects that tend to place them in a passive role that relies on marriage as the most suitable life option. Another study, also considering macrolevel data, is offered by Rosemberg. Her overview of the educational conditions of women in Brazil cuts through the apparent progress of women in gaining access to all levels of the educational system and reveals how gender discrimination strongly interacts with race. Education and income differentials are, consequently, more strongly evident among black women, who evince narrower occupational distributions than do white women and men of either color.

A relatively common subject of inquiry on the question of gender and education has been the examination of sexual stereotypes in the curriculum, particularly in textbooks. In the Latin American context, this has been done at least in Chile (Magendzo, 1970; Ochoa, 1983), Peru (Anderson and Herencia, 1983), Argentina (Wainerman and Barck, 1984), Brazil (Pinto, 1982), and Colombia (Silva, 1979). However, very little has been done about modifying teaching practices involving sexual stereotypes. Such is the effort undertaken by Bonder, who conducted intensive experimental workshops with women primary teachers for the purposes of making them aware of their gender-based values and attitudes and providing them with the skills and knowledge to modify their sexually stereotyped teaching practices as well as their own lives as gendered subjects. The significant attitudinal changes obtained by Bonder through the workshops cast an optimistic light on the process of social transformation regarding gender issues.

Another issue seldom explored in the study of gender and education concerns the participation of women in teachers' unions. This participation is crucial because it has the potential to enable women both to develop an agenda that responds to their gender interests and to modify the teaching profession so that it incorporates both male and female definitions of "teaching" and "teachers." Cortina's study of the powerful National Syndicate of Educational Workers in Mexico is one of the first of its kind. It identifies the dynamics that characterize union participation, finding that women tend to define themselves as rank-and-file members only, while men tend to see women mostly in social responsibilities within the union and block the few efforts by women to fill more critical positions. The result of these forces is that although women constitute the majority of union members, they occupy very few of the leading policymaking positions.

The study by Schmukler is a phenomenological study of how parents—essentially women—link with school authorities. Understanding this linking process is essential to visualizing the possibilities of change in the educational system that may be brought about through parental participation. Presumably group discussions by parents can aid in the identification of major issues that need change or improvement. But the detailed observation of these school-community meetings and how mothers participate in their agendas provides incisive knowledge of how the school controls participation by mothers and modifies it into support for school activities and avoidance of personal problems. Schmukler's study also shows how women—already fragmented in their private world—enter into bilateral (mother-school) negotiations that prevent the development of either collective or political actors. Several paths exist to the organization of women for education. They can play their maternal roles in bringing out problems their children face in school. This action can be political if they present particular requests and mobilize to negotiate with educational authorities. Schmukler's study also shows the need for microsocial democratization (at home) before schools can be democratized. In the absence of this process, mothers engage in bilateral relations and play roles subservient to school authorities. They do not enter into the definition of problems but rather see as their main responsibility the absence of problems for the school. This means that they accept the status quo defined by the school and concentrate on ensuring their children's success under the terms set by the school.

Two chapters offer contributions in the field of popular education. Valdes, in her description and analysis of the evolution of a rural school for women in Chile, offers valuable insights into the potential and limits of educational interventions among adult working women. She shows that among women workers the discussion of gender must be conducted within the specific framework of their respective occupations because the realities of low-income women are extremely varied and work experiences permeate their understanding of their social conditions. She shows also that the rural school's effectiveness relies on the intense, personal experience it provides for a few days to the women; at the same time, this experience—by offering women a space of tranquility and reflection—constitutes such a unique experience that women seem unable to relate it to their ordinary lives when they return to their homes and communities. This finding identifies one more important problem to be faced in programs seeking to alter gender conditions through collective action.

The other chapter, by Fink, explains the forms and objectives of "popular education" programs for women. It presents an overview of their implementation in Latin America, underscoring the critical role that nongovernmental organizations (NGOs) have played in their success. Although Fink highlights the creativity and usefulness of these programs for improving the conditions of low-income women by facilitating the acquisition of important skills and attitudes at the individual level, she notes that these programs face many obstacles in linking microlevel changes to macrolevel social transformations and in combining critical gender consciousness with the acquisition of skills for ordinary life.

▲ Conclusion

The chapters in this book reveal a bittersweet picture of women's conditions in Latin America. Women are doing much better than before in terms of access to education and years of education attained, but problematical situations remain in several areas: content of curriculum materials; the social and organizational arrangements used in schools, classrooms, and teachers' unions; the presence of women in teachers' unions; women's literacy rates; and the design and scope of nonformal educational programs.

The manifestation of the problems that women face is rather subtle and comes in small doses—but it is persistent and cumulative. Like the grains of rice given almost one by one to beggars in front of Buddhist temples in Nepal but that by the end of the day have grown to a reasonable pile, women's experiences within the relations of gender are seldom dramatic. Nonetheless, the wide array of gender-loaded influences does accumulate and creates a normalcy that is then accepted as the only possible state of affairs.

This is not to say that no women escape these influences. Obviously some do, and some of these go on to write and contribute to books such as this one. But the majority of women grow with social norms and develop social expectations that leave little room for "unconventional" ways of being and thinking.

On the other hand, despite the strong force of the invisible gender practices and relations, women—as any other subjugated group—are capable of acquiring a consciousness of their problem and taking the initiative to modify it. Evidence to this effect is provided by the efforts of Bonder in Argentina with the intensive workshops for teachers in the sexual stereotypes of textbooks and teaching practices, and of Valdes in Chile with the rural school for women. Nonformal education, particularly popular education for adult women, has shown considerable impact. In light of the scarce support by the state for programs that will enable women to shake off their old identities and roles, these programs hold much promise.

The chapters here reveal interesting tensions and contradictions. Women in occupational training are preparing themselves for a job, and having a nondomestic role is helpful. As de Beauvoir remarked long ago, "Work is not a panacea but is the first condition for emancipation" (cited in Marks and de Courtivron, 1980, p. 148). At the same time, these women are being trained in conventional (feminine) occupations and see their salary as complementary to that of the husband.

Women may participate in union activities, but domestic work prevails in defining what roles they can perform most efficiently. Women can participate in university politics, but these are defined in gender-blind fashion. Literacy offers an opportunity for women to decode the world, but the messages of many of these programs are stiflingly conservative.

Mothers, doubly marginalized as women and as parents of schoolchildren, can do very little to affect the education of their children; their own participation is fragmented, and the majority of them tend to be silent and passive for fear of teacher reprisals. Nonetheless, it is possible to encourage group action and address collective problems. Mothers participate more than fathers in school because it constitutes an extension of their domestic role. At the same time, the extension of this role leads them to argue for the resolution of individual problems, which places them in the position of subjects of the school system. They do not move into content change or into questioning the gender nature of the schools, particularly that of the administration. They concentrate on ensuring success of their children by avoidance of school failure.

I nevertheless choose to end with an optimistic note by echoing the observations of Connell (1989) that we should not see schools merely as reproducers of patriarchy: "The effect of such a frame of thought on educational practice is, quite simply, demobilizing. It implies a pessimistic view of teachers, takes an ironic view of the consequences of their work, and tends to view pupils as passively receiving a social imprint" (p. 2). An understanding of the potential and limitations of existing educational programs for women should enable us to identify reliable and effective allies and thus advance in the creation of an altered reality.

▲ Notes

1. It is interesting to observe that it makes very little difference for the treatment of gender in the curriculum whether the regime is liberal democratic, socialist, or authoritarian. Rossetti's review of educational programs in Chile found that, in all cases, the invisibility of gender continued.

2. One man was asked to produce an article for this collection. His heavy research duties and other priorities prevented him from making a contribution.

▲ References

Althusser, Louis. *Lenin and Philosophy and Other Essays*. New York: Monthly Review Press, 1971.

Anderson, Jeanine, and Cristina Herencia. *L'image de la femme et de l'homme dans les livres scolaires péruviens*. Paris: UNESCO, 1983.

Baudelot, Christian, and Roger Establet. *La escuela capitalista*. Mexico, D.F.: Siglo XXI, 1975.

Birgin, Alejandra, and Marta Kisilevsky. *Asisten las niñas a escuelas para varones?* Buenos Aires: FLACSO, September 1989.

Bourdieu, Pierre, and Jean-Claude Passeron. *Reproduction*. Beverly Hills, Calif.: Sage, 1977.

Bowles, Samuel, and Herbert Gintis. *Schooling in Capitalist America*. New York: Harper and Row, 1976.

Carnoy, Martin. "Education, Economy, and the State." In Michael Apple (ed.), *Cultural and Economic Reproduction in Education*. London: Routledge and Kegan Paul, 1982.

———. "Preface." In Carlos Torres, *The Politics of Nonformal Education in Latin America*. New York: Praeger, 1990.

Carnoy, Martin, and Henry Levin. *The Dialectics of Education and Work*. Stanford, Calif.: Stanford University Press, 1982.

Connell, Robert. "Sociology of Education and Curriculum Politics." Macquarie University, Australia, mimeo, 1989.

Gertler, Paul, and Paul Glewwe. "Gender Differences and the Willingness to Pay for Education: Evidence from Rural Peru." Washington, D.C.: World Bank, mimeo, March 1990.

Gramsci, Antonio. *Selections from Prison Notebooks.* New York: International Publishers, 1971.

Hargreaves, Andy. "The Micro-Macro Problem in the Sociology of Education." In Robert Burgess (ed.), *Issues in Educational Research: Qualitative Methods.* London: Falmer Press, 1985.

Jimenez, Emmanuel, and Marlaine Lockheed. "Enhancing Girls' Learning Through Single-Sex Education: Evidence and a Policy Conundrum." *Educational Evaluation and Policy Analysis* 2, no. 2 (Summer 1989), pp. 117–142.

Lee, Valerie, and Marlaine Lockheed. "The Effects of Single-Sex Schooling on Achievement and Attitudes in Nigeria." *Comparative Education Review* 34, no. 2 (May 1990), pp. 209–232.

Livingston, D. W., and Meg Luxton. "Gender Consciousness at Work: Modification of the Male Breadwinner Norm Among Steelworkers and Their Spouses." *Canadian Review of Sociology and Anthropology* 25, no. 2 (1989), pp. 240–275.

Magendzo, Salomon. "Relación entre estereotipos de roles sexuales y libros de enseñanza." In *Educación y realidad socioeconómica.* Mexico, D.F.: Centro de Estudios Educativos, 1970.

Marks, Elaine, and Isabelle de Courtivron. *New French Feminisms: An Anthology.* Amherst: University of Massachusetts Press, 1980.

Morales-Gómez, Daniel, and Carlos Torres. *The State Corporate Politics and Educational Policy-Making in Mexico.* New York: Praeger, 1990.

Ochoa, Jorge. *La sociedad vista desde los textos escolares.* Documento de Trabajo no. 4. Santiago: CIDE, 1983.

Pinto, Regina Pahim. A imagem da mulher atraves dos livros didáticos. *Boletín Bibliográfico de Biblioteca Mario de Andrade* 43, nos. 3/4, 1982, pp. 126–131.

Rosetti, Josefina. "La educación de las mujeres en Chile contemporáneo." In Centro de Estudios de la Mujer, *Mundo de mujer: Continuidad y cambio.* Santiago: Centro de Estudios de la Mujer, 1988.

Scott, Sue. "Feminist Research and Qualitative Methods: A Discussion of Some of the Issues." In Robert Burgess (ed.), *Issues in Educational Research: Qualitative Methods.* London: Falmer Press, 1985.

Silva, Renán. "Imagen de la mujer en los textos escolares." *Revista Colombiana de Educación* 4, 2d semester (1979), pp. 9–52.

Strober, Myra. "Toward a General Theory for Occupational Sex Segregation: The Case for Public School Teaching." In Barbara Reskin (ed.), *Sex Segregation in the Workplace: Trends, Explanations, Remedies.* Washington, D.C.: National Academy Press, 1984.

Torres, Carlos. *The Politics of Nonformal Education in Latin America.* New York: Praeger, 1990.

UNESCO. *1988 Statistical Yearbook.* Paris: UNESCO, 1988.

Wainerman, Catalina, and Rebeca Barck. *La división sexual del trabajo en los libros de lectura de la escuela primaria argentina: Un caso de inmutabilidad secular.* Buenos Aires: Centro de Estudios de Población, 1984.

PART 1

Education, the State, and the Economy

▲ 1

Women and Literacy in Latin America

Nelly P. Stromquist

One of the most basic conceptual skills, literacy, is more evenly distributed across gender in Latin America than in any other developing region. The continent has a literacy gender gap of only 3 percent, in contrast with 21 percent each in Asia and Africa.

Yet before complacency sets in, it is important to realize that this gender differential reflects a chronic condition of a predominantly rural and destitute population of women, in which monolinguism, exhaustive domestic tasks, and racial subordination often form a composite set of obstacles that prevents the acquisition of literacy skills.

The gender gap is strong in rural areas. But it is not simply that the countryside is more "backward" than the city. In many Latin American countries rural life is also characterized by poverty and limited social services, including education. Under those circumstances, women's labor is in great demand for household maintenance.

Clearly the elimination of illiteracy among women will necessitate the elimination of poverty and the redefinition of women's role in society. This solution may be encouraged by other observers of educational systems, but many states do not see it in their best interests to provide literacy for their marginal people, particularly marginal women. Seldom do states oppose the provision of literacy programs, yet seldom do they fund these programs to ensure effective implementation. Thus, the state-offered literacy programs are extremely limited given the existing number of illiterates. And although states offer literacy programs for women, the content of these programs is defined on the basis of traditional women's roles, with women treated exclusively in their capacity as mothers and home managers. The content of literacy programs offered by the state tends to solidify status quo definitions and social representations of women. This content, which inculcates passivity above all, sets up major obstacles to the attainment of effective literacy. In a more diffuse sense, significant obstacles derive from industrial-based models of national development that place priority on the creation of a trained urban labor force, from the social and personal constraints imposed by the current external financial debt, and from the enduring gender ideologies that justify the current sexual division of labor. Under present

19

conditions, the prospects for a definitive reduction of illiteracy among Latin American women are slim.

—Editor

▲   Among all three developing regions—Asia, Africa, and Latin America—one usually recognizes Latin America as the most advanced. With the highest income per capita among the Third World regions, the powerful financial corporations of Sao Paulo and its multiple industrial plants, the gigantic size of Mexico City, and the cosmopolitan life of Buenos Aires, Latin America evokes images of widespread westernization, industrialization, and modernization.

Yet another feature of Latin America is its great diversity. The people in Latin America range from large autochthonous cultures (e.g., in Bolivia, Peru, and Mexico), to those basically European in origin (in Costa Rica and Argentina), to those with a large number of Afro-American inhabitants (in Cuba and Brazil). Not only are the countries different in terms of the people inhabiting them, but their income is one of the most unequally distributed in the world. In this unjust region, the share of wealth by the lowest 20 percent of its population is lower than in either Africa or Asia by approximately half (Sheahan, 1987).

The educational attainment of the population tends to be uneven both among and within countries. Some countries have levels of participation at the university level that surpass those of several European countries; others have literacy levels industrialized countries had more than 100 years ago. In the area of literacy, some progress is taking place. The illiteracy rate for Latin America and the Caribbean in 1985 was 17.3 percent, down from 27.3 percent in 1970. In both years, however, the absolute number of illiterates has been the same: about 44 million (UNESCO, 1988). In this context, illiteracy is a chronic situation. In some Latin American countries, it affects the indigenous populations never fully incorporated into the national system. In others, it hits populations that suffer from uneven distribution of land and inequitable access to the provision of social services, particularly education, housing, and health care. Illiteracy also affects unstable low-income populations. In Mexico, for instance, illiteracy is very high among the migrant workers in agricultural production (*población golondrina*), estimated to be 700,000, and among the semiproletarian population that works temporarily in agricultural fields in the United States, estimated to be 5 million (Schmelkes, 1988).

Although illiteracy levels are relatively low in Latin America compared with those in other developing regions, it must be remembered that in this region illiteracy is occurring parallel to a process of progressively higher levels of education being reached by other social groups. Thus the polarization of the population is increasing, as pockets of illiterates continue to exist while the number of those with complete secondary and university education grows (Tedesco, 1984; Braslavsky, 1988). The implications for socioeconomic and political development derived from a highly polarized population in terms of skills, aspirations, and social affiliation have not been systematically explored; yet it is clear that they forecast serious problems in promoting consensus about national "needs" and "objectives."

Access to primary education has improved greatly in Latin America, and many countries boast of servicing at least 99 percent of the school-age population. Nevertheless, the formal system still faces serious problems of retention, particularly in the first years of primary schooling (Sirvert, 1983; Namo de Mello, 1988). In 12 of 24 countries in Latin America and the Caribbean no more than 70 percent of the children complete primary schooling. Dropout rates are particularly severe between the first and second grades: In half of the Latin American countries more than 10 percent of the students leave school at this transition, and in some countries the rate exceeds 30 percent (REDALF, 1989). Even an advanced country such as Argentina faces serious dropout problems. In 1980 only 46 percent of its primary school population completed studies (Braslavsky, 1988). In contemporary Brazil one-third of the children between 7 and 14 years of age are outside the school (da Silva, 1988).

Numerous educational reforms have described the failure of children to stay in school as the outcome of factors such as "irrelevant content," "lack of fit between education and work," and "poor organization and administration of the educational system" (Sirvert, 1983). Unquestionably, many educational systems in the region are weak in their offerings and management. Yet the generalized poor performance is symptomatic of more profound problems. In the first place, the formal educational system is clearly segregated by class. Upper and, increasingly, middle social classes send their children to private schools; public schools have become the site for the education of the poor. Private schools, having access to greater resources in terms of teaching personnel, materials, and school facilities, are able to provide an education usually superior to that available through the public school system. Moreover, the education of the elite meets worldwide standards. For those children who remain in the public school system, the prospects for a good education—even for basic literacy—are inauspicious: There are crowded schools in the cities, incomplete and badly equipped schools in the rural areas, and untrained teachers or poorly paid teachers who develop a low identification with their profession or who leave for other employment when the opportunity arises.

The public school systems in the region receive a proportion of their national budgets that ranges from 12 to 25 percent. This proportion at first sight appears reasonable, but when examined in light of the student population it must serve, the amount that the governments spend per student is minuscule. The average per-pupil expenditure for primary schooling in the Latin American region is approximately $100 per year. The comparison with the United States—where the average yearly expenditure per student at the primary level is approximately $3,700 (National Center for Educational Statistics, 1989)[1]—reveals a 37-fold difference. This differential, it must be noted, is higher than the differential in average per capita income between the Latin American region and the United States.

Preschool gives an advance opportunity for learning. The concept, however, is having an unintended effect in Latin America. Preschools there are far from servicing the entire population; most of them are private and serve families with at least middle incomes. Data from Argentina reveal that almost all of the centers for children between 3 and 4 years of age and the majority of those for children between 4 and 5 years of age are private and require tuition fees. In that country, 6 of 10 children attend preschool, with many of them attending at least two years. In contrast, 4 of 10 are not attending at all (Tedesco et al., 1983). The absence of preschools among the poor hurts low-income children's chances of succeeding in school or at least becoming literate. Their prevalence among the rich ensures not only that these people will succeed in school but also that they will progress much faster than the poor.

▲ Rural/Urban Literacy Gap

Adult illiteracy is predominant in rural areas, a fact evident in all Latin American countries—and a phenomenon observed worldwide.

An adult's failure to read is associated with poverty, but it is also associated with a poor school environment. In rural areas there is a notorious lack of educational infrastructure, and the teachers who serve there usually have the lowest qualifications in the teaching force. Data for Peru show high rates of teacher and student absenteeism and high rates of student dropout. Moreover, about 65 percent of the teachers lack proper training, and many schools are one-classroom schools (Kalinowski, 1989). It has been estimated that in rural Peru 49 percent finish primary school and only 4 percent complete high school (Kalinowski, 1989, p. 21). Also, very little learning time occurs in rural schools. An observational study by Hornberger (1987) estimated that only 6 percent of the time spent in rural Peruvian schools and classrooms is really "academic learning time."[2] Given these conditions, it is not surprising that in Peru the rates of rural/urban illiteracy have remained constant in the last two decades for which census data are available. In 1972 the proportion of illiteracy was 72 percent in the rural regions; by 1981 it was 70 percent (Kalinowski, 1989). Peru, unfortunately, does not represent an isolated instance. Mexico reported a national primary completion rate of 52.1 percent in 1986 but the much lower completion rate of 10 percent among indigenous schools (Schmelkes, 1988, p. 215).

It has been observed that literacy materials offer poor content because they often present messages and realities devoid of familiar meaning to the neoliterates. Braslavsky (1988) notes deficient literacy materials in several provinces of Argentina. Mexico, which has an active National Institute of Adult Education, still has literacy materials for only 17 of its 56 ethnic groups, as it has not yet developed writing systems for some of these languages. Further, despite its large migrant population, it has no educational programs addressed to that group (Schmelkes, 1988).

Unquestionably, literacy materials could be better designed, yet it is important to see them as consequences of a lack of attention to the problem of illiteracy rather than as a cause for its existence. Marginal and oppressed nationalities within various countries have no political power, and thus their voice, language, and culture are not reflected in educational programs, much less in textbooks. There is a strong association between countries with a large core of indigenous people—generally economically and politically weak—and a high illiteracy rate (see Table 1.1). Such is clearly the case for Guatemala, Bolivia, Peru, Ecuador, and Mexico—all countries with sizable non-Spanish-speaking populations.

There is also an association between poverty and illiteracy independent of linguistic characteristics. Honduras, El Salvador, and Brazil—countries with an exploited rural population, usually with no access to land and dependent upon manual labor for survival—are also afflicted by high rural illiteracy rates, reaching at least 46 percent (see Table 1.2).

▲ Literacy Programs and Women

It is clear that the condition of women's literacy is tied to the condition of men's literacy, which in turn is affected mostly by poverty and social class location. Yet gender differences in illiteracy rates are considerable. According to official statistics (UNESCO, 1988) women in Latin America have an illiteracy rate of 19 percent compared with 15 percent for men. Yet, these figures, derived from census data, notoriously misrepresent the condition of indigenous and rural women. Individuals with solid experience in literacy programs hold that women's literacy rates are usually overestimated in the official counts.

Many articulate voices have decried the condition of the downtrodden, marginal, and oppressed classes in Latin America, yet their discourse makes no distinction between men and women. The absence of specific reference to women prevails today even in publications that explicitly address the relationship between education and democracy (see, e.g., Braslavsky et al., 1989; Braslavsky and Filmus, 1988). By implication, women do not face a separate reality, or their problem is not considered serious enough to merit discussion.

In the history of formal adult education in Latin America, literacy

Table 1.1. Proportion of Indigenous and Illiterate Population per Country

Country	Indigenous as Percent of Population	Illiterate as Percent of Population
Guatemala	59.7	54.0
Bolivia	59.2	36.8
Peru	36.8	17.4
Ecuador	33.9	25.8
Mexico	12.4	18.2
Panama	6.8	15.4
Chile	5.7	11.0
Honduras	3.2	43.1
El Salvador	2.3	38.0
Paraguay	2.3	19.9
Colombia	2.2	19.2
Nicaragua	1.8	42.5
Argentina	1.5	6.1
Costa Rica	0.6	11.6
Brazil	0.2	25.5

Source: UNESCO (1987) and Mayer and Masferrer (1979), cited in CEAAL (1990).

programs focusing on women as beneficiaries are a relatively new phenomenon. Their emergence can be linked to the feminist movement that introduced a widespread awareness of women's subordination in the 1970s. However, as discussed later in this chapter, many of these programs still convey traditional gender roles.

Why do women have lower literacy skills than men? The explanation lies in social causes rather than factors of individual ability. In the rural areas, the sexual division of labor that imposes upon girls and women many domestic duties and responsibilities acts as a major impediment to their further schooling. Girls may attend the first years of schooling, but soon tend to be withdrawn from classes. Today over 90 percent of rural women have attended school at some point in their lives (Gertler and Glewwe, 1990), but research on the obstacles to adult women's literacy in the region has not yet been conducted. Glimpses about these impediments come from anecdotal sources or from studies that describe experiences mainly at the primary level. Hornberger's observation of classroom practices in rural Peru (1987) detected that domestic tasks continue to be conducted by girls even while at school— they help baby-sit the teacher's children or they bring their own siblings to school on their backs.

A literacy campaign was conducted by the government of Ecuador during the period June–September 1989. Through the collaboration of 73,000 literacy teachers (of whom 67,000 were high school students), the program served about 200,000 literacy students. Data from 55 accounts based on visits to the literacy sites by the pedagogical director of the campaign indicate that many of the participants were women. A common obstacle to their participation was opposition by husbands to their leaving the house (because of fear that the women would develop some romantic affair or because they were needed at home to take care of the house and children). Many of the women who did attend the program stated that they were unable to attend regularly because of maternal duties with children and having to perform domestic tasks such as cooking (R. M. Torres, 1990).

The data in Table 1.2 reveal that in all cases of rural residence, women's illiteracy is consistently higher than that of men. Gender differentials range from 0.5 percent (Argentina and Costa Rica) to 16.4 percent (Mexico); these differentials are greater when a large segment of the population speaks a nonofficial language.

Linguistic differences tend to affect women more than men because women, having a more restricted geographical mobility and less access to jobs outside the home, do not interact with people who speak the official language. (For an account of this phenomenon, see the study by Rockhill, 1987, of Latin immigrant women in the United States.) Thus, they develop a more limited competency in the official language of the country; they develop also less need to become literate. Their limited physical world brings them into fewer contacts than men with written messages (e.g., signs on streets and stores, use of money, exposure to mass media); therefore, they have a more limited encounter with "literacy events," which have been found to function as powerful antecedents of literacy.

In Peru women represent 73 percent of the illiterate population, with the great majority of them monolingual in Quechua. Data from national censuses in that country indicate the proportion of illiterates who are women is growing, having moved from 62.4 percent in 1940 to 67.8 percent in 1961 and to 73.1 percent in 1981 (Kalinowski, 1989).

As shown in Table 1.3, rural areas have greater levels of illiteracy than urban areas, regardless of sex—although urban women do not improve the statistics for their sex quite as much as urban men do for theirs (a 27.5 percent illiteracy gap exists between urban and rural women, compared with a 25.4 percent gap between urban and rural men). It is striking, however, to observe that the gender gap in rural areas (12 percent) is double that in urban areas. The disadvantage of rural women is most likely due to the sexual division of labor that places upon them major burdens for domestic work, subsistence production, and various family responsibilities.

▲ The State and Women's Literacy

Literacy programs conducted by governmental agencies have offered and continue to offer messages that are extremely traditional for women in terms of the social and gender ideology aspects of men's and women's roles and in

Table 1.2. Rates of Male and Female Rural Illiteracy by Country, Latin America

Country	Male Rural Illiteracy Rate	Female Rural Illiteracy Rate	Gender Gap[a]
Guatemala	66.6	77.6	11.0
Bolivia	53.2	68.5	15.3
Peru	37.7	53.1	15.4
Ecuador	38.2	44.4	6.2
Mexico	39.8	56.2	16.4
Panama	27.2	29.8	2.6
Chile	25.6	27.9	2.3
Honduras	54.4	56.8	2.4
El Salvador	53.0	57.2	4.2
Paraguay	25.9	32.3	6.4
Colombia	34.7	36.8	2.1
Nicaragua	65.4	67.0	1.6
Argentina	14.6	15.1	0.5
Costa Rica	17.0	17.5	0.5
Brazil	46.4	48.1	1.7

Source: UNESCO, cited in CEAAL (1990).
[a]Gender gap to the disadvantage of women.

distinctive notions of femininity and masculinity. A review of materials used in the literacy programs in Argentina in 1986 found that most phrases in the primers were derived from historical themes and events involving male heroes. The primer's pictures showed men always working and women preparing *mate* (a beverage), cooking, or taking care of children (Braslavsky, 1988, p. 51). As has been documented in other developing countries (see references mentioned in Stromquist, 1989), programs run by the state are often cast in conventional gender roles, depicting women in predominantly domestic activities. These programs generally provide women with knowledge pertaining to basic "female" tasks such as nutrition, child health, and family planning. Even content that has emancipatory features, such as "civic education," has been construed in traditional terms when offered by the state. For instance, such a program for rural women in Peru, conducted jointly by the Ministry of Education (MED) and UNESCO, states in a module on the family that both spouses have equal rights and duties in family decisions and that unmarried people who live together for two years acquire goods and rights as if they were married. The same primer also states that abortion is illegal and that a woman is subject to imprisonment for at least four years if she aborts (MED, 1989). In other words, crucial information affecting women's control over their own bodies is presented as a given, without discussing its implications for women. When discussing existing laws, programs run by the state limit themselves to presenting them without questioning the basis upon which they were built and without raising the possibility that they can be transformed.

Table 1.3. Illiteracy Levels by Gender and Rural/Urban Residence, Latin America (percent)

Country	Urban		Rural	
	Men	Women	Men	Women
Guatemala	20.0	35.5	59.9	77.6
Bolivia	6.2	23.2	37.3	68.5
Peru	3.4	11.8	22.2	53.1
Ecuador	6.9	12.2	32.3	44.4
Mexico	3.6	12.5	23.4	56.2
Panama	4.8	5.6	24.9	29.8
Chile	5.4	7.7	23.6	27.9
Honduras	17.6	24.0	52.1	56.8
El Salvador	12.7	22.2	48.9	57.2
Paraguay	7.4	14.7	19.7	32.3
Colombia	9.0	13.0	32.8	36.8
Nicaragua	16.1	22.1	63.8	67.0
Argentina	3.6	4.5	14.2	5.1
Costa Rica	4.0	5.7	16.6	17.5
Brazil	14.2	19.3	44.8	44.8
Average rural/urban illiteracy gap - Men			25.4	
Average rural/urban illiteracy gap - Women			27.5	
Average gender gap in urban areas			6.3	
Average gender gap in rural areas			12.0	

Source: UNESCO (1987) and Mayer and Masferrer (1979), cited in CEAAL (1990).

In Latin America, nongovernmental organizations (NGOs) have emerged to provide alternative educational programs of a clearly emancipatory nature. "Popular education" distinguishes itself by introducing political awareness and the need for mobilization among the marginal social classes. In all Latin American countries, NGOs offer literacy classes, often truly innovative in objectives and methodology. Yet these programs are seldom especially designed to address women's needs and concerns. In this regard, the rhetoric of popular education is more sensitive to women than is its practice. On the other hand, there are many "popular education" programs run by women. These emphasize raising gender consciousness through a number of issues such as health, housing, and income generation. Few address literacy; thus, the neediest of needy do not become targeted for assistance and do not become incorporated into efforts to help them.

Studies of adult education in Latin America using a political-economy perspective contend that the state considers literacy an important tool to socialize individuals perceived to be outside the mainstream of the political legitimation process. For instance, it has been argued that through literacy programs, the Mexican state ensures the reproduction of its corporatist power structure (Morales-Gómez and Torres, 1990). These authors maintain that the state has engaged in the "provision of literacy training programs that create the illusion of social and economic equality of opportunity and mobility" (Morales-Gómez and Torres, 1990, p. 211). This assertion suggests that a significant deployment of resources by the state has taken place in the interests of literacy. But this is not borne out by the empirical evidence. Traditionally there has been weak governmental support for literacy, and even less for programs that consider the particular conditions of women and the need for a transformation of social relations. Support for literacy programs rarely surpasses 3 percent of most national educational budgets, and reports by those who have closely followed actual expenditures indicate that the resources actually disbursed are often less than the officially budgeted amounts. However, this observation must be counterweighed by the fact that literacy programs tend to be inexpensive because literacy teachers—the largest single cost—are often paid pittances. Thus, governments may obtain much visibility (and thus legitimacy) through small investments. An issue that remains unclear in the understanding of state behaviors in the provision of literacy is its traditionally limited coverage: If adult education programs incorporate marginal people as subject citizens who will accept their situation in life or believe they can succeed only if they try harder, why don't states have more of these programs?

The current world economic crisis, particularly severe in Africa and Latin America, will most likely reduce the already meager state expenditures on literacy. Because those with literacy needs are the poorest and most disadvantaged groups in any country, they also have the least political leverage to become an important constituency. In assessing the low attention given to literacy by the state, C. Torres notes that the literacy clientele is

> composed of peasant and indigenous people; urban marginals; self-employed people in lower rank positions (e.g., street vendors); urban lower-wage workers, usually located in competitive industries and in the service sector (as opposed to those located in monopolized industries and the higher levels of government bureaucracy); people working in personal services in urban and sometimes rural areas (e.g., household jobs, house-cleaning, housekeeping); and the lowest levels of the urban industrial petite bourgeoisie, particularly in those countries with the lowest industrial development. These people could be expected to demand adult education from the State, but they failed to do so because their structural position within the subordinate classes, and their lack of political organization and power, meant they did not participate in the class alliance that gave rise to the political regimes that increased import-substitution industrialization (i.e., developmentalist regimes) (C. Torres, 1990, p. 34).

With the current economic crisis, survival needs will be even greater among the poor. As noted by a member of an NGO in Peru actively committed to literacy programs:

The economic situation prevails [over other conditions], forcing children to work from early ages, in the countryside as well as in the city. Today, as a result of the economic crisis, dropping out of school has increased. Who is able to buy books and uniforms, to afford bus fares and tuition fees (in the case of private schools)? We do not need a formal study to know that education is becoming increasingly elitist, that it is increasingly the privilege of social classes that can afford the expenses necessary to guarantee a good education for their children. If the State is not capable of guaranteeing the minimal general education for children in ages 8–10, can it guarantee the education of adults and neo-literates? (*Jornada*, 1989).

Under current conditions, most international attention is going to formal education. The new slogan, "education for all"—a strategy adopted by four of the major development and donor agencies (the World Bank, UNDP, UNESCO, and UNICEF)—makes no clear and direct reference to the problem of adult illiteracy. At the international meeting held in Jomtien, Thailand, to discuss a plan of action for "education for all," only UNESCO—the agency with the smallest financial resources for education—reportedly expressed a commitment to address literacy (*NORRAG News*, 1990).

▲ Conclusion

In many countries the literacy gap between rural and urban areas, which seriously affects women, is likely to persist. Various forces account for this: national development models that give priority to industrial development and to men as workers; the inability of poor families to provide their children with a literate environment or to send children to preschool to attenuate disadvantaged home effects; the early incorporation of girls and boys into domestic duties in low-income families; and the lack of programs targeting women as beneficiaries.

The illiteracy problem of women is situated at the crossroads of class and gender subordination. That illiteracy is a sociopolitical and structural problem has been said many times before. It is a correct diagnosis and one that demands a complex and sustained solution. It appears with increasing clarity that the "illiteracy" problem will not go away until other social measures affecting the economic level, social acceptance, and life chances of marginal individuals are in place. Whether only a revolutionary society can accomplish this is a matter of political strategy beyond the scope of this chapter. What can be stated in conclusion is that the elimination of illiteracy among women will call for more than a redistribution of income and other resources. It will call also for a different social ordering, one in which poor women have overcome ideologies and social representations of men as powerful and assertive and women as their abnegating, self-effacing companions.

Governments and organized citizens need to reflect on their current national development strategies. On the one hand, increasing the numbers of those who get secondary and higher education increases the numbers of people with higher skills and reduces wage differentials. On the other hand, to reduce poverty there should be first an initial emphasis on universal literacy and primary education (Sheahan, 1987). Clearly, poverty and illiteracy feed each other, and to break this vicious circle might mean acting simultaneously on both.

The intimate relationship between primary education and adult literacy has been known for many years. Yet educational policies invariably serve mostly the young, ignoring that their skills will be lost if their parents are not brought into the literacy world at the same time. Earlier UNESCO resolutions and experts such as Ferreiro (1988) have recognized the need for a two-pronged approach to literacy. It is evident that it is necessary to work both at the primary level and with the education of adults (specifically parents). Parents who are not habitual readers can hardly create reading environments for their children. A recent empirical investigation (Alvarez, 1985) further substantiates this. The study was based on a sample of 2,400 children of ages 7 to 14 in 18 rural municipalities in Colombia. Using logit regression analysis, Alvarez found that if the head of household was illiterate, the probability of the children reaching third grade decreased by 9 percent.

The International Literacy Year (1990), or ILY, sponsored by UNESCO, has created the opportunity to express concern for problems of illiteracy, to have international meetings with high visibility, to issue beautiful posters, and to have charming ideas such as the "book voyage."[3] In all, UNESCO attracted only $375,000 to implement the ILY. It remains to be seen, however, how this rediscovery of literacy will be followed by national and international budget allocations to address the needs of those who cannot read. The prospects for any considerable attention to literacy are weak; in the case of women, they appear even weaker.

▲ Notes

1. US statistics combine elementary and secondary school expenditures because the reporting is by school district. The combined per-student expenditure for 1989 was $4,700; the elementary school costs were calculated by assuming secondary school costs to be 25 percent higher than those for primary school, a proportion frequently quoted by school authorities.

2. Hornberger considers as academic learning time only the time the teacher was delivering a lesson, not when the students were working independently in their notebooks or copying materials from the blackboard to their notebooks. This definition of academic learning time may have underestimated the actual learning that occurred in the observed classrooms.

3. The "book voyage" was an international project involving a series of books in which people who have recently learned to read and write drew or expressed messages in their own language to share with others around the world.

These books traveled from literacy center to literacy center, from country to country, during the UN ILY; in the end, national and international books were produced (*International Literacy Year 1990*, 1989).

▲ References

Alvarez, Elsa Ramírez de. *Educación y trabajo: Dimensiones de la vida infantil en el medio rural*. Annex 3. Bogota: Pontificia Universidad Javeriana, mimeo, October 1985.

Braslavsky, Cecilia. "Perspectivas de la educación y de la alfabetización en Argentina en el marco de la transición a la democracia." In UNESCO/OREALC, *Alternativas de alfabetización en América Latina y el Caribe*. Santiago: UNESCO/OREALC, 1988.

Braslavsky, Cecilia, and Daniel Filmus. *Respuestas a la crisis educativa*. Buenos Aires: FLACSO/CLACSO, 1988.

Braslavsky, Cecilia, Luiz Antonio Cunha, Carlos Filgueira, and Rodolfo Lemez. *Educación en la transición a la democracia: Casos de Argentina, Brasil y Uruguay*. Santiago: UNESCO/OREALC, 1989.

Carnoy, Martin. "Education, Economy, and the State." In Michael Apple (ed.), *Cultural and Economic Reproduction in Education*. London: Routledge and Kegan Paul, 1982.

CEAAL (Consejo de Educación de Adultos de América Latina). *Carta mensual*. Santiago: CEAAL, February 1990.

da Silva, Teresa. "Lo ya hecho y lo que queda por hacer para alfabetizar a la población brasileña." In UNESCO/OREALC, *Alternativas de alfabetización en América Latina y el Caribe*. Santiago: UNESCO/OREALC, 1988.

Ferreiro, Emilia. "Alternativas a la comprensión del analfabetismo en la región." In UNESCO/OREALC, *Alternativas de alfabetización en América Latina y el Caribe*. Santiago: UNESCO/OREALC, 1988.

Gertler, Paul, and Paul Glewwe. "Gender Differences and the Willingness to Pay for Education: Evidence from Rural Peru." Washington, D.C.: World Bank, mimeo, March 1990.

Hornberger, Nancy. "Schooltime, Classtime, and Academic Learning Time in Rural Highland Puno, Peru." *Anthropology and Education Quarterly* 18, no. 3 (September 1987), pp. 207–220.

International Literacy Year 1990. Newsletter of the International Task Force on Literacy, no. 7, December 1989.

Jornada. "1990. Año Internacional de la Alfabetización." Lima: Accion Educativa, May 1989.

Kalinowski, Dina. *Alfabetización con video: Una propuesta, una realidad*. Lima: Ministerio de Educacion, 1989.

Mayer, Enrique, and Elio Masferrer. "La población indígena de América en 1978." *América Indígena* 30, no. 2 (1979).

MED (Ministerio de Educación). *Cartilla de alfabetización: Mujer y familia*. Lima: Proyecto de Alfabetización y Educación Cívica. Peru: Sede Huancayo, Ministerio de Educación, 1989.

Mello, Guiomar Namo de. "Enseñanza primaria: Las estrategias de la transición democrática." In Cecilia Braslavsky and Daniel Filmus (eds.), *Respuestas a la crisis educativa*. Buenos Aires: FLACSO/CLACSO, 1988.

Morales-Gómez, Daniel, and Carlos Torres. *The State, Corporatist Politics, and Educational Policy-Making in Mexico*. New York: Praeger, 1990.

National Center for Education Statistics. *The Condition of Education 1990.* Washington, D.C.: U.S. Department of Education, 1989.

NORRAG News. "What Happened at Jomtien and the Beginnings of Follow-up." No. 8, June 1990.

REDALF (Red Regional de Capacitación de Personal y Apoyos Específicos en los Programes de Alfabetización y Educación de Adultos). *Educación de adultos: La acción de la REDALF.* Santiago: REDALF, UNESCO, 1989.

Rockhill, Kathleen. "Gender, Language, and the Politics of Literacy." *British Journal of Sociology of Education* 8, no. 2 (1987), pp. 153–167.

Schmelkes, Sylvia. "La política educativa mexicana y la atención prioritaria a las poblaciones marginadas." In UNESCO/OREALC, *Alternativas de alfabetización en América Latina y el Caribe.* Santiago: UNESCO/OREALC, 1988.

Sheahan, John. *Patterns of Development in Latin America.* Princeton: Princeton University Press, 1987.

Sirvert, María Teresa. *La mujer y el proyecto principal de educación en América Latina y el Caribe.* Santiago: UNESCO, May 1983.

Stromquist, Nelly. "Challenges to the Attainment of Women's Literacy." Paper presented at the symposium on "Women and Literacy: Yesterday, Today, and Tomorrow," Nordic Association for the Study of Education in Developing Countries, Hasselby (Sweden), June 1989.

Tedesco, Juan Carlos. "La universidad: Problema de todos." *Educación Hoy* 14, nos. 83–84, May–December 1984.

Tedesco, Juan Carlos, Cecilia Braslavsky, and R. Carciofi. *El proyecto educativo autoritario: Argentina 1976–1982.* Buenos Aires: FLACSO-GEL, 1983.

Torres, Carlos. *The Politics of Nonformal Education in Latin America.* New York: Praeger, 1990.

Torres, Rosa María. *El nombre de Ramona Cuji.* Quito: Editorial El Conejo, 1990.

UNESCO. *Compendium of Statistics on Illiteracy.* No. 30. Paris: Division of Statistics on Education, Office of Statistics, UNESCO, 1988.

UNESCO/OREALC and Ministerio de Educación. *La alfabetización en el grupo de los 8.* Lima: Ministerio de Educacion, 1987.

▲2

Education, Democratization, and Inequality in Brazil

Fulvia Rosemberg

A consequence of powerlessness is not being able to attract research attention to problems one considers important. In the case of women, many important educational issues remain understudied. Yet, as Rosemberg's study shows, available census data can be analyzed to understand gender conditions. Her study further explores the intersection between gender and ethnicity, a phenomenon especially relevant in a country such as Brazil.

Women have been gaining increased access to education in that country, and they now represent fully half of all students. Inequalities emerge in years of educational attainment of men and women, in fields of study pursued by the two genders, and in the remuneration similar levels of education produce for men and women.

These findings are well known in the context of other countries. Rosemberg's contribution resides in showing that the gender hierarchy—at least in the Brazilian context—is subordinate to the race hierarchy. The inferior remuneration of women versus men is more pronounced than that of blacks versus whites, an intriguing outcome given the fact that blacks as a group attend poorer schools than whites. Without access to more direct data, we can only surmise that society determines values regardless of actual training and that women learn, through schooling and other social experiences, not to question monetary rewards. That this phenomenon occurs in other countries of the region is suggested by a study by David Post (1990), which found that girls in Peru across all social classes expected to earn less than boys.

—Editor

▲ In Brazil the post of minister of education has been held by a woman, and women have been and still are in charge of state and municipal education offices. Women have figured prominently in the formulation of educational policies and in the administration of the country's educational system. In 1980 they accounted for 87 percent of Brazil's teachers,[1] and half of all Brazilian students were women in 1982. In spite of these facts and figures, it can be said that the system of formal education in Brazil discriminates against women. How can this apparent paradox be explained?

As in other countries around the world, sexual discrimination in education has shifted in Brazil. Rather than hindering women's access to the educational system, it now affects those within the system. Although access to education has increased admirably in Brazil, the education of men and of women is fundamentally different. Despite the principle of coeducation, a veritable sexual ghetto exists in schools. By not adopting an antisexist stance, Brazilian schools continue to reinforce sexual stereotypes. The labor market also persists in its discriminatory recognition of the education of men and women. Men have access to better occupational opportunities, and they receive more compensation for services rendered.

▲ Educational Situation of the Brazilian Population

Over the past several decades Brazil has embraced a project for national development that has led to intense urbanization and the pursuit of a modern, expanding economy. The nation responded to the economic, social, and cultural demands that urbanization creates by expanding its educational opportunities and by scarcely altering an educational system that had been inadequate for centuries.[2]

Brazil has succeeded in democratizing and modernizing education considerably. A good indicator of educational opportunities in Brazil is the schooling index, the ratio of schooled individuals to the general population. It jumped from 9.05 per 100 in 1940 to 21.84 in 1980 (Rosemberg and Pinto, 1985, p. 19).

Despite these advances, the level of education in Brazil remains low. The population 5 years and older has on the average only 4.5 years of schooling in 1987. Recent surveys also point to many persistent and crucial distortions in the education system. For instance, it is estimated that one-fourth of Brazilians 10 years of age and older cannot read or write (Ferrari, 1985, p. 36). Even among youths 15 to 24, the most literate age group, the illiteracy rate is still high, at 10.6 percent in 1987.

In 1980, 23 percent of Brazilian children between the ages of 7 and 14 did not have access to a school, and in elementary schools, one-fourth of all students failed a grade and had to repeat. Of 100 children enrolled in first grade in 1978, only 5.9 entered the first year of university in 1989.

As in other dimensions of social life, educational opportunities are not equally distributed among the different segments of the Brazilian population. White urban residents in the south have access to the best education (Rosemberg and Pinto, 1985, pp. 31–37). There is also a strong correlation between education and the family's socioeconomic status. Generally speaking, in families that make at most the equivalent of two minimum-salary incomes, dependents receive at most elementary education. Only those students whose families make more than the equivalent of five minimum salaries really consider higher education.

In essence, despite educational reforms and the relative increase of educational opportunities, the Brazilian system of education still withholds education from large segments of the population and favors others, conferring an elite status on a fortunate few. This elitism within the system has compelled Brazilian educators to create theoretical systems for analysis, definitions of priorities, and political-action proposals. Some educators say that the Brazilian educational system must make knowledge heretofore available only to elite groups available to all students (Barreto et al., 1979; Mello, 1982; Saviani, 1983). Instruction in reading, writing, and arithmetic has become the battle cry of some educators who wish to eliminate what they consider to be nonessential instruction from the system. In this realignment of educational priorities, there is a risk that, once again, gender and racial discriminations will be overlooked.

▲ Educational Situation of Brazilian Women

The few surveys of women's education in Brazil concentrate on limited themes and have been developed in conjunction with studies that pertain to general education. Although the studies address issues ignored in the past, many of them are fashioned directly or indirectly by theoretical models developed in the male universe, and as a result they reflect the concept that the goal of education is the production of skilled labor (Salm, 1980, p. 28). Clearly, such models ignore the possibility that education is also interdependent with many other conditions, such as the availability of economic resources. It is also evident that many studies attribute the same significance to both the education of men and the education of women. For instance, studies do not consider the fact that for adolescent girls of certain classes, the primary role of school has been that of guardian and protector. At conferences and seminars on education, rescuing the question of women's education from the common grave of other themes has been an almost impossible endeavor. Analyzing the specifics of the education of women is clearly not a priority for researchers, nor for the government agencies responsible for funding research.

General research pertaining to the Brazilian woman is equally limited. In keeping with the tendency of feminism to favor the working woman, "woman and work" was the main theme of research until the end of the 1970s (Costa, 1985). Such favoritism hindered any attempt to push beyond work-related considerations. In addition, Brazilian educational statistics have not always included data pertaining to the sex variable.

The absence of studies, census information, and research pertaining to the educational situation of black women is even more accentuated.[3] Researchers have seldom debated racial discrimination. Until recently, white feminists practically ignored the specific conditions of discrimination suffered by black Brazilian women. The absence of debate results in part from the generally promoted myth that Brazil is the kingdom of racial democracy. Why discuss something that is not a problem? Why research racial differences in the kingdom of equality if that will call attention to discrimination? Only six of Brazil's nine national censuses have gathered information on race, and even that information was nonspecific. Ministry of Education officials do not include the racial origins of students and teachers in their annual report on Brazil's education system.[4]

The Brazilian system of education also conceals its prejudice against blacks by subordinating racial discrimination to class origin. The reasoning is that because most of the black population is poor, observed differences between blacks and whites can be attributed to poverty, not to race. This is a comfortable way of thinking that thrusts racial discrimination in education into limbo and begs the issue of educational priorities.

Schooling and Literacy

Women have benefited from the expansion of education in Brazil and now participate in the school system in the same proportions as men. In 1987, 51.5 percent of the 34.4 million students in Brazil were women. Although women have yet to enter all levels of education in the same numbers as men do (see Table 2.1), statistics indicate a tendency toward equalization. In 1987, 44.6 percent more women and 38.8 percent more men entered all levels of education than in 1970.

Women also account for much of the increase in literacy over the past several decades.[5] Whereas 8.2 percent more men were literate than women in

Table 2.1. Female Participation as a Proportion of Students Age 5 and Older, Brazil 1970, 1980, and 1987 (percentages)

School Level	1970	1980	1987
Elementary	49.2	50.1	50.9
Adult elementary (accelerated program)	40.8	48.7	—
Secondary	50.7	53.4	58.5
Adult secondary (accelerated program)	35.4	40.6	—
College preparatory	36.4	47.2	—
Higher education			
Undergraduate level	42.4	49.2	52.6
M.A. level	—	46.0	—

Sources: Fundação IBGE, *Censo Demográfico 1970, Brasil* and *Censo Demográfico 1980, Brasil*; Fundação IBGE, *PNAD 1987, Brasil* (excluding rural population).

1940, the percentage difference in 1980 was a mere 1.3 percent for the population five years of age and older (see Table 2.2).

As in other Latin American countries, the Brazilian women most likely to be illiterate are those who are poor, older, black, and live in rural regions. Some 1987 figures (for the population five years of age and older) illuminate this point:

1. In the northeast, 1 of every 2 women is illiterate, compared with the southwest, where the rate is 1 in 5.
2. In rural areas, 1 in 2 women is illiterate; the rate in urban areas is 1 in 5.
3. Illiteracy is more prevalent among Brazilians 50 years of age and older, 34 percent of whom are illiterate; the group with the highest rate of literacy is women between the ages of 15 and 19, only 8 percent of whom are illiterate.
4. One of every three black women is illiterate, whereas one of every five white women is illiterate.

Instruction

Educational attainment (years of school completed) is extremely low for both male and female populations; nonetheless, it has been increasing slowly. Statistics indicate that men and women have almost equal access to education, yet significant differences persist among the races. On the average, black women remain in school for 3.1 years, while white women remain in school for 5.3 years (see Table 2.3).

Different paths, different destinations. Previous studies have shown that the education system formerly discriminated against women by preventing access to schools (Rosemberg, 1982; Rosemberg and Pinto, 1985), but sexual discrimination now seems to affect those within the education system by supporting fundamental differences in societal expectations for men and women. Men tend to enter technical and scientific fields, while women enter such fields as the humanities, education, and health (see Table 2.4). Schools seem to be laying a comfortable trap for women, encouraging them to choose areas of study that prepare them for a variety of types of work, even if it means they will eventually accept jobs for which they are overqualified. For example, a degree in the humanities prepares students for many types of jobs. However, because jobs in the humanities are not specialized and there is a large work force available to fulfill them, they do not pay as much as jobs that require technical knowledge, most of which are held by technically trained men.

There is some indication that the black population falls into the same trap.[6] On the one hand, the white male population concentrates on university

Table 2.2. Literacy Rates Among Brazilian Population, 1940–1980 (percent)

Age Group	1940 Census			1950 Census			1960 Census			1970 Census			1980 Census		
	A	B	C	A	B	C	A	B	C	A	B	C	A	B	C
5 to 9	13.5	14.1	50.4	12.6	13.4	50.9	18.9	19.6	50.0	28.8	30.2	50.7	28.3	30.4	51.2
10 to 14	39.3	40.3	50.3	42.8	44.7	50.9	59.1	61.1	50.7	68.3	71.8	51.2	71.6	76.7	51.5
15 to 19	46.2	44.5	50.5	52.6	52.8	52.0	65.1	66.8	52.5	74.0	76.8	52.2	81.2	85.7	52.0
20 to 29	51.6	41.0	45.7	57.4	49.4	47.8	68.7	63.0	49.6	73.4	70.1	50.1	83.5	83.0	50.6
30 to 39	54.0	36.7	40.2	57.1	43.4	43.1	67.9	57.1	—	71.1	62.7	47.6	78.1	73.9	49.3
40 to 49	50.8	31.8	36.6	54.7	37.3	39.2	62.4	48.6	—	66.7	55.6	45.0	73.1	65.4	47.5
50 to 59	49.1	30.0	36.5	52.0	32.5	37.3	—	—	—	61.6	47.6	43.0	67.7	57.8	46.5
60 +	43.1	25.7	40.3	45.9	28.9	40.6	—	—	—	54.5	39.0	43.0	55.7	43.6	46.6
Unknown Age	56.2	44.2	48.5	36.8	25.4	44.5	46.3	41.2	48.1	34.0	30.4	46.7	48.7	43.9	46.5
Total	42.3	34.1	44.7	46.0	39.3	46.4	55.7	50.6	47.8	62.0	58.7	49.0	68.6	67.3	50.1

Sources: Fundação IBGE, demographic censuses for 1940, 1950, 1960, 1970, and 1980, Brazil.
Note: A = male literacy; B = female literacy; C = female percentage of the total literacy figure. Also, the 1960 census grouped the ages differently, making it impossible to have a full breakdown.

Table 2.3. Average Years of Schooling of People Age 10 and Older by Region, Race, and Sex, Brazil, 1987

Region	Men	Women	Total	White			Black			Mixed		
				M	W	T	M	W	T	M	W	T
North[a]	4.9	5.0	5.0	5.8	6.0	5.9	3.3	3.8	3.5	4.6	4.7	4.6
Northeast	2.8	3.3	3.1	3.8	4.2	4.0	2.1	2.3	2.2	2.4	2.9	2.6
Southeast	5.3	5.1	5.2	5.9	5.7	5.8	3.7	3.5	3.6	4.1	4.1	4.1
South	5.0	4.9	4.9	5.3	5.2	5.2	3.8	3.5	3.7	3.2	3.1	3.1
Center-West	4.6	4.8	4.7	5.4	5.6	5.5	3.0	2.9	3.0	3.8	4.1	3.9
Total Brazil	4.5	4.6	4.5	5.4	5.3	5.4	3.2	3.1	3.1	3.3	3.5	3.4

Source: Fundação IBGE, 1987.
[a]Excludes the rural population of this region.

studies that are directed toward technical specialization, which leads in turn to higher-paying jobs; on the other, black women tend to enroll in education, the humanities, and social sciences and for the most part are destined to become teachers (see Table 2.5). The paths of black men and white women seem to lie between these two extremes. Many black men enroll in business administration, economics, and accounting programs, and these majors prepare them for a relatively wide spectrum of jobs, just as schooling in the humanities, social sciences, and education does for women.

Obviously, Brazilian schools do not force their students to follow certain careers,[7] but a student's liberty to choose his or her career is determined by the socialization experience. Social institutions encourage black men, white women, and especially black women to assume the jobs in which they are most likely to succeed.

Educational qualifications: A necessary yet insufficient tool. A recent series of studies shows that the labor market does not give consistent recognition to the education that is acquired by different segments of the population. Several studies show that women are paid less than men even when they have the same education, and that the "contrast between salaries for men and women is even clearer when dealing with those who have secondary and university education" (Bruschini, 1985, p. 52).

Studies of the social situation of black Brazilians also indicate that although education grants them social mobility, it does not guarantee them the same benefits enjoyed by whites (Hasenbalg, 1983, p. 183; Carneiro and Santos, 1985, p. 6). The studies suggest that whites not only make more money than blacks of the same educational level, but that the difference increases with the level of education (Oliveira, 1985; Hasenbalg, 1983; Silva, 1980).

Data pertaining to years of education, earnings, sex, and racial origin for

Table 2.4. **Women's Participation in Levels and Fields of Education, Brazil 1970 and 1980 (population 10 years and older, by percent)**

	1970	1980
General Schooling	49.9	50.2
Elementary	49.9	50.5
Secondary	54.2	47.6
Trade/Vocational Schooling	—	63.1
Agricultural	4.3	9.5
Commercial	28.7[a]	42.7
Industrial	11.7	19.9
Health	88.0[b]	70.7
Military	4.6	34.1
Education (Elementary)	94.7	95.8
Other	26.2	48.0
University Level[c]	—	44.6
Biological & Health Sciences	—	40.6
Medicine	10.7	24.0
Physical Education	54.7	52.6
Exact & Technological Sciences	—	18.2
Agrarian Sciences	—	9.7
Humanities and Social Science	—	53.8
Psychology	—	86.2
Education and Art	—	84.4
National Defense	—	1.1
Other	—	51.3
Masters and Doctorate Degrees[d]	—	32.0
Biological & Health Sciences	—	27.8
Exact & Technological Sciences	—	17.1
Agrarian Sciences	—	11.3
Humanities and Social Science	—	38.2
Education and Art	—	70.2
Undetermined	—	51.2

Source: Fundação IBGE, demographic censuses for 1970 and 1980.

[a]Covers commercial and science-related statistics.

[b]Refers only to nursing.

[c]1970 percentages could not be calculated due to different grouping of the various fields of education.

[d]The 1970 census did not register this information.

the state of Sao Paulo show that for each level of education there is a hierarchy of average salary: White men are at the top, followed by black men, white women, and finally, receiving the lowest salaries, black women (see Table 2.6). In other words, the earnings of white women and black women are lower than those of white men and black men with the same education.

These statistics[8] give rise to the following points:

Table 2.5. Fields of Higher Education According to Sex and Race, Sao Paulo, 1980
(percentages)

Field	Black Men	White Men	Black Women	White Women
Engineering	10.0	27.3	—	—
Law	20.0	27.3	6.7	21.1
Medicine	—	13.6	—	5.3
Dentistry	—	—	6.7	—
Business administration, economics, and accounting	35.0	22.7	6.7	5.3
Humanities, social sciences, and education	10.0	4.5	73.3	47.4
Exact and biological sciences (except medicine)	10.0	4.5	—	10.5
Others	15.0	—	6.7	10.5
Total	100.0	100.0	100.0	100.0

Source: Counselors and family members of the Council of the Feminine Condition and members of the black community.

Table 2.6. Average Earnings of Individuals Age 10 and Older by Level of
Instruction, Years of Schooling, Race, and Sex, Sao Paulo, 1980
(in cruzeiros)

Years of Schooling	Academic Level	Men		Women	
		White	Black	White	Black
0 to 3	Incomplete elementary	10,390	8,334	4,965	4,461
4 to 7		14,544	10,447	6,852	5,483
8 to 10	Complete elementary	19,578	13,267	9,526	7,379
11	Complete high school	32,078	19,692	14,919	10,890
12 to 13	Incomplete university	32,326	23,040	14,728	12,361
14 and over	Complete university	66,880	40,014	24,750	20,380
Average		19,530	10,178	9,996	5,680

Source: Special tabulations of data from Fundação IBGE, *Censo Demografico 1980, Brasil.*

1. The greatest discrepancy in earnings appears in a comparison of the earnings of white men and black women, especially in jobs requiring higher education. In the economically active population (EAP) with the highest degree of schooling, black women earn 30.5 percent of what white men earn.

2. The least accentuated discrepancy in salary appears in the comparison of white women and black women, even among those with high levels of education.

3. For all levels of education, the difference between the salaries of white men and the salaries of black men is less than the difference between the salaries of white men and those of white women.

4. The difference between the salaries of white men and those of white
women is greater than the difference between the salaries of black
men and those of black women. White women earn less than 50
percent of what white men earn, while black women earn slightly
more than 50 percent of what black men earn.

One of the widespread arguments supporting these discrepancies claims
that men and women and blacks and whites have different work schedules—
that black men and all women earn less than white men because they work
less. Recent studies have shown that this is not true and that, in fact, the
black population tends to work longer hours than does the white population.[9]
According to several studies of the Brazilian labor force,[10] salary
differences are the result of discrimination against different populations
within the labor market. Also, wage inequality may reflect discrimination in
the educational system because whites and blacks, men and women, do not
go to the same schools, just as the poor do not attend the same schools that
the rich attend. The same educational level can conceal different levels of
training, whether it be in the quality of instruction or in the types of courses
that schools provide their students. Rosenberg, analyzing schools in the city
of Sao Paulo in 1981, observed that the "underprivileged population" was
serviced by "underprivileged schools" that were unable to offer the necessities
for adequate learning.[11] Information gathered on the different schools attended
by whites and blacks suggests a similar trend: Many more black students
attend poor-quality schools than do whites. As a result, the education system
has been providing white students with better training, so whites have an
advantage when competing for jobs (Rosemberg, 1986).

In addition, by the nature of the courses they offer, different schools
prepare students for certain types of careers. As already demonstrated, schools
tend to prepare women and blacks for jobs of lesser importance within the
labor market.

▲ Conclusion

Those who seek to establish a truly democratic society have denounced the
roles that schools play in reinforcing dominant ideology. As one researcher
has stated:

> When a social organization is racist, it not only displays discriminatory
> practices but also limits the motivation and aspirations of blacks. The
> black population's ascendent social mobility is limited by both white
> discrimination and internalization (by the majority) of an unfavorable
> self-image. This negative view of the blacks begins in school books,
> being permanently conveyed by the racist aesthetics of mass media and
> incorporated into a set of stereotypes and popular representations. Thus,

there is a mutual reinforcement of discriminatory practices, the tendency to avoid discriminatory situations, and symbolic violence against blacks regulating their aspirations according to the impositions of the dominant racial group and its definitions of "appropriate place" for colored people (Hasenbalg, 1983, p. 91).

Recent literature has revealed that educational structures are also responsible for transmitting bipolarized sexual models. There is evidence that sexist patterns exist in student/teacher relationships, a condition that reflects not only society's discriminatory values but those of the educational system as well. There is also strong evidence that the curricula and didactic material used at all educational levels, from preschool to university, discriminate against women.

The Brazilian educational system must recognize the existence of economic, racial, and sexual discrimination and take mobilizing action. Given that blacks and women are often channeled into fields of learning that prepare them for jobs that pay less than those held by white males, there would be little sense in establishing racial and sexual quotas in universities. Because women and blacks often receive academic preparation inferior to that of white males, there also would be little sense in establishing labor quotas. Rather, equal education must begin with a deep debate of the conditions and gender ideology underlying education.

▲ Notes

1. These figures and others presented throughout this chapter come from the Fundação IBGE 1970 and 1980 demographic censuses and the 1982 PNAD, wherever another source is not stated.
2. Following is a brief description of the Brazilian educational system: *elementary education*—duration of 8 years, designed to prepare children and preadolescents in the 7–14 age bracket, mandatory; *secondary education*—duration of 3 or 4 years, designed to prepare adolescents, not compulsory. Elementary education beyond general instruction should provide vocational inquiry and work initiation. Secondary education's main objective is to prepare for a profession.

There is also a supplemental educational system of elementary and secondary education for youths and adults designed to offer them the education not acquired at the right time to complete unfinished schooling, or to perfect and update acquired information.

Higher education—access is not automatic. A student must take a selective exam (*vestibular*). Higher education is composed of undergraduate studies (university level), certification, graduate studies (master's and doctorate), extension, in-service training, and specialization.

The Brazilian educational system is made up of (1) private groups—responsible for 20 percent of the enrollment in 1982 and (2) public groups, accounting for the remainder. The latter are classified according to whether they are funded by municipal, state, or federal government. The administrative responsibilities are distributed according to educational levels and the various geographic regions of the country. Administratively, the formal higher educational system is subordinate to the Ministry of Education at the federal level and to the Offices of Education at the state and municipal levels.

3. Currently, sectors of civil society concerned about racist manifestations in Brazil have used the expression *black population* when referring to blacks and mulattoes. The combination of the two groups recognizes that racial, social, economic, cultural, educational, and symbolic discrimination—contrary to general assumption—does not spare offspring of mixed marriages.

4. The Statistics Service of Education and Culture (SEEC/MEC, connected with the Ministry of Education) is responsible for educational statistics at the federal level.

5. The 1970 and 1930 censuses considered literate all people able to read and write at least a simple message in their language.

6. Information about the presence of racial segments in fields of higher education was collected from counselors and family members of the Council of Feminine Condition and the Council of the Black Community for the State of Sao Paulo.

7. Selective educational orientation can be detected at the high school level: public schools, where the greatest percentage of students is black, are not only scarce in neighborhoods of greater black populational density, but they do not offer the same professionalizing options as do the private schools (see Franco, 1983).

8. These figures immediately confirm comments already made by Carlos Hasenbalg and Nelson do Valle Silva (1984, p. 42): "Considering the different positions white women and black men hold as family providers and the low earnings black women contribute to the family's support, it is possible to conclude that there is strong inter-racial disparity in the distribution of family earnings." They do not, however, validate the hierarchy of privileges for the four population segments, based on race and sex association, currently promoted (Hasenbalg and Silva, 1984; Carneiro and Santos, 1985): white men, white women, black men, and black women. On the contrary, these figures suggest that despite the equal educational opportunities for men and women and the ever-greater access of white women to higher levels of education, the labor market still treats women as second-class workers.

9. Average weekly hours worked by people in Greater Sao Paulo were 44.7 among blacks and 43.1 among whites; median weekly work hours were 47.7 among blacks and 44.8 among whites (figures for the period October 1984–July 1985, SEADE/DIEESE, 1985, p. 17).

10. Cristina Bruschini (1985) points to occupational segregation as one of the factors responsible for salary variance observed between the sexes: "As long as job openings for women are very limited and the number of workers grows, female salaries will continue to be proportionately smaller than those of men. There are too many workers available for 'women's jobs' at the same time that the positions carry less prestige because they reflect women's position in society" (Bruschini, 1985, pp. 50–51). Later the author adds: "Other factors besides occupational segregation can have an important role in explaining salary discrimination: Women's limited access to administrative and supervisory positions; their difficulty in making demands, a direct consequence of the socializing process that wants women to be docile and submissive; the smaller political-syndicated tradition of tertiary activities, where women are concentrated, as compared to those of the transforming industry" (Bruschini, 1985, p. 51; see also Paiva, 1981).

Nelson do Valle Silva's studies are also directed to interpreting salary

differences between whites and blacks in the light of racial discrimination by the labor market. In the conclusion of his study about black men residing in Greater Rio de Janeiro the author states:
These observations have some theoretical and practical implications. Although inferences taken from data for the period can be very risky, the data does not support the hypothesis that, when non-whites [the term Silva uses to refer to the black population segment] invest in education, imposed obstacles will be removed. On the contrary, they seem to indicate that, at least in the short run, as long as the *market structures* [emphasis added] are maintained, the salary differential between races can increase when non-whites increase their educational level, as the figures show that these differentials increase with the degree of schooling. Therefore, prospects of racial equality in Brazil seem quite remote despite the extraordinary tenacity of the "racial democracy" myth (Silva, 1980, p. 43).
11. Maria Malta Campos, researching the struggle for elementary education in two neighborhoods adjacent to Sao Paulo, also verifies that "the one-school appearance is deceiving. It actually encompasses various possible routes, maintained by various mechanisms considered 'inefficient' or 'poorly adjusted' but integral parts of a class-determined society's educational system" (1982, p. 341).

▲ References

Barreto, Elba Siqueira de Sa, et al., 1979. "Ensino de 1o. e 2o. graus: Intencao e realidade." *Cadernos de Pesquisa*, no. 30, pp. 21–40.
Barroso, Carmen L. de Melo (ed.), 1982. *Mulher, sociedade e estado no Brasil.* Sao Paulo: Brasiliense/UNICEF.
Bruschini, Cristina, 1985. *Mulher e trabalho: Uma avaliação da decada da mulher, 1975 a 1985.* Sao Paulo: NOBEL.
Campos, Maria Machado Malta, 1982. "Escola e participação popular: A luta por educação elementar em dois bairros de Sao Paulo." Ph.D. thesis, University of São Paulo.
Carneiro, Sueli, and Thereza Santos, 1985. *Mulher negra: Politica governamental e a mulher.* Sao Paulo: NOBEL/Conselho Estadual da Condição Feminina.
Costa, Albertina de Oliveira, 1985. "Pesquisa sobre mulher no Brasil do limbo ao gueto." *Cadernos de Pesquisa*, vol. 54, pp. 5-15.
Ferrari, Alceu R., 1985. "Analfabetismo no Brasil: Tendencia secular avanços recentes: resultados preliminares." *Cadernos de Pesquisa*, vol. 52, pp. 35–49.
Franco, Maria Laura P. Barbosa, 1983. "O ensino de 2o grau: Democratização? Profissionalização? Ou nem uma coisa nem outra?" *Cadernos de Pesquisa*, vol. 47, pp. 18–31.
Fundação IBGE, 1987. *Pesquisa Nacional por amostra de domicilios, 1987, Brasil, Cor da População.* (Rio de Janeiro, Fundacao IBGE, 1987).
Gouveia, Aparecida Joly, 1980. "Origem social, escolaridade e ocupação." *Cadernos de Pesquisa*, vol. 32, pp. 3–30.
Hasenbalg, Carlos A., 1983. "1976—As desigualdades sociais revisitadas." In *Movimentos sociais urbanos, minorias étnicas e outros estudos: Ciências Sociais Hoje*, vol. 2. Brasilia: ANPOCS.
Hasenbalg, Carlos A., and Nelson do Valle Silva, 1984. *Industrializacao,*

emprego e estratificação social no Brasil. Rio de Janeiro: Marco Zero.

Kerstenetzky, Isaac, et al., 1979. "Indicadores sociais da educação." In Brasilia Senado Federal, Comissão de Educação e Cultura, *Projeto educação: Conferências, pronunciamentos e depoimentos*. Brasilia: Senado Federal, vol. 3, pp. 17–93.

Lewin, Helena, 1977. *Mão de obra no Brasil: Um inventário crítico*. Petropolis: Vozes.

Madeira, Felicia, 1984. *A integração trabalho-escola na vida do menor*. Sao Paulo: FCC)

Mello, Guiomar Namo de, 1982. *Magistério de 1o. grau: Da competência técnica ao compromiso político*. Sao Paulo: Autores Associados/Cortez.

Miranda, Glaura Vasques de, 1975. "A educação da mulher brasileira e sua participação nas atividades econômicas em 1970." *Cadernos de Pesquisa*, vol. 15, pp. 21–36.

NEM/Pontificia Universidade Católica do Rio de Janeiro, 1984. *Avaliação da década da mulher no Brasil: 1976–1985*. Rio de Janeiro, PUC.

Oliveira, Lucia Elena, 1985. *O lugar do negro na força de trabalho*. Rio de Janeiro: IBGE.

Paiva, Paulo de T. A. "A mulher no mercado de travalho urbano." In *Encontro nacional de estudos populacionais*. Sao Paulo, ABEP, 1981.

Post, David. "The Social Demand for Education in Peru: Students' Choices and State Autonomy," *Sociology of Education*, vol. 63, 1990, pp. 258–271.

Rezende, Jorge de, and Vera Regina de Souza Dias, 1976. "Analise da relação 'educação-ocupação' de acordo com algumas características demogrâficas." In *Encontro brasileiro de estudos populacionais*. Rio de Janeiro: IBGE, pp. 370–384.

Rosemberg, Fulvia, 1982. *A educação da mulher no Brasil*. São Paulo: Global.

Rosemberg, Fulvia, Regina P. Pinto, and Esmeralda V. Negrao, 1986. *Diagnóstico sobre a situação educacional de negros (pretos e pardos) no estado de São Paulo*, vol. 2. São Paulo: Fundação Carlos Chagas.

Rosemberg, Fulvia, Edith Piza, and Maria Montenegro, 1985. *A educação da mulher*. São Paulo: Nobel.

Rosenberg, Lia, 1981. "Educação e desigualdade social: Rendimento escolar de alunos de diferentes origens sociais." M.A. thesis, Pontificia Universidade Católica, Sao Paulo.

Salm, Claudio, 1980. *Escola e trabalho*. São Paulo: Cortez/Autores Associados.

Saviani, Dermeval, 1983. *Escola e democracia*. São Paulo: Cortez/Autores Associados.

SEADE/DIEESE (Fundação Sistema Estadual de Análise de Dados and Departamento Intersindical de Estatística e Estudos Socio-Econômicos), 1985. *Pesquisa de emprego e desemprego na Grande Sao Paulo*, vol. 10.

Silva, Nelson do Valle, 1980. "O preço da cor: Diferenciais raciais na distribuição da renda no Brasil." *Pesquisa Planejamento Econômico*, vol. 10, no. 1, pp. 21–24.

▲ 3

Educational Legitimation of Women's Economic Subordination in Argentina

Cecilia Braslavsky

Braslavsky's study combines census data and survey data. Her analysis of macrolevel census data is juxtaposed with the current socioeconomic structure and the social functions of education. She connects the presence of sex stereotypes in textbooks to the existence of social norms about women's proper role at home and in society.

Although Argentina has extremely high levels of women participating in education, Braslavsky explains that their participation in a school system that continues to present images of women as passive and devoted to home and family has not eroded the existence of a type of domesticity that functions to exclude women from the public sphere.

Her cross-sectional research, which observes students at two points in their high school experience—the first and the last year of studies—provides evidence of disparate academic achievement, depending on the socioeconomic status of the school's student body. Although low-income students seem to be slightly more aware than their high-income peers of inequalities in society, all students tend to believe that individual characteristics determine academic success. The egalitarian myth, then, is strong at the individual level, and girls tend to endorse it even more than do boys.

The comparison between first-year and fifth-year students does not reveal a definite pattern in the perceptions of school failure and value orientations of students, which leads Braslavsky to conclude that the five-year school experience does not substantially modify the distribution of perceptions based on gender and socioeconomic positions students bring to school.

—Editor

▲ Educational research in Latin American countries has frequently adopted the theoretical, methodological, and thematic issues that have originated in central industrial countries (Tedesco, 1987; Braslavsky and Filmus, 1988). In a country where, first, there are 1.7 million illiterates, approximately 300,000 children between 6 and 12 years of age who do not attend school,

47

and 4.8 million adults who have not completed primary education, and where, second, these unfavorable tendencies are shared equally by men and women, it might be argued that an interest in women's education might reflect a tendency to adopt foreign fashions rather than a genuine belief in its importance.

In the case of Argentina, closer scrutiny reveals that a preoccupation with the link between women and education is necessary. Traditional gender analysis, which follows closely the pattern of central countries, and the research on women's education that has emerged in those societies are no longer sufficient to achieve an exhaustive understanding of this relationship. Consequently, it is desirable to expand the range of inquiry to include not only research on the education of women but two other areas of concern: the economic and social structure, and the social function of education and the educational system. These areas are examined in this chapter in the context of Argentina.

The focus here is on the relationships that exist between the education of the entire population and the maintenance of an unfair system of opportunities in society for women, the purpose being to determine the extent to which the education of the entire population is conditioned by differing perceptions on the part of young people of both sexes. Thus, this discussion proceeds through the history of schooling in Argentina from a gender perspective to examine an important way in which women's identity has been constrained and how this condition is maintained: the relegation of women to marginal economic status and their restriction to the domestic sphere. Surveys of some recent studies on the education of women in Argentina are then followed by original data that serve as a base to attempt to clarify and establish the relationship between the entire population's education and the persistent, powerful segregation of women from economic life and activity.

▲ Educational Equality: Beliefs and Facts

Women's Unequal Access and Opportunity

Argentina is one of the Latin American countries that underwent early modernization.[1] This process included an expansion of schooling for children and young people, though it was unable to eradicate fully the existing marginalization. Notwithstanding the vicissitudes of political climate and leadership as well as various economic upheavals, the modernization process continues today (Tedesco, Braslavsky, and Carciofi, 1984).

The national census of 1962 reveals that almost the entire population of children between the ages of 6 and 12 entered primary school and that a significant percentage of young people beyond 13 years of age attended secondary school. At that time, the percentages of male and female attendance at primary and secondary school were similar, although men had a considerable advantage over women in university-level education. From 1960 on, the secondary level of the Argentine educational system continued to expand, accompanied by a dramatic increase in higher- and university-level enrollment. Young women not only participated in this increase—they were, in fact, the main beneficiaries; the proportion of women who received a university education increased at a faster rate than that of men.

The strong presence of women at all levels of the educational system, particularly at higher and university levels, coincided with the myth of Argentina as an egalitarian country. However, additional data gathered from subsequent population censuses, particularly the one conducted in 1980, indicate that the relatively equal participation of women in education does not correspond to a subsequent equal participation in other arenas of social life.

In fact, data from the 1980 census demonstrate that a significant percentage of young women remain at home (see Table 3.1). It is likely that many of them do not have a valid reason to stay home. For example, the number of young people 14–19 years of age who stay home (21 percent or 293,642) is equivalent to the sum of the women of the same age who are mothers (and not working) and the working women who could be mothers of young children (225,838, a figure computed on the basis of additional census data). This coincidence could lead to the hypothesis that the women who stay at home do so to engage in domestic work and take care of their families, particularly to replace their mothers in domestic chores as their mothers reenter the work force. It is known, however, that not all of the working women ages 45–49 have children 14–19 years of age, and that some of these women have more than one child. It is also known that among the 14- to 19-year-old daughters of women 45–49 years of age, there are girls who work outside the home. Finally, it is known that there is no unequivocal correspondence between the homes in which girls 14–19 years of age carry out household chores, and homes in which girls of this age are mothers themselves or daughters of working mothers who are not at home. A similar case can be made for the group of women 20–24 years of age (see Braslavsky, 1985a).

The preceding observations lend credence to the assertion that the advancement of women within the educational system has not been accompanied by an equivalent advancement in economic participation. Moreover, in Argentina there are limited choices for regular societal participation for any woman who neither works nor studies. For example, the organization of political parties is conducted around students and unions. Among women with higher incomes, groups have been developed to assist the needy sectors of society by providing recreational activities. It would not be accurate, however, to assert that the women who develop them represent a numerically significant segment of society.

The analysis of the participation of young women in Argentine society

Table 3.1. Activities of the Argentine Population by Age Group, Sex, and Urban/ Rural Residence

Age Group		Total			Economically Active Population (%)[a]		
		Total	Women	Men	Total	Women	Men
14 and above	Total						
	1960	14,232,200	7,147,475	7,054,722	52.9	23.1	83.0
	1980	20,136,213	10,228,771	9,707,442	50.3	26.1	75.0
	Urban						
	1960	10,912,241	5,644,607	5,267,631	51.7	25.3	74.9
	1980	16,818,276	8,817,902	8,000,374	50.2	28.6	74.0
	Rural						
	1960	3,319,959	1,502,571	1,817,008	56.8	15.5	97.0
	1980	3,317,937	1,410,869	1,707,068	51.1	16.7	79.5
14–24	Total						
	1960	3,584,004	1,811,429	1,772,575	55.2	34.6	76.3
	1980	5,030,180	2,522,643	2,512,537	47.9	32.5	63.4
	Urban						
	1960	2,561,300	1,335,533	1,225,767	54.3	38.2	71.9
	1980	4,157,017	2,199,941	2,037,076	47.9	34.8	61.6
	Rural						
	1960	1,022,704	475,896	546,805	57.5	24.5	86.2
	1980	873,163	402,702	475,461	47.8	20.6	70.8
14–19	Total						
	1960	2,052,884	1,035,439	1,017,445	48.2	30.8	66.0
	1980	2,811,023	1,398,296	1,412,727	35.5	24.7	46.1
	Urban						
	1960	1,439,180	752,287	686,893	45.3	32.8	59.0
	1980	2,292,204	1,163,938	1,123,266	34.3	25.8	43.0
	Rural						
	1960	613,704	283,152	330,552	55.0	25.4	80.4
	1980	518,819	234,358	284,461	40.5	19.2	58.1
20–24	Total						
	1960	1,531,120	775,990	755,130	64.6	39.7	90.3
	1980	2,223,157	1,124,347	1,099,810	63.6	42.2	85.5
	Urban						
	1960	1,122,210	583,246	538,874	65.8	45.1	88.3
	1980	1,364,813	956,003	908,810	64.7	45.7	84.7
	Rural						
	1960	409,000	192,744	216,256	61.3	23.2	95.2
	1980	359,344	168,344	191,000	58.2	22.5	89.7

Source: Population and Household Censuses, 1960 and 1980.
[a]Percentages for the economically active and inactive population total 100 for the total, women, and men breakdowns respectively.

suggests that among those who take care of home chores and duties, there are two groups. The first group is composed of those who fulfill functions that are socially meaningful, although not altogether personally fulfilling for many of them (Jelín and Feijóo, 1983). They take care of their little brothers

Table 3.1 Continued

| | | | Economically Inactive Population (%)[a] | | | | | |
| | Student | | | Home Care | | | Unspecified | |
Total	Women	Men	Total	Women	Men	Total	Women	Men
4.4	4.4	4.4	33.8	67.2	—	8.9	5.3	10.8
7.6	7.8	7.4	27.4	52.9	0.7	14.7	12.4	16.9
—	—	—	—	—	—	—	—	—
8.2	8.3	8.0	26.5	50.2	0.4	15.1	13.1	17.6
—	—	—	—	—	—	—	—	—
4.7	4.8	4.5	31.9	69.3	0.9	12.4	9.2	15.1
17.2	16.9	17.5	23.1	45.6	—	4.5	2.8	6.2
28.9	30.2	27.5	15.9	31.2	0.5	7.3	6.0	8.6
—	—	—	—	—	—	—	—	—
31.6	32.9	30.2	14.0	27.1	0.4	6.5	5.3	7.8
—	—	—	—	—	—	—	—	—
16.2	16.4	13.9	24.9	53.1	0.9	11.2	10.0	14.4
27.7	27.2	26.9	19.3	38.3	—	5.6	3.8	8.0
44.5	46.8	42.2	10.8	21.1	0.6	9.2	7.4	12.0
—	—	—	—	—	—	—	—	—
48.7	50.9	46.5	8.8	16.9	0.4	8.2	6.4	10.1
—	—	—	—	—	—	—	—	—
25.8	26.3	25.5	19.6	42.0	1.1	14.0	12.5	15.3
4.0	3.3	4.7	28.1	55.4	—	3.3	1.6	—
9.1	9.6	8.6	22.3	43.8	0.4	4.9	4.4	5.3
—	—	—	—	—	—	—	—	—
10.4	10.9	10.0	20.4	39.4	0.3	4.5	4.0	5.0
—	—	—	—	—	—	—	—	—
2.2	2.6	1.9	32.4	68.5	0.6	7.2	6.4	7.8

and sisters, cook and feed the family, and care for their own children.[2] The second group, in contrast, simply stays at home, idle, sometimes waiting for marriage to happen—indeed, waiting for the opportunity to fulfill the functions that have already been assumed by the first group. Some, however, are simply without any life project altogether (CEPAL, 1983).

Although the personal and social implications of the two situations are very different (Braslavsky, 1986, 53ff.), women in both seem to accept a high degree of passivity. In other words, even though some of the 762,690 young women taking care of the home might concur with some qualitative research findings suggesting that they do not readily accept their lot, the majority unquestionably accept the premise of "domesticity"—which means women confined, both with respect to ideology and practice, to their own homes, and to the moral authority which this entails.[3] By surrendering to this "excluding domesticity," young men and women also accept one of the multiple forms of differential participation in society. In doing so, women accept the rules of economic dependence upon their parents and husbands and the accompanying forms of noneconomic dependence usually reflected in physical domination through violence.[4] Moreover, when young women and young girls endorse the option of an excluding domesticity, they also accept the many ways of social discrimination that have become crystallized within Argentine society following the period of social change and expansion that occurred between 1930 and 1965 (Braslavsky, 1986).[5]

This acceptance of domestic roles, with the concomitant exclusion from other roles that it implies, has occurred for a multitude of reasons. Some of these reasons are based upon conditions that exist within the educational system. There are two major conditions in schools that promote this acceptance: First, educational systems convey a sexist message. Second, the educational process encourages students to accept a variety of types of discrimination, one of which is the restriction of women to exclusively domestic roles. Recent and still incipient educational research in Argentina has provided some evidence for the existence of a sexist message being conveyed within the educational system and for a process that encourages students to accept various kinds of discrimination. The next sections present the evidence for these assertions.

The Sexist Message Within Argentina's Educational System

Recent studies conducted in Argentina provide evidence that women attending school are being educated to assume a domestic role. Catalina Wainerman and Rebeca Berck de Raijman (1984) show that the textbooks used in primary schools contain text and pictures that differentiate between male and female activities. The males are portrayed as working people, while the females are shown cooking, taking care of children, and performing other household duties.

Mabel Grillo (1987) demonstrates through quantitative research carried out in Rio Cuarto (Province of Cordoba) that the portrayal of women in the schools (public and private) under investigation corresponds to the traditional feminine stereotype:

> In the maintenance of discipline, it was generally observed that, when
> girls were found talking in class, they were penalized as strictly as when
> boys were discovered committing serious misdeeds, such as hitting or
> tripping other students; in other words, female teachers apply different
> standards of disciplinary maintenance on the basis of gender. This
> distinction can be linked, in the context of prevailing sex stereotypes,
> to the acceptance of the aggressive nature of men vs. the submissive and
> obedient character of women. The fact that reference is made to the
> "girls' ways" when teachers discipline girls confirms this notion
> (Grillo, 1987, p. 43).

In the various topics discussed during class, the role of "mother" is identified exclusively with emotional qualities: kindness, warmth, and affection. Furthermore, the activities of "motherhood" that are emphasized focus mainly upon providing domestic and personal care. Analysis of the syntax and morphology of teacher-constructed sentences revealed that female characters were portrayed as being passive and limited to a domestic environment. Male characters were shown possessing abilities associated with adventure and risk.

These characteristics are found in the treatment of subject matter in class and in teacher comments. In this respect, standards related to the "inevitable," "self-evident," "taken-for-granted" qualities associated with the sexes were recorded: Interest in adventure, employment, and valor are the proper domain of men; interest in household duties, personal care, marriage, and family are the natural concerns of women. On the other hand, "none of the cases studied demonstrated any opposing views about the feminine stereotype. Nor did any of the comments or incidents observed suggest that women's issues could be the theme or subject of dialogue inside the classroom" (Grillo, 1987, pp. 31–32). This synthesized interpretation of the limited research findings regarding the sexist message conveyed in the Argentine educational system indicates clearly that both sexes of young people are educated and conditioned to accept the role of women as being restricted to domesticity.

The presence of a sexist message conveyed throughout the educational system has led those educational researchers and politicians who are concerned with the attainment of greater social justice and equity to suggest a series of steps that would help to educate young people in a different way. Many of these steps coincide with the proposals provided in several regional forums (see Braslavsky, 1986). Included among these are the transformation of the schools' curricula and textbooks. Also proposed is the organization of study and discussion groups among teachers, so that they can become aware of the messages they convey and thus also be able to evaluate the consequences of these messages. Undoubtedly, these are necessary steps. However, the evidence provided later in the chapter suggests that these steps are insufficient.

Legitimation of Women's Unequal Status in Society

In contrast to the previously mentioned research studies, which emphasize the socialization of young people of both sexes toward the acceptance of role differentiation in later, postschool life, the study discussed in the next section deals with the experience of students as they pass through high school. This analysis reveals that the educational experience produces homogeneous social images (or representations) among students beyond their gender affiliation and shows that these representations are not directly associated with the roles that each gender must fulfill but rather with the social structure and the relationship that exists between the school and the community. This educational experience leads to the crystallization of discriminatory forms of social integration, thus offering differential opportunities for participation for men and women. Moreover, these homogeneous representations are also the product of a "deep penetration" (O'Donnell, 1984) of the hegemonic pedagogical ideology in Argentina, an ideology that complements in a perverse way the socialization of both genders.

▲ The Data Base:
The National Secondary Education Program

The original data presented in this study come from a research project carried out from 1984 to 1987 by the Latin American Social Science Faculty (Facultad Latinoamericana de Ciencias Sociales, FLACSO) with the support of the International Development Research Center (Canada). During these three years, the research team of the educational section of FLACSO studied the experience of adolescents in a diverse set of schools. These educational settings offered opportunities and choices of differing quality to both children and young people. These opportunities existed clearly in direct relation to their social origin (the best choices going to the highest social sectors, the worst choices going to the lowest). It was also clear that these institutional settings did not contribute to the ultimate objective of schooling: teaching and learning. Rather, the achievement results could be attributed to the individual effort of students. The study attempted to determine the extent to which young people accepted the segregation and alienation of responsibilities conveyed to them through the processes of teaching and learning, and whether that acceptance increased or decreased proportionately as students approached completion of their program of studies. For this purpose, students were chosen from the first and last years of several high schools, drawn from among the various types of schools previously identified. These students were asked to give their opinions about a series of questions, which could be used as indicators of their degree of acceptance of various social norms.[6] The results from this survey involved 589 youths; the characteristics of this sample are presented in Table 3.2.

Table 3.2. Sample Composition by School, Sex, Socioeconomic Status (SES), and Grade (percent except where noted)

Grade	School 1		School 2		School 3		School 4		School 5	
	Men	Women	Men	Women	Men	Women	Men	Women	Men	Women
First grade										
Low SES	80	81	69	73	67	61	23	16	6	4
Medium	5	6	17	9	17	22	18	38	13	17
High	10	5	14	9	17	13	59	46	81	74
Unclassified	—	7	—	8	—	4	—	—	—	4
Total	100	100	100	100	100	100	100	100	100	100
Absolute numbers	20	59	29	53	42	82	39	50	32	23
Fifth grade										
Low SES	47	77	50	33	50	46	19	34	—	—
Medium	27	15	50	58	15	39	29	31	25	20
High	27	4	—	—	25	15	53	28	75	80
Unclassified	—	4	—	8	—	—	—	6	5	—
Total	100	100	100	100	100	100	100	100	100	100
Absolute numbers	15	26	8	12	12	13	17	32	20	5

The differences among the social and educational origins of the students, obvious in the case of both men and women, correspond to the characteristics of the neighborhood of the school. School 1, where most of the students come from low-income sectors, has the poorest building, the teachers with the greatest number of teaching hours, and the most difficult conditions of physical access. It is located on a dirt street, in the outskirts of Buenos Aires, and depends on the support of a poor community to improve teaching conditions. At the other extreme is School 5, which enrolls students from families with the highest income and educational levels; it has a majestic building, teachers with few teaching hours (because they have outside income), and easy conditions of physical access. It is located in La Plata City's downtown area, the capital of Buenos Aires Province. It depends on the university for support and has its own budget to improve teaching conditions. Between these extremes, there are three schools, ranging from two classic schools for low-middle classes (Schools 2 and 3), with solid buildings that, nonetheless, have limited supplies and poor upkeep, to another traditional school of La Plata City, supported by a well-off community. All five schools offer a high school diploma. Consequently, the future of their graduates is linked to the possibility of their being able to continue studies at the university level.

The students who attend these five different schools evince distinct academic achievement. As can be expected, those who attend School 1 repeat courses with much greater frequency than those in other schools (see Table 3.3) and, if they continue in school, reach levels of achievement similar to those attained by students who attend Schools 4 and 5. The price to be paid for this achievement, however, is that students in School 1 must distance themselves from the ideas and feelings of the other young people from the same origins, who have not been able to remain in the educational system (Bravslavsky and Filmus, 1987). The question to be asked is whether the students are aware of the differing risks of failure associated with their origins.

Symbolic Equality as Legitimating All Actual Inequality

Argentina's educational system was formed and experienced its first wave of expansion in a historic period during which positivism was the dominant intellectual current (Weinberg, 1983). It was then believed that education should and could make a great contribution to the development of the nation and its people. In fact, education contributed to both of these developments in rather different ways, as the social classes became more differentiated and the economic relations became more complex in a process that increasingly linked Argentina to the world centers of power.

Within the ideological and political spheres of production, the function of education was conceived in accordance with these goals and accepted as proper by the people in general, not only as a result of ideological pressure but because of the correspondence between the beliefs about education and the prevailing economic tendencies of that period. The more educated members of the population had, for example, greater opportunities for better jobs than the people with less education (Llomovatte, 1987).

An additional period of significant expansion of the educational system occurred during the years when democracy was established, after the promulgation, in 1916, of the Saenz Peña Law of Secret Voting, which was obligatory for men. The expansion was determined, on the one hand, by industrialization efforts to replace imports (1930–1955) and, on the other, by a stage of economic growth (1958–1966) involving various development strategies, not only in Argentina but also in Latin America (Wiñar, 1974).

In all of these events a positivist current of thought prevailed: Education could and must contribute to the development of the country and to the individual, although this "development" was called by many names. This core thought was supplemented by additional ideas, some of which were also drawn from positivism but some of which emerged through later theories. These ideas often did not consider the possible failure of the educational system to meet such expectations. Among these ideas, the following are most evident: (1) Schools offer to all young people the same learning

Table 3.3. Repetition Rates Among Students in the Last Year of High School (percent)

Repetition Rate	School 1		School 2		School 3		School 4		School 5	
	Men	Women	Men	Women	Men	Women	Men	Women	Men	Women
First-time repeaters	63	59	45	45	21	26	6	6	—	—
Two-time repeaters	27	21	6	4	11	5	—	—	—	—
Total	100	100	100	100	100	100	100	100	—	—

possibilities; and (2) the differing opportunities to take advantage of these possibilities and conditions result from the abilities, "assets", and "willpower" possessed by the students or from the amount of effort they exert.

The Myth of Equality

One of the key postulates of pedagogical positivism assumes that the supply of learning opportunities will be directly associated with the use made of and advantage taken of those opportunities. In other words, it is believed that if the system merely offers equal learning opportunities, all students have the same possibilities to make use of them. The adoption of this assumption by those who develop educational policy resulted in the proposal to organize a single primary school system for the entire population. This meant that all of the country's primary schools were to possess buildings with identical facilities, teachers with equal training, and similar equipment of similar quality. All schools were to have an auditorium, a large campus, a music room, maps, blackboards, chalk, laboratory (stuffed) animals, and laboratory equipment.

This proposal gained strength by the end of the last century, and it was subsequently sanctioned by law. Both girls and boys were expected to attend these primary schools, learn the same things, and be there for the same number of class hours. The single difference (not an incidental one) was that girls were expected to do fancy needlework and embroidery, while the boys were to engage in carpentry or some other activity properly associated with a masculine role.

Somewhat paradoxically, it is evident from the history of Argentina's educational system that the primary level has been organized as a highly segmented subsystem, with each school being very different from the others. There are a number of very clear manifestations of these differences. For example, there are many schools that offer only part-time classes, wherein boys and girls attend classes for only two or three hours per day (260,000 students from Buenos Aires province currently attend these kinds of institutions). In contrast, there are other schools—mostly private—where students attend eight hours per day.

The evidence from the FLACSO study indicates that this school differentiation continues in the high schools. It is well known that most of the students who attend the worst high schools come from those sectors of society with the lowest income and lowest educational levels. Furthermore, they demonstrate the highest rates of grade repetition and dropping out, regardless of personal effort by individual students. Because of this high proportion of repetition and dropping out, these students are unable to enter the university (see Tedesco, Braslavsky, and Carciofi, 1984; Klubitschko, 1980; and Braslavsky, 1987).

Given the existence of this strongly segmented primary educational subsystem, it is possible to conclude that, quite contrary to the pedagogical message of positivism, other conditions obtain. As some students observed: "In Argentine society, there are the rich and the poor, and they each are treated differently at school"; "rich people have more opportunities to go to school than poor people"; "high schools differentiate individuals according to social origins"; "sheer individual effort is not sufficient to be successful at school"; and finally, "effort is not enough to assure that the individual can attend university." Notwithstanding all this, substantial percentages of young people of both sexes today hold opposite views, believing that schools are egalitarian, open to all, and nondiscriminatory and that effort can bring success (see Table 3.4).

It is highly probable that the cause for the persistence of the egalitarian myth can be found, specifically, in the existence of gender segmentation—and in the successful maintenance among young people of a state of ignorance regarding its existence. Both of these factors lead young people to compare themselves only with peers who attend the same institutions and who thus are considered equal. They do not have the opportunity to relate to young people from other institutions, who come from other social and economic sectors. In this sense, the myth of equal educational opportunity persists for young people of differing social status, in a society that, in fact, does not offer the same educational opportunities to all.

The Myth of Individual Agency

The myth of individual agency includes many elements. When a young person believes that if a student perseveres and studies diligently, he or she will almost certainly be able to attend university, this conviction implies not only a fundamental belief in equality with respect to educational opportunity. It also suggests that the possibility of attending a university is dependent upon personal effort.

The myth of individual effort, however, is expressed quite independently of whether or not a student drops out of school. A significant percentage of

Table 3.4. Agreement by Students with Opinions Regarding Society, School Norms, and School Failure, by Sex and Type of School (in percentages)

Opinion	Grade	School 1		School 2		School 3		School 4		School 5	
		Men	Women	Men	Women	Men	Women	Men	Women	Men	Women
There are rich and poor people in society. In school, we are all equal.	1	90	86	72	93	81	90	87	90	63	83
	5	73	77	75	100	75	69	75	81	25	25
In the past only rich people went to school; today schools are for all.	1	100	95	79	89	81	83	92	92	78	87
	5	80	84	100	100	83	62	81	78	50	20
Today, high schools make no distinctions of religion, race, or social class.	1	74	76	52	53	71	67	64	80	78	78
	5	87	92	100	100	100	77	69	81	30	20
Any student can succeed in school; he/she need only do his/her best.	1	74	93	79	96	93	89	80	80	91	70
	5	87	92	88	100	92	100	75	98	75	80
If a student does his/her best, he/she can certainly be admitted to a university.	1	95	95	93	100	98	93	97	92	97	91
	5	80	85	100	83	100	92	94	94	90	100

the adolescents and young people of both sexes believe that the unpleasantness of school, the lack of enthusiasm for studies, and the lack of academic ability are the primary causes for student withdrawal from school (see Table 3.5). Nevertheless, it seems that the myth of individual effort is not as widespread as the egalitarian myth. Its existence is most evident in those schools that enroll people from diverse socioeconomic and educational origins, including those that, as in School 1, enroll students who come from the poorest sectors of society but who go on to the high school level.

Equal Processing of Different Messages

The studies outlined previously regarding the unequal socialization carried out through the educational system have not clarified the effects upon the attitudes of students that derive from the messages conveyed by textbooks and female teachers. Those studies suggest that by the mere fact that the messages directed toward men and women are different, each group will develop different values as well as different attitudes and aptitudes. Empirical evidence gathered in the National Secondary Education Program regarding the values held by male and female students relating to school matters, which presage the values they will hold toward analogous social matters, suggests a contrary hypothesis. In other words, there is evidence that both men and women construct their assumptions and shape their social behaviors through a series of mediations between what is offered to them in written or oral form and what is provided to them by social participation, involving all of their life experiences. As a result of these mediations, girls, for example, may not be as obedient and submissive as the manner in which they are conditioned by female teachers would predict. Moreover, those same female teachers and professionals may not, in fact, act in this manner in their own social practices.[7]

The study data indicate a similar tendency among the students of first and fifth year of high school of both sexes toward considering that good behavior in school obviates problems or that schools should have stricter discipline (see Table 3.6). However, in some instances (fifth-year students in Schools 3, 4, and 5 for the first and second statement), women showed a greater tendency to accept order and discipline as important for educational success.

One reason Argentine women may not develop values based on disciplinary norms could stem from their marked protagonism in some significant social movements during the years of the authoritarian government and the beginning of the country's transition toward democracy. Argentine women, supposedly socialized to accept the existing order, headed the movement in favor of human rights through diverse associations to locate children and adults who "disappeared" during the 1975–1983 period. This is also linked to the greater resistance by female students to the treatment of

Table 3.5. Causes of Student Dropout as Perceived by Students, by Grade, Type of School, and Sex (percent agreement)

Grade and Cause	School 1		School 2		School 3		School 4		School 5	
	Men	Women	Men	Women	Men	Women	Men	Women	Men	Women
First grade										
Students do not like or want to study	42	32	41	28	33	24	46	38	19	26
Economic reasons	32	51	41	59	48	57	31	34	56	35
Lack of ability	21	14	7	7	14	11	8	24	13	13
Other	5	3	11	6	5	8	15	4	12	26
Total	100	100	100	100	100	100	100	100	100	100
Fifth grade										
Students do not like or want to study	33	38	88	67	58	23	19	44	10	60
Economic reasons	53	42	12	25	25	77	38	47	75	40
Lack of ability	13	—	—	—	8	—	31	9	5	—
Other	1	20	—	8	8	—	12	—	10	—
Total	100	100	100	100	100	100	100	100	100	100

Table 3.6. Value Orientations Toward Order and Discipline, by Student Grade, Type of School, and Sex (percent agreement)

Value Orientation	Grade	School 1		School 2		School 3		School 4		School 5	
		Men	Women	Men	Women	Men	Women	Men	Women	Men	Women
In order not to have problems at school, it is extremely important to have good behavior.	1	58	49	28	28	32	28	21	36	22	35
	5	47	35	50	42	58	62	38	56	35	60
School discipline should be more strict.	1	47	38	38	38	26	42	33	26	9	9
	5	20	8	25	17	8	16	13	25	10	20

political themes in the schools, though this occurs in only a few cases (see Table 3.7).

With respect to the political issue, Argentine society seems to resemble other Latin American countries in its distrust of traditional procedures for channeling participation into political parties with single platforms (Calderón and Jelín, 1987). In this regard, adolescents also may have lost some of their trust in political parties, a distrust originally derived from the fear of retaliation to previous generations suffered for their political affiliations and struggles (see Seoane and Ruiz Nunez, 1986). Consequently, adolescents prefer to confront political issues in the protected environment of the classroom, through the daily presentation of ideas by young party militants to their classmates. Women manifest this behavior more frequently than their male counterparts.

▲ Altering the School Message

The assertion that the study of the education of women has been influenced in recent years by a theoretical position espousing a particular perspective does not need to be supported by bibliographical references. This perspective emphasized the existence of mechanisms of discriminatory socialization by sex, and of sexist assumptions harbored by society. The use of this perspective is extremely important in bringing forth the significant differences that emerge as a result of differing sexual socialization. Schools have played a fundamental role in the permanence of this disparity.

However, the focus on socialization separates this process from a fundamental one that in fact subsumes it: the existence of an extensive series of differing opportunities within society that become progressively more fixed and entrenched. This inequity affects women in a particular way. Essentially, it consists in not allowing women to break away from the home environment at the same rate at which they have been able to free themselves from educational inequalities. This, however, is not much more serious than the difficulties youngsters experience in finding a job for the first time, or when children commit themselves exclusively to their studies without the need to work from a very early age.[8]

This line of reasoning suggests that women accept this situation not only because they accept acting as women and must, consequently, remain at home, but also because they accept that there are extremely limited social opportunities available to them, as well as other opportunities that are unequally apportioned to them and to men. In doing so, they reproduce, on an individual basis, the secular message conveyed to them by the schools concerning their social disadvantages. This message, which is based upon an assumption of the inequality of women (and many other social groups and sectors within Argentine society), implicitly states: "We are all equal, and

Table 3.7. Value Orientations About Introducing Politics into School, by Student Grade, Type of School, and Sex (percent agreement)

Opinion	Grade	School 1		School 2		School 3		School 4		School 5	
		Men	Women	Men	Women	Men	Women	Men	Women	Men	Women
It is all right for students who have a preference for a political party to engage in political activities in school.	1	42	15	24	11	36	17	18	4	31	9
	5	13	4	—	—	42	15	56	16	30	—
It is important for the working class to discuss the political situation of the country.	1	32	39	48	40	48	35	49	50	53	65
	5	67	72	88	84	92	93	100	81	90	100

our own success or failure depends on our own endeavors; this is the law of the school, and it should also be the law of life." If this were truly the case, efforts to abolish sexually differentiated messages could have two very different but equally paradoxical effects upon the possibilities of improved social opportunities for women.

As a first option, women could feel equal to men and convince themselves that they have the same rights and possibilities for social participation. Furthermore, their lack of opportunity is merely a correlate of the overall lack of opportunity that exists for everyone in society, and they should, consequently, accept their exclusive domestic role, just as others accept unemployment or underemployment. They would not accept this role merely because they are socialized to do so as women, or because they are inclined to accept the status quo or present social order, but because they are socialized as youngsters to accept overall social disadvantage as a consequence of the failure to apply individual willpower to improve their personal outlook for the future. The educational system would play a fundamental role in this socialization.

As a second option, some women might be able to command a greater degree of participation in economic activity, by paying the price of relegating the remaining areas of societal participation to other men and women, thereby creating an even more unfair social situation. The educational system would also play a significant role in the acceptance of this dynamic.

It is clear that if the entire set of messages and behaviors promoted by the daily practice of teachers is not altered, then the modification of sexist patterns will have no other effect than the two just described. The first will involve a strengthening of conformism and social paralysis; the second will increase the degree of social injustice and promote equal distribution of this injustice to all members of society.

Understandably, the statements cited in this chapter support the preceding reflections and assertions only in a very general and partial manner. Consequently, the last few paragraphs have the character of preliminary conclusions. They are intended to stimulate the development of an increased understanding of the different socialization experienced by children and young people, both male and female, in the schools of Argentina and Latin America. The points are intended, furthermore, to promote serious reflection upon the roles schools play in conveying notions that legitimate the many inequalities and miseries of society. The proposals that could emerge from such reflection may help to generate an all-encompassing awareness of the practice and the actions of the sectors of society concerned with the quality of life experienced by the entire population and with the establishment of social equity.

▲ Notes

1. Regarding this process, see also Germani, 1965; CEPAL, 1985.
2. The performance of domestic tasks begins very early. Mary, a nine-year-old girl from a working-class neighborhood in Buenos Aires, describes a typical day in this manner: "I get up, make the beds up, go to school; afterward I take care of my little brothers and sisters . . . I change them and give them milk; I watch TV."
3. These differential notions, accepted and disseminated by the church and Catholic laymen, greatly influenced the mothers that socialized today's youth.
4. Violence and its dangerous character exercised by husbands toward wives became public in Argentina with the case of Monzon, a world boxing champion, who during the summer of 1988 killed his wife and threw the body from a balcony to make it appear to be an accident.
5. The most recent studies about the socioeconomic structure and situation in Argentina refer not only to the crystallization of this differential insertion but also to the deepening of the differences in the quality of life among the various social strata; there is also a clear regressive tendency in the social distribution of income (Altimir, 1986).
6. Other results from the same research program can be seen in Braslavsky, 1985a; Filmus, 1988; Llomovatte, 1987; Braslavsky and Filmus, 1987; and Entel and Braslavsky, 1987.
7. Primary and secondary school teachers are women who work and thus avoid, albeit not entirely, fitting into the traditional stereotype. In fact, they led in 1988 one of the most sustained and serious labor disputes in Argentina: a 37-day strike that placed the viability of the academic year in danger.
8. In this respect, some data are available about youth unemployment and underemployment, rates of which reached 11 percent in some cities during 1984 (Braslavsky, 1984). There are also data on child labor (Llomovatte, 1986).

▲ References

Altimir, C. "Estimaciones de la distribución del ingreso en la Argentina, 1953–1980." *Desarrollo económico*, no. 100, Buenos Aires, 1986.
Braslavsky, Cecilia. *Mujer y educación: Desigualdades educativas en América Latina y el Caribe*. Santiago: UNESCO, 1984.
———. "Las mujeres jóvenes entre la participación y la reclusión." In CEPAL, *Mujeres jóvenes en América Latina: Aportes para una discusión*. Montevideo: ARCA/Foro Juvenil, 1985a.
———. *La discriminación educativa en Argentina*. Buenos Aires: FLACSO/GEL, 1985b.
———. *La juventud argentina: Informe de situación*. Buenos Aires: CEAAL, 1986.
———. "Perspectivas de la educación y de la alfabetización en Argentina en el marco de la transición a la democracia." UNESCO/OREALC, *Seminario regional sobre alternativas de alfabetização para a America Latina e o Caribe*. Brasilia: UNESCO/OREALC, May 1987.
Braslavsky, Cecilia, and Daniel Filmus. *Ultimo año de colegio secundario y discriminación educativa*. Documentos e informes de investigación no. 50. Buenos Aires: FLACSO, 1987.
———. *Respuestas a la crisis educativa*. Buenos Aires: CANTARO, 1988.
Calderón, F., and Elizabeth Jelín. *Clases y movimientos sociales en América Latina: Perspectivas y realidades*. Buenos Aires: Estudios CEDES, 1987.
CEPAL (Comisión Económica para la América Latina). *Mujeres jóvenes en América Latina: Aportes para una discusión*. Montevideo: ARCA/Foro Juvenil, 1985.
———. "Notas respecto a las estrategias de ejecución para el adelanto de la mujer hasta el año 100." Report presented at the Group of Experts meetings held in Santiago, December 3–5, 1983.
Entel, A., and Cecilia Braslavsky. *Cartas al presidente*. Buenos Aires: Editorial De la Flor, 1987.
Filmus, Daniel. "Primer año del colegio secundario y discriminación educativa." In Cecilia Braslavsky and Daniel Filmus (eds.), *Respuestas a la crisis educativa*. Buenos Aires: CANTARO, 1988.
Germani, Gino. *Estructura social de la Argentina*. Buenos Aires: Raigal, 1965.
Grillo, M. "La imagen de la mujer que se transmite en las aulas de la escuela primaria en Argentina." Report presented to CONICET, Rio Cuarto, mimeo, 1987.
Jelín, Elizabeth, and María del Carmen Feijóo. "Presiones cruzadas: Trabajo y familia en la vida de las mujeres." In *El deber ser y el hacer de las mujeres: Dos estudios de caso en la Argentina*. Mexico, D.F.: El Colegio de Mexico/PISPAL, 1983.
Klubitschko, D. *El origen social de los estudiantes de la Universidad de Buenos Aires*. Buenos Aires: DEALC, 1980.
Llomovatte, S. *Adolescentes trabajadores*. Buenos Aires: FLACSO, 1986.
———. *Escuela media y trabajo*. Documentos e informes de investigación no. 51. Buenos Aires: FLACSO, 1987.
O'Donnell, Guillermo. *Democracia en la Argentina: Micro y macro*. Buenos Aires: Contrapunto, 1984.
Seoane, M., and H. Ruiz Nuñez. *La noche de los lápices*. Buenos Aires: Contrapunto, 1986.
Tedesco, Juan Carlos. *El desafío educativo: Calidad y democracia*. Buenos Aires: GEL, 1987.

Tedesco, Juan Carlos, Cecilia Braslavsky, and R. Carciofi. *El proyecto educativo autoritario: Argentina 1976–1982.* Buenos Aires: FLACSO/GEL, 1984.

Wainerman, Catalina. "El mundo de las ideas y los valores: Mujer y trabajo." In *El deber ser y el hacer de las mujeres: Dos estudios de caso en la Argentina.* Mexico: El Colegio de México/PISPAL, 1983.

Wainerman, Catalina, and Rebeca Berck de Raijman. *La división sexual del trabajo en los libros de lectura de la escuela primaria argentina: Un caso de inmutabilidad secular.* Cuaderno no. 42. Buenos Aires: CENEP, 1984.

Weinberg, G. *Modelos educativos en América Latina.* Buenos Aires: Kapelusz, 1983.

Wiñar, D. "Aspectos sociales del desarrollo educativo 1900–1970," Revista del Centro de Estudios Educativos, vol. 4, no. 4, Mexico, 1974.

▲ 4

Gender, Education, and Employment in Central America: Whose Work Counts?

Lisa Catanzarite

This chapter examines the relationship between education and work. Although the association between them tends indeed to be positive, Catanzarite shows this is true only of formal, not informal, service occupations. Within the formal sector the association is not strictly linear; rather, a curvilinear pattern emerges as women with both high and low levels of education tend to participate more than those with in-between levels.

Theories of female participation tend to assume that women are dependent on men's wages and that their participation in the labor force is essentially a question of aspirations and opportunity cost calculations. Catanzarite argues instead that for poor women work is a necessity for family survival. Therefore, at that level, the association between education and work is irrelevant. Further, women in the informal sector—regardless of educational level—are paid less than men. These findings are important because the informal sector is expanding and women's participation in it is already greater than men's. In addition, educated women tend to have more stable employment than uneducated women, but many educated women end up in the informal sector of the economy.

Catanzarite's study calls for a reformulation of economic theory to include women's particular role in family survival. It challenges the notion that education will facilitate women's incorporation into the labor force and generate greater income. Neither of these claims is true when women face unstable employment, a strong feature of informal-sector participation. In consequence, the improvement of women's conditions lies not in greater education but in the improvement of wages and the creation of more stable jobs for women, many of whom find their incorporation in the labor force precarious.

—Editor

▲ Is it truly the case that "education drives women toward the labor market" (Wainerman, 1980, p. S182)? Bowen and Finegan's (1966) study established the basis for the idea that women's educational attainment is positively associated with labor force participation. Academics and policy planners have used this argument to promote increased educational opportunities for women in Third World countries. Certainly, such efforts are commendable. At the societal level, expansion of female education is a progressive political and economic force. Similarly, at the individual level, education can empower women. And, surely, better-educated women have greater labor market opportunities than poorly educated women.

Attempts to increase women's educational opportunities should not, however, lead to an exaggerated faith in the magic of education for women. The education–labor force participation link is weak, and its application, especially to Third World countries, should be carefully examined. The notion that education increases the probability of women's labor force participation obscures the experiences of disadvantaged, poorly educated women. Further, reliance on official data sources, notorious for their underenumeration of women's employment, compounds this danger.

This study provides an overview of education and labor force participation by gender in the five Central American countries (Costa Rica, El Salvador, Guatemala, Honduras, and Nicaragua). Census data suggest a positive association between women's educational attainment and labor force participation. However, methodological issues in the measurement of female labor force participation and use of alternative data sources are considerations that cast doubt on the apparent trend. The theoretical rationale for a positive association between women's educational attainment and labor force participation has not been adequately established (Standing, 1976, 1982), and I argue that its application is highly problematic for these countries.

▲ Theoretical Framework

The landmark Bowen and Finnegan (1966) analysis was limited to U.S. married women, with husband present and no children under age 6. For these women, education was positively associated with labor force participation. Other empirical evidence for the association between women's education and labor force participation has been extremely mixed, particularly for Third World countries; studies of different countries show positive, negative, and curvilinear associations (see, inter alia, the reviews in Ram, 1980; and Standing, 1982).

Rationales for the predicted positive association include, on the supply side, the opportunity costs and aspirations arguments: Because better-educated women have higher potential earnings than the poorly educated, their opportunity costs for economic inactivity are higher; and because education increases income aspirations, the higher expectations of better-educated women will induce them to seek employment.[1] On the demand side is the relative employment opportunities argument: There is a higher demand for better-educated labor than for less-educated labor (see Standing, 1982; Standing, 1976 for reviews).

Standing (1976, 1982) proposes a revision of the education–female labor force participation model, based on the aspirations and relative employment opportunities arguments. In his version, equalization of educational and training opportunities between females and males should increase female labor force participation and increase the likelihood of a positive relation between educational attainment and such participation.[2] The underlying logic is that equalization of access to educational resources should increase women's access to labor market resources and decrease sexual dualism in the labor market.[3]

But structural differences in labor market outcomes for women and men are not determined solely by educational qualifications.[4] For example, in Albelda's (1986) analysis of U.S. data, changes in educational dissimilarity by gender did not affect levels of occupational segregation between women and men. Standing's model (1976, 1982) predicts that in countries where educational attainment is equalizing for women and men, female labor force participation will increase and education will be positively related to women's labor force participation. Published data from the five Central American countries, reviewed later in this chapter, appear to support Standing's view. These countries showed relatively small gender gaps in educational attainment by the 1970s, and, indeed, available data suggest both that female labor force participation has increased and that it is positively related to educational attainment. A closer examination of the pertinent data suggests, however, major flaws in the enumeration of women in agricultural and informal-sector employment. This raises important questions regarding both the reliability of empirical findings on the relationship of education to female labor force participation and the applicability of the theoretical model (even Standing's revised model) that suggests a positive association.

Existing arguments regarding women's labor force participation give little or no attention to individual economic need.[5] Most perspectives assume that women's earnings are not important to household survival, and most arguments view women as wives. Clearly, the opportunity costs and aspirations arguments are pertinent only for those women whose family support (from a male partner or from other family members) is sufficient for survival. There is probably a threshold point of family earnings above which these arguments become relevant for women. For poor women, however, economic need will be the driving force for labor market participation.

To the extent that education is related to social class background, there is a competing, negative association between education and labor force participation.[6] Poorly educated lower-class women who are in marital or consensual unions are more likely than higher-class women to be involved with men whose earnings are insufficient for family survival,[7] and lower-class women who do not have a male partner (but may have dependent children) are less likely to be supported by their family of origin than are higher-class women.

Theorizing on the relationship between education and women's labor force participation has given inadequate attention both to social class background[8] and to family structure. Because models have tended to assume that women are married and that men's earnings are sufficient for family survival,[9] the emphasis has been on individual aspirations and opportunity costs as the major influences on women's economic behavior.

▲ The Central American Case

In Central America, family structures and fertility patterns, the large proportion of lower-class persons, gender-specific migration patterns, and gender-specific demand for labor in rural and urban areas make the likelihood of a positive education–labor force participation association questionable. The analysis of the data presented in this chapter leads me to argue that the underenumeration of women in the labor force occurs with unstable employment. I conclude that the assertion that education drives women toward the labor market should be reconsidered and that policy attention should be focused on disadvantaged women whose economic activity has not been appropriately recognized.

Family Structures and Fertility

The normative family structure of male-headed households is not universally realized. In Central America (as is true elsewhere), women who do not have male partners often have children to support, and this is particularly true among lower-class women.

With respect to the urban poor, Nieves found in her 1979 study of shantytowns in San Salvador that 21 percent of the households in her sample were consanguineous, connected through women's bloodlines, with no husband/father present. The men in these households (usually sons, brothers, uncles, nephews) tended to be economically inactive and not contributing to household income. Roberts (1970, as per Nieves, 1979) found that 17 percent of his Guatemala City sample of households in the mid-1960s were headed by women with children and no spouses. In 1959, González (1970, as per Nieves, 1979) found much higher rates in black Carib communities on the Atlantic coast of Guatemala, with 45 percent of households in Livingston headed by women with children. And "studies carried out in Costa Rica report that consanguineous households prevail in urban settlements" (Nieves, 1979, p. 139, citing López de Piza, 1977).

In rural areas as well, women are often heads of household. Buvinic (1982) reports that in rural areas of Honduras, fertility was similar for women with and without a male partner present—that is, the ratio of number of children to years of fertility was the same for both groups.

Other data on illegitimate births give an indication of women's potential need for earnings. In 1984, 37.2 percent of births were illegitimate in Costa Rica, and 67.4 percent were so classified in El Salvador (United Nations, 1986, p. 856).[10]

Class Structure and Poverty

In Central America, lower-class individuals constitute the vast majority of the population. Estimates of the percentage of the population that was lower class in 1970 ranged from a low of 76.9 percent in Costa Rica to a high of 88.2 percent in Guatemala (Wilkie and Ochoa, 1985, p. 273, citing Filgueira and Genelitti, 1981, p. 53; data available on all five Central American countries). Another measure of stratification is poverty estimates, available for Costa Rica and Honduras. About 1970, the percentage of households below the poverty line was estimated at 24 percent for Costa Rica and 65 percent for Honduras, with rates higher in rural than urban areas (Wilkie and Ochoa, 1985, p. 278, citing Altimir, 1979, p. 63).

Educational Attainment

Data on educational attainment by gender are provided in Table 4.1. (For Costa Rica, El Salvador, Guatemala, and Nicaragua, the data are available for the 1950s and 1970s; for Honduras, data are available for the 1960s, 1970s, and 1980s.) The data indicate that gender differences in educational attainment in the earlier period were fairly small relative to other Third World countries (compare Smock, 1981). Further, the differences diminished somewhat over time. Hence, by the 1970s and 1980s, women's access to educational resources was, overall, fairly similar to that of men. Standing's (1976, 1982) hypothesis, then, would suggest that education and labor force participation should be positively related. (Data presented later compare overall educational attainment with that of the population considered economically active.) It is also important to note the much lower levels of educational attainment in rural than urban areas, a factor pertinent for agricultural workers and rural-urban migrants.

Labor Force Participation

An overview of changes in labor force participation by gender is provided in Table 4.2. The figures represent the percentages of all females and males (including children) who were economically active in 1950, 1960, and 1980 in each of the five Central American countries.

Table 4.1. Educational Attainment by Gender Among Population Age 25 and Older (percent)

Year and Country		Gender	Pop. (1000s)	Incomplete Primary	Complete Primary	Secondary[a]	Tertiary[a]
Costa Rica							
1950	Total	MF	276	62.5	33.2	2.8	1.5
		F	149	63.0	33.4	2.7	1.0
1973	Total	MF	658	65.2	17.8	11.2	5.8
		F	331	65.8	17.7	11.0	5.4
	Urban	MF	298	44.6	24.8	19.9	10.6
		F	162	47.4	24.4	19.0	9.3
	Rural	MF	360	82.4	12.1	3.8	1.8
		F	170	83.4	11.4	3.4	1.7
El Salvador							
1973	Total	MF	1240	—	93.0 —[b]	6.1	.9
1980[b]	Total	MF	3132	90.9	—	6.9[c] —	2.3 —
		F	1635	91.4	—	6.6 —	1.9 —
Guatemala							
1950	Total	MF	1028	88.5	10.1	1.0	.5
		F	510	89.6	9.4	.9	.1
1973	Total	MF	1786	—	93.9 —	4.9	1.2
		F	898	—	94.7 —	4.8	.5
	Urban	MF	640	—	85.2 —	11.8	2.9
	Rural	MF	1146	—	98.7 —	1.1	.2
Honduras							
1961	Total	MF	615	84.8	12.6	2.1	.5
		F	314	85.8	12.2	1.9	.1
1974	Total	MF	858	87.6	6.0	5.3	1.0
		F	440	88.4	6.0	5.2	.4
	Urban	MF	280	70.6	12.5	13.9	3.0
		F	152	73.9	12.0	13.0	1.1
	Rural	MF	579	95.9	2.9	1.2	.1
		F	288	96.1	2.8	1.1	0.0
1983	Total	MF	n/a	84.8	—	4.3[c] —	10.9 —
		F	n/a	85.2	—	4.4 —	10.5 —
Nicaragua							
1950	Total	MF	390	84.2	14.4	1.0	.4
		F	204	84.6	14.7	.7	.1
1971	Total	MF	593	73.2	—	22.5 — —	4.4 —

Sources: UNESCO (1964, 1987); Wilkie and Ochoa (1984).

[a]For secondary and tertiary education figures, the earlier census shows highest year completed; the later censuses show highest year attended.

[b]The 1980 data for El Salvador are for the population 10 years of age and older; thus figures are not comparable to those for the population 25 years of age and older.

[c]These figures show primary complete combined with the first cycle of secondary education. In the following column, the second cycle of secondary education is combined with the figure for tertiary education.

Except for Guatemala and Honduras, the general tendency was for female labor force participation to increase between 1950 and 1980.[11] This might suggest that equity in access to educational resources (as shown in Table 4.1)

Table 4.2. Economically Active Population by Gender (percent of total population)

	1950[a]		1960[b]		1980	
	Women	Men	Women	Men	Women	Men
Costa Rica	10.4	57.6	9.6	49.5	17.2	52.4
El Salvador	11.6	59.3	11.3	53.6	24.0	47.5
Guatemala	9.0	59.8	7.9	54.6	8.7	54.2
Honduras	41.8	52.8	7.7	52.7	9.5	49.2
Nicaragua	8.6	54.5	12.3	50.0	13.3	51.4

Sources: ILO (1955, 1960, 1970, 1982).
Note: "Economically active" is defined in text below.
[a]1950 figures for Costa Rica, El Salvador, and Nicaragua exclude population under 15 years of age.
[b]1960 figures are 1963 for Costa Rica, 1961 for El Salvador, and 1964 for Guatemala.

could have been related to an increase in labor force participation. However, the figures on female labor force participation are problematic, making assessments of change in overall employment subject to question.

The data for Honduras show a dramatic decrease in the percentage of economically active females, from 41.8 percent in 1950 to 9.5 percent in 1980. This apparent change is indicative of the problems associated with measuring women's labor force participation and is important because it provides an alternative estimate of female labor force participation.

The discrepancy probably results from a shift in the census definition of "economically active" in agriculture. The later censuses adopted a definition that included only those individuals who worked full-time, full-year. Problems of underrepresentation of women's economic activity in agriculture are noted throughout the literature (e.g., Boserup, 1970; PREALC, 1978; Dixon, 1982; Buvinic, 1982).

Women's labor force participation is underrepresented not only in agricultural work but also in informal-sector activity.[12] Men's employment is underestimated in the informal sector as well, but the problem is more severe for women because urban women are disproportionately located in this sector; only their work as domestic servants is regularly counted.

Agricultural Work

Undercounting of women's labor force participation in agriculture is of critical importance in the predominantly rural economies of Central America, where male agricultural workers constituted from 43.3 percent (Costa Rica in 1973) to 69.6 percent (Honduras in 1973) of all economically active males. The reported percentage of economically active women engaged in agricultural work ranged from 2.9 percent in Costa Rica (1973) to 13.6 percent in El Salvador (1978; data on all five countries from the International Labour Organisation, 1976, 1977, 1979, 1980). The wide disparity in educational attainment between rural and urban areas implies that agricultural workers have some of the lowest educational levels.

Women perform a variety of economic activities in agriculture, but their wage employment is highly seasonal. Discontinuous employment contributes to the underenumeration of female workers in census data. Women are generally employed for specified periods of the year, usually at harvest. Recent censuses base the definition of economic activity on work done during the previous week rather than for the entire year, a measurement approach that misses the full extent of women's participation in agriculture.

In general, females have few opportunities for stable employment in rural areas. Women are generally employed only at certain stages of the production process; opportunities for men are more regular and more numerous (PREALC, 1978, p. 72). For example, in Costa Rica, women "work as salaried laborers . . . in the harvesting of coffee during three consecutive months of the year, six days a week and up to ten hours a day" (Buvinic, 1982, p. 105). A similar situation exists in cotton production in Honduras:

> Although the preparation of land and the sowing are performed by men with tractors, there are four stages in the cotton cycle, which lasts six months, in which "manpower" is needed. In this, women carry out probably 50% of the work: in the selection and removal of plants while the sprouts are small; in the fertilization stage two months prior to the sowing when they apply powders to the plants; during the weeding process that lasts throughout the whole cycle; and during the harvest time when they pick the mature cotton for three months (AID, 1978, p. 4).

Buvinic's (1982) study of female employment in several rural areas of Honduras showed that women workers in coffee and tobacco harvesting worked 5.4 months and 3 months per year, respectively, and worked for lower wages than men. Based on her case study, Buvinic estimated that the number of women employed in agriculture in the Copan region in 1974 was approximately 11,640, far higher than the census estimate of 642 (Buvinic, 1982). Further, Buvinic noted that women were engaged in a variety of wage-earning activities in the rural informal sector; they predominated as artisans and operators (Buvinic, 1982, citing data from an unpublished study of the Center for Industrial Technical Cooperation, Tegucigalpa, Honduras, 1978), as well as in small markets and the cigar industry (Buvinic, 1982).

Rural-Urban Migration

The unstable nature of women's paid work in rural areas translates into severe seasonal unemployment (PREALC, 1978, p. 72) and contributes to a gender difference in rates of rural-urban migration. As is common in other areas of Latin America, rates of migration to the urban areas of Costa Rica, El Salvador, and Nicaragua were consistently higher for women than men (Elizaga, 1970, pp. 21, 31). Roberts (1973, as per Nieves, 1979) also found that in Guatemala, females migrated to the cities more frequently and at younger ages than males. Geographic mobility of these relatively poorly educated women, in combination with their form of insertion in the urban labor market, may also contribute to the underenumeration problem.

Informal-Sector Work

The general pattern suggested by studies of migrants in Latin American cities is a pronounced tendency for females to engage in domestic service and, moreover, "a wide difference in the employment profile of native and migrant women and, among the latter, between the recent and earlier arrivals" (Jelín, 1977, p. 133). Notably, the consistent differences in the employment patterns of native and migrant women are not matched by patterns of male employment; studies of male employment "have shown no clear pattern of differentials between male migrants and natives" (Jelín, 1977, p. 33). Migrant status and the presumably low levels of education that accompany it do not appear to affect adversely the labor market position of men as much as they do that of women.

The tendency for migrant women to be employed as domestic servants is consistent with findings that the urban informal sector is largely comprised of rural-urban migrants. In San Salvador, "the proportion of migrants who had been resident more than 10 years and were engaged in informal activities was still as high as 50 per cent compared with nearly 70 per cent of those who had arrived during the past year and 39 per cent for natives of the city" (Souza and Tokman, 1976, p. 360).[13]

The urban informal sector is a critically important area of women's economic activity. In San Salvador, one study estimated that 63 percent of all women residents worked in the informal sector (Souza and Tokman, 1976, p. 360). This figure is in marked contrast to the overall 24 percent rate of female labor force participation given in 1980 census data (see Table 4.2). Moreover, the finding that more women work in the informal than the formal sector remains true even when domestic service (the single most common occupation for women) is excluded from informal-sector activities (Souza and Tokman, 1976, p. 359).

Workers in the informal sector, like workers in agriculture, tend to be very poorly educated. In San Salvador 73 percent of informal-sector workers had three or fewer years of education (PREALC, 1975). Underenumeration of female workers in the informal sector, as in agricultural employment, can thus have profound implications for the association between education and labor force participation.

▲ Relation of Education to Labor Force Participation

Table 4.3 presents available census data on educational levels for the female and male labor force. The Nicaraguan data are about 1970; data for the other countries are about 1960 because 1970 data were not broken down by gender in the statistical reports for that year.

The data show that the women defined by the census as economically active were, on average, better educated than women as a group (compare Table 4.3 with Table 4.1). According to these data, there is a much higher percentage of better-educated women in the labor force than among the population as a whole. Further, although women overall were slightly less educated than men, the women considered economically active tended to be better educated than their male counterparts. The percentage of economically active women with three or fewer years of education was lower than the percentage of economically active men at the same educational level.[14]

Thus, the data suggest that the female labor force has an overrepresentation of better-educated women, that better-educated women are more likely to work than poorly educated women, and that the relationship between education and labor force participation is positive. Similarly, one study, using census data for San Jose (Costa Rica), found a positive association between educational attainment and urban female labor force participation, with women who had secondary education being the most likely to work (Uthoff and González, 1978). This study also found that the composition of the female labor force shifted between 1963 and 1973 so that better-educated women formed a larger percentage of workers than those who were poorly educated.[15] These data also suggest that it may have been increasingly difficult for poorly educated women to find "legitimate" work.[16]

Census data, then, suggest a positive association between education and labor force participation for women. However, as previously mentioned, those groups of women engaged in agricultural and urban informal sector activity, whose participation is undercounted, are precisely the groups with the lowest educational attainment levels.

Correcting the low estimates in the censuses of women's participation would have the effect of altering the observed positive association between education and labor force participation. It is likely that if the large numbers of poorly educated women in agricultural and informal-sector work were included, the relationship between education and labor force participation in the Central American countries would approximate more nearly a curvilinear than a straight positive association, with both poorly educated and well-educated women being more likely to work than women with average levels of education. (This is a preliminary suggestion; case studies that adopt an alternative definition of labor force participation[17] are recommended to test whether this idea would be borne out in direct empirical investigations.)

Table 4.3. Educational Level of the Economically Active Population by Gender, About 1960 (percent)

Country and Gender	Total			Years of School Completed			
		0–3	4–6	7–9	10–12	13+	N/A
Costa Rica							
Women	100.0	34.6	40.8	9.3	6.4	8.8	0.3
Men	100.0	54.0	35.2	4.8	3.5	2.3	0.2
Total	100.0	50.6	36.2	5.6	4.0	3.4	0.2
El Salvador							
Women	100.0	68.9	18.4	6.7	5.3	0.1	0.5
Men	100.0	80.8	13.4	2.5	1.7	0.6	1.0
Total	100.0	78.4	14.2	3.2	2.3	0.5	0.9
Guatemala							
Women	100.0	20.1	18.5	5.1	5.9	1.0	49.3
Men	100.0	24.9	10.4	1.9	1.2	0.9	60.7
Total	100.0	24.4	11.4	2.9	1.8	0.9	59.3
Honduras							
Women	100.0	63.0	20.5	4.6	8.8	0.5	2.7
Men	100.0	83.0	11.0	1.2	1.6	0.7	2.6
Total	100.0	80.4	12.3	1.7	2.6	0.6	2.6
Nicaragua[a]							
Women	100.0	53.7	27.4	6.8	6.7	2.0	3.3
Men	100.0	69.9	17.7	3.8	2.5	2.3	3.8
Total	100.0	66.4	19.8	4.5	3.4	2.3	3.7

Source: CEPAL (1975), based on national censuses.
[a]Figures for Nicaragua are for 1970.

▲ Measurement of Economic Activity and Women's Employment Position

Why is women's economic activity in agriculture and in the urban informal sector so grossly undercounted? In addition to political factors that influence the ways in which different people's economic activity is defined,[18] the answer has to do with the unstable nature of women's employment in these areas. With respect to the latter, most women have few options for stable employment in Latin America:

> Women are concentrated in a group of "feminine" occupations that is relatively limited. This is true for all educational levels, in that if women reach middle or higher levels of education they tend to be concentrated in a determined set of professional activities: secretarial, teaching, paramedical, etc., which in certain measure counteracts the impact of variables like years of education and earnings capacity in

relation to the professional activities of men (PREALC, 1978, pp. 127–128).

Well-educated women are disadvantaged relative to men by virtue of the high degree of gender segregation in stable occupations (Boulding et al., 1976, p. 132). Segregation results in lower wages in female-dominated occupations.[19]

For poorly educated women, particularly older women, segregation is compounded by the problem of access to stable employment, because many low-level female-dominated occupations are relatively unstable. Arizpe, noting that Latin American women's involvement in the labor force declines after age 25, argues that there is a corresponding increase in informal activities (1977, p. 29). Studies conducted by PREALC have shown high concentrations of both younger and older workers in the informal sector; in San Salvador the former tended to be domestic servants and blue-collar workers in small enterprises, while the latter tended to be self-employed (Souza and Tokman, 1976, pp. 359–360). Particularly for poorly educated older women, whose range of options for employment in stable work is extremely limited and whose education levels are likely to be lower than those of younger women, informal-sector activity represents an area where they can essentially create their own demand. "From the point of view of the labor market, [the informal sector's] essential characteristic is the facility of entry" (PREALC, 1978, p. 73).

However, this characteristic is indicative of the precarious position of informal-sector workers, whose share of total employment is growing. The percentage of the economically active population involved in informal-sector activities rose in all the Central American countries over the 1950–1980 period (PREALC, 1982, pp. 47, 55, 57, 60, 67).[20]

Informal-sector activity is characterized by uninstitutionalized, small-scale operations, with low technology. As a result, wages are generally lower than in the formal sector (see Table 4.4). The same instability that contributes to underenumeration also contributes to low wages. As shown in the table, mean earnings at almost every level of education are markedly lower in the informal sector than the formal sector. Female earnings are lower than male earnings for all formal-sector workers. This is also true for most informal-sector workers.[21] Thus, activity in the informal sector is remunerated more poorly than in the formal sector, regardless of educational level, and women are generally remunerated more poorly than men.

Clearly, the most disadvantaged urban workers are women in the informal sector, where most urban women are employed. Further, a disproportionate number of these women are heads of household. Souza and Tokman's study of San Salvador showed that the informal sector contained a higher percentage of heads of household than the economy as a whole, and they suggested that "the informal sector employs a high

Table 4.4. Average Remuneration by Sector, Gender, and Type of Job, San Salvador (colones per week)

Years of Education	All Jobs		White-Collar Jobs Men and Women		Men		Blue-Collar Jobs Men and Women		Men	
	I	F	I	F	I	F	I	F	I	F
0–3	20	44	14	55	22	58	21	37	25	39
4–6	28	53	35	69	44	77	27	40	30	42
7–9	66	70	41	75	38	80	42	35	42	37
10–12	132	108	51	114	41	136	—	49	—	55
13+	212	237	64	227	82	280	—	—	—	—
All Workers	38	100	38	108	43	124	27	39	30	41

Source: PREALC (1975).
Note: I = informal sector; F = formal sector.

percentage of young and/or female heads of families" (Souza and Tokman, 1976, p. 360).

▲ Conclusion

Education appears to be more relevant to stable labor force participation for women than for men in Central America. Women engaged in stable employment tend to have considerably more education than women engaged in the unstable work that is undercounted by the census. For men, however, education has been a less important criterion for obtaining stable employment. Of course, those who are impacted most heavily by this disparity are poorly educated women, whose family situation often requires them to work.

Theoretical research on education and labor force participation would benefit from a consideration of the experiences of different groups of women, especially lower-class and Third World women. The simple positive association between education and labor force participation found in studies that rely on census data obscures the reality facing poorly educated, Third World women by implying that it is education that serves to bring women into the labor force. Education does appear to be related to employment in stable labor market sectors. But the data reported by the census make it appear that few poorly educated women engage in economic activity, thereby supporting underdeveloped theoretical models and focusing policy attention on (1) those women who are considered economically active and (2) strategies to bring other women into the labor force. If, as I and others have suggested, poorly educated women are already in the labor force in much larger numbers than are revealed by census data, a more fruitful emphasis would be to seek means of improving wages and stability for them.

▲ Notes

Special thanks go to Nelly Stromquist for her comments, suggestions, and encouragement on this chapter. Thanks also to Angela Valenzuela for her helpful comments and suggestions on the final draft. I would also like to extend my appreciation to Martin Carnoy, Elizabeth Cohen, Edmundo Fuenzalida, Francisco Ramirez, and Martha Roldan for their comments on earlier papers upon which this chapter is based.

An earlier version of this chapter was presented at the Western Region Conference of the Comparative International Education Society, Los Angeles, California, November 13, 1987. Another version constituted my master's thesis in the International Development Education Program at Stanford University in August 1986.

1. Standing notes that aspirations also may lead to a reluctance to work in the informal sector, and that a "status frustration effect" makes conceivable a negative association between education and labor force participation (Standing, 1976, 1982).

2. Such a pattern would be consistent with that found in industrialized countries (Standing, 1976, p. 295).

3. Equalization also should make men less able to meet the increased income aspirations of their wives, contributing to the likelihood of dual-earner families (Standing, 1976).

4. Abundant literature on employment discrimination, dual and segmented labor markets, and occupational segregation suggests that features of the labor market other than individual qualifications impact access to labor market resources.

5. Standing (1982) differs from his earlier work (Standing, 1976) in acknowledging that there is a "tendency for the least educated to belong to households in which incomes are very low, making labour force participation a necessary condition for survival" (1982, p. 153). This recognition, however, does not lead him to alter his proposition regarding the likely positive association between education and female labor force participation.

6. As Ram (1980) notes, an education–labor force participation association is not necessarily causal. "Even if a positive covariance between education and female market activity rate is observed, it would not necessarily reflect the effect of education; the correlation may be due to the operation of other variables that affect both education and labor force participation, for example, aspiration levels, connections, or opportunities" (p. S64). Another variable that may affect the correlation is social class background.

7. With respect to unemployment partners, Bowen and Finnegan (1966) found that the percentage of wives with impecunious husbands in the United States tended "to be higher among married women with little schooling than among those with much," and this factor tended "to increase participation" (p. 578).

8. In a somewhat similar vein, Papanek (1985) argues that "one of the least

understood processes is the interaction between gender and class as it is revealed in the linkages between formal schooling and remunerated work" (p. 317).

9. Similarly, for young women, support by fathers and male family members is assumed to be sufficient.

10. Note that consensual unions are relatively common in Central America, and it is not clear what proportion of "illegitimate" births are to women in consensual unions versus to women with no partner. Marriage rates per thousand individuals were 8.5 for Costa Rica and 3.5 for El Salvador in 1984. The corresponding U.S. rate in 1984 was 10.5 (Wilkie and Ochoa, 1989, p. 142).

11. It is not clear whether the apparent decline in female labor force participation in Guatemala may have been an artifact of changes in measurement.

12. Informal-sector activity is difficult to measure and requires the use of indirect indicators. According to Souza and Tokman (1976), "The sector may be defined as comprising all those engaged in domestic service, casual laborers, the self-employed, and employers, white-collar, blue-collar and family workers in enterprises with a total staff of not more than four persons" (p. 356). Whereas this definition overestimates informal-sector activity, agricultural employment remains underestimated.

13. See ibid. for the definition of informal sector activity used in this study.

14. The exception is Guatemala, but data on it are incomplete, with information on educational levels missing for 60.7 percent of the work force.

15. Uthoff and González's (1978) Table 3 provides the following information on the breakdown of the female labor force, aged 15–49, by educational level, in San Jose, Costa Rica:

Yrs. of Ed.	1963	1973
0–3	26.4%	13.9%
4–6	43.0%	41.3%
7+	30.6%	44.8%

The trend for better-educated women to compose a larger share of the female labor force results in part from an overall increase in educational attainment in the population. This is not the sole reason, however, because the same trend is apparent for older cohorts. Women who were 25 and over in 1963 presumably did not experience much change in educational attainment over the ten-year period, yet there was a tendency for poorly educated workers to decline in representation in these (artificial) cohorts:

Age Group in 1963	Yrs. of Ed.	1963	1973*
25–29	0–3	24.7%	19.0%
	4–6	32.9%	38.6%
	7+	42.4%	42.4%
30–34	0–3	27.9%	24.6%
	4–6	42.9%	39.6%
	7+	29.2%	35.8%
35–39	0–3	29.2%	19.1%
	4–6	40.9%	51.7%
	7+	29.9%	29.2%

*The 1973 figures are for the age group that is 10 years older than the 1963 group. These are not necessarily the same women.

16. A changing and differential demand for well-educated and poorly educated female labor, reflected in census data, is consistent with Papanek's work on other regions of the Third World. She notes that in South and Southeast Asia, as well as in Egypt, there has been a "rapid rise in demand for educated female labor in the modern sector of the economy and . . . declining demand for less educated women workers" (Papanek, 1985, p. 319).

17. Dixon (1982) discusses studies that use alternative measures of labor force participation, particularly in agriculture. Deere (1982) and Wainerman and Recchini de Lattes (1981) suggest that the form of the census taker's questioning can significantly alter estimates of female economic activity (both provided per Dixon, 1982). Dixon also cites empirical evidence that alternative time references produced vastly different estimates of rural labor force participation.

18. This is true both for census takers and for respondents. As already noted, alternative definitions of economic activity influence estimates of labor force participation. Further, individual women (and men, since their reports of family members' activities are sometimes used), when asked about women's primary occupation, will often respond that the woman is a housewife or is inactive, despite significant economic activity. (See Dixon, 1982, for a fuller discussion.)

19. Bergmann (1974) has argued that when a group of workers has access only to a limited range of occupations, competition and overcrowding will depress wages in those occupations, and wages will be inflated in the occupations to which they do not have access. Consistent with this argument, several empirical studies have found that a high proportion of women in an occupation depresses wages over time (Catanzarite, 1987; Snyder and Hudis, 1976; Treiman and Terrell, 1975).

20. PREALC (1982) data showed an increase despite the fact that "the international agencies that are the source of these data define informal employment . . . [as excluding] . . . informal wage workers, that is, those who are hired casually and lack social security protection. . . . In Latin America, . . . this assumption leads to a gross underestimate of informal employment because a large proportion of wage laborers are employed in microenterprises that are either legally exempted from the existing labor legislation or simply do not observe it" (Portes and Sassen-Koob, 1987, p. 35).

21. More precisely, in the informal sector, women's earnings are lower than men's in blue-collar jobs at all levels of education, except in the category of 7–9 years of education, where earnings are equal for women and men. In white-collar jobs, women's earnings are lower than men's for individuals with 0–3, 4–6, and greater than 13 years of education; among workers with 7–9 and 10–12 years of schooling, women's earnings are somewhat higher than men's. One can reasonably conclude that most women workers in the informal sector earn less than their male counterparts because most informal-sector jobs are blue collar and most workers have less than 7 years of education. As noted previously, 73 percent of informal sector workers in San Salvador had three or fewer years of education (PREALC, 1975).

▲ References

AID (Agencia para el Desarollo Internacional). *Diagnóstico para el sector agrícola para Honduras*. Washington, D.C.: AID, 1978.

Altimir, Oscar. *La dimensión de la pobreza en América Latina, no. 27*. Santiago, Chile: Economic Commission for Latin America, 1979.

Albelda, Randy. "Occupational Segregation by Race and Gender, 1958–1981," *Industrial and Labor Relations Review*, vol. 39, no. 3, April 1986, pp. 404–411.

Arizpe, Lourdes. "Women in the Informal Labor Sector: The Case of Mexico City." *Signs*. 1977, no. 3, pp. 25–37.

Bergmann, Barbara R. "Occupational Segregation, Wages, and Profits When Employers Discriminate by Race or Sex." *Eastern Economics Journal*, 1974, no. 1, pp. 103–110.

Boserup, Ester. *Woman's Role in Economic Development*. New York: St. Martin's Press, 1970.

Boulding, Elise, Shirley A. Nuss, Dorothy Lee Carson, and Michael A. Greenstein. *Handbook of International Data on Women*. New York: Halsted Press, 1976.

Bowen, William G., and T. Aldrich Finnegan. "Educational Attainment and Labor Force Participation." *American Economic Review*, 1966, vol. 65, no. 2, pp. 567–582.

Buvinic, Mayra. "La productora invisible en el agro centroamericano: Un estudio de caso en Honduras." In Magdalena Leon (ed.), *Debate sobre la mujer en América Latina y el Caribe*, no. 2, pp. 103–113. Bogota: ACEP, 1982.

Catanzarite, Lisa M. "Gender Composition, Education, and Work Dimensions in Occupations." Paper presented at the annual meeting of the American Sociological Association, Chicago, Illinois, 1987.

CEPAL (Comisión Económica para América Latina). *Mujeres en América Latina: Aportes para una discusión*. Mexico: Fondo de Cultura Económica, 1975.

Deere, Carmen Diana. "The Division of Labor by Sex in Agriculture: A Peruvian Case Study." *Economic Development and Cultural Change*, vol. 30, no. 4, 1982, pp. 795–811.

Dixon, Ruth. "Women in Agriculture: Counting the Labor Force in Developing Countries." *Population and Development Review*, 1982, vol. 8, no. 3, pp. 539–566.

Elizaga, Juan C. *Migraciones a las áreas metropolitanas de América Latina*. Santiago, Chile: Centro Latinoamericano de Demografía (CELADE), 1970.

Filgueira, Carlos, and Carlo Genelitti. *Estratificación y movilidad ocupacional en América Latina*. Santiago: Economic Commission for Latin America, 1981.

González, Nancie L. "Toward a Definition of Matrifocality." In N. E. Whitten, Jr., and J. F. Szwed (eds.), *Afro-American Anthropology*. New York: Free Press, 1970.

ILO (International Labour Organisation). *Yearbook of Labor Statistics*. Geneva: ILO, 1955, 1960, 1970, 1976, 1977, 1979, 1980, 1982.

Jelín, Elizabeth. "Migration and Labor Force Participation of Latin American Women: The Domestic Servants in the Cities." *Signs*, 1977, vol. 3, no. 1, pp. 129–141.

López de Piza, Eugenia. "La familia matrifocal como mecanismo de adaptación de la mujer a su marginalidad." Paper presented at the first Mexican–Central American symposium on research on women, Mexico City, November 7–9, 1977.

Nieves, Isabel. "Household Arrangements and Multiple Jobs in San Salvador." *Signs*, 1979, vol. 5, no. 11, pp. 134–142.

Papanek, Hanna. "Class and Gender in Education-Employment Linkages." *Comparative Education Review*, 1985, vol. 29, no. 3, pp. 317–346.

Portes, Alejandro, and Saskia Sassen-Koob. "Making It Underground: Comparative Material on the Informal Sector in Western Market

Economies." *American Journal of Sociology*, 1987, vol. 93, no. 1, pp. 30-61.

PREALC (Programa Regional del Empleo para América Latina y el Caribe). *Situación y perspectivas sobre el empleo en El Salvador*. Santiago: Oficina Internacional del Trabajo, 1975.

———. *Investigaciones sobre empleo: Participación laboral femenina y diferencias de remuneraciones según sexo en América Latina*. Oficina Internacional del Trabajo, 1978.

———. *Mercado de trabajo en Cifras 1950–1980*. Oficina Internacional del Trabajo, 1982.

Ram, Rati. "Sex Differences in the Labor Market Outcomes of Education." *Comparative Education Review*, 1980, vol. 24, no. 2, part 2, pp. S53–S77.

Roberts, Bryan. "The Social Organization of Low-Income Urban Families." In Richard N. Adams (ed.), *Crucifixion by Power*. Austin: University of Texas Press, 1970.

———. *Organizing Strangers: Poor Families in Guatemala City*. Austin: University of Texas Press, 1973.

Smock, Audrey. *Women's Education in Developing Countries: Opportunities and Outcomes*. New York: Praeger, 1981.

Snyder, David, and Paula Hudis. "Occupational Income and the Effects of Minority Competition and Segregation: A Reanalysis and Some New Evidence." *American Sociological Review*, 1976, vol. 41, pp. 209–234.

Souza, Paulo R., and Victor E. Tokman. "The Informal Urban Sector in Latin America." *International Labour Review*, 1976, vol. 114, no. 3, pp. 355–365.

Standing, Guy. "Education and Female Participation in the Labour Force." *International Labour Review*, 1976, vol. 114, no. 3, pp. 281–297.

———. "The Impact of Education on Participation." In Guy Standing (ed.), *Labor Force Participation and Development*. Geneva: International Labor Office, 1982.

Treiman, Donald, and Kermit Terrell. "Women, Work, and Wages: Trends in the Female Occupational Structure." In Kenneth Land and Seymour Spilerman (eds.), *Social Indicator Models*. New York: Russell Sage, 1975.

United Nations. *Demographic Yearbook*. New York: United Nations, 1986.

UNESCO (United Nations Educational, Scientific, and Cultural Organization). *Statistical Yearbook*. Paris: UNESCO, 1964, 1987.

Uthoff, Andras, and Gerardo González. "Mexico and Costa Rica: Some Evidence on Women's Participation in Economic Activity." In Guy Standing and Glen Sheehan (eds.), *Labor Force Participation in Low-Income Countries*. Geneva: International Labor Organization, 1978.

Wainerman, Catalina. "The Impact of Education on the Female Labor Force in Argentina and Paraguay." *Comparative Education Review*, 1980, vol. 24, no. 2, part 2, pp. S180–S195.

Wainerman, Catalina, and Zulma Recchini de Lattes. *El trabajo femenino en el banquillo de los acusados: La medición censal en América Latina*. Mexico: Editorial Terra Nova and the Population Council, 1981.

Wilkie, James W., and Enrique Ochoa (eds.). *Statistical Abstract of Latin America 22*. Los Angeles: University of California Los Angeles, Latin American Center Publications, 1984.

———. *Statistical Abstract of Latin America 23*. Los Angeles: University of California Los Angeles, Latin American Center Publications, 1985.

———. *Statistical Abstract of Latin America 27*. Los Angeles: University of California Los Angeles, Latin American Center Publications, 1989.

PART 2

Women and the Formal Education System

▲ 5

Coeducational Settings and Educational and Social Outcomes in Peru

Violeta Sara-Lafosse

The study by Sara-Lafosse is unusual in that it considers benefits other than academic achievement for the development of boys and girls in schools. Her findings have to be appreciated in the context of a Latin society that is *machista* in nature and in which strong beliefs about the sexual division of labor prevail.

Research in other countries indicates that boys tend to benefit from both single-sex and coeducational schools. They accrue benefits under both settings from the preferential treatment they tend to receive from both men and women teachers. Research that controls for factors such as socioeconomic status has also shown that in some countries girls register greater gains in academic achievement when they attend single-sex schools.

Although coeducational schools may be in some instances detrimental to girls' cognitive growth and may send hidden curricula messages reinforcing women's subordination, particularly through the modeling of men in important administrative positions, the coexistence of girls and boys in settings defined as serious and formal tends to reduce the myths of masculinity and femininity that set the genders apart from each other.

Sara-Lafosse's study shows that student perceptions of equal abilities by both sexes along a wide range of dimensions (intellectual to artistic) tend to be higher among students with substantial exposure to coeducational schooling than among those whose experience has been limited mostly to single-sex schools. Her data also show that levels of aggression—an essential feature of *machista* behavior—and the belief that housework is solely a woman's task diminish for boys in coeducational schools. For those who think of the many virtues in single-sex schooling, Sara-Lafosse presents a view of other gains that accrue when there is a more open contact between male and female students.

—Editor

▲ The statistically verified lower educational level of women in comparison with men has generated considerable concern about the education of women. However, this imbalance varies from one country to another. In some countries, it is apparent in the first few grades of primary education; in other countries, it is manifested in the lower number of women who graduate in certain fields at the university level. In the former case, there might be unanimous concern; in the latter, the level of concern will depend on one's notion of the place of women in society.

Women have experienced neglect regarding educational matters, a condition they share with many other social minorities. Minorities may be composed of racial or ethnic groups, but they may also be constituted by social categories. The struggle for equality of educational opportunities is clear and rather widely shared in the case of racial or ethnic minorities. In the case of socially defined minorities or, in a narrower sense, occupational groups, the converse is true: No demands are usually made to remedy educational disadvantages of peasants and workers because it is assumed they will make little use of the education provided for them.

People often react to the education of women in a similar manner. This occurs because in most societies there is a sexual division of labor, according to which women have been assigned a role that they alone must fulfill, while men have been assigned another role that they monopolize. However, both roles are not equivalent, neither in the power they provide nor in the level of education required.

The preceding thoughts provide an increased understanding of the objections that are voiced in efforts to raise the educational standard of women—for example, that when women obtain access to all educational levels and specialties, they will invariably attempt to acquire the employment positions and higher levels of authority that have been heretofore reserved exclusively for men. This condition will present a twofold problem: Not only will women occupy those positions previously reserved for men, but in so doing, women will neglect and leave undone all the other activities now currently reserved for them.

The problem, as stated, can be resolved only if it is realized that heretofore both women and men have been socialized to play and fulfill certain roles; consequently, any changes brought about in the education of women must be accompanied by changes in the education of men. This is the only way to bring about effective change in a harmonious manner and to avoid unnecessary gender conflicts.

Men and women maintain permanent relations in the family sphere, but other cross-gender relations are becoming increasingly more frequent in several areas of social life. In order to preserve the hierarchical organization of gender relations, men must internalize a sense of superiority to justify their authoritarian behavior. Conversely, women are conditioned to acquire a sense of inferiority so that without protest or resistance they may be placed in a subordinate position.

Both the new education of women and the new education of men assume that the hierarchical relations between men and women should be reconsidered for them to learn to live together as peers. This means that both genders must learn how to perform all kinds of tasks, without considering as unworthy of men those tasks that the current division of labor has assigned to women. This further implies the abandonment of many stereotypes about femininity and masculinity that previously have been assumed to be natural "realities" rather than social consequences. It is these stereotypes—products of the social construction by particular organized groups and certainly not social facts emerging from each culture and society as a result of democratic processes—that must be abandoned.

▲ School and Gendered Education

Both family and school compete with each other in the education of children and adolescents. However, the family has an advantage over the school in two ways: First, it shelters the child during his or her first years of life, years during which the basic personality structure of the child is established, including the identification with a particular gender; second, it establishes a strong emotional bond between the child and the adult. The school, on the other hand, introduces the child to relationships with his or her peers and encourages him or her to live together with strangers, with whom the child must learn to interact and who, in turn, are going to know and appreciate him or her.

The family and the school are social institutions that have emerged from the culture of which they are a part. If the society is based upon a division of labor according to gender, then this division is an important element not only in the relations within the family but also in the structuring and content of the educational system.

To the extent that the sexual division of labor is taken as a given by the family, it will result in the acquisition of a different education for men and women beginning with early childhood. This education means not only that the genders will behave in a different way but that the relationship between them will be characterized by patterns that establish the subordination and servitude of women by men.

In the Latin American context, one of the most effective ways by which the school system ensures the sexual division of labor is through single-sex education. This arrangement not only promotes different educational programs, but it also (and perhaps this is its most harmful effect) encourages individuals to associate only with members of their own gender, thereby diminishing or eliminating altogether the possibility of developing egalitarian relationships with members of the other gender.

It is in this context that coeducation has the power to question the hierarchical division of labor. Specifically, it allows men and women to be educated together in a situation based not upon domination and subordination by gender but upon freedom from bias and the acknowledgment that men and women can relate to each other as peers. This observation suggests that it is meaningful to raise a number of questions concerning the maintenance of separate school systems both in several Latin American countries and within certain social classes.

The prevailing interactions between genders in society and the system of coeducation have been investigated by UNESCO and other international organizations. They all conclude that if the social environment is diversified, the environment of the school also tends to be diversified. In other words, "the more that women participate on equal terms with men in the activities of daily life, work, politics, business, culture, and entertainment, the more it will be considered normal that the school environment be coeducational at all levels" (De Grandpré, 1973, p. 73).

The preceding assertions are in complete agreement with the definition of education provided by Durkheim after examining education through history: "Education is the action performed by adult generations upon those who are still found not yet ready for the social life; it has the purpose of stirring up and developing in the child a certain number of physical, intellectual, and moral conditions, which are demanded by the political society as a whole, and by the particular environment to which every child, individually, is destined" (Durkheim, 1975, p. 53). When applying this definition to the examination of educational realities, it should be remembered that if male and female roles are differentiated in every Latin American political society and within several social contexts, then to accomplish this differentiation, it is necessary to create an educational system that develops different physical, intellectual, and moral conditions.

▲ Coeducation and Change in Gender Roles

The investigation of gender roles in single-sex educational schools, compared with those that are coeducational, makes it possible to specify the ways in which coeducation helps to transform such roles. This study is based on a representative sample of students in their senior year of high school and teachers in public schools in Lima. Data were also obtained from fathers or mothers of the same sample of students.

To observe whether the coeducational experience produces changes, it is necessary to know the initial parameters. Thus, taken as the point of departure are the perceptions parents and teachers have of certain behaviors and attitudes according to gender. For example, some teachers state that "girls are kind and docile, much more calm," while the boys "are on the go." Parents in turn state that girls are "modest, reserved, well-mannered," while boys are "rough, restless, aggressive." These commonly held views provide a general idea of the way adults perceive young people comparatively, how they view men and women in terms of some of the basic personality characteristics, and how these characteristics are assigned to one or the other sex as something innate or natural.

Examined in the study discussed here are data with respect to how male and female students view themselves, in single-sex as well as in coeducational schools, and the perceptions parents and teachers have about the influence of the educational system on the way students interact with each other and related behaviors. It should be noted that young people's *self-perception* is as important as the perception they have regarding the other gender. Also important are the relationships they maintain with each other in the areas of friendship and romantic relations.

The level of participation and the degree of aggressiveness are two of the indicators chosen to measure the students' self-perception. Student participation was examined with respect to four indicators: asking the teacher questions in class, expressing ideas in class, protesting against injustices, and speaking in public meetings. Asking questions in class was also considered to be an indicator of the relative autonomy students possess with regard to speaking in public. This assertion can be tested by examining the reasons that one-fifth of the student body does not ask any questions: fear, shyness, bashfulness, anxiety about being made the object of peer ridicule, or teacher's dislike. The same factors are involved in explaining why ideas are not expressed in class, although there are also students who do not express themselves because they lack critical ability and initiative and invariably assert that "what the teacher says is right."

Protesting against injustices is one of the most heterogeneous indicators. Consequently, it is also one of the richest sources of information because, through an examination of the reasons that students do or do not protest, it is possible to discover not only attitudes toward autonomy and independence, or submission and dependency, but also what relationships exist among students and between teachers and students. This behavior is normally distributed: One-fourth of the students never protest; one-third always protest; the rest protest only in certain circumstances. The reasons students do not protest might include fear of teacher reprisal or overall indifference to situations in which they are not directly affected. Also, protests may reflect individualism or solidarity, depending upon whether this protest reflects the individual's or peer group's rejection of discrimination and the demand that individual rights be respected. Half of the students in the sample protest occasionally or always because of what might be termed "a matter of principle."

Performance in public meetings, whether individual or collective, is rejected by one-tenth of the students and embraced with interest by the rest. However, only one-third of the students have actually been mobilized. Usually, the reasons for avoiding speaking in public meetings are shyness, bashfulness, and fear.

Scores for each of the four indicators were used to measure the degree of participation of the students and to group them into three categories: low, medium, and high participation. With this information, the data were compared according to sex and according to the type of school (single-sex or coeducational) attended by the students. The totals for female and male participation make it clear that 40 percent of the female students have low participation, whereas less than 33 percent of the males report a similar level. In other words, women more frequently than men express fear, shyness, and bashfulness, have less of an ability to criticize and initiate action, and/or manifest a higher degree of submissive and dependent attitudes.

The type of school is associated very differently with the degree of participation by gender. Boys who study with girls participate to a greater extent than those who attend schools for boys only. The presence of female schoolmates encourages them to participate to a greater extent. In the case of women, coeducation has a polarizing effect, producing both high levels and low levels of participation—the presence of men stimulates the participation of some girls, but discourages the participation of others. (This latter group of girls will require a separate analysis to understand the power of family conditioning, which is extremely varied with respect to the acceptance of female participation).

Aggressive behavior is one of the most distinguishing characteristics associated with "masculinity"; conversely, its absence is considered a distinguishing characteristic of femininity. At the same time, it is the masculine behavior that has the most damaging effect upon women. In this study, aggressive behavior was operationalized according to four indicators: frequency and reasons given for engaging in physical fights, the various ways identified for conflict resolution, acceptance and justification of coarse language, and the frequency and justification for the imposition of will by force.

Coming to blows during a student fight was admitted by only one-fourth of those who were interviewed, and of these, half said this had happened only once. The reasons for becoming involved in this kind of fight are not serious, according to some students. Others believe fights are caused by personal offenses and, particularly, by attacks incurred upon family members. The possibility of solving these conflicts nonviolently is admitted by three-fourths of those students who engage in fights; the others, in one way or another, justify their aggressive behavior.

Expressing oneself through coarse language is a form of aggression and, consequently, one of its indicators. This type of behavior is manifested by more than half of the students. A few confess they talk this way all the time, but the majority state they talk coarsely only once in a while. However, although most of the students do not justify their behavior, one-third of them assert that it is a way to prevent being abused by others or that it is an expression of their own lack of self-control.

Domineering behavior—the imposition of one's will upon another—is admitted by only one-tenth of the students. However, there are others who, although they are not domineering with their friends, behave this way at home. In other words, greater solidarity exists among groups of friends than with family members (de Hoyos and de Hoyos, 1966).

Explanations for this type of behavior are usually given in terms of personality traits ("I like to be obeyed") or justified in terms of social necessity ("one must know how to impose upon others"; "one has to be inconsiderate"). Conversely, those who are not domineering explain their behavior as an expression of respect for the ideas of other people ("we are all equal").

This quantitative synthesis of the selected indicators allows the establishment of three categories of student aggressiveness: low, medium, and high. According to the data, two-thirds of the student body manifest low aggressive behavior; one-fourth demonstrate medium aggressiveness; and only one-tenth are represented as highly aggressive.

Overall, the data reveal significant patterns when aggressiveness is compared by school type (see Table 5.1). Most girls in single-sex schools (97 percent) report low levels of aggressiveness, whereas a significant number of boys in single-sex schools (28 percent) report high aggressiveness. When students attend coeducational schools, girls still report low aggressiveness (92 percent), but a few (2 percent) now report high aggressiveness. For boys, the proportion reporting high aggressiveness diminishes considerably (to 13 percent).

The data confirm that there is an important association between the degree of coeducation in schools and the level of students' aggressiveness. However, what is most interesting from this difference in setting is that it has one effect among girls and an opposite effect among boys. In other words, coeducation liberates, to a small degree, the aggressive impulse in girls, whereas it encourages a restraining of that impulse in boys. The very fact of living together requires that girls develop their aggressiveness somewhat and that boys repress theirs.

The discovery of the effect of behavior convergence upon the two genders as a result of coeducation has also uncovered and clarified the closed environmental character of single-sex schools, in which those gender characteristics culturally imposed are promoted and confirmed as essential and necessary to the identity of men and women. These characteristics are sometimes emphasized to such an extreme degree that anyone who deviates even slightly from them is considered to be abnormal or homosexual.

The innate abilities of an individual are dependent upon genetic factors. Furthermore, the variations existing among individuals present wide ranges both for men and women. It is within the school that the individual has an opportunity to develop different aspects of those abilities in a variety of directions, in a more complete and systematic manner than that provided at home. However, the possibilities for the individual's development depend

Table 5.1. Students' Level of Aggressiveness According to Sex and Level of Coeducation (in percentages)

Aggressiveness Level	Women Students' Level of Coeducation				Men Students' Level of Coeducation				Total
	Nil	Inc.	Comp.	Total	Nil	Inc.	Comp.	Total	
Low	97	84	32	92	36	41	46	42	65
Medium	3	16	6	7	43	37	41	40	25
High	—	—	2	1	21	21	13	18	10
Total	100	100	100	100	100	99	100	100	100
Absolute numbers	58	37	65	160	77	43	56	176	336
Gamma coefficient	0.71				−0.15				

Note: Inc. = incomplete coeducational experience; Comp. = complete coeducational experience.

upon the economic and cultural conditions existing within society. Our society is in a state of cultural transition that, with respect to gender roles, is marked by a tendency toward less differentiation between genders.

In this study, students were asked their self-perceptions regarding their abilities vis-à-vis equality and gender in relation to four areas of ability: intellectual, artistic, athletic, and development of friendships. The responses of the students as members of a particular gender group vary according to the particular attribute or quality under examination (see Table 5.2). The attribute receiving the most consensus for being equally distributed among men and women is intelligence, though only slightly more than 67 percent of all students perceive this to be the case. The ability to become good friends places second, with about 60 percent of all students perceiving it as a quality not subject to gender differentiation. The remaining two attributes receive much less agreement: Nearly one-half of the students perceive both genders as having equal artistic aptitude, and a little more than 40 percent feel that both genders are equally athletic.

Analysis indicates that perceptions of relative equality are greater among girls than among boys in all or most of the abilities investigated. Most of the women perceive equality for all attributes, with 78 percent perceiving this with regard to intellectual ability. About 60 percent of boys perceive themselves to be of equal intelligence to girls, and about 33 percent consider men more intelligent than women. Once again, it is possible to demonstrate the existence of stereotypes of masculine superiority that are used to justify authoritarian behavior and to explain the fewer educational opportunities available to women than to men. It can also be seen that girls do not share these stereotypes to the same extent: Only 14 percent believe men are more

Table 5.2. Students' Perceptions of Equal Male-Female Ability According to Sex and
Degree of Coeducation (in percentages)

Aspects of Equal Ability	Women Students' Level of Coeducation				Men Students' Level of Coeducation			
	Nil	Inc.	Comp.	Total	Nil	Inc.	Comp.	Total
Intellectual	75	84	76	78	61	49	67	60
Artistic	51	51	62	55	43	29	42	39
Athletic	48	46	56	51	34	30	34	33
Friendship	66	49	52	56	56	55	63	58
Total	100	100	100	100	100	100	100	100
Absolute numbers	59	37	66	162	76	43	56	175

Note: Percentages refer only to the students' perceptions of equality in each of the aspects
measured. Students' perceptions of inequality between the sexes are not considered here.
Inc. = incomplete coeducational experience; Comp. = complete coeducational experience.

intelligent than women, and some women perceive themselves to be more
intelligent than men.

The influence of coeducation upon the perception of gender equality
among students with respect to ability is highly significant in some areas and
less significant in others. It is important to note that in order for coeducation
to have an influence, it is likely that it must be all-encompassing. In other
words, it must be without courses of study or activities that separate students
by gender.

The perception of equality with respect to intellectual ability is
significantly higher for men than women in coeducational schools, and men
in coeducational schools believe women to be their intellectual equals to a
greater extent than do men in single-sex schools. The ability of men to
become good friends with women as well as men is also perceived to be
higher among men in coeducational schools, in contrast to all-men schools;
however, women's perception of this quality is lower in coeducational
schools. It is interesting to note that boys have a greater tendency to believe
in their superior intellectual ability regardless of school type. Girls, in
contrast, tend to believe that women have a greater ability to develop good
friendships in both types of schools; boys' perception is favorable toward
their own gender when they are in boys-only schools, but shifts to favor
women when they are in coeducational schools.

Artistic and athletic ability are perceived to be equal by more girls than
boys. This perception is greater in coeducational schools than in girls'
schools; there is less variation among the boys' perception. Considerable
diversity exists about artistic ability. Girls favor themselves in all types of
schools. Boys favor themselves in boys-only schools; they favor women in

coeducational schools. With respect to athletic ability, both boys and girls in all types of schools favor men.

Relationship Between the Genders

This relationship has been analyzed with respect to two factors: friendship and falling in love. Women's education requires that the ability to relate to men on an equal level be learned, principally by relating to them as human beings and, consequently, as friends. This education must ensure that the sexual impulse is channeled in such a way that it becomes a complete expression of personal and social development, not merely a biological function. A woman educated in this manner requires a man who is educated according to the same principles.

The hierarchical gender roles that still exist in Latin America do not favor personal relationships based upon equality but rather those that are authoritarian and procedural. This is reflected in the manner in which young people at school relate to each other. They show an inability to establish friendships between genders and a tendency to feel attracted only in reference to physical attributes. Nonhierarchical relationships require the ability to become friends with persons of a different sex, as well as the ability to feel attracted to them by personal qualities, love, and understanding.

Groups of friends acquire a special importance among adolescents and, depending on their composition, may have varying effects. Mixed groups facilitate a fluid interaction among young people of both sexes, whereas exclusive groups of either boys or girls constitute closed spaces where, as students search for affirmation of their gender identity, various stereotypes are developed about the opposite gender and substantial barriers are erected against the possibility of establishing spontaneous and full relationships.

The type of school is influential in conditioning the ways in which students participate in friendship groups outside the schools. In single-sex schools the situation is marked by sexual differentiation: About 25 percent of the girls are not a part of any group of friends, but only 5 percent of the boys find themselves in that situation. What is even more remarkable is the contrast in the proportion of students who participate in friendship groups of only their own gender—20 percent of the girls and more than half of the boys. The high degree of participation among male students in single-sex schools is particularly significant because these male peer groups represent the principal reference group for the macho subculture in Latin America. In contrast, in coeducational schools, there is less differentiation between boys and girls with respect to friends, and most of the social participation, for either sex, occurs in mixed-gender groups.

Students in either single-sex or coeducational schools may form friendship groups outside the schools that are in turn either single-sex or mixed. Information about the activities of groups of friends provides additional data of interest. Activities include going to parties, playing games, and having fun, but there are also some activities that are less common. These have been classified into three categories (Table 5.3), the first of which involves activities that include as a means of entertainment "having a drink together," "having a high time" with girls, and carrying on "mischief." The second category includes not only activities such as having fun together but also studying together, helping each other with their homework and their troubles, and hearing lectures outside the school. Within the third category are activities that include concern for their building (when they live in apartments), the neighborhood block, and the country's problems and difficulties. They actualize their concerns about community welfare by forming cultural clubs and theater clubs or by volunteering in church cathechism programs.

Additional data regarding friendships for entertainment purposes indicate that only among the boys-only groups do students admit to drinking in groups or of committing acts of mischief. The number of cases is not considerable. Nonetheless, it is evident that the proportion of answers in connection with these acts is higher in boys-only schools than in coeducational schools. It is also important to note that the data reported in Table 5.3 indicate a substantial increase in the number of social activities among girls in coeducational schools. For their part, almost half of the boys report social activities in coeducational schools. In brief, it can be said that the presence of men encourages women to emerge from their private sphere and participate in social life, either within exclusively female or mixed groups.

The other variable analyzed here is attraction between young people and the impulse to develop romances or reject them. The findings demonstrate that half of the students have had the experience of being involved in a romance, though this experience occurs more frequently among boys than among girls. This difference is explained by the fact that the number of girls who rejected becoming involved in a romance is much greater than the number of boys who were not accepted.

The type of school conditions the romantic behavior of students regardless of gender. In coeducational schools, there is a high rate of girls as well as boys who have never been romantically involved, compared with students in single-sex schools. Likewise, the proportion of male and female students who have had some romantic experience is smaller than that of their counterparts in single-sex schools.

These data are extremely interesting because they counter the belief of parents that romantic involvements are primarily a characteristic of coeducational schools. The data indicate that precisely the opposite is true. On the other hand, when students of coeducational schools do initiate romances, they do not necessarily develop them with their schoolmates; about 40 percent become involved with friends or acquaintances outside of school.

Table 5.3. Purpose of Friendship Groups According to Type of School and Sex of
           Group (in percentages)

Purpose of Friendship Group	Type of School							Total
	Women-only Sex of Group		Men-only Sex of Group		Coeducational Sex of Group			
	Women	Mixed	Men	Mixed	Women	Men	Mixed	
Entertainment	—	—	10	—	—	11	—	3
Individual betterment	73	88	53	68	67	53	54	61
For social betterment	27	12	37	32	33	36	46	36
Total	100	100	100	100	100	100	100	100
Absolute numbers	11	33	38	34	30	36	107	289

The reasons for either accepting or rejecting romantic involvement are also conditioned by the type of school. Female rejection of macho behavior is found in 33 percent of the girls in girls-only schools but in only 20 percent of the girls in coeducational schools. In contrast, there are very few males who admit to not having been chosen as someone's boyfriend, especially among the boys in single-sex schools.

The reasons why a male is chosen as a boyfriend or why he is able to have romantic experiences are diverse, ranging from very serious to extremely trivial. Some boys claim that they view romance as an amusement, as a way to satisfy curiosity, or as a means of "having a high time" with girls. (This includes those boys who have multiple relationships occurring at the same time.) Others point to physical attraction or compatibility. A third group refers to characteristics such as quietness, cheerfulness, and pleasantness. Finally, there is a fourth group that states, "We understand each other" or "We feel the same way about each other."

This crucial area of adolescent experience—romance—does vary between males and females and also by type of school. The data indicate that 20 percent of the students become romantically involved as a kind of entertainment, and that the proportion is greater for boys in single-sex schools, where 25 percent of the males believe that falling in love is a kind of pastime or diversion. The data about girls are more diverse: Two-fifths of females in single-sex schools accept a boyfriend because of physical attraction; 33 percent of those in coeducational schools refer to the boyfriend's personal qualities. Among males, most of those in single-sex schools believe they are accepted because of their personal qualities; only among the males from coeducational schools is there a significant proportion who refer to mutual love and understanding as reasons for falling in love.

The data illuminate the significant effects of coeducation upon the ability of students to develop knowledge about both genders. Females stop perceiving boys according to stereotypes and begin to discover personal qualities in them that are divorced from physical characteristics. Males, on the other hand, stop perceiving themselves as objects of admiration, and begin to appreciate the value of genuine personal encounters, characterized by the giving and receiving of love and affection.

▲ Parents' and Teachers' Perceptions

Information from parents and teachers regarding male and female students was obtained through questions probing some perceived differences among young people of different genders. First, it was found that the majority of teachers and parents consider that both male and female students demonstrate different behaviors depending upon whether they are educated separately or together. Second, more than 80 percent of the teachers assert that this difference exists, whereas a little more than half of the parents believe this to be the case.

The analysis now clusters behaviors ascribed to one or another gender into four categories according to the answers provided by parents and teachers. The first category concerns behavior that is considered "proper" or "improper," based upon social definitions of masculinity or femininity. According to these definitions, female students are "feminine" because they are modest, circumspect, delicate, polite, less bright, easily dominated, etc. Conversely, they are considered to be "mannish" if they perform "manly" tasks, are strong and valiant in front of men, coarse and rude, etc. The definitions of masculinity are the inverse of the definitions of femininity. Males are macho if they are aggressive, rude, coarse, domineering, do not deprive themselves, and do not control themselves. They are not manly or are "non-macho" if they are quiet, docile, moderate, repressed, weak of character, reserved, and have false manners.

The second category of behavior refers to the way that males and females relate to each other. There is a significant contrast in attitudes within this category. At one extreme are those who contend that boys, as well as girls, are timid and bashful and that girls isolate themselves because they are fearful and distrustful of boys. On the opposite end are those who state that boys and girls perform equally, that boys and girls demonstrate solidarity and respect for each other, that boys and girls can be good friends, and so on.

The third category refers to those behaviors that are associated with school achievement. Competition between boys and girls is viewed either as encouraging or discouraging, depending on whether the presence of the other gender is considered to be beneficial or disturbing.

The fourth category refers to behaviors related to discipline and responsibility, which are classified as either proper or improper.

Parents' and teachers' perceptions regarding all of these behaviors among young people are similar in some aspects and different in others. With respect to behaviors that are regarded as "proper" for a given gender, almost 33 percent of all parents believe that female students who study in girls-only schools are more "feminine" than those who study at mixed schools (Table 5.4); this perception is shared by less than 20 percent of teachers with a similar schooling experience (Table 5.5).

Both parents and teachers perceive boys in single-sex schools to be more masculine (more "macho") than those in coeducational schools. Approximately 42 percent of the parents with single-sex schooling experience and 55 percent of the teachers with a similar experience agree with this perception of masculinity. It should be noted that included among behaviors considered "nonmacho" is behavior indicating "the danger of becoming a homosexual" and that parents feel this is primarily a danger at coeducational schools, whereas teachers feel that the risk exists mostly in boys-only schools.

The data indicate that parents are more concerned about the masculinity of their sons than the femininity of their daughters. At the same time, however, the form of masculinity that is endorsed presents features characteristic of a macho subculture. Consequently, this notion of masculinity will condition the men's image of women and the type of relationships men will want to establish with them.

Developing social ties with friends of the opposite sex is believed to be more prominent in the coeducational experience, according to parents and teachers. About half of all teachers recognize this experience for girls. In contrast, one-third of all teachers point out that girls educated in girls-only schools are timid in dealing with males. About two-thirds of all parents consider boys to be more sociable with girls in coeducational schools, and 20 percent consider boys who attend boys-only schools to be timid.

As for behavior associated with school achievement, parents and teachers have opposing perceptions concerning the influence of the type of school. Parents feel that coeducational schools have a negative influence upon performance; teachers view them as more positive for school achievement. The case is similar with respect to improper behavior: Parents ascribe this behavior largely to coeducational schools; teachers believe that separate schools foster improper behavior. This perception of teachers corresponds to the self-perception of male students about aggressive behavior; it is greater in boys-only schools than in coeducational schools.

The existence of contrasting opinions between teachers and parents leads to the possible conclusion that the presence of stereotypes may prejudice them in one direction or another concerning male and female behavior in separate and coeducational schools. The risk that opinions are based upon stereotypes is greatest among those parents whose experience is limited by their having sent their children to only one type of school and among

Table 5.4. Student Behaviors Perceived by Parents According to Students' Sex and Parental Experience with Coeducational Schools (in percentages)

Types of Behavior	Students in Single-Sex Schools Parental Experience			Students in Coeducational Schools Parental Experience		
	Single-sex Only	Single and Coeducational	Co-educational Only	Single-sex Only	Single and Coeducational	Co-educational Only
Women Behaviors						
"Feminine"	43	35	25	—	—	5
"Nonfeminine"	2	3	8	2	13	11
Inhibited	15	16	29	2	5	1
Social	—	—	—	31	42	51
Improper	5	10	12	62	33	23
Proper	35	36	26	2	7	9
Total	100 (40)	100 (69)	100 (65)	100 (39)	100 (69)	100 (65)
Men Behaviors						
"Macho"	42	41	42	6	3	2
"Nonmacho"	—	8	8	16	26	15
Inhibited	17	20	22	3	2	3
Social	5	—	3	24	39	46
Improper	11	12	13	43	24	19
Proper	25	19	12	8	6	15
Total	100 (36)	100 (64)	100 (67)	100 (37)	100 (62)	100 (65)

Note: Figures in parentheses represent absolute numbers.

teachers who have taught exclusively in either separate or coeducational schools.

Comparison of parents' and teachers' degree of experience with coeducation shows that the proportion of parents who value "femininity" as the main characteristic of women in separate schools increases to more than 40 percent for those whose educational experience with their children is limited to separate schools. This perception is less pronounced and does not vary much among teachers. The macho behavior of males in separate schools is similarly perceived by parents regardless of their schooling experience. The perception of student behavior that reflects macho attitudes decreases among those teachers whose experience is limited to separate schools, although this perception is generally higher among teachers than parents.

From these findings, it can be concluded that parents who ascribe to girls-only schools the ability to develop characteristics considered feminine

Table 5.5. Student Behaviors Perceived by Teachers According to Students' Sex and Teachers' Professional Experience with Coeducational Schools

Types of Behavior	Students in Single-Sex Schools Teacher Experience			Students in Coeducational Schools Teacher Experience		
	Single-sex Only	Single and Coeducational	Co-educational Only	Single-sex Only	Single and Coeducational	Co-educational Only
Women Behaviors						
"Feminine"	17	16	20	—	—	—
"Nonfeminine"	4	5	1	4	8	9
Inhibited	21	27	38	15	12	14
Social	—	—	—	33	51	53
Improper	21	24	15	30	8	11
Proper	37	28	26	18	21	13
Total	100 (24)	100 (133)	100 (86)	100 (27)	100 (136)	100 (88)
Men Behaviors						
"Macho"	55	62	63	7	4	2
"Nonmacho"	4	4	1	35	35	37
Inhibited	10	12	15	—	4	6
Social	—	—	—	31	37	38
Improper	24	14	12	10	7	6
Proper	7	8	9	17	13	12
Total	100 (29)	100 (138)	100 (91)	100 (29)	100 (138)	100 (90)

Note: Figures in parentheses represent absolute numbers.

do so on the basis of a stereotype that cannot be verified in the real world. Moreover, this assertion is confirmed by the opinions of teachers: Of those who have had the experience of teaching in both women's schools and coeducational schools, only 17 percent ascribe the development of feminine qualities to separate schools. As for the macho character of males, it is important to point out that parents see it as a needed quality for men, but teachers see it as a negative trait. This is particularly obvious when the teachers become familiar with nonmacho behaviors among students in coeducational schools.

A positive relationship with girls is also valued for male students, but parents who know both types of schools value this as more important than do parents who are familiar only with single-sex schools. The majority of parents and teachers believe that a positive relationship with boys is the most important trait of female students in mixed school. The proportion who hold this opinion decreases, however, to less than one-third among those who do not have this experience.

About 33 percent of the parents who are familiar with both types of school consider that female students' "improper" behaviors occur in coeducational schools, but 62 percent of those who have experience only with separate schools believe this to be the case. This divergence demonstrates that the latter's view is a result of bias. In the case of teachers, 30 percent of those with less experience have a biased view concerning improper behaviors, whereas only 8 percent of the teachers with more experience hold the same opinion. In contrast, 20 percent of the teachers with exposure to both types of school feel that female students of mixed schools demonstrate "proper" behavior. There is a similar negative bias expressed by parents in reference to the improper behavior of male students in coeducational schools—more than 40 percent for those who have no experience with such schools, and less than 26 percent for parents whose children have been educated in both types of schools. Among teachers with a more diverse experience, only half as many complain about male students' improper behavior in coeducational schools as opposed to those who perceive that proper behavior occurs there.

In summary, it is evident that the supposed disadvantages of coeducation, as they are perceived by parents, do not have a grounded foundation because most of the parents who cite these disadvantages have no experience with the schools they criticize. Teachers appear more objective because of their experience with student behavior in the classroom, whereas parents are only able to judge indirectly from the behavior they observe in their children or through the information their children give them.

▲ Changing Domestic and Occupational Roles

The sharing of chores and tasks at home is the strongest expression of a change in gender roles. In order to learn about students' behavior and experience in relation to their roles at home, students in the study were examined about their participation in fulfilling domestic chores at home and their rejection or acceptance of the provision in a relatively recent Peruvian Civil Code (November 1984) that emphasizes the equality of male and female responsibilities toward the fulfillment of housework and child care.

The traditional division of labor, which assigns house chores to women, is apparent in Peruvian society because 97 percent of female students in our sample fulfill this role, regardless of the type of school they attend. However, a change is occurring in males' participation in the fulfillment of these tasks: Of men in men's schools, 83 percent participate, and this percentage increases to 90 percent in coeducational schools.

The motivations that determine either the acceptance or rejection of the law about family responsibilities give insight into student perceptions of family life, marriage, and values such as equality and solidarity and their application to gender relationships. These perceptions range from considering women to be solely responsible for housework, to considering that an "equality of rights" exists between husband and wife and that husbands must share in the performance of household chores so that women are not oppressed. Between these two extremes are opinions that "help" from husbands is desirable in special circumstances or as a means of benefiting children and the family.

Analysis of the probable impact of coeducation upon student views of house chores indicates the importance of examining these views according to student gender. Female students' views do not vary between different types of schools, with the exception of those women who are motivated to eradicate the oppression of women: In separate schools only 3 percent hold this opinion, whereas in coeducational schools 14 percent think in this manner. In other words, it is evident that coeducational schools provide a more favorable environment for women to become aware of their rights. Nonetheless, males' views are certainly influenced by coeducation, particularly in regard to the assertion that housework is the sole responsibility of women: In coeducational schools only 5 percent of male students hold this view; the figure doubles in boys-only schools.

Discrimination by gender in Peruvian society is facilitated by employment as both a means of subsistence and personal fulfillment. In Peru, as in many other countries, there are specific jobs, occupations, and professions considered to be either typically masculine or feminine. Within the context of the present study, in order to ascertain the changes occurring in gender roles, students' occupational expectations were analyzed and classified according to their degree of femininity.

The influence of coeducation is felt to a much greater degree by boys than by girls. Among male students in men's schools, more than 80 percent restrict their occupational goals to the army, navy, air force, engineering , and computer science—careers generally considered masculine. In coeducational schools, less than 67 percent of the male students state these occupational goals. Among this latter group, medical, legal, and similar careers appeal to the rest of the students (including four who aspire to become teachers).

The lower percentage of stereotyped occupational desires among males who study in coeducational schools suggests that their exposure to female peers makes them value those qualities that have been traditionally associated with women. Furthermore, males develop an appreciation for those occupations whose fulfillment requires those qualities. Thus, when men do not monopolize the more technical occupations, room is left for women to fill these positions.

▲ Conclusion

The results obtained in this study lead to the conclusion that coeducation has a positive effect upon women's education. At the same time, it is clear that its impact is positive not only for women but also for society in general because changes in gender roles are encouraged. This results in a questioning of the way in which labor is currently divided by gender and, indirectly, to an expansion of the democratic process in society.

Finally, coeducation makes another critical contribution: Changes brought about are not the result of conflict; rather, they occur as a result of young people discovering satisfaction in a new way of being and a new way of relating to each other, without gender distinctions.

▲ References

De Grandpré, Marcel. *La coeducation dans les écoles des 45 pays.* Quebec: Editions Paulines, 1973.
de Hoyos, Arturo, and Genevieve de Hoyos. "Amigo System and Alienation of the Wife in the Conjugal Mexican Family." In Bernard Faber (ed.), *Kinship and Family Organization.* New York: John Wiley, 1966.
Durkheim, Emile. *Educación y sociología.* Barcelona: Editorial Península, 1975.

▲ 6

Gender and Power in the Teachers' Union of Mexico

Regina Cortina

Women represent the largest group among primary school teachers in many countries of the world. Although this means that potentially they could play a decisive role within their profession, this is in fact seldom the case.

A case study of the participation of women teachers as union members and leaders is provided in Cortina's chapter. Through her examination of the National Union of Education Workers in Mexico, the largest union and unquestionably one of the most powerful in Mexico, Cortina explains how the high participation of women in union membership has not been reflected in leadership positions. This situation is complex and results not only from women's self-exclusion based on prevailing norms of "virtuous women" who must refrain from meeting with men in awkward settings, but also from women's everyday constraints as they feel responsible for the domestic life of their families. The limitations women face are further fostered by the male leadership of unions that, consciously or unconsciously, draws upon women's norms of passivity and devotion to gear their involvement into supportive activities for the union. Thus, women's units in the union ironically end up playing social auxiliary roles rather than providing substantive political input. The recent demise of the women's units, however, might also signal a defensive response on the part of male leadership to preclude the emergence of effective space for women.

Cortina's qualitative investigation provides insights into how gender as a system of power relations contributes to maintain political structures and social inequalities. Women teachers show little knowledge of the female leaders representing them; female leaders, in turn, show little awareness of feminist ideas or of the need to address problems salient among women. Thus, reproduction of the status quo continues.

—Editor

▲ To understand women's work in Mexican education, it is necessary to grasp the political and institutional realities that shape their lives as professional educators. The control of Mexican public education is highly centralized at the national level. Two institutions set policy and direct the daily activities of education across the entire nation: the Secretaría de Educación Pública (SEP) and the Sindicato Nacional de Trabajadores de la Educación (SNTE). The latter, the national teachers' union, is the largest, and one of the most powerful unions within the Mexican political system. Composed mainly of teachers but also other employees within SEP, it has become a dominant influence in the training, working conditions, and professional advancement of teachers.

Since their creation at the end of World War II, unions in Mexico have been instrumental in the maintenance of political control at the state and party levels. In their early days, unions were useful for integrating national and regional power blocs. But as decades have gone by, they have become a conservative force against present state aims of modernization and democratization. In the case of SNTE, the union carries out grassroots and organizational work for the dominant political party, the Partido Revolucionario Institucional (PRI). The membership of SNTE, estimated at 645,000, of whom women are the majority, represents 40 percent of all public employees in Mexico.[1]

The size and national character of SNTE make it an excellent case for studying the culture of the union to learn how women experience it, how the participation of women and men within the union differs, and how gender relations are constructed in union life. In the extensive literature on unions and the labor movement in Latin America, only a few studies have looked closely at the participation of women in the organized labor movement.[2] To explore the participation of women in union life, this chapter considers women in the teachers' union, analyzing the stance of the leadership toward women and how the culture of the union influences women's participation or nonparticipation in union activities.

▲ Teaching and the Quest for Women's Rights

For women, teaching and political mobilization have had a long-standing association in Mexican history since the Revolution. The teaching profession has been central to the quest of Mexican women for equal rights and better treatment as workers. As far back as the First Feminist Congress of Yucatan in 1916, when Mexican women came together to discuss their social and political rights, a large proportion of the participants were teachers. Among the issues discussed in the congress were the right of women to education and their right to work. Female teachers also stood out in the movement during the 1930s to obtain full citizenship and the right to vote for women. More than 50,000 women participated in the Frente Unico Pro Derechos de la Mujer (United Front for Women's Rights) between 1935 and 1938.[3] As a consequence of the social programs of that period under President Lázaro Cardenas, female teachers today are entitled to maternity leave and free child day care, plus all the social benefits provided by law for unionized state employees: retirement after thirty years of service, social security, paid vacations, low-interest loans, and equal pay for employees working at the same level, whether male or female.[4]

The work done by different feminist organizations led directly to the incorporation of women into the institutionalized interest groups within the PRI. Through the activities of women's organizations in the 1930s, a women's section was founded in the Partido Nacional Revolucionario (PNR), the original precursor of the PRI. This was accomplished after Cárdenas promised in his first presidential address in 1935 to help with the political organization of women, even though women did not yet have political rights (Garrido, 1982). A women's section exists today in the PRI and in most Mexican unions. As in the case of unions and other organizations attached to the dominant party, the women's section has conveyed the votes of women members to elections in exchange for elective and administrative positions in very small numbers. As is true for the SNTE, female leaders from the women's section of the PRI are advanced to elective or administrative positions. Women are represented through a separate category within the party structure, however, as peasants and workers are. It is through this mechanism that a few women have had access to political power, generally sitting on the committee that represents women's interests.

By thus isolating female leaders structurally, the party circumscribes women in the political structure and defuses demands from the rank and file. Female leaders within the PRI continually debate whether the creation of a women's section has been beneficial. Some female party leaders argue that the political participation of women cannot come about within separate organizations. Other leaders contend that women are not yet in a condition of equality and thus need an organization to support them.[5] In any case, the women's section of the PRI has provided a space for women to gain experience and to move into more important political positions.

Despite the creation of a women's section in the dominant political party, women were not enfranchised until 1953. The denial of the right to vote for women in the 1930s resulted from the political crisis that marked the end of the Cárdenas administration and the intensification of Mexican industrialization at the outset of World War II. At that time the Partido de la Revolución Mexicana (PRM), the ruling party that preceded and in 1946 was transformed into the PRI, reversed the proposal developed by the Cárdenas administration to legislate expanded political rights for women. A plausible hypothesis for this abandonment, as Luis Javier Garrido has argued in his account of the transformation of the PRM at that time, is that since its beginning the United Front for Women's Rights was linked to the Communist party. With the policy of Unidad Nacional, the national consolidation, which also entailed the exclusion of Communists from the party ranks, the work of the women's section of the party was restricted, and women thereafter were pictured routinely as conservatives (Garrido, 1982). The anti-Communist vendetta did much more than purge radical leadership from the national party. The ideological changes at the party level stalled the mobilization of women toward gaining the right to vote. As the party forced its cadres to conform to a unified but exclusionary pattern of leadership, the political aims of women were constrained.

Largely as a result of the social programs of the Cárdenas period and the mobilization of women at that time, women teachers have become a relatively privileged group among women workers in Mexico. As state employees, they receive salaries equal to those of men for the same years of experience and education. Most important, women gained legal equality in public employment during those momentous years of state building a half-century ago. Yet they were still limited in the profession, not so much by overt legal discrimination as by the more subtle political and institutional constraints over which they had—and to this day still have—little control.

▲ Union Politics and Public Education

The structure of occupational opportunity in Mexican education is highly formal and institutionalized nationally. Most teachers in Mexican public education start as preschool or elementary school teachers. With time and experience they can slowly advance, becoming school principals at the lower levels, then teachers in the junior high schools, and then principals at this level. After that, if they advance further, they become supervisors for schools in a given area. From there they might continue to advance to administrative positions in SEP or follow a political career within the union.[6]

The careers of most union leaders begin at the school level. They are elected by their coworkers in the school; then they become union representatives at the delegation level. The delegations, the smallest units of the union, are organized by school zone or workplace. After a successful career at the school and delegation levels, union representatives are selected by the section for active participation within it. The sections comprise delegations in each state of the nation or in the Federal District. Within the section there are three levels of participation. First, the executive committee is formed by the general secretary of the section and more than twenty other secretaries. Second, each secretary has assistants and negotiators who solve teachers' problems in the different government offices. The positions of assistants and negotiators are used as a training ground for the future secretaries. Third, the coordinators are teachers directly involved in the schools, acting as a link between the schools and the executive committees at the delegation level within the union. The identification of leaders with the rank and file comes from their having advanced from within the system—they know what it means to be a teacher. It takes many years of investing one's time and energies to achieve these positions of leadership.

The avenues to power and social mobility within the union are shaped by union politics. Since its creation, the union has been controlled by two factions closely allied with the PRI. The dominant faction from 1949 to 1972 was a group led by Jesus Robles Martínez; since 1972 it has been a group called Vanguardia Revolucionaria, led by Carlos Jonguitud Barrios. SNTE is controlled from the top by the national executive committee, and in all its decisions the union has a steeply pyramidal structure of control.

Although most leaders of SNTE are members of the PRI as well, union leadership is more complex and pluralistic than is commonly believed. Various political groups maintain positions of their own and have representatives on SNTE's executive committee at both the national and section levels. Among these is the Movimiento Revolucionario del Magisterio, which emerged from the Ninth Section in Mexico City and has been a significant presence in union politics for more than thirty years. Another group is the Coordinadora Nacional de Trabajadores de la Educación, which emerged in the late 1970s. These two groups have been the best organized of the dissident movements in the history of the teachers' union.[7]

In the sections that follow I characterize the participation of women in union life, first by focusing on women members of Vanguardia Revolucionaria, the power bloc that controls SNTE, and second by exploring the participation of women within the dissident movements.

▲ Women and Union Leadership

The organizational structure of SNTE reflects the structure of the profession, not only its levels but its types of control. In the 1977–1978 school year, union statistics showed that it had 548,356 members, 52 percent of whom were women (SNTE, 1977). Its membership consists of preschool and elementary school teachers, secondary school teachers, normal school teachers, and administrative personnel. The union includes employees of the federal, state, and municipal governments and of private schools. Its members are distributed in fifty-five sections divided by location and type of control. As stated earlier, each section is divided into delegations, which are organized by school zone or workplace. Members of delegations and sections choose representatives for executive committees to represent them in the governance of the union. In Mexico City there are three sections of federal employees: the Ninth Section, for preschool and elementary school teachers; the Tenth Section, for secondary education; and a section for administrative personnel. The two sections that represent teachers in Mexico City have the most members and are the most important sections.

To examine the participation of women in the leadership of the union, we now delve into the Ninth Section of the SNTE. Union statistics show that in 1977–1978 this section had 42,918 members, 74 percent of whom were women (SNTE, 1977, p. 15). During the six-year period from 1976 to 1982, two women served in the first triennium and only one woman in the second triennium as elected members on SNTE's national executive committee, which has a total of twenty-five members. In the Ninth Section, five women were on the section's executive commitee in both trienniums, out of twenty-eight members. The Ninth Section offers an illuminating case for research because it is in Mexico City, the core of the highly centralized national education system. The Ninth Section of the SNTE, moreover, has a long history of political participation by teachers and, as noted earlier, has the highest proportion of women and is the power base of Vanguardia.

The interview data upon which the following interpretation is based are from preschool and elementary school teachers in Mexico City, specifically twenty-two women and twenty-one men in comparable positions; thus, the total number of Mexican educators interviewed for the study was forty-three.[8]

The teachers' union is generally seen as a man's world in Mexico. Very few women ever become part of its leadership. A woman who has been teaching since 1929 and a supervisor for the last twenty years expressed the general consensus on the lack of female participation in the union leadership this way: "Men act in other spheres where women cannot go—because women have not lost all their decorum, and they cannot go to meet with men in the cantina to deal with certain problems, or they cannot be in many other places. There has always been a fence that hinders women from becoming involved."[9]

Referring to the participation of women in the leadership of the union from the male leaders' point of view, a former general secretary of the union asserted that "they do not want, or did not want, to be elected into the leadership of the union."[10] At the same time, a school principal suggested that "women are the ones who have given men the political power within the union. All male leaders have been launched by women, and they know that."[11]

A woman who worked in SEP clarified what the school principal was saying by recalling her days as an elementary school teacher during the early 1970s in one of the northern states. Most women, she observed, were interested in their own school and in the children they taught, and they were not so concerned with power relations in the profession. For women the union "was something remote, a group of male teachers who were fighting each other, and every two or three years, I don't remember, we had a free day and we had to go vote. . . . I was never interested." One of her memories was of a time when someone had to be elected as representative for the union delegation:

We chose a male professor from the school across from us. We chose him because we—I and all the other women who taught in our school—did not want to do it. No one was attracted to the position of union representative. It was an annoyance because you had to go to the union and pay attention to teachers' problems, all of which meant extra work. We proposed the man instead. He was very happy, and we elected him.[12]

But as a female leader of the union pointed out, women have also been blocked from positions of responsibility by the male leaders, and only inferior positions—never the decisionmaking positions such as secretary in the executive committee at the sectional and national levels—have been open to them. Nevertheless, using her own experience as an example, the leader thought that the participation of women in union activities had changed because before, "our only role was to listen."[13] This leader is referring to the increased participation of women at all levels of union policymaking since the 1970s. In previous years, one or two women at the most were secretaries in the sectional or national committees; also, different types of assignments were given to men or women leaders, with men in charge of the crucial political decisions, while women tended to focus on organizing meetings, arranging for transportation and meals, and so on.

Most of the power within the union has been concentrated in the hands of men, even though women constitute a majority of the teachers. For this reason, and because they are uncomfortable with the ways that men use their power as union leaders, women have not felt welcome in the union. In the interviews they tended to agree that union leaders were all too ready to exchange sexual favors for services. A young woman working as an assistant in the union recounted that older female teachers were constantly telling her that "in the union we only suffer disrespect." She added that things have changed for women in the union. Many young women today will visit the union offices on professional business, although some of them still go accompanied by their father or brother.[14]

Repeatedly, leaders mentioned a difference between elementary and preschool teachers in their union participation. Preschool teachers are mostly women from a slightly higher social background than elementary school teachers, and among preschool teachers there has not been a tradition of union participation. Preschool teachers in the past tended to see their work as temporary, and they usually remained teachers only until they were married or became mothers. In the case of elementary school teaching, there is a lifelong pattern of participation within the teaching profession. A preschool teacher and leader of the union said, "Preschool teachers are not politically conscious because they come from more privileged groups and they do not have a working-class consciousness." She added, "I left the normal school without knowing that there was a union."[15] These differences can be explained by distribution of the preschool and elementary normal schools: The normal schools for preschool teachers have always been concentrated in the urban areas, and women who attend them are from middle-class backgrounds for the most part. In the view of both labor leaders and officials from SEP, this pattern has changed rapidly over the last few years as public education has expanded and the social class differences between preschool and elementary school teachers have decreased.

In 1972, Vanguardia Revolucionaria took control of the leadership and became the dominant faction within the union. As is the case with the PRI, Vanguardia Revolucionaria generally presents itself as embodying the ideals of the Mexican Revolution. Since Vanguardia Revolucionaria took power, the union has lost some of the pluralism that used to characterize it, for the members of this group have tended to recirculate themselves in the higher positions of union leadership. Moreover, the leaders have been attempting to improve the image that the rank and file has of them by increasing the participation of women in union life, changing the women's view of the union, and making women feel at ease when they go to the union to conduct their professional business. A female leader in the union said that for Carlos Jonguitud Barrios, the president of Vanguardia Revolucionaria, the participation of women in the union is deeply important. He told her that the "time has arrived for women to assume strength to defend the position of women, of union women, of political women. This does not conflict with their functions as mother and teacher, nor with their femininity. . . . Women can struggle side by side with men without losing their femininity."[16]

Describing the rise of women to the leadership of the union, a school principal said, "Women arrive through the same channels that men do, and with the same alliances."[17] What this means is that female leaders as well as male leaders form part of Vanguardia Revolucionaria. As is true of the male leaders, the same women have tended to rotate in the positions of leadership within the union and the section. Three of the women who were on the executive committee of the Ninth Section when interviewed had been secretaries in the same section during the previous triennium. The other two had been assistants and negotiators undergoing training to advance to leadership roles. As in the case of the males, they were chosen by the leadership for these positions; and as with most of the cadres of Vanguardia Revolucionaria, they came from the middle-level positions such as school principals and supervisors. All of them agreed that within the section executive committee, men and women participated equally. Women spoke up and were not relegated to secondary functions. These women leaders, however, were a small minority on the executive committee, which represents a key section of the union, in which the vast majority of the rank and file are women.

In the literature on the political participation of women in Latin America, it has been argued that the marginalization of women from power occurs because of traditional values within the family, which limit behavior and serve as a barrier to women in public and political institutions.[18] Against this prevailing explanation, it is useful to develop a more elaborate view of the complex realities that women face in professional life. A female leader of the Ninth Section represents the perspective of a woman who had advanced to a position of power:

> Years ago, when I began going to the organization, the atmosphere was not healthy, although we cannot say that today it is excellent. . . . For this reason, in those years I did not want to participate directly. I liked to participate in congresses, academic meetings, and sports events organized by the union . . . but not direct participation. I felt that it was not the moment yet for a woman to be there, . . . sometimes women were not treated with respect, . . . the males as leaders felt very powerful and were domineering and behaved improperly toward women. Things have changed, they have improved, women have increased their participation in the union. The latest general secretary of the union has attempted to erase the image that existed, that within the union there was no respect for women teachers. The affection, good treatment, and respect toward women teachers have increased.

In describing this improved treatment, this woman also went beyond the theme of traditional values and expressed the limited perspective of the union leadership with its emphasis on domesticity and motherhood. For example, she observed, "A special celebration for those who are mothers is organized by the union on Mothers Day . . . to give women the place they deserve, because if they are not honored among us, then even less [so will they be] within society at large." One could argue that the union was merely responding to the accepted cultural role of women in Mexican society, but in fact the union leaders quite consciously instituted this practice instead of other forms of participation that women in the rank and file actively sought. Imposed under such circumstances, the celebration of domesticity becomes a means of deflecting female aspirations for a greater share of power in the decisions of the union to which they belong, and the practice thus reveals the undemocratic climate within the union. The ways in which the male union leadership uses social rituals to attract the participation of the female rank and file is analyzed further later in this section.

The same leader explained how the structure of opportunity for advancement to leadership positions has changed with the increasing importance of educational credentials. "When I began participating in the leadership of the union," she recalled, "I did it through my academic credentials; I did not advance only through a political career. This was helpful because I was able to get involved without having to put up with the unhealthy environment that existed."[19] As Peter H. Smith and Roderic Camp have found in studying the political elite in Mexico, education is the most important variable for explaining access to the political elite. Not only educational credentials matter, of course; the privileged access to certain institutions and the personal contacts that develop while in those institutions are essential.[20]

The same pattern appears in the case of some women who join the union leadership. But the male political culture that surrounds power in the union has thrown social barriers in front of women that are not barriers for men. A secretary of the Ninth Section of the union remembered how, after several years of participating in union-sponsored events for teachers, she decided to participate more directly in the leadership of the union, encouraged by the persistence of one of her fellow students in the normal school who at that time was a member of the executive committee of the Ninth Section:

> An old friend of mine, who was on the executive committee and had known me since we were students, insisted that I participate more and assured me that the men there were going to respect me as a woman. I was having doubts about becoming more deeply involved in the union because I was different. For example, the leaders of the union used to party a lot. . . . After the meetings they always got together, drank and stayed until very late at night. I used to stay only for a little while— because you have to do it in order to find your way in. But it is a world of men. . . . I could have succumbed to their ways. My goal was to become part of a working team, both as a professional and within the union, without having to give up my image and convictions.[21]

In contrast to this female leader, many more women have been reluctant even to try to participate, thus limiting their aspirations and careers. Exclusion results in part because the women enter a social world clearly dominated by men. Women are afraid; they confront obstacles, both internally generated and externally imposed, to participating openly in that world. At the same time, there is a long history of corruption and sexual harassment by union leaders. Not only is it common knowledge that union leaders will sell the permanent jobs and the promotions that women seek, but it is also well known that some male leaders are ready to exchange promotions or jobs for sexual favors. One of the dissident leaders, when interviewed, recalled that when protesting teachers took over the building of one of the union sections, they found "the bedroom of promotions."[22]

Just when women were beginning in very small numbers to enter the leadership of SNTE, the male-dominated leadership decided in 1977 to break up the women's office of the union. This office has existed in all unions in Mexico, as well as in the PRI, since the Cardenas administration in the 1930s. SNTE is the only union in Mexico that has made this decision, and it is also the union with the largest percentage of women in it. The female leaders within the Ninth Section were not involved in the controversy.

The leadership of SNTE dissolved the women's office of the union on the grounds that if most of the rank and file are women, they do not need a separate bureau. One of the leaders explained why there should not be a women's office within the union: "The organization has set hierarchies in terms of the importance of the struggle for all teachers. That is why I cannot struggle according to my own interests . . . and I cannot work with groups of women only."[23] This ironic proclamation of the equality of men and women in union affairs brings up difficult questions. Do women need separate representation? Does the female rank and file benefit from the participation of a few women in the ruling elite? What role do female teachers play within the union? How will women as a subordinated group gain power in existing institutions and within the political structure of Mexico? The interviews with union leaders did not provide evidence that female leaders were concerned with these questions.

The evidence provided by the interviews showed that there is little communication between the female leaders and the female rank and file. Nonetheless, the female leaders are serving a certain function in the attempt of the leadership to improve its image in front of the rank and file. One female leader recalled that Vanguardia Revolucionaria's President Barrios told her that "the image of the organization will change greatly when women enter and participate with all the honesty and devotion that characterize them."[24] A dissident leader noted, "In the promotion of social trade-unionism and its style of politics, they [Vanguardia Revolucionaria] have women play a central role."[25]

This expedient use of female leadership in a male-dominated institution does not mean that the situation of women has failed to change. The traditional conception of women's political participation within the PRI was that of voluntary public assistance; today, women have access to real opportunities. Still, as one male dissident leader asserted, "It is more a treatment of courtesy than of equality."[26] The entrance of women for the first time into the leadership, a man's world as it is currently set up, has not been without problems, but as one of the interviewed women said, "I have been on several teams in which all were men but me. It is difficult because they want you to follow their ways instead of letting you follow your own, and as a woman you need to search for new ways of participating." She continued by saying that in the Ninth Section there is only one place to be if female leaders wish to gain more power within the executive committee, and that is in the chair of the general secretary. "All of us want that position," she added, but "who knows if the moment has arrived yet for a woman to be there?"[27]

Wary of such aspirations, the leadership has been attempting to construct a carefully limited sphere for increasing the participation of women in the union. Most of the efforts of the union are designed to attract the participation of women through social rituals such as the celebration of Mother's Day and other get-togethers. There is also a tendency toward using the union as a center for innocuous social activities, reflected in an increase in the number of breakfasts and lunches organized by the union. Most female teachers can attend these without any constraints, but such participation is misleading because it has replaced the function of union assemblies bringing together the leadership and the rank and file to discuss general issues of concern in employment and union politics. The use of the union for social activities has been a way of maintaining the legitimacy of the organization while restricting rank-and-file participation in union decisions and policies. Limiting women's role thus helps to fragment the power of workers in a section of the union where the majority of members are women.[28]

Along similar lines, the number of women who attend the national congress may well have increased in recent years, but it is evident from women's own accounts and by looking at the photographs of such occasions that women are involved in activities different from those of men. In addition to the disproportionately small number of women delegates, many other female teachers participate in the congress, serving coffee, handling the microphones, acting as hostesses—roles that show a constricted view of women's participation in the life of the union, one that maintains traditional functions such as domestic chores that are associated with the home. "The participation of women in the union is decorative," said a young teacher referring to the union congresses. Challenging these practices in the culture of the union, a dissident leader said that the union leadership has a "perverted view" of women's participation in union politics.[29]

More than half of the women interviewed had participated in union activities in one way or another during their careers. Except for the leaders of the Ninth Section, they had participated primarily in union-sponsored events—social reunions, sports competitions, cultural activities—or at the delegation level. Others had participated in the dissident movements.

▲ Women in Dissident Movements

The officially sanctioned participation of women in SNTE is only one component of their political participation. Because of the historical conditions under which the union emerged in the 1940s and the fact that it was an organization created from the top down, there always has been a wide gulf between the rank and file and the leadership. As in other unions in Mexico, rank-and-file participation in the life of the organization is limited.[30] Women have always participated from below, from the rank and file, and they have shown great solidarity with dissident movements even when there has been little direct participation by women in the leadership of these movements.

In the late 1950s a movement arose among elementary school teachers in Mexico City to democratize the life of the union. Organized by Movimiento Revolucionario del Magisterio, the insurgent faction fought for the leadership of SNTE's powerful Ninth Section. Under the leadership of Othon Salazar, teachers mobilized against the union leadership, its antidemocratic forms of control, its close relationship to the party, and its corruption. Most of the teachers in the section went on strike for more than six weeks, closing schools in Mexico City; a sit-in on the patio of the SEP building followed.

As a result, their wages were increased. But the leadership of this opposition group, though strongly supported by the rank and file, did not manage to become part of the executive committee of the Ninth Section. In fact, Salazar was incarcerated on grounds of subversion. Since that time, the members of Movimiento Revolucionario del Magisterio have chosen to make their voice heard within the existing structure of the union and to seek positions in the section and national committees.

During those years, when teachers demonstrated in favor of a democratization of the leadership of SNTE, women participated actively. A leader at that time described the vehemence with which women participated and the central role they had in launching the movement:

> The movement of 1958 had a strong moral overtone. We were seeking to purify the ruling body, not to change the political structure. This had a special rank and file, which was fighting against the abuses of the "gun-slingers" [*casta pistoleril*] who used women, who gave them permanent jobs in exchange for going out with them, against all the disdain and ill treatment heaped upon women. We had important and decisive participation by women and enthusiasm of women in the struggle, in the brigades, even though it was more difficult for women because of their family responsibilities. During the sit-in of 1958, the female teachers went even with their children and their families.[31]

The opposition movement of the late 1970s emerged from the rank and file in the less developed and more rural states of Mexico. Between June 1979 and February 1981 there were teacher strikes of thirty days on the average in several different states: Chiapas, Oaxaca, Mexico, Hidalgo, and Guerrero. The initial reason for the movement was a delay in teachers' paychecks. These protests then snowballed into a movement for democratization of the union, producing the most massive protest demonstrations by teachers since the creation of SNTE in 1943. Protesting teachers created a parallel organization, the Coordinadora Nacional de Trabajadores de la Educación, to mediate between themselves, SEP, and SNTE. This popular struggle has developed new and varied ways of showing its opposition—such as sit-ins, demonstrations, political advertisements, control of the workplace—that are similar to those currently used by other independent unions.

The Coordinadora is quite possibly the strongest reaction against the union leadership during the entire history of the teachers' union. It has called into question the ways in which the relationship between union leadership and the rank and file is structured for the educational profession in Mexico. The Coordinadora has become a powerful, if still somewhat fragile, organization in its own right, with at least 200,000 members. Two sections of the union, Oaxaca and Chiapas, are in control of the Coordinadora. Its delegates were allowed to attend SNTE's national congress in February 1983, and as a result one of its leaders now sits on the national executive committee. The leadership was, then, at least partly incorporated into the power structure that controls SNTE.

As the leadership of the union sees it, if there has not been any more broadly based protest movement in the Ninth Section, it is because of the work that the union does in each school to minimize tension. In the view of the dissident leaders, it is because of the tight control placed upon teachers by the union. One of the sections where greatest mobilization has occurred is in the north of Mexico City—Section 36 of Valle de Mexico. This section is located in the working-class neighborhoods surrounding Mexico City. A teacher relates her history of participation in the movements taking place there:

> There is much fear . . . but a large majority of women are participating in politics now . . . I have had intense political participation . . . although not openly because I think I don't have enough knowledge to do it. . . . I see other fellow teachers standing up in meetings and speaking . . . they can be strongly criticized. You need to have a very clear mind, be articulate, and have a good knowledge of the situation, and I do not have enough time to prepare myself for that. . . . I have been a political dissident because I see it is necessary . . . because those are my ideals. As a working-class person, I have suffered in my own skin all the injustices. . . . This is what has led me to participate in politics . . . in order to defend my rights. In the school where I work, we are all dissidents for those same reasons . . . we have been struggling and fighting for years to secure a permanent job that was opened up to us by the SEP and then was taken away by the union because they said we were not worthy of it. One problem after another has led us to keep on with the struggle. . . . I have been in demonstrations, meetings, brigades and sit-ins. Last November [1981] we sat down in the street, right in front of the riot police for three days and two nights. I told my mother that if something happens to me, please take care of my children. I know it is dangerous, but I am defending my rights and I am struggling for them.[32]

In the past, the role of women as rank-and-file members of the union was kept in silence. But as indicated by the preceding discussion about the two most important dissenting movements that have arisen from the rank and file, women have had a central if not yet fully documented role. There are marked differences between their opposition in the 1950s and more recently. In the 1950s women were organized from the top down by a political party, whereas today their popular mobilization resembles other urban popular movements sweeping across Latin America (Jelín, 1987). In both cases, immediate circumstances such as the deterioration of wages and threats to their standard of living prompt women to action. When they act in times of crisis, women in the dissident movements confront both the political structure and the institutional culture that together act to devalue their worth and frustrate their aspirations throughout their careers.

▲ Conclusion: Women and Power in Politics

In the 1930s female teachers mobilized to incorporate women into the organized structure of power in Mexico. In the decades that followed, women moved in small numbers to positions of authority inside the government, the PRI, and its related organizations, such as labor unions. Beyond offering a particular case study of SNTE—one of the mainstays of PRI—in this chapter, I have attempted to illuminate both the achievements and the hopes of women after half a century of active participation. A few women do hold positions of power within the political structure. Nevertheless, the dominant male leadership typecasts the participation of women in union life, reverting to stereotypes when dealing with the aspirations of women. Women are seen as inferior, less capable of holding power, more suited to supporting—in culturally acceptable ways—the men who hold power within the union. In reaction to this stereotypical image of women imposed by the union culture, female educators make choices that have the effect of excluding them from leadership positions because women do not identify with that image.

It is revealing that the officially sanctioned participation of women in the union occurs primarily through social events organized by the leadership. In an organization numerically dominated by women, the emphasis on social activities has resulted in restricted rank-and-file participation in union decisions and policies. A major outcome of antidemocratic processes within the union is that workers have lost their bargaining position as a collective group. They have been atomized and must approach the union leadership as individuals seeking benefits and favors. The policies of the male leadership and the demands they place on SEP and PRI on behalf of rank-and-file teachers do not address the obvious and pressing needs of women as workers. There is, for example, little union support to increase the availability of child day care, to expand preschool education, or to develop more adequate health care services. Reflecting the extreme fragmentation of collective power in bargaining with the male-dominated union leadership, even the few women who have achieved leadership positions do not express feminist ideals or show a clear concern for mobilizing to expand women's opportunities. For the many more women who constitute the majority of the teaching profession, the success of those few who have become part of the leadership has not changed the constraints that shape their professional lives.

Women as a group are not organized, and at best they play a carefully circumscribed role in union life. As I have argued here, the union leadership purposefully draws upon cultural stereotypes about women, even when promoting their participation in leadership roles. The few women who have advanced to such roles have been promoted because of their traditionally female image of honesty and devotion, and as a way of legitimizing the leadership in front of the rank and file. But if union culture accounts for the nonparticipation of women in union politics, women's active participation in dissident movements shows their interest in changing the institution that controls them as professional teachers. Their quest serves as a reminder that legal equality for women marks only the starting point of further efforts to remake the institutions that shape the work of women.

In summary, women who seek to advance their careers in the education profession of Mexico suffer two types of constraints: those related to the mechanisms of control within the union, and those more closely related to their own socialization as women. On the union side, women face a tight structure of control in which jobs and promotions are used for political purposes, with personal favors often more important than concrete achievements. With regard to their own socialization, women feel uncomfortable participating in an institutional culture that undervalues them; frequently, they prefer to retreat from the culture of male power that they encounter when they seek professional opportunity.[33]

This analysis of gender and power within the teachers' union shows that in spite of the fact that gender has rarely been included in the study of labor organizations in Mexico and Latin America, gender as a system of power relations plays a crucial role in the maintenance of existing political structures and the social inequality these structures help to perpetuate.

▲ Notes

1. The SNTE membership figure is from Parra (1985).

2. José A. Alonso has written several pieces on the presence of women in the garment workers union; among them see Alonso (1983). Also on garment workers see Carillo (1988). On the participation of women in unions in other countries in Latin America, see Jelín (1987).

3. On the participation of Mexican teachers in the feminist movement during the first half of the century, see Macías (1982); also Foppa (1979).

4. Entitlement to these benefits does not, however, necessarily mean provision of services by the government. In the case of childcare, for example, the demand greatly exceeds government-sponsored services. Women see this gap between rhetoric and reality as a major problem in their conditions of employment, impeding professional advancement at all levels.

5. Interview E-4, Mexico City, September 1982. See note 8 for methodological information.

6. In another essay I have reviewed the literature on the participation of women in the teaching profession of Mexico since the turn of the twentieth century, analyzed how the postsecondary educational opportunities for women shape their careers within the teaching profession, and examined their role as leaders within SEP; see Cortina (1989).

7. For an account of teacher mobilization in the 1950s, see Loyo Brambila (1979); on the movement since 1979, see Salinas Alvarez and Imaz Gisper (1984).

8. All interviews cited in this chapter are from my doctoral dissertation (1985). Unless otherwise indicated, all translations from Spanish are my own.

The dissertation uses interviews, union materials and publications, government documents, direct observation of activities, newspapers, and secondary literature. To complement traditional sources of documentation, I conducted interviews in 1981–1983; in all there were 43 interviews: 11 of male and female teachers, 9 of past and present labor leaders, 3 of principals and supervisors, 13 of past and present officials from the Secretaría de Educación Pública, and 5 of other informed sources. My 43 interviews are complemented by 32 oral life-history interviews of teachers made by the Centro de Estudios Contemporáneos of the Instituto Nacional de Antropología e Historia. An additional source of evidence was the direct observation of activities that came along with the interviews, such as daily activities in the union and visits to the schools.

9. Interview C-1, Mexico City, July 1982.

10. Interview with Professor Gaudencio Peraza, general secretary of the National Executive Committee of SNTE (1945–1949), Departamento de Estudios Contemporáneos, INAH, interview PHO/3/21 by Marcela Tostada, June–August 1979, p. 395.

11. Interview C-2, Mexico City, July 1982.

12. Interview D-12, Mexico City, September 1982.

13. Interview A-3, Mexico City, August 1982.

14. Interview D-13, Mexico City, July 1982.

15. Interview A-2, Mexico City, August 1982.

16. Interview A-3, Mexico City, August 1982.

17. Interview C-2, Mexico City, July 1982.

18. For a review article on the topic, see Jaquette (1986). One of the few detailed studies on the political participation of women in Latin America is Chaney (1979). Chaney's conclusion is that Latin American societies "define women's public activity as an extension of their traditional family role to the public arena" (p. 158).

19. Interview A-3, Mexico City, July 1982.

20. See Smith (1979), especially chapter 9, "The Rules of the Game"; and Camp (1984).

21. Interview A-3, Mexico City, July 1982.

22. Interview A-10, Mexico City, August 1982.

23. Interview A-2, Mexico City, August 1982. This point was confirmed by Interview A-4, Mexico City, August 1982.

24. Interview A-3, Mexico City, July 1982.

25. Interview A-5, Mexico City, August 1982.

26. Interview A-5, Mexico City, August 1982.

27. Interview A-3, Mexico City, July 1982.

28. To identify discrimination in union activities, two union publications were closely examined to evaluate the image of women that is projected through these media: *Reivindicación* and *Magisterio. Reivindicación* served as the house organ for SNTE from the founding of the union until the teachers' conflict of 1958, at which time it was discontinued and the new magazine *Magisterio* emerged.

29. Interview D-3, Mexico City, August 1982.

30. For an analysis of the history of unions in relation to that of the PRI, see Garrido (1982).

31. Interview A-5, Mexico City, August 1982. For an account of the teacher mobilization of 1958, see Loyo Brambila (1979).

32. Interview D-8, Mexico City, August 1982. On the movement since 1979, see Hernández (1981).

33. On the institutional culture of SNTE, see Cortina (1989a).

▲ References

Alonso, José. "The Domestic Clothing Workers in the Mexican Metropolis and Their Relations to Dependent Capitalism." In June Nash and Maria Patricia Fernandez-Kelly (eds.), *Women, Men, and the International Division of Labor*. Albany: State University of New York, 1983.

Camp, Roderic. *The Making of a Government: Political Leaders in Modern Mexico*. Tucson: University of Arizona Press, 1984.

Carillo, Teresa. "Working Women and the '19 of September' Mexican Garment Workers Union: The Significance of Gender." Unpublished paper, 1988.

Chaney, Elsa. *Supermadre: Women in Politics in Latin America*. Austin: University of Texas Press, 1979.

Cortina, Regina. "La vida profesional del maestro mexicano y su sindicato." *Estudios Sociológicos*, 1989a, vol. 19, pp. 79-103.

———. "Power, Gender, and Education: Unionized Teachers in Mexico City." Unpublished doctoral dissertation, Stanford University, 1985.

———. "Women as Leaders in Mexican Education." *Comparative Education Review*, 1989b, vol. 33, no. 3, pp. 357–376.

Foppa, Alaide. "The First Feminist Congress in Mexico." *Signs*, 1979, vol. 5, pp. 192–199.

Garrido, Luis. *El partido de la revolución institucionalizada: La formación del nuevo régimen (1928–1945)*. Mexico City: Sigloveintiuno, 1982.

Hernández, Luis (ed.). *Las luchas magisteriales 1979–1981*. Mexico: Macehual, 1981.

Jaquette, Jane S. "Female Political Participation in Latin America: Raising Feminist Issues." In Lynn Iglitzin and Ruth Ross (eds.), *Women in the World: 1975–1985, the Women's Decade*. Santa Barbara, Calif.: ABC-CLIO Press, 1986.

Jelín, Elizabeth (ed.). *Ciudadanía e identidad: Las mujeres en los movimientos sociales latino-americanos*. Ginebra: Instituto de Investigaciones de las Naciones Unidas para el Desarrollo Social, 1987.

Loyo Brambila, Aurora. *El movimiento magisterial de 1958 en México*. Mexico: Era, 1979.

Macias, Anna. *Against All Odds: The Feminist Movement in Mexico to 1940*. Westport, Conn.: Greenwood Press, 1982.

Parra, Manuel German. "Historia del movimiento sindical de los trabajadores del estado," *El Cotidiano*, vol. 2, no. 7, 1985.

Salinas Alvarez, Samuel, and Carlos Imaz Gisper. *Maestros y Estado*, vols. I and II. (Mexico City, Editorial Linea, 1984).

SNTE (Sindicato Nacional de Trabajadores de la Educación). *Cuántos somos?* Mexico: SNTE, 1977.

Smith, Peter. *Labyrinths of Power: Political Recruitment in Twentieth-Century Mexico*. Princeton: Princeton University Press, 1979.

▲ 7

Gender Inequalities and the Expansion of Higher Education in Costa Rica

Haydée M. Mendiola

This chapter examines the changes in the participation of women in higher education that derive from a major expansion of the university system in Costa Rica. This rich quantitative study compares enrollment changes over a seven-year interval and traces university graduates as they join the labor force.

Mendiola finds no changes in the participation rates of men and women as new types of universities are created. This supports findings detected in other countries, namely that as more men seek higher education, so too do more women. The principle of homogamous marriage may be at work, a concept that deserves further consideration.

A positive result from the expansion of university education is that women tend to increase their chances of completing their studies and moving into a more diversified set of fields of study. On the other hand, women from upper classes are the ones who move into the new fields, including nonconventional fields for women.

The Costa Rican data also show that access to higher education does not result in the same benefits for men and women. Different types of educational institutions produce different levels of financial compensation in the labor force for their graduates, an effect that is more marked among women than among men.

In all, the chapter warns us that the process of social and gender stratification is an enduring one and that university expansion alone does not significantly alter the field-of-study choices and income of lower sectors of society.

—Editor

▲ This chapter discusses gender differences in the educational and labor market outcomes of higher education expansion in Costa Rica. The focus is on the impact that mass higher education has had on female participation in university education and market activity.

In the early 1970s, Costa Rica instituted a reform of its higher education system that transformed the university from an elite to a mass institution.[1] The ostensible purpose of this reform was to offer equal opportunity of access to higher education, independently of students' socioeconomic origins.[2] Prior to this reform, the Costa Rican postsecondary education system was composed of one public university, the University of Costa Rica; one teacher-training college; and eleven private centers that offered short programs, primarily in business and secretarial courses. During the 1970s, the postsecondary education system expanded rapidly. In less than ten years the percentage of the relevant age cohort attending a higher education institution grew from 8 to 27 percent (World Bank, 1985). University enrollments alone increased from 17,645 students in 1972 to 44,915 at the end of the decade. By 1978, the country had thirty postsecondary institutions. The Costa Rican higher education system now included five universities, four of them public and one private. Three of the public universities offered their services in fourteen locations, while the Open University made higher education available throughout the country. The single private university served the major cities.

This reform of higher education was implemented at a time when Costa Rican society was undergoing profound political and economic transformations. During this period, a new direction was given to economic policy in order to develop a state accumulation process,[3] and the relationship among dominant social groups was redefined. The expansion of higher education was part of this new development strategy. On the one hand, it would provide the required educated human resources; on the other, it would eliminate social conflict by satisfying the increased demand for higher education as individuals sought social mobility and a more equitable income redistribution.

This chapter analyzes the impact that the particular form of public university expansion generated by this reform had on female higher education access and achievement and on market participation. It answers questions such as the following: Has the disparity between male and female participation in higher education narrowed with university expansion? With the proliferation of universities, does the distribution of men and women vary significantly from one higher education institution to another according to the quality of these institutions? Have sex differences in field-of-study choice and graduation rates changed after the reform, and, if so, in what ways? Do the labor force participation effects of the reform differ for males and females, and, if so, what explanation could be offered for the difference? Have the different occupational distributions of men and women changed after the reform and why? How do the income effects of higher education expansion differ by gender and why?

▲ Methodology

In order to answer these questions, this study used data covering two cohorts of university entrants—one before and the other after the 1970s higher education reform. Also used were follow-up data of both sets of former students into the 1986 labor market. The preform incoming students were selected at random within the University of Costa Rica. For the reform generation, all four public higher education institutions—the University of Costa Rica, the Technological Institute, the National University, and the Open University—were included in the study, and individuals were selected at random within each of the universities. Both samples represent about 10 percent of the total of entering freshmen in 1972 and 1979.[4]

The data for the study come from four sources: (1) the 1972 and 1979 university information forms of entering freshmen; (2) students' academic records; (3) the national register of births; (4) and a follow-up study conducted in 1986 of those former students who are now in the labor force. The university information forms allowed the researcher to identify the students' educational plans, gender, family socioeconomic status, high school records, and parents' name, address, and similar matters. From the academic records it was possible to determine whether the student had graduated, dropped out, or continued in the university; and in the case of those who completed a degree, it was also possible to identify the field of graduation. From the national register of births the researcher obtained each student's national identification number so as not to confuse him or her with another person with the same name when doing the follow-up. The purpose of the follow-up study was to obtain information on the occupational attainments of the students since university graduation.

The follow-up study was conducted using two sources of information: June 1986 national payrolls and a telephone survey. The national payrolls, obtained from the Costa Rican Social Security Agency, provided information regarding graduates' monthly income and place of work. The telephone survey had three purposes: (1) to identify the type of position the subjects in the sample were occupying (because information about occupation did not appear in the payrolls); (2) to follow up on those former students who could not be found in the Social Security Agency's data bank; and (3) to double-check the information obtained from the Social Security Agency (in about 20 percent of the cases).[5]

Statistical Techniques

Throughout the study four statistical procedures were used: (1) tabular analysis, (2) chi-square tests of association, (3) Cramer's V test, and (4) multiple regression. The first permitted general comparisons across cohorts.

The second was used to examine gross relationships between gender and higher education institution attended, field-of-study choice, academic status, labor force participation, type of workplace, and occupation. The third was used to assess whether the degree of association between gender and educational and labor market outcome variables had become more pronounced across cohorts. The fourth was used to investigate the simultaneous effects of the key variables on male and female graduates' income.

Variables and Operational Definitions

The variables employed in this study are sex of the student, the socioeconomic status and income of the student's family, the university attended, and the student's academic status; and, for those who graduated, the field of graduation, income, place of work, and type of occupation.

The variable *gender* refers to the sex of the student. It is a dummy variable with a value of 0 for males and a value of 1 for females.

In order to measure *socioeconomic status* (SES), a composite index was constructed on the basis of family income, head-of-family education, and head-of-family occupation. It was assumed that a combination of these three factors presents a more accurate profile of the student's family background than any one factor alone. Points were assigned to each of the categories of the three variables, with 1 being the lowest position and 6 the highest. A composite score was created by adding up the values for each individual in the sample. Total scores ranged from 3 to 18 points. In order to obtain a social stratification model, a symmetrical rank distribution for the sample was selected, assuming an approximated normal distribution of students across socioeconomic strata. The SES index was used for compiling all tables.

The variable *family income* is the 1972 or 1979 monthly income of the student's family, measured by gross earnings from salaries and fees in Costa Rican colones. This variable was used as a proxy for graduates' socioeconomic background in the regression equations. For both the preform and reform generation, family income was found to have a strong positive correlation with the SES index (.91 and .95, respectively). Family income instead of the SES index was used for the equations because of its greater variance.

The variable *university attended* refers to the quality of the university attended by the student. The quality of the higher education institutions is measured by two separate variables: (1) the percentage of professors with a master's degree or a doctorate and (2) the admission requirements of each institution.[6] Points were assigned to each of these two variables, 1 being the lowest and 4 the highest. The values obtained by each university were added, and the universities were arranged in order from the highest to the lowest score. This is the order in which they appear in the tables that follow.

In the regression equations, *university attended* was defined as a set of dummy variables where the University of Costa Rica is the base category. The UCR was selected as the standard for comparison because it is the higher education institution with the largest number of students.

The variable *academic status* refers to the academic standing of the student, based on whether the student graduated, continued in the university as of July 1986, or dropped out.

The variable *graduate's income* refers to the June 1986 monthly income of the graduate, measured by gross earnings from salaries and fees in Costa Rican colones. It is unknown, however, if this income was derived from full- or part-time work.

The variable *field of study* is the field of graduation of the student. In the regression equations the term is defined as a set of dummy variables in which the social sciences area is the base category. This area of study was chosen as the standard for comparison because it has the largest number of graduates.

The variable *graduate's place of work* refers to the sector of the economy—public or private—where the graduate worked in June 1986. It is a dummy variable with a value of 0 for the public sector and a value of 1 for the private sector.

The variable *graduate's type of occupation* has three categories: self-employed, employed with managerial or supervisory responsibilities, and employed without managerial or supervisory responsibilities. In the regression equations the term is defined as a set of dummy variables where the third category was selected as the standard for comparison.

▲ Results: Prereform and Reform Generations Compared

Gender, Higher Education Access, and Achievement

Table 7.1 shows the percentage of male and female students who enrolled for the first time in the university in 1972 and 1979. With respect to the gender composition of the student population, this table indicates that the gap between male and female enrollments, as a percentage of their cohort, did not narrow with mass expansion of the university system. Both in 1972 and 1979, freshmen enrollment rates for males and females were 56 and 44 percent, respectively.[7] These findings suggest that the expansionary reform of the 1970s did not bring about any substantial changes in the percentage distribution of entering students by gender. Although the reform permitted larger numbers of women to gain access to the university because of an absolute increase in university entrants, it also continued to reproduce the existing gender disparity. Nevertheless, it is important to observe that, contrary to what other studies have shown,[8] in Costa Rica, at least, the expansion of the higher education system did not benefit males more than females.

The results summarized in Table 7.2 show that with the creation of new

Table 7.1. Gender Distribution of Entering Freshmen (percent)

Gender	UCR 1972	University System 1979
Males	55.6	56
Females	44.4	44
Total	100	100

Table 7.2. Distribution of Students by Gender and Higher Education Institution Attended, 1979 (percent)

Institution	Female	Male	Total
UCR	47	53	100
ITCR	25	75	100
UNA	51	49	100
UNED	34	66	100
Column percent of total sample	43.7	56.3	100
X_2=24.09	df=3	$p<.001$	

higher education institutions, gender differentiation among universities has occurred. Two institutions—the Technological Institute (ITCR) and the Open University (UNED)—have a predominantly male population (75 and 66 percent, respectively), while the University of Costa Rica (UCR) and the National University (UNA) have a more even distribution of male and female students.

However, no particular pattern between men and women in university attended was found. This appears to suggest that gender differentiation among higher education institutions is not related to university status. The University of Costa Rica, which is the most prestigious higher education institution in the country, has a larger representation of female freshmen and a smaller proportion of first-year male students relative to the total sample percentage. On the other hand, in the Open University (UNED)—the least attractive of the higher education institutions in terms of academic excellence—men exceed the male proportion of the total sample by 10 percent.

Gender differences in university choice seem to be more related to the field of specialization chosen. Most of the ITCR's program offerings are in engineering, a field in which women in Costa Rica have been traditionally underrepresented. The UNED offers courses in educational, public banking, and business administration; all of these are fields in which men tend to predominate. The fact that the UNA has a greater proportion of women than the university system as a whole can also be explained by the numerous teacher-education programs it offers, an occupation which, in Costa Rica, is female dominated.

Before the patterns between men and women in field of graduation are discussed, it is important to look at the association between gender and academic status. Table 7.3 shows that this relationship strengthened after the reform. In the 1972 cohort no statistically significant differences were found in the percentage distribution of students by gender and academic status. Both men and women appear to have graduated, dropped out, or continued in the system at the same rates.

The class of 1979, however, shows a significant relationship between gender and academic condition. Even though greater gender differentiation occurred after the reform regarding this aspect, it appears to have favored women over men. Although females constituted 44 percent of the freshman class, they represented 50 percent of those who graduated. Males, on the other hand, made up 56 percent of the entering class, but accounted for only 50 percent of the graduates. In the case of dropouts, the inverse relationship can be established—men abandoned their studies at higher rates than females. It is also important to note that as of July 1986 the proportion of women who continued studying was significantly higher than that of men. In other words, female students in the postreform cohort persisted in their studies and graduated at higher rates than men.

According to the literature on gender and education,[9] this finding could be explained in market terms. Because working-class families do not possess sufficient economic resources to send all of their offspring to the university, parents prefer to educate their sons on the assumption that the gain from higher education is greater for males than for females. The supposition is that the education of women is consumption because they will later be confined to reproductive roles. In consequence, a high percentage of those women who enter the university are allegedly from upper socioeconomic strata and so can remain much longer within the system and graduate at higher rates. However, in the sample this does not appear to be the case. No significant association was found between gender and socioeconomic status of first-year students. Perhaps a reason for women's persistence and successful graduation is that female students are under less pressure to join the labor force while studying, irrespective of socioeconomic status.

Table 7.4 shows the percentage distribution of graduates by field of specialization and gender for each of the two cohorts. Note that despite the fact that in both groups there is a significant relationship between gender and field of graduation, this association is less pronounced for graduates of the reform generation.

In both groups women are disproportionately represented in education, social work, nursing, and arts and letters; they are overrepresented in

Table 7.3. Distribution of Students by Gender and Academic Status, 1972 and 1979 (percent)

Academic Status	1972 Cohort			1979 Cohort		
	Male	Female		Male	Female	
Graduated	52	48	100	50	50	100
Continued	65	35	100	49	51	100
Dropped out	58	42	100	61	39	100
Column percent of total sample	56	44	100	56	44	100

X_2=2.3 df=2 $p>.05$ X_2=11.8 df=2 $p<.005$
Cramer's V=.065   Cramer's V=.108

proportion to the total sample in the social sciences and law; and they are underrepresented in architecture, engineering, and agricultural sciences. Both cohorts reveal a high representation of women in all of the fields leading to lower, less-prestigious positions or to occupations with the fewest opportunities for employment. This phenomenon could be explained by looking at the effect of discrimination on the demand and supply sides. If women are aware that once in the labor market they will be denied entry into certain prestigious occupations, then most of them will choose to graduate from fields that will lead to occupations where such barriers do not exist or are minimal.

However, in health and basic sciences, fields which in most other countries are traditionally male provinces, women have predominated, and their representation has increased over cohorts. At the same time, although architecture, engineering, and the agricultural sciences remain a male's domain, the 1979 cohort shows a slight improvement in the percentage of women graduating in these fields. In short, it appears that the 1970s higher education reform slightly facilitated women's opportunities in terms of field-of-study choice.

These findings, however, are somewhat less encouraging once the intersection of class and gender is taken into consideration. The study reveals that the social stratification of women by field-of-study choice has been accentuated by university expansion. For 1972 cohort female graduates, no significant association was found between socioeconomic status and field of graduation. In the case of the reform generation, this relationship was found to be significant. Upper-class women make up 43 percent of female graduates in architecture and engineering, 41 percent in health sciences, 56 percent in law, and 100 percent in basic sciences. By contrast, women from the lower stratum graduated at higher rates in fields such as nursing, education, and social work and in topography and other technical fields. These results show

Table 7.4. Distribution of Students by Gender and Field of Study, 1972 and 1979 Cohorts (percent)

Field of Study	1972 Cohort			1979 Cohort		
	Male	Female		Male	Female	
Architecture/engineering	96 (43)	4 (2)	100	73 (33)	27 (12)	100
Health sciences	47 (16)	53 (18)	100	39 (9)	61 (14)	100
Law	55 (6)	45 (5)	100	53 (10)	47 (9)	100
Basic sciences	43 (9)	57 (12)	100	29 (2)	71 (5)	100
Agricultural sciences	86 (12)	14 (2)	100	72 (20)	28 (8)	100
Social sciences	57 (31)	43 (23)	100	48 (24)	52 (26)	100
Arts/letters	13 (2)	87 (14)	100	14 (1)	86 (6)	100
Nursing	0 (0)	100 (1)	100	0 (0)	100 (2)	100
Education/social work	9 (3)	91 (31)	100	12 (3)	88 (22)	100
Topography/other technical	100 (1)	0 (0)	100	100 (2)	0 (0)	100
Column percent of total sample	52	48	100	50	50	100

$X_2 = 82.2$ $df=9$ $p<.001$ Cramer's $V=.593$

$X_2 = 82.2$ $df=9$ $p<.001$ Cramer's $V=.494$

Note: Figures in parentheses represent number of responses.

that the reform of the 1970s had different impacts on women of different social classes. Women benefited from the reform in terms of field-of-study choice, but the benefit appears to have more to do with being upper class than with being female. Analyzed in the next section is what these results mean in terms of labor market activity and income.

Gender and Market Activity

With respect to those graduates economically inactive or unemployed,[10] the study found 8.77 percent of all 1972 cohort graduates in that situation. However, if males and females are taken separately, the picture is very different. Of all female graduates, 16.22 percent are not participating in the labor force, compared with only 1.71 percent of all men. Among 1979 cohort graduates, the difference in inactivity rates between men and women is not as pronounced. Of all graduates in the sample, 9.6 percent are economically inactive or unemployed. Of the total female graduates, 12.63 percent are not working, compared with 6.9 percent of men. This difference in market participation among women of the two cohorts is probably explained more by the presence of children than by any other factor. In Costa Rica, family burdens tend to keep women away from the labor market regardless of their educational level. Hence, because of age differences, women graduates from the older cohort are more likely to have quit work for the purpose of child rearing than are women from the younger generation.

It is also important to observe that, contrary to what was expected from the study, no association was found between women's labor market activity and socioeconomic status. For both cohorts the proportion of women not in the labor force differed across socioeconomic strata, suggesting a curvilinear relationship in which middle-class women represent the largest proportion of those economically inactive. However, that relationship was not found to be statistically significant. These findings contradict data from a study by Standing and Sheehan (1978, pp. 36–38), in which a negative linear relationship was found between (highly educated) female market participation rates and income. According to data provided by those authors, in Costa Rica the rate of (educated) female labor market activity decreases as income increases.

Table 7.5 suggests that the degree of association between gender and type of workplace has weakened. Although in the private sector the preference for hiring men more than women has not changed across cohorts, in the public sector women from the reform generation have been absorbed at higher rates than their older counterparts and have come to compose half of public employees in their cohort. In other words, no sex differences in public-employment rates were found among 1979 cohort graduates. These results can be explained in two ways. On the demand side, the small size of the private sector and its slow rate of growth in the past years severely limit its

Table 7.5. Distribution in the Labor Force by Gender and 1986 Workplace, 1972 and
1979 Cohorts (percent)

Workplace	1972 Cohort			1979 Cohort		
	Male	Female		Male	Female	
Private	57	43	100	57	43	100
Public	55	45	100	50	50	100
Not working	10	90	100	37	63	100
Column Percent of total sample	52	48	100	50	50	100

$$X_2=7.5 \quad df=2 \quad p<.005 \qquad X_2=2.89 \quad df=2 \quad p>.05$$
$$\text{Cramer's } V=.179 \qquad \text{Cramer's } V=.153$$

ability to absorb prospective workers, whether male or female. However, because of employers' preference for recruiting males, and because the nature of the educational training women receive and their family responsibilities place them at a disadvantage in competing for openings in this sector, prospective male employees are recruited at much higher rates than women. Hence, the increase in female market participation within the younger cohort forces public-sector employers to hire from a larger pool of prospective female workers. On the supply side, it is probable that women, particularly married ones, prefer public-sector employment because of the many advantages it offers to them, such as maternity provision, more stable employment, larger number of holidays, and a more flexible schedule. Furthermore, it appears that in the public sector women are more likely to compete on equal terms with men.

Nevertheless, a tabular analysis of women's socioeconomic status by type of workplace shows a significant association between both of these variables. A similar pattern found in both cohorts suggests that upper-class women are concentrated at higher rates in the private sector, working-class women have a much higher representation in the public sector, and the distribution of middle-class women in both sectors is more or less the same. These findings reveal that recruiting patterns in both the private and the public sector vary across socioeconomic strata. The hierarchical needs of private-sector employers lead not only to discriminatory practices by gender but also by class, leaving working-class women almost no chance of being hired. Furthermore, according to results from the study, the relationship between women's class and workplace strengthened after the reform. Thus, it seems that with university expansion has come increased dependence on class background for obtaining a job in the private sector.

With respect to the distribution of occupations between the sexes, Table

7.6 reveals a significant relationship between graduates' gender and occupation for both groups under study. Larger proportions of men are self-employed or occupying managerial positions, while women are primarily unemployed or occupying positions in lower echelons. From the demand side, one possible interpretation for the underrepresentation of female labor in managerial positions is the belief that women are likely to leave the job because of domestic responsibilities. It is obviously easier for the employer to find a replacement for someone in a lower-status occupation than for someone in a key managerial position. Another possible explanation, this time from the supply side, is that many of these women are burdened with domestic chores and are forced to reduce their salaried labor to less than full-time. In other words, unequal status for educated women in Costa Rica's work force is most probably a function both of discriminatory practices imposed by employers and of the sexual division of labor that gives women prime responsibility for the family.

However, the same table suggests that the structure of job opportunities for educated women has slightly improved across cohorts. On the one hand, the percentage of women who are economically inactive or unemployed has decreased considerably; on the other, the proportion of females in managerial or supervisory positions has increased. Unfortunately, these findings probably suggest not an amelioration of women's position in the labor market but that with seniority, occupational differences between men and women become more pronounced. Because of the age difference between both cohorts, it is to be expected that more women from the older group are married and have greater domestic responsibilities. Hence, either because women have left their jobs for the purpose of child rearing, or because they frequently place their domestic responsibilities above their commitment to work, the difference between male-female occupational distributions in their cohort has become more pronounced.

Gender and Its Effect on Income Inequality

Table 7.7 presents the estimates of male and female earnings functions of prereform graduates. Two findings are particularly worthy of attention. The first is that the family income elasticity of graduates' 1986 income is significant for males but not for females. Women's income is not affected by socioeconomic background (see equation B4 in the table), but equation A4 shows that every 100 percent increase in family income (other things being equal) would yield a 10 percent increase in male graduates' monthly income.

One possible interpretation for this finding is that in Costa Rica, families in the upper-middle and upper class tend to consider a son's career as a necessity but a daughter's as optional. Daughters, in the long run, are expected to marry and become homemakers; sons are prepared to become the sole breadwinners of their families. Parents will then put more effort into

Table 7.6. Distribution in the Labor Force by Gender and 1986 Occupation, 1972 and 1979 Cohorts (percent)

Occupation	1972 Cohort			1979 Cohort		
	Male	Female		Male	Female	
Self-employed	68	32	100	63	37	100
Managerial and Supervisory	79	21	100	64	36	100
Employed, Nonmanagerial	49	51	100	50	50	100
Not working	10	90	100	37	63	100
Column percent of total sample	52	48	100	50	50	100

$$X_2=26 \quad df=5 \quad p<.001 \qquad X_2=15.6 \quad df=7 \quad p<.05$$
$$\text{Cramer's } V=.332 \qquad \text{Cramer's } V=.259$$

helping their sons find the best job possible or into financing their installation as self-employed professionals than they will their daughters.

A different interpretation is that upper-income families can provide support for their daughters—even married ones—so that they need not work as much or in the most demanding occupations. Hence, upper-class educated women have the luxury of working for self-fulfillment and not because of need. A third interpretation is that the social networks of the wealthy are effective but that they function primarily for the men.

The second finding worthy of notice is that although type of workplace—public or private—does not have an effect on male graduates' income (see equation A4), it is negative and significant in the case of female graduates. Women working in the private sector can expect a monthly salary about 13 percent lower than that of women working in the public sector, other things remaining the same. These workplace results coincide with those of the previous section in the sense that gender-discriminatory practices are more pronounced in the private sector than in public employment.

The "occupation" categories in equations A4 and B4 show that when all other explanatory factors are fixed at their means, more income inequality by occupation is present among women than among men. Male graduates who are self-employed do not have incomes significantly different from those of men who are employed without managerial responsibilities; only men employed in supervisory or managerial positions have salaries significantly higher (about 28 percent) than those of the rest of their counterparts. By contrast, women who are self-employed have incomes 27 percent higher than those of women who are employed without managerial responsibilities, and female supervisors or managers earn salaries significantly above (36 percent)

Table 7.7. Male and Female Graduates Log(x) of 1986 Income Equations, 1972 Cohort

Sample (N=size)	Equation	log(x) Family Income	Architecture/ Engineering	Health Sciences	Law	Basic Sciences	Agricultural Sciences
Male	A1[a]	.198[a]	—	—	—	—	—
Graduates	A2[a]	.136[a]	.120[a]	.159[a]	.121	−.175	−.073
(122)	A3[a]	.112[a]	.123[a]	.164[a]	.086	−.151	−.068
	A4[a]	.103[a]	.157[a]	.202[a]	.110	−.062	.012
Female	B1	.093	—	—	—	—	—
Graduates	B2	.030	—	.137[a]	.209[a]	−.159	—
(113)	B3[a]	.045	—	.153	.234[a]	−.162	—
	B4[a]	.075	—	.234[a]	.229[a]	−.052	—

[a]Statistically significant at the .05 level.

Table 7.8. Male and Female Graduates Log(x) of 1986 Income Equations, 1979 Cohort

Sample (N=size)	Equation	log(x) Family Income	ITCR	UNA	UNED	Architecture/ Engineering	Health Sciences	Law	Basic Sciences
Male	C1[a]	.156[a]	−.000	−.000	−.000	—	—	—	—
Graduates	C2[a]	.043	−.315[a]	−.218[a]	−.107	—	—	—	—
(116)	C3[a]	.036	−.211[a]	−.077	−.032	.057	.103	.170[a]	.011
	C4[a]	.035	−.208[a]	−.075	−.023	.045	.120	.162[a]	−.016
	C5[a]	.007	−.225[a]	−.131	.050	.114[a]	.207[a]	.173[a]	−.081
Female	D1	.118	—	—	—	—	—	—	—
Graduates	D2	.006	−.225[a]	−.602[a]	−.124	—	—	—	—
(116)	D3[a]	−.060	−.296[a]	−.408[a]	.085	.217	.258[a]	.394[a]	.175
	D4[a]	−.060	−.296[a]	−.407[a]	.085	.217	.256[a]	.394[a]	.176
	D5[a]	−.023	−.373[a]	−.325[a]	.158	.337[a]	.331[a]	.470[a]	.321

[a]Statistically significant at the .05 level.

Table 7.7 continued

Arts/Letters	Nursing	Education/Social Work	Topography/Other Technical	Workplace	Occupation Managerial/Supervisory	Self-Employed	Constant	R2
—	—	—	—	—	—	—	3.851	.159
-.026	—	-.195[a]	-.342[a]	—	—	—	4.044	.380
.011	—	-.175[a]	-.354[a]	.075	—	—	4.101	.394
.075	—	-.116	-.251[a]	.018	.276[a]	.099	4.042	.543
—	—	—	—	—	—	—	3.995	.034
-.190[a]	-.096	-.176[a]	—	—	—	—	4.273	.315
-.170	-.095	-.161[a]	—	.053	—	—	4.228	.322
-.025	-.025	-.038	—	-.128[a]	.361[a]	.269[a]	4.017	.471

Table 7.8 continued

Agricultural Sciences	Arts/Letters	Nursing	Education/Social Work	Topography/Other Technical	Workplace	Occupation Managerial/Supervisory	Self-Employed	Constant	R2
—	—	—	—	—	—	—	—	3.806	.101
—	—	—	—	—	—	—	—	4.291	.358
-.094	—	—	-.120	-.128	—	—	—	4.271	.473
-.111	—	—	-.121	-.133	.048	—	—	4.250	.483
-.019	—	—	-.061	.006	.005	.219[a]	.175[a]	4.321	.595
—	—	—	—	—	—	—	—	3.856	.030
—	—	—	—	—	—	—	—	4.333	.260
-.001	-.026	.031	-.192[a]	-.118	—	—	—	4.490	.550
-.013	-.026	.030	-.192[a]	-.120	-.004	—	—	4.490	.550
.048	.097	.159	-.098	-.004	-.089[a]	.456[a]	.149	4.258	.548

those of women employed without management responsibilities. Note also that the difference in average percentage levels between males and females of the managerial and supervisory category is considerable, showing that the effect of a managerial or supervisory position on graduates' income is much stronger for women than for men. One possible interpretation of these findings is that the average monthly income of a woman employed without managerial responsibilities is substantially lower than that of her male counterpart. It is then evident that the effect of being self-employed or occupying a supervisory or managerial position will be more pronounced for women than for men.

With respect to field of graduation, the most significant finding is that when all other variables are held constant, male lawyers' incomes do not differ significantly from those of a social sciences graduate, but in the case of women, a law degree guarantees an income 23 percent above that of a graduate in the social sciences. At the same time, both males and females with degrees in health sciences can expect a monthly income about 20 percent higher than that of a social sciences graduate. This would seem to suggest that a degree in a liberal profession (architecture, engineering, health sciences, and law) allows women to have more nearly full access to the labor force and to stable full-time employment.

The estimated earnings functions for male and female graduates from the 1979 cohort are shown by equations C5 (males) and D5 (females) in Table 7.8. The most interesting aspect is that the effect of "type of higher education institution attended" and "field of graduation" on the 1986 natural logarithm of graduates' income is greater for women than for men.

Women who graduate from the National University (UNA) or the Technological Institute (ITCR) can expect monthly incomes around 35 percent lower than those of their University of Costa Rica (UCR) counterparts. At the same time, only men who graduate from the Technological Institute have significantly lower (22.5 percent) incomes than UCR male graduates. Notice also that the negative effect of the Technological Institute is considerably weaker for males than for females.[11] This would appear to suggest that through the creation of new higher education institutions, the reform of the 1970s produced more income inequality between male and female graduates.

With regard to the field-of-graduation effect, it is important to note that only a degree in the liberal professions has a positive and significant effect on the natural logarithm of graduates' income. This effect, however, is more pronounced for female than for male graduates. This seems to indicate that even if income disparities between male and female graduates are present, a degree in one of the liberal professions would permit women to equalize their monthly income with that of male colleagues.

The table also shows that the natural logarithm of family income is more important in explaining male than female income differentials.

Although in equations C5 and D5 the family income elasticity of graduates' income is significant, equation C1 shows that before the variable of institution attended is controlled, the impact of the natural logarithm of family income on the natural logarithm of male graduates' income is both positive and significant.[12] Every 100 percent increase in family income is associated with an increment of 16 percent in male graduates' income. Equation D1, however, is insignificant. This shows that before other variables are controlled, the natural logarithm of family income is not a significant predictor of female graduates' income. These results appear to imply that parents' attitudes toward their daughters' career development did not change from one cohort to the other.

The type of workplace is also another important explanatory factor for male and female graduates' income differences. In the case of female graduates, being employed in the private sector contributes negatively to monthly income. For men, however, working in the public or the private sector does not affect monthly earnings. Thus, there is the same sexual division of labor between public and private as in the 1972 cohort.

For the 1979 cohort, being self-employed or in a managerial or supervisory position significantly increases male graduates' income. But for women, only a job at a managerial or supervisory echelon contributes positively to monthly earnings. The effect of this type of occupation, however, is much stronger for women than for men. This seems to indicate that male income differences by type of occupation are not as pronounced as they are for women.

In a comparison between the two cohorts, the first and most important finding is that in the 1979 cohort (Table 7.8), male and female graduates from the Technological Institute (ITRC) and female graduates from the National University (UNA) have significantly lower incomes than their University of Costa Rica (UCR) counterparts. This indicates that in addition to other income differentials already in existence in the 1972 cohort, the creation of new higher education institutions produced a new form of labor market discrimination among university system graduates, particularly among women.

The regression of the natural logarithm of family income on the natural logarithm of male graduates' income also shows some variation between cohorts. Family income appears to have greater relative importance for men from the older cohort (equation A4, Table 7.7) than for those from the younger one (equation C5, Table 7.8). A possible interpretation for this variation is that as male graduates get older, the effect of socioeconomic background on income becomes more pronounced. Because graduates from the 1979 cohort have not been in the labor force long enough, it is still very difficult to pick up the family income effect, a limitation accepted in this study. With respect to women, no variation was found between cohorts. In neither of the two groups is the natural logarithm of family income a significant predictor of the natural logarithm of female graduates' income.

Note also that although the field-of-graduation effect on men's monthly income has not changed much over cohorts (equations A4 in Table 7.7 and C5 in Table 7.8), it has increased substantially in the case of women. The most salient example is the case of women lawyers. A law graduate from the 1972 cohort has a monthly income about 23 percent higher than that of a social sciences graduate (equation B4 in Table 7.7). But a colleague of hers from the 1979 cohort is earning 47 percent more than a graduate in the social sciences (equation D5 in Table 7.8).

The vast expansion of programs in the social sciences that took place after the reform could shed some light on this finding. If the supply of social science graduates increased as a product of the reform, the salaries offered to these young professionals undoubtedly dropped. This would explain why income differentials between graduates in the liberal professions and graduates in the social sciences have become more pronounced over cohorts. However, this interpretation does not account for gender differences. A more thorough analysis of the data, one in which each of the fields in this area of study is analyzed separately, would be necessary in order to understand fully the causes of gender differences.

As for effects of occupation, for males the impact of being self-employed on the natural logarithm of 1986 income is significant only for the younger group (equations A4 in Table 7.7 and C5 in Table 7.8), thus suggesting an increment of this effect over cohorts. It is interesting to observe, however, that for women the opposite is true (equations B4 in Table 7.7 and D5 in Table 7.8). The effect of being self-employed is significant only for women from the older group. With respect to the impact of a managerial or supervisory position, both male and female earnings functions show some variation over cohorts. These results indicate that relative to graduates employed without managerial responsibilities, the effect of a managerial position on the natural logarithm of male graduates' income has dropped from one cohort to the other. For women, on the contrary, the effect of a position at a managerial or supervisory level is stronger for graduates from the younger cohort than for those who entered the university in 1972.

Last, for both men and women, no important variation of the effect of the workplace variable on the natural logarithm of graduates' income was found from one cohort to the other.

▲ Conclusion

With the expansion of the Costa Rican university system, gender differences in regard to educational access or achievement were not modified. In certain cases women made some relative gains, and in others their situation remained about the same.

Despite the fact that the male-female distribution of prereform and reform freshmen did not change, in absolute terms more women gained access to higher education than before. At the same time, female students after university expansion were not found to be concentrated in lower-status institutions, nor were they found to drop out at higher rates than men. Significant differences were revealed in the percentage distribution of men and women by academic status, but this relationship slightly favored women over men.

Although in both cohorts women were overrepresented in fields leading to less-prestigious positions, a slight improvement in the number of women graduating from fields such as engineering, architecture, medicine, and basic sciences was found among reform graduates. Nevertheless, the study reveals that those women who majored in these fields were primarily from the upper or middle class. It would thus appear that the social stratification of women by field-of-study choice was accentuated by university expansion.

The labor market outcomes of university expansion, however, reveal greater gender segregation. The study found that discriminatory practices in the private sector by gender and social class have increased over cohorts. At the same time, male-female income differentials have been shown to be more pronounced among graduates from the postreform period. In addition to the effects of field of graduation, type of workplace, and occupation, the negative impact on income of having attended a university of lesser status has been much stronger for women than for men.

The reform of the 1970s, therefore, did not necessarily improve women's opportunities. Although in absolute terms more female students were able to enroll and graduate from the Costa Rican higher education system than ever before, the labor market made the final adjustment by segregating women into lower status occupations, by differentiating them according to their social background, and by accentuating income inequality. It would then appear that no matter how much education is made available and accessible to Costa Rican women, they will continue to have relatively poor opportunities in the labor market, unless changes in the structure of work and in the process of development facilitate the incorporation of educated women into the labor force.

▲ Notes

1. Contrary to what happened in most of Latin America, where the enrollment explosion took place at advanced levels before primary education became universal, in Costa Rica this process took place after elementary education had been made universal and after secondary education had been extended to the great majority of the school-age population. Within a

single century, the Costa Rican educational system changed from being a minor public institution to becoming the largest one in the country. In 1870, Costa Rica had only 69 schools with an enrollment of 5,000 students. By 1981, 100 percent of the national population between the ages of 6 and 12 was enrolled in elementary education, and 50 percent of the population between the ages of 13 and 18 was enrolled in secondary education. In this sense, Costa Rican education followed a development pattern similar to that of industrialized societies.

2. See Paniagua (1988); see also Universidad de Costa Rica (1979), pp. 9–10.

3. For a comprehensive discussion of this development pattern, see Sojo (1984) and Vega (1986).

4. In 1972, 4,743 new students were admitted to the single university, the University of Costa Rica. In 1979, 10,876 new students were admitted to the university system. Of these, 5,677 gained admission to the University of Costa Rica, 1,087 were admitted to the Technological Institute, 2,066 enrolled in the National University, and 2,046 entered the Open University. Consejo Nacional de Rectores (1979), p. 38.

5. It is important to mention that when individuals surveyed were asked their monthly income, almost 75 percent mentioned an amount considerably lower than reported to the Social Security Agency. Thus, using this source of data was important in the study because this type of information provided more valid evidence than could personal or telephone interviews.

6. The information needed for this classification was taken from two sources: Consejo Nacional de Rectores (1982), p. 97; and Consejo Nacional de Rectores (1985). *Análisis de la matrícula y de la admisión en las instituciones universitarias estatales, 1974–1984* (San Jose, Costa Rica: OPES, 1985).

7. These figures place Costa Rica among those countries with the highest share of female tertiary students. Around 1970, the distribution of female participation in higher education in 128 countries was as follows: "under 10 percent, 13 countries; 10–19 percent, 28; 20–29 percent, 30; 30–39 percent, 24; 40–49 percent, 28; 50–59 percent, 4; and over 60 percent, one country." See Bowman and Anderson (1980), pp. S13–S32.

8. Several authors have argued that as school enrollments have doubled and tripled in most Third World countries, the expansion has favored males more than females. See, for example, Deblé (1981); Smock (1981); and Finn, Dulberg, and Reis (1979).

9. See Acker (1984); Bowman and Anderson (1980); Kelly (1984); Woodhall (1973); and Wickramsinghe and Radcliffe (1979).

10. From the way the sample was taken, it was impossible to distinguish between those who are not working because they cannot find a job and those who are not working because they do not desire to do so. Hence, all people not in the labor force are referred to as being economically inactive or unemployed.

11. As stated in the previous section, the insignificant effect of an Open University degree on graduates' 1986 natural logarithm of income is believed to result from the inadequate size of the sample of UNED graduates. The UNED proved to be the higher education institution with the highest dropout rate. Out of the 220 UNED students in the sample, only 3 percent of them had graduated in 1986.

12. When the variable of institution attended is controlled (see equation C.2), the family income elasticity of male graduates' income becomes insignificant. This indicates that the effect of family income on male graduates' income is mediated by the higher education institution attended.

▲ References

Acker, Sandra. "Sociology, Gender and Education." In S. Acker (ed.), *World Yearbook of Education*. New York: Nicholas Publishing, 1984, pp. 64–77.

Bowman, Mary Jean, and C. A. Anderson. "The Participation of Women in Education in the Third World." *Comparative Education Review*, 1980, vol. 24, no. 2, part 2, pp. S13–32.

Consejo Nacional de Rectores (OPES). *Proyecciones de la matrícula de la educación postsecundaria en Costa Rica, 1980–1985*. San Jose: OPES, 1979.

———. *Estadística de la educación superior*. San Jose: OPES, 1982.

———. *Proyecciones de la matrícula y de la admisión en las instituciones universitarias estatales, 1974–1984*. San Jose: OPES, 1985.

Deblé, Isabel. *The School Education of Girls*. Paris: UNESCO, 1981.

Finn, J. D., L. Dulberg, and J. Reis. "Sex Differences in Educational Attainment: A Cross-National Perspective." *Harvard Educational Review*, 1979, vol. 49, pp. 477-503.

Kelly, Gail. "Access to Education in the Third World: Myths and Realities." In Sandra Acker (ed.), *World Yearbook of Education*. New York: Nicholas Publishing, 1984, pp. 81–89.

Paniagua, Carlos. "Higher Education and the State in Costa Rica." Stanford University, unpublished doctoral dissertation, 1988.

Smock, Audrey. *Women's Education in Developing Countries: Opportunities and Outcomes*. New York: Praeger, 1981.

Sojo, Ana. *Estado empresario y lucha política en Costa Rica*. San Jose: EDUCA, 1984.

Standing, G., and G. Sheehan (eds.). *Labor Force Participation in Low-Income Countries*. Geneva: International Labor Office, 1978.

Universidad de Costa Rica. *Acuerdos definitivos originados en el tercer congreso universitario*. San Jose: Oficina de Publicaciones de la UCR, 1979.

Vega, Jose L. *Hacia una interpretación del desarrollo costarricence*. San Jose: Porvenir, 1986.

Wickramasinghe, S., and D. Radcliffe. "Women and Education in South Asia." *Canadian and International Journal of Education*, 1979, vol. 8, no. 2, pp. 117–125.

Woodhall, Margaret. "Investment in Women: A Reappraisal of the Concept of Human Capital." *International Review of Education*, 1973, vol. 19, no. 1, pp. 9–29.

World Bank. *World Development Report*. New York: Oxford University Press, 1985.

▲ 8

Feminist Reflections on the Politics of the Peruvian University

Nelly P. Stromquist

This chapter examines a highly politicized university setting in order to detect the extent to which feminist currents have had an impact on the curriculum or the sociopolitical agenda of the university. In Peru, university students are highly sensitive to the questions of social, economic, and ethnic inequalities in the rest of society—a feature that long has characterized them. This sensitivity to social disparities, unfortunately, has not been extended to gender issues.

Despite the fact that several fields have a large female enrollment and that women participate to a moderate degree in university politics, the political agenda is defined in the Marxist context of a class struggle, with feminist concerns dismissed as petty bourgeois. Women students who seek acceptance must then suppress these concerns.

Stromquist discusses the various factors that account for the low attention to gender issues in the university. Salient among these issues is the strong reliance on Marxism as a theoretical framework. Because it emphasizes the mode of production rather than the interplay between production and reproduction, this framework is compatible with existing patriarchal ideologies that leave little space for the development of a feminist agenda.

In consequence, politics at the university channels student activism into protecting the disadvantaged groups of society, yet it categorizes these people essentially in terms of their occupational roles as workers and peasants, not as gendered social actors. Ironically, although Peru has a well-developed feminist movement, with several large and stable groups and sustained publications, neither the university programs nor the activities within it reflect gender-related concerns.

—*Editor*

It is not even possible to talk about the political dimension in education; it is political throughout.
—Paulo Freire

▲   In an ever-modernizing world, higher education is undoubtedly very desirable because formal knowledge and credentials are socially and economically rewarded. Thus, it becomes a crucial means for individuals to attain prestige and power. For women, higher education offers a great promise, not only in terms of providing highly esteemed credentials but also in terms of conveying a critical knowledge of society that will allow them to understand and change the conditions of subordination they face. But if women are to improve their conditions, they need to engage in collective action rather than merely in individual promotion. This means that women must not only use university resources to acquire knowledge and skills but use the university itself as a terrain both to create new conditions for women's education and to practice political action.

Contrary to the North American model that concentrates on the provision of profession-related knowledge but eschews student involvement in national and international political issues, the Latin American university has been characterized by frequent student engagement in political acts either to shape conditions within the university or to influence national events.

The early Peruvian university, modeled after the Spanish University of Salamanca, was male, authoritarian, and upper class in its origins. Indeed, although Peru has one of the oldest universities in Latin America (San Marcos, founded in 1551), women were not entitled to enter the university until 1908. Bernales (1978b) further describes the early university as characterized by a "religious and juridical orientation and a theological and literary concept of teaching" (p. 9).

With minor modifications, the university remained medieval in its orientation until 1919, when the incipient modernization of Peru and the model university reform provided by the Cordoba (Argentina) movement of 1918 led to a student movement that demanded—and successfully obtained—significant changes in the objectives and functioning of the Peruvian university. Among the main features of the reformed university were that it would

- Be autonomous, free of political influence and pressure by the government
- Have co-government, meaning participation of students—in addition to professors and university workers—in governance
- Be sensitive to the interests of the people via its active involvement in extension programs
- Be critical of the political regimes and in particular of dictatorships
- Assign a strong protagonistic role to students
  (Ikonicoff, 1983, quoting Luis Alberto Sánchez)

The 1919 reform modified the nature of the university, but some observers question whether the university became seriously concerned with national issues. Bernales, a persistent analyst of university students, states:

> During a long time people believed the mirage that the university reform
> was a struggle to have a university of the people and for the people. In
> fact, this was never what the reform was about. The reform sought a
> modernization, which included as a sui generis feature the desire of the
> student movement to be recognized as a specific and important political
> actor (Bernales, 1978b, p. 3).

Although the features of the 1919 university reform have been
implemented with varying degrees of fidelity, they introduced into the
university a strong sensitivity regarding national conditions. It is undeniable
that students in Peruvian universities are socialized into a model of political
activism common to other Latin American countries but extremely rare in
other parts of the world. Moreover, one of the features of the early university
reform movement—the university's autonomy—is now firmly inscribed in
Peru's current constitution. Article 31 reads: "Each university is autonomous
in academic, economic, normative and administrative matters within the
limits of the law. They are free to organize, develop, and evaluate their
academic research programs, and extension programs" (quoted in Espinoza,
1985). These prerogatives may not surprise the U.S. reader, but in a country
with very centralized primary and secondary education systems, the freedoms
of the university are unparalleled.

Given the strong tradition of political mobilization among Peruvian
university students, it is of interest to review the nature and objectives that
have characterized the various university movements in that country. It is
especially useful to examine to what extent female students have participated
in them or gender issues have been part of the local or national problems
identified by students. It is also useful to identify to what degree the
university. as a center of higher learning, has been a source of feminist ideas
and knowledge. The understanding of this historical experience should enable
us to anticipate the future role of the university in the improvement of
women's conditions and to identify a number of useful actions the university
could take on this matter.

▲ Women in the Peruvian University

Discussions about university politics generally focus on student politics, but
the university comprises two very different populations, students and faculty,
each with a set of distinct and often competing objectives. These groups,
therefore, are analyzed separately.

Students

In the last three decades, the Peruvian university has experienced an
impressive expansion, showing an average annual rate of growth of 10.6

percent compared with 3.9 percent for primary schooling and 9.0 percent for secondary schooling during the period 1960–1984 (Fernandez, 1987).[1] Table 8.1 shows the Peruvian university enrollment across two decades; as can be observed, the student population almost quadrupled between 1961 and 1972 and doubled between 1972 and 1981.

According to most observers, the university expansion can be traced to social demand pressures rather than to the identification of specific fields linked to development needs. A study by the National Interuniversity Commission, the body in charge of coordinating the activities of the Peruvian universities, notes that careers linked to national development, such as electrical engineering, oil engineering, mechanical engineering, and forestry, have very little social demand; each enrolls fewer than 1 percent of the students (Comision Nacional Interuniversitaria, July 1981). In other words, although the university claims to play a pertinent role in the industrial development of the country, in fact its careers have been oriented toward the satisfaction of personal interests.[2]

From only 12 universities in 1960, enrolling a total 30,000 students, in subsequent years—during the civilian government of Belaúnde (1965–1968)—the number of universities rose to 30 and enrolled more than 100,000 (Castillo et al., 1985). Peru today has the distinction of being among the five Latin American countries with the largest number of universities. Between 1970 and 1979 the demand for higher education tripled. There were 64,312 candidates for admission into 30 universities in 1970 and 204,889 candidates for 32 universities in 1979. During that period the number of those admitted doubled, from 23,914 in 1970 to 45,684 in 1979 (Comisión Nacional Interuniversitaria, 1986), indicating that the demand increasingly exceeds the supply.

By 1987 there were 46 universities, of which 32 were located in cities other than Lima, thus considerably decentralizing higher education in Peru (see Table 8.2). The number of private universities also increased, and according to 1985 data, these universities enrolled 109,586 (47 percent) of the 234,882 students.

The expansion democratized the university system in terms of making higher education available to a larger proportion of the population. It further democratized the social composition of the student body, which has become increasingly representative of lower social class segments. Statistics about the social composition of students are not available, but various observers affirm that this new social composition is evident.

The expansion of the university has also benefited women. Although still in the minority, women composed 38 percent of the 1981 university enrollment (Francke, 1985).[3] However, expansion of women's higher education has not led to a reconfiguration of the student gender composition in the various fields of study. Traditionally "feminine" careers have continued to attract women, and traditionally "masculine" fields still attract mostly

Table 8.1. University Student Population Growth, 1961 to 1981

Year	Total Enrollment	Rate of Total Growth	Women	Rate of Female Growth
1961	35,018	100% base	9,041 (26)[a]	100% base
1972	132,188	377	40,485 (31)[a]	448
1981[b]	277,338	792	na	—

Source: Comisión Nacional Interuniversitaria, 1982.
[a]Figures in parentheses indicate the percentage of women.
[b]Estimated.

Table 8.2. Peruvian Universities by Private or Public Status, 1985

Type of University	Lima	Other Cities	Total
Public	6	21	27
Private	8	11	19

Source: Comisión Nacional Interuniversitaria, 1986.

men. Women compose 98 percent of the students in obstetrics and social work and 95 percent of the nursing students. They are 64 percent of the students in psychology and 55 percent of those in education. In contrast, women represent a small proportion of those in engineering: 2 percent of the students in mining engineering, 8 percent in civil engineering, and 10 percent in oil engineering (Francke, 1985). As Table 8.3 shows, the proportion of women in the various fields has remained constant over a twenty-year period, except for significant gains made in the field of medicine. The most recent data available by gender indicate that the proportion of women in education increased and that the proportion of those in medicine decreased during the 1970–1979 period. The maintenance of the career choice patterns among Peruvian women is intriguing because this period not only coincided with a progressive social period in Peru, fostered by the 1968–1975 military revolution of Velasco Alvarado, but it was also a time during which the women's movement created great ferment among middle-class women. Although the feminist movement in Peru was becoming one of the strongest in Latin America and leading to the emergence of grassroots groups and feminist organizations, the university—judging from career choices—seemed impervious to the new social ideas.

Because the expansion of the public universities was not accompanied by concomitant state financial support, there was a considerable deterioration of university teaching and research. In 1986 the Peruvian public university received 59 percent less than it received per student in 1960 (Comisión Nacional Interuniversitaria, 1986). With the exodus of many students into

Table 8.3. Women's Absolute Enrollment and as a Proportion of Field Enrollment in the University

Field	1960	1965	1968	1970	1979
Science	1,223 (33)	1,121 (33)	1,452 (30)	(31)	—
Education	3,234 (51)	10,516 (44)	14,477 (45)	(46)	8,267 (56)
Humanities	2,680 (23)	5,076 (23)	9,048 (26)	(26)	—
Engineering and architecture	250 (4)	429 (4)	864 (5)	(6)	—
Medicine	543 (14)	1,050 (24)	1,774 (30)	(30)	1,640 (26)

Sources: Data for 1960, 1965, and 1968 from CONUP (1969); for 1970 from CONUP (1971); for 1979 from Comisión Nacional Interuniversitaria (December 1981).
Note: Figures in parentheses represent percentages.

private universities, the public university was politicized toward the left and radical left of the political spectrum (Bernales, 1978a). Since the mid-1960s this politicization has affected course content; according to Espinoza (1985), freedom of expression does not exist in the field of philosophy in several universities because only Marxism is covered in those courses. This condition has worsened as non-Marxist philosophers have left public schools to teach in less conflictive and better-paid private universities. Marxist orientations are also predominant in the faculty of education and of history (Portocarrero and Oliart, 1986–1987). Various university professors affirm that not only is political activism high in the public universities but that it has become strongly identified with Marxism-Leninism. Often, students in radical political groups interrupt classes for several minutes to explain their objectives and analysis of the Peruvian situation to classmates.

Women have traditionally played secondary roles in university politics. They do not seem to have occupied leading positions in the student federations or in the various political parties operating in the university. Positions such as treasurer, calling for honesty and responsibility, however, have often been filled by women.

Faculty

With the expansion of the universities in the 1960s, the teaching staff also changed to become "less aristocratic in origin and attitude" (Bernales, 1974). But in terms of gender parity, the staff remains predominantly male, with women representing 18 percent of the teaching body. Statistics for faculty status (permanent or temporary) indicate that women tend to be underrepresented as permanent faculty staff.[4] Table 8.4 shows the most recent figures for the country as a whole. It should be remembered that these figures hide important differences between universities; according to Bernales (1974),

Table 8.4. University Faculty by Gender and Status, 1982

Staff	Women	Men	Total
Permanent staff	1,636 (56)	9,195 (67)	10,831 (65)
Short-term contract	1,305 (44)	4,512 (33)	5,817 (35)
Total	2,941 (100)	13,707 (100)	16,648 (100)

Source: Adapted from Comisión Nacional Interuniversitaria (1984).
Note: Figures in parentheses indicate percentages.

short-term faculty constitute as much as 90 percent of the teaching staff in some universities—a situation that continues to characterize low-prestige universities.

In the case of permanent professors, women represent only a small proportion of the full professors. (Table 8.5). There are more men and women in the lower hierarchies, but women represent only 9 percent of all full professors and 14 percent of all associate professors.

No statistics are available showing the gender breakdown of the faculties in the various fields. It is highly probable, however, that most female professors are found in the careers that are typically "feminine." If that is the case, there would be very few women in departments such as sociology, history, and anthropology, which are potentially rich fields for revealing social myths and prejudices about gender.

Although it would be inaccurate to claim that every woman is a feminist, it can be argued that the reduced number of women in the Peruvian university faculty has had a dampening effect on the identification of issues dealing with women's problems and in the design of courses and academic activities to treat them. Working in a setting where the gender composition makes it unlikely that such issues will be addressed, female professors probably learn to be prudent—and eventually silent and undemanding.

With professors not raising important gender concerns, students are not likely to raise them either. Students who depart from the norm usually conduct their studies without major support or interaction with advisers and dissertation committee members. As a result, few dissertations will deal with women's issues. A more general result is that the generation of knowledge about women's conditions does not take place in the university but away from it, either in centers that are closely linked to feminist practice (and that sometimes do not properly or exhaustively reflect on their own actions) or in research development centers (that conduct important studies that are, unfortunately, seldom mainstreamed into university curricula).

In Peru today, the universities do not offer courses in women's studies. A few female professors are introducing discussions of women's issues in their courses, and one university, the Catholic University of Peru (in Lima),

Table 8.5. Permanent Professors by Gender and Ranking, 1982

Ranking	Women	Men	Total
Full professor	255 (16)	2,676 (29)	2,931 (27)
Associate	442 (27)	2,691 (29)	3,133 (29)
Assistant	593 (36)	2,984 (32)	3,577 (11)
Teaching assistant	346 (21)	844 (9)	1,190 (11)
Total	1,036 (100)	9,195 (99)	10,831 (100)

Source: Comisión Nacional Interuniversitaria (1984).
Note: Figures in parentheses indicate percentages. Total for men does not reach 100 because
of rounding.

has offered a course on the sociology of women since 1983.[5] Other efforts by
university faculty related to women's concerns include the organization of
workshops and conferences where feminists and other researchers discuss
recent developments. Such events are relatively rare, with the most important
one being an international congress about research on Andean women
cosponsored by the Catholic University of Peru in 1982. Topics discussed at
the conference included remunerated work, peasant conditions, ideology and
socialization, and family and survival strategies. Some discussion of
educational issues (e.g., sexual stereotypes in textbooks) took place; issues
regarding higher education were not considered (for a full account on this
meeting, see Anderson, 1983).[6]

Nature of Politics in the Peruvian University

The persistence of women in traditional fields of study, the weak presence of
women in university positions of importance, and the lack of attention to
gender as a legitimate area of knowledge can be analyzed in several ways. On
the one hand, women can be viewed as failing to use the university as an
arena for political action and for the expression of sex-specific demands. On
the other, women's failure to make gains can be attributed to blockage by
male-dominated student politics. To evaluate these interpretations requires
looking at the past.

Politics in the Peruvian university has gone through various definitions
and stages. In its first stage, from 1919 through the 1950s, the university
was an important institution for both the development and functioning of the
national political parties; it was the source of ideas for the renewal of
political parties, whether by creating new parties or by exerting a strong
influence on existing ones. An important example is the creation of Alianza
Popular Revolucionaria Americana (APRA) by the then student leader Victor
Raul Haya de la Torres in 1924 (Ikonicoff, 1983). During that period,

students were often consulted about party policies and strategies. APRA, which has been termed the "archetypical populist party in Latin America" (Jaquette, 1973, p. 346), offered a "feminist platform." It included demands for female suffrage, election and appointment of women to government positions, equal pay for equal work, maternity benefits, and guarantees of civil rights to married women (Jaquette, 1973, p. 346).

Although APRA manifested some concern for women, the dominant analytical framework it used to examine the Peruvian reality has always been that the main conflicts in society derive from the process of production; thus the party has emphasized the role of worker and, to a lesser degree, peasants in the process of social transformation. According to Haya de la Torres, the first president of the Federation of University Students and the longtime APRA's leader, the key national political problem was the socioeconomic exploitation by a minority, and the most advisable strategy was a united front of workers and students to defeat the dominant classes. Within this strategy, an important objective was to "transform the university student into an intellectual worker with class consciousness. To turn professionals into revolutionary agents and servants of the majority of society, i.e., the exploited classes" (quoted in Bernales, 1978a).

Thus, when university students spoke of social change, operationally they had in mind joining efforts with workers and peasants—often male. One instance of this type of effort was the creation in the 1920s of "people's universities," also known as the Gonzales Prada Popular Universities, which Bernales considers "one of the richest experiences of the alliance between students and workers and peasants" (1974, p. 28).[7] Some APRA women served as instructors "imparting training, doctrine, and revolutionary consciousness to radical groups" in the Pan-American efforts of the party (Jaquette, 1973, p. 346). But, for reasons still unexplained, the participation of women in the movement declined by the 1930s. From the 1920s to the end of the 1950s, university politics were dominated by APRA. Dealing often with military and repressive governments, students concentrated their efforts on either protecting their fragile rights for university autonomy or criticizing unconstitutional acts taken by both the civilian and military governments in power. Thus, the pattern for student political action during that time was reactive, not proactive, a pattern that has been somewhat modified today. It has been estimated that the university has enjoyed autonomy, cogovernance, and freedom of speech no more than ten years since the university reform took place (Cruz and Carpio, 1981).

From the 1960s, both inspired and surprised by the success of the Cuban Revolution, the university student movement in Peru became radical. APRA lost its hegemony, and various of its former student members formed new parties endorsing rural guerrilla struggle. Other students, affiliated with the Communist Party, took sides in the Sino-Soviet split, which led to the creation of several factions, each of them more likely to endorse armed struggle than its party of origin. The two main guerrilla groups active in 1964–1965—Movimiento de Izquierda Revolucionaria (MIR) and Ejército de Liberación Nacional (ELN)—did not include the liberation of women in their political statements, yet "women fought in at least one MIR unit" (Jaquette, 1973, pp. 348–349).

In the 1960s numerous radical groups emerged in the university. Added to the confrontations between communist and democratic groups, such as APRA, Popular Action, and the Popular Christian Party, was conflict among the various Peruvian Communist Party factions: Red Fatherland (Patria Roja), Red Flag (Bandera Roja), Red Star (Estrella Roja), Revolutionary Vanguard, and Shining Path (Sendero Luminoso). What these groups have in common, despite significant strategic discrepancies, is a weak social base. Also, they have changed student politics, moving from the defensive side (e.g., protesting government threats to increase bus fares, and government arrest of union leaders) to an offensive position, which manifests itself both in the struggle for a new society and in the adoption of physical violence as a means to achieve change. Shining Path, the strongest of these groups, grew considerably in influence in the 1980s. It was particularly active at the University of Huamanga in Ayacucho, where it reportedly ran "popular schools" for adolescents (Espinoza, 1985). Now the movement operates clandestinely and its political platform is only partially known. What is known does not treat gender issues, though women, and particularly female university students, have been reported to be engaged in the movement at levels that surpass previous female participation in radical political action (Guardia, 1985; Castillo et al., 1985).

Some recognition of women operates among the radical student groups. In 1983 the First National Conference of the Revolutionary Communist Youth (Juventud Communista Revolucionaria, JCR), the youth section of Partido Comunista Revolucionario, a splinter group of Revolutionary Vanguard, took place. Its statements admitted that the popular movement was composed of "workers' unions, peasant syndicates, neighborhood associations, Christian communities, progressive professionals, and mothers' clubs" (Carpio et al., 1983, n.p.). Mentioned last—but mentioned—are women. The problem is not recognized as a gender but a class problem because the mothers' clubs in this reference are those active in marginal neighborhoods. Nonetheless, the explicit mention of women as social actors is a new and positive development. The JCR's plan of action refers to the need to form "new men and new women," a gender-specific reference new in radical politics. The three main objectives of the JCR regarding the university were defined as being (1) to make the university a collective organic intellectual to serve the people and achieve independent national development; (2) to form a legitimate university government; and (3) to make the university a militant institution in favor of human rights, popular freedom, and national sovereignty.

The first and third objectives could in principle address women's issues, but this is not the case. The elaboration of the first talks about the university signing bilateral agreements with popular institutions such as peasant communities, neighborhood associations, and production cooperatives to support their productive and welfare activities. The discussion of the third point deals with protecting human and civil rights, fighting the influence of imperialism, giving the university a more independent political voice, and promoting a Latin American consciousness. As can be seen, references to women's concerns are lost when the objectives come to a more operational level.

On the whole, it is clear that the leadership of political activity by university students has been in the hands of male students and that many of their initiatives have been related to internal affairs, such as the protection of university autonomy and protests against insufficient economic resources, poor teachers, and deficiencies in student facilities (e.g., food, lodging, health, sports, and counseling services). Some protest has also occurred against what students perceive as "drastic changes in curriculum and methodology," which refers to the creation of elective courses that student leaders believe "dilute the curriculum." The university students have also taken action regarding issues external to the university, such as the protection of human rights, illegal and unconstitutional acts by various regimes, and economic decisions harmful to low-income groups (e.g., price increases in bus fares and staple foods). Common tools for influence have been the appeal to public opinion by means of street demonstrations and solidarity strikes, by which university students have stopped classes in order to join strikes conducted by factory workers, peasants, and miners.

In characterizing the political action of Latin American university students, Ikonicoff (1983) states that although their discourse emphasizes class conflicts, students have shown a tendency to define themselves as students rather than members of a particular social class. This is less true for Peru, certainly less true at present. The radical position of several student groups today in favor of joining guerrilla movements in both urban and rural settings and thus abandoning their university studies is evidence that for some the role of student is not the most important. These students are a minority of the student body, but their drastic actions have definitely created a new form of student political activism.

University students as a group, however, have yet to act on behalf of women's rights or even women-initiated demands (e.g., for greater public services in housing, transportation, and water). A number of university students—mostly females—have joined feminist grassroots groups and organizations, where they actively participate in development and research activities, but such involvement is the exception.

The university is, nonetheless, a source of important political socialization, and faculty members in certain departments, particularly philosophy and history, convey counterhegemonic messages. This is evident in an investigation carried out by Portocarrero and Oliart comparing the messages transmitted by Peruvian textbooks on history and civics with images that the student had of Peru as a nation. The study, based on a 1963 nationwide sample of senior high school students, reports an intriguing finding: The textbooks portrayed Peru as a socially and racially integrated country, in which exploitation and injustice would soon disappear. Yet when the students were asked about their beliefs, the majority felt that the upper classes had played a negative role in the development of the country, that Peru was a country whose human and natural resources have been either scarcely utilized or not utilized at all, and that the main motives behind the actions of politicians had been to obtain personal and group rather than nationwide benefits (Portocarrero and Oliart, 1986–1987, pp. 80–82). This student perception, clearly at odds with the image portrayed in the textbooks, was termed by the researchers the "critical idea." In tracing the emergence of this "critical idea," Portocarrero and Oliart identified its main transmitters as being high school teachers and, in turn, the faculties of education in the various Peruvian universities:

> Those who develop and disseminate the critical idea are mainly the high school teachers. In the national universities, the faculty of education, and in particular the area of historical-social studies, is normally the center of attraction for the poorest students. The reasons for this appeal are related to the low-demanding character of the studies and the possibility of obtaining a job that even though poorly paid is stable and which, at least until the 70s, was easy to get. In this manner, for the sons of peasants or the daughters of white-collar workers and small businessmen the teaching career becomes an attractive alternative. Because of its social composition, the type of studies that they follow, and the poor economic prospects that this profession offers, the faculty of education is one of the most radical in the university. Courses in dialectic and historic materialism are compulsory and the teaching of history is under the influence, if not the domination, of Marxism (1986–1987, p. 11.)

Portocarrero and Oliart also noted that the expansion of the Peruvian university, though massive, has been especially strong in the area of education. Table 8.6 reveals the growth within the five major fields around which the university is organized.

This being the case, it can therefore be asserted that the university produces high school teachers who will present a critical analysis of Peruvian reality and thus promote elements of political discontinuity and tension in society—elements that could create conditions for social transformation in Peru. It remains to be seen, however, whether this tension and the fact that women compose at least 55 percent of faculties of education will be conducive to an identification of gender issues in student politics.

Table 8.6. Total Enrollment Figures by Field of Study, 1960 to 1968

Year	Sciences	Education	Humanities	Engineering/ Architecture	Medicine	Total
1960	2,664	6,381	11,855	6,303	3,780	30,983
1965	3,367	23,730	22,481	10,534	4,429	64,541
1968	4,760	31,953	34,695	16,487	6,008	93,903

Source: CONUP (1969).

Reasons for Lack of Attention to Gender Issues

With the present economic crisis, it is extremely difficult for young people—even those with higher degrees—to find suitable jobs. Economic frustrations are leading to political radicalization, a phenomenon that can be observed through the continuing support that guerrilla movements such as Shining Path and the more recent Tupac Amaru receive from young people. In these groups, it is known that female participation is considerable and that several women play leading roles (Guardia, 1985; Castillo et al., 1985); at the same time, there is no evidence that women's demands per se have been incorporated into the platform of these groups.

Why are university students relatively inactive with regard to women's concerns? Several competing explanations can be advanced, all of them plausible, but there is not yet empirical research to support them.

Marxism as a form of patriarchal hegemony. Marxism appeals to university students because it deals with social justice and the need for change. Yet it defines inequalities only in terms of wealth; thus, the importance of the difference between workers and the owners of capital is central. Differences of power and status are not conceived of in terms of gender.

Under a Gramscian approach, it could be stated that a major reason for the nontreatment of gender is that the traditional Marxist approach prevailing in Peruvian universities defines the problems of injustice and inequality in society as determined primarily, if not exclusively, by economic forces. The mode of production—the economic structure—is seen as the main source for the emergence of conflict between human beings and thus solely accountable for the existence of exploitative relations in which some rule and others are ruled. In this view of the world, the only struggle worth examining and pursuing is that between workers and capitalists. Other societal forces causing subordination and exploitation are ignored. Ideological forces, particularly the existence of patriarchal ideologies that assert the inferiority of women and enforce it in all domains of social relations, are discarded as inventions of the superstructure and thus guaranteed to disappear when the fundamental contradictions (capital versus labor) are resolved.

The emphasis on economics in this traditional interpretation of Marxism has led to the rejection of politics and ideology as areas with distinct autonomy. Mouffe identifies two problematic facets of traditional Marxism derived from ignoring the role of ideology:

> The first one consists in seeing a causal link between the structure and the superstructure and in viewing the latter purely as a mechanical reflection of the economic base. This leads to a vision of ideological superstructures as epiphenomena which play no part in the historical process. The second facet is not concerned with the role of the superstructures but their actual nature, and here they are conceived as being determined by the position of the subjects in the relations of production. The second aspect is not identifiable with the first since here it is in fact possible to attribute "differential time sequence" and even a certain efficacy to the ideological superstructures (1979, p. 169).

Several Marxist-inspired thinkers have recognized the importance of ideology as a major force in the construction of relations in society, but they have not admitted the existence of a patriarchal ideology. Among these are Antonio Gramsci and Louis Althusser, both of whom have repeatedly noted the role of ideology in serving as an effective and nonviolent form of coercion in reproducing the dominant worldview. However, Marxist interpretations prevailing in Peruvian universities are still those attached to early Marxism-Leninism. In this interpretation, economic determinants are decisive and ideology (including patriarchal ideologies) is seen as only a tool of domination by the bourgeoisie. Ideologies are not seen as existing among the dominated, nor are the dominated seen as sharing some elements of these ideologies, such as patriarchy.

University students, by denying the importance of gender issues, ironically continue to impose patriarchal hegemony, which by definition sees the world from a male perspective and accepts women's subordination as a given. By emphasizing the aspects of production of remunerated work and reproduction of the labor force over those concerning the production of domestic work and the reproduction of ideologies, gender analysis becomes subsumed within the class struggle. Women's concerns then become "divisive" to the class struggle and a distraction from "serious political priorities," a view that can be easily detected among many male Peruvian politicians and intellectuals of the Left and that seems to be accepted even by female participants in leftist parties.

A feminist observer of student politics in San Marcos explains the absence of a feminist agenda as follows:

> A feminist discourse does emerge but is identified as being petty

bourgeois. And although the implementation of feminism in Peru indicates that it is interested in reaching the marginal sectors, its language is too violent for the San Marcos woman. For her the academic mantel that offers San Marcos is most important. How to reconcile a discourse in which the body and sexuality appear free and full of joy with political questions and a commitment toward the disadvantaged social groups. . . ? Undoubtedly, despite her almost totally nonexistent leadership, she wants to participate in political changes. And, it could be that if she is needed as a "political cadre," it is because they think that women are more idealistic and more manipulable and will not seek inside the political groups a power that they are not trying to exercise in other areas (Figueroa, 1986, p. 42).

In Figueroa's opinion, therefore, female students find it difficult to challenge the patriarchal ideology, and many of them, to win acceptance by their male peers, fall into traditional feminine molds.

Derivative reasons. Other reasons for the lack of attention to gender issues are more derivative in nature. Some emerge from the existence of patriarchal hegemony; others seem to be a product of certain organizational characteristics of the Peruvian university. They include the following:

• First, university student demonstrations in favor of other groups are made possible through the existence of informal networks between the university and trade unions and political parties. Because many female workers are not organized politically, their participation in parties and labor unions is minimal, and thus they have not succeeded in developing informational networks with university students. Conversely, with the political leadership in the hands of male students, contacts with women's groups are limited and their demands neither well known nor understood.

• Second, the absence of either a significant number of female faculty or at least a critical group of feminist scholars within the university has not promoted the emergence of curricula sensitive to women's issues, which in turn has not promoted among students the identification of gender concerns or the discussion of theories and empirical findings regarding gender differences.

• Third, the fact that many faculty members work part-time or hold more than one job detracts from their looking into new social areas of inquiry. This produces a lag between changes occurring in society and changes being incorporated into the university's curricula. This condition affects all kinds of social changes, not just those related to women, but it might explain why the university has been slower than other groups in society to adopt a feminist position or cover gender issues in its academic programs.

• Fourth, student movements are by nature crisis oriented. The women's struggle for a just social order, in contrast, is a protracted struggle to be fought not only for a long time but also on the basis of day-to-day issues. The drama involved in crisis politics is not found in struggling for women's equality, and this may lend gender issues limited appeal within student politics.

• Fifth, the high concentration of female students in five academic fields (social work, obstetrics, nursing, education, and psychology) means that women exist in different physical and intellectual spheres in the university. It is likely that women in "traditional" fields accept dominant social definitions about the "proper" role of women, which includes a reluctance to challenge and contradict male leadership. It is doubtful that in the "feminine" spheres significant counterhegemonic socialization occurs. The Peruvian university presents curious anomalies, such as highly politicized departments, including those in which women are present in large numbers, and yet there is no visible feminist agenda. It seems reasonable, therefore, to argue that the work of challenging gender relations will fall upon the few women in the less gender-stereotyped fields. But here, because women are relatively few, their chances for influence are slight.

Redressing Gender Inequality

Can the university be made to play a progressive gender role, or is it best to leave it alone? The question is obviously rhetorical. Given the university's role in creating or at least certifying professionals, higher education is critical to the improvement of women's conditions. One particular feature of the Peruvian university, also true of universities in many developing countries, is that most of the high school teachers are trained in the university. Intervention at the university level, therefore, would affect a critical space where counterhegemonic knowledge, if produced, would influence other levels of the educational system.

It must be remembered that universities continue to be bastions of male power. As a US feminist aptly put it, "Universities are male institutions with women in them." Because sophisticated knowledge is highly rewarded, power is created at the university. Such being the case, the university is highly controlled in terms of who can become providers of knowledge.

How can the university change? The recruitment of more women, including gender-sensitive women, as faculty members would seem an imperative first step. But the current economic crisis has forced many universities in Peru not to hire new people and even to reduce their operational budgets. The extremely limited financial resources, combined with inflation, render unlikely the addition of new faculty, male or female. It is obvious that a solution to the current economic crisis will have to be found so that needed financial support of the university may occur.

Even in the absence of large numbers of female faculty, one could work with the existing teaching cadres. Incentives could be provided so that teachers could engage in innovative courses and projects dealing with women's issues. These incentives do not have to be monetary; they could be expressed in terms of symbolic rewards that carry internal recognition within the university, or there could be small financial awards, such as allowing teachers to attend professional meetings or giving them annual allowances for the acquisition of books for private use. Another way of encouraging innovative behavior in the university would be for it to open its doors more often to feminists. These women could teach and explain their activities and research. Both students and faculty members could take initiatives in this regard.

The university's extension work with the community could be redefined so that it covers not only workers and peasants but also women, both in rural and urban areas. Here again both students and faculty members could initiate action.

University statistics should consider gender breakdowns by field, both for students and for faculty. Also, these statistics should include social class characteristics in order to do follow-ups of the extent to which the university is becoming more accessible to lower-income sectors and less oriented to class origins. The existence of better information should allow a better identification of student admission and faculty hiring policies.

Pressure could be exerted on international organizations to produce and sponsor research more pertinent to women's needs. Here joint action by feminists inside and outside the university could occur. Professional networks could be developed with progressive universities in other parts of the world. Networking requires financial resources, however small, for photocopying of publications and mailing; funds might be obtained from supportive international agencies.

▲ Conclusion

As discussed in this chapter, the Peruvian university does not address gender issues. Yet most of the Peruvian feminist intellectuals are graduates of Peruvian universities. Exactly how these women developed their feminist consciousness has not been the subject of research, but several characteristics are certain: The feminists are recognized as competent professionals in their respective fields; many of them were militants in leftist political parties; they tend to come from middle rather than upper and lower social classes. It is also clear that much of their education in feminist theory and empirical studies was done after the university and through individual and collective efforts in feminist groups. In this respect, the role of higher education appears to have been important not in the content it addressed but in the provision of general knowledge, tight reasoning, and use of evidence. Higher education gave the feminists tools that enabled them afterward to put together a critique from the fragmented pieces of their subordination and oppression. Why some female university graduates broke through the patriarchal ideology barrier is not yet understood, and this should constitute the subject of future gender research.

The Latin American university—the Peruvian university in particular— has played an important political role in the support of democratic rights and the protection of oppressed groups such as workers and peasants. University student leaders see themselves as progressive, even revolutionary, yet their views are predicated on a male conception of the world based on the public sphere of production, and they have not proposed strategies for the deconstruction of gender.

In the decision to consider women a nonissue at the university level, it is the students who have played a significant role; the state has not. Although the Peruvian university benefits from a considerable degree of autonomy vis-à-vis the regimes that have governed Peru, this autonomy has resulted in the emergence of a critical but gender-excluding political philosophy.

In his analysis of the state, Gramsci (1971) notes that the state uses schools to create hegemony and argues that to create counterhegemonic forces, progressive individuals may have to work outside educational institutions. Applying this analysis to the problems women face makes sense, not because the State is the oppressive force but rather because the current intellectuals of the university—the students and the professors—have defined the world in a way that leaves almost no space for women's concerns.

The new social composition of the Peruvian university has helped to radicalize its demands. Now much more attention than before is given to the Indian problem, which does not emerge as a question of revindication of peasants but rather as a matter of fundamental Peruvian identity. Racial problems are being linked—and rightly so—to class problems. Therefore, it is likely that in the university, the gender question may continue to receive a very low priority, despite the fact that women are numerous in one of the most politically radical departments, education.

There is reason to believe that some faculties devote particular attention to the discussion of social and economic problems affecting the country. It is likely, however, that because of the dominance of the Marxist-Leninist paradigm, with its emphasis on economic forces over ideological considerations, women's issues will not receive the full attention they deserve.

It might also be that a time lag operates between social movements and the university's recognition and endorsement of them. In the meantime, it must be underscored that it is women who have graduated from the university but whose life experiences have taught them about gender inequalities and discrimination. These women are conducting the most fruitful tasks for the improvement and transformation of women's conditions.

A more fundamental question to be raised is whether the university can be made to play a substantial role in the transformation of gender relations or whether the political involvement of university students is a temporary role, with little impact, meant basically to be a rite of passage from adolescence to adulthood.

In the meantime, I believe feminists in Peru have adopted a correct path by creating their own political and social space and by developing increasing contacts between middle-class and popular feminists. University students, mostly females, are coming to join the feminist movement, and this is a modest but nonetheless promising first step.

The statement by Paulo Freire at the beginning of this chapter is apt—education is indeed political. But politics can be defined in such a way as to preclude women's concerns. The politics of gender-blind issues characterizes the Peruvian university, and no inroads have yet been made in these conditions. Significant improvements will not take place until feminism and traditional Marxism cease being parallel and become intersecting social movements.

▲ Notes

1. This phenomenon of a greater university expansion, incidentally, is also evident in many other developing countries. In observing the tremendous university expansion in Latin America in the 1960s and 1970s, McGinn (1982) notes that several explanations have been advanced: that the expansion was a desire to promote social justice, that it was prompted by the need to have the trained personnel needed for economic development, and that it was a demagogic recourse to hide the unavoidable tendency of capitalism toward greater wealth and greater poverty. All of these explanations, however, imply that supply rather than demand forces drive growth and thus that the state was the major protagonist. Tedesco (1985) and others agree that the state was the most dynamic actor, but underscore that popular demands unleashed a powerful pressure that had to be satisfied.

2. A counterargument to the criticism that universities are not producing the cadres in science and technology needed by developing countries is offered by Ikonicoff (1983), who cites studies indicating that 50 percent of the brain drain occurs precisely in the fields considered "modern" or "strategic" for development and that 20 to 30 percent of the engineering graduates emigrate, which means that if the university were to produce more experts in these fields, it would simply lose them to developed countries.

3. It should be noted that the participation of women in other institutions or postsecondary institutions, such as secretarial schools, has been greater than that of men, with women representing 51 percent of that enrollment.

4. The statistics on faculty include the teaching assistant position (*jefe de practicas*). In Peru this position is considered a regular teaching job rather than part of a financial aid package consisting of tuition and varied teaching duties as in the United States. A *jefe de practicas* is usually a recent graduate or a student in the last year of studies.

5. In August 1991, the Catholic University of Peru initiated a non-degree program on gender studies. It is addressed to professional women with a bachelor's degree and has the financial support of the Ford Foundation.

6. The lack of attention to the study of higher education as it relates to women's conditions or possibilities for social changes in the treatment of gender is being corrected in developed countries. In Latin America, however, practically nothing exists. A recent comparative study on postgraduate education conducted by the UNESCO Regional Center for Higher Education in Latin America and the Caribbean (CRESALC) is disappointing in its coverage of women. Two of the four case studies reviewed, Mexico and Brazil, discuss the growth and characteristics of postgraduate studies and explore the possible contributions of advanced study to scientific and technological development. They disregard issues such as student and faculty composition in the new fields. See Córdova et al. (1986) for Brazil; see Wuest Silva (1986) for Mexico.

7. At the same time, Bernales observes that the worker-student alliance functioned in an ad hoc and fragmented fashion. Moreover, he affirms that the university students tended to behave paternalistically, recognizing in theory that the proletariat was the revolutionary force but in practice adopting the position that the student could illuminate the masses from above.

▲ References

Anderson, Jeanine (ed.). *Congreso de investigación acerca de la mujer en la región andina*. Lima: Asociación Perú-Mujer, 1983.

Bernales, Enrique. *Movimientos sociales y movimientos universitarios en el Perú*. Lima: Pontificia Universidad Católica del Perú, 1974.

———. *Expansión y redefinición del sistema universitario del Perú en un contexto de modernización*. Lima: Pontificia Universidad Católica del Perú, 1978a.

———. *Origen y evolución de la universidad en el Perú*. Lima: Pontificia Universidad Católica del Perú, 1978b.

Carpio, Neptalí, Gastón Wilka, and Pedro Francke. *La generación del 80*. Lima: Dirección Nacional Provisional, JCR, 1983.

Castillo, Carlos, Carlos Alvarez, and Hernán Fernández. "Un mundo complejo y poco conocido." *Autoeducación*, no. 12, Jan.–Mar. 1985.

Comisión Nacional Interuniversitaria. *Ingresados*, 1970–1979. Documento de trabajo no. 33. Lima: Departamento de Estadística e Información, Comisión Nacional Interuniversitaria, July 1981.

———. *Estadísticas 27*. Lima: Comisión Nacional Interuniversitaria, December 1981.

———. *Estadísticas 38*. Lima: Comisión Nacional Interuniversitaria, December 1983.

———. *Estadísticas 43*. Lima: Comisión Nacional Interuniversitaria, September 1984.

———. *Estadísticas 51*. Lima: Comisión Nacional Interuniversitaria, September 1986.

Córdova, Rogerio de Andrade, Divonzir Gusso, and Sergio Vasconcelos de Luna. *Postgrado en América Latina: Investigación sobre el caso de Brasil*. Caracas: CRESALC-UNESCO, 1986.

Cruz, Antonio, and Neptalí Carpio. *Movimiento universitario en el Perú*, 1909–1980. Lima: Publicaciones de Investigación Universitaria, 1981.

Espinoza, Nicéforo. *Nuevos rumbos de la educación nacional*. Lima: Editorial Escuela Nueva, S.A., 1985.

Fernández, Hernán. "La situación educativa de la mujer en el Perú." Lima: INIDE, mimeo, 1987.

Figueroa, Blanca. "Las sanmarquinas de hoy." *La Casona*, no. 42, April 1986.

Francke, Marfil. *Las mujeres en el Perú*. Lima: Centro de la Mujer Peruana Flora Tristán, March 1985.

Gramsci, Antonio. *Selections from Prison Notebooks*. New York: International Publishers, 1971.

Guardia, Sara Beatríz. *Mujer peruana: El otro lado de la historia*. Lima: Empresa Editorial Humboldt, 1985.

Ikonicoff, Moisés. "Rôle de l'université et des étudiants dans le développement de l'Amerique Latine." Paris: Institut International de Planification de l'Education, mimeo, 1983.

Jaquette, Jane. "Women in Revolutionary Movements in Latin America." *Journal of Marriage and the Family*, no. 35, May 1973, pp. 344–354.

McGinn, Noel. "Los alcances limitados de la reforma de la educación superior." *Educación*, 1982, vol. 26, no. 89, pp. 54–70.

Mouffe, Chantal. "Hegemony and Ideology in Gramsci." In Chantal Mouffe (ed.), *Gramsci and Marxist Theory*. London: Routledge and Kegan Paul, 1979.

Portocarrero, Gonzalo, and Patricia Oliart. "El Perú segun sus jóvenes." *Quéhacer*, December 1986–January 1987, no. 44, pp. 76–93.

Scott, Alison. "Desarrollo dependiente y la segregación ocupacional por sexo." *Debates en Sociología*, 1984, no. 10, pp. 5–60.

Tedesco, Juan Carlos. "Reproductivismo educativo y sectores populares en América Latina." In Felicia Reicher Madeira and Guiomar Namo de Mello (eds.), *Educaçao na América Latina*. Sao Paulo: Cortez Editora, 1985.

Wuest Silva, Teresa (ed.). *Postgrado en América Latina: Investigación sobre el caso de México*. Caracas: CRESALC-UNESCO, 1986.

PART 3

Adult Women and Educational Efforts

▲ 9

Women and Popular Education in Latin America

Marcy Fink

Marcy Fink's chapter examines the concept of nonformal education and particularly "popular education." It maps both conceptually and descriptively the features and achievements of popular education—a type of education that is expanding and becoming more refined in Latin America and yet remains relatively unknown in the United States.

In a detailed description of popular education programs, Fink notes the variety they offer in characteristics, content, and strategies. Notwithstanding this variability, they all share the objectives of providing women an educational alternative to that provided by the formal educational system, which tends to be prescriptive of women's traditional norms and roles. Whether using games, theater, or more common didactic approaches, popular education for women seeks their acquisition of emancipatory skills.

Fink provides various arguments to support the case that adult women's education must be central in the process of social transformation. It must affect domestic relations and mothers in them. Intervening for adult women will accelerate the process of social change by creating a new socialization process for children, by encouraging mothers to reduce their enforcement of the sexual division of labor at home, and by evincing new forms of questioning of male power, thereby renegotiating domestic relations.

This chapter also highlights the major tensions within popular education. A key weakness so far has been the lack of linkage between local activities and social policy. Yet from a feminist perspective, this may also be a strength. By conducting work in areas in which the state does not intervene, popular education has opened spaces for contestation that will make the state respond not by policy but through the acceptance of new issues.

—Editor

▲ The proliferation of "nonformal" and "popular education" programs in Latin America has expanded opportunities for the social, economic, and political participation of women in society and has served as a significant vehicle for personal growth. Such programs, outside the formal educational structures and largely based on grassroots efforts, have also played a key role in the development of collective strategies for survival in the face of the economic crisis looming over Latin America since the early 1980s. These programs have had an impact on the local level, serving as a springboard for the expansion of community and political organizing to address local needs. But they are much less effective in linking community level self-help initiatives with more macrolevel obstacles and opportunities for women's participation in society.

Several studies reveal that Third World development programs tend largely to exclude women, under the assumption that men are household heads, principal producers, and the decisionmakers in the family unit. In so doing, they have failed to provide opportunities to enhance contributions by women. Greater attention should be paid to the gender dimension in the design of antipoverty strategies and nonformal training programs so that they in fact address the social and economic constraints that women face.

The following is an examination of the strengths and limitations of nonformal education programs for Latin American women, with particular emphasis on the Latin American concept of "popular education."

▲ Background

The term "nonformal education" was probably first popularized by Philip Coombs in 1968 as "any organized, systematic educational activity carried on outside the framework of the formal system to provide selected types of learning to particular subgroups in the population" (La Belle, 1986, p. 2). Such programs emerged in Latin America in the late 1960s in large part as a response to the failure of schools to make educational opportunities available and relevant to poor and marginalized sectors of the population. Societal and family structures in Latin America, for example, place a low priority on schooling for young women.

Nonformal education programs run by nongovernmental organizations (NGOs) have greatly expanded since the late 1960s, playing an increasingly important role in community organizing as well as national and international development work. They have taken a variety of shapes and forms, from vocational training and literacy work to community-run health education programs. The common thread linking these efforts is that they are a local-level activity, characterized by highly motivated and involved learners—a reflection of both the participatory learning methodology and the tie between educational content and immediate needs.

▲ Nonformal Education Projects Aimed at Women

Nonformal education opportunities for women vary substantially, shaped in large measure by the character of the agency involved. The three principal actors in the arena of nonformal education are the national government and its various ministries, the international nongovernmental organizations (NGOs), and the national Latin American NGOs. Except in some socialist or post-revolutionary societies, government-administered nonformal educational projects tend to emphasize skills development within the traditional domain of women, such as health and home economics (Stromquist, 1986). This focus tends to reinforce societal norms that leave women subjugated by a dominant male role in society.

Before the mid-1970s, those who formulated development policy as well as practitioners paid minimal attention to the contribution made by women to national economies. Projects targeting women were conceived of as "welfare efforts to provide health services and food to children" (Tinker, 1987, p. 1). With the United Nation's designation of 1975 as International Women's Year, and subsequent world conferences in 1980 and 1985 as part of the UN Decade for Women, new attention to and research examining women's roles began to change that perspective.

Although studies documenting women's multifaceted roles became available, this awareness did not translate into concrete program strategies. Governmental and nongovernmental agencies continued to target men in training programs, failing to recognize women's contributions as economic producers and the importance of their knowledge base to the survival of the family unit. Mayra Buvinic and Margaret Lycette's 1988 research on women and poverty in the Third World closely examined the characteristics of female poverty and the importance of women's economic contribution to the household. They recommended prioritizing antipoverty strategies that expand women's economic opportunities and earnings, but not focusing those strategies on the household. Such opportunities for training and economic improvement must, they concluded, address the social, economic, and legal constraints that women face.

Beyond limited access, women's participation in development and training programs is inhibited by a series of factors, among them educational requirements, time constraints resulting from family obligations, lack of inexpensive transportation, curricula that fail to address specific needs of women, and the tendency of women to attend programs of short duration, which generally do not lead to higher-paying jobs (Buvinic and Lycette, 1988).

Some nongovernmental organizations, such as the International Women's Tribune Center (New York) and OEF International (Washington, D.C.), have shown a greater disposition to deal with these variables, providing training for women in less traditional areas that offer a greater likelihood for economic stability. There has been an increasing focus among NGOs on the "informal sector"—in Latin America this labor force is 50 to 60 percent women. Such training for income-generation and small-enterprise development entails skills related to carrying out feasibility studies, managing businesses, and marketing products. Much effort has been dedicated to seeking successful formulas and components to such programs.

Beyond the need for resources and technical ability, training in leadership and management skills is an essential component to any significant enhancement of societal contributions by women. Based upon her study of thirty-one multilateral and bilateral development agencies and the projects they fund, Nelly Stromquist contends that "the success of these projects is characterized not only by the attainment of profits by participating women, but also their involvement in decisions regarding the functioning of the project instead of being mere beneficiaries" (Stromquist, 1986, p. 6).

▲ Popular Versus Nonformal Education

Although the terms "nonformal education" and "popular education" are at times used interchangeably in the United States, a distinction should be made because of the role popular education identifies for itself as an instrument for social and structural change. Differences are implicit in their nomenclature: "Nonformal education" emphasizes the mode of learning; "popular education" focuses on the sector involved. Nonformal education tends to focus on the individual and specific technical skills development; popular education looks at community and organizational training needs, emphasizing the skills needed to bring about improvements in economic and social well-being as a whole. According to Chilean Jorge Osorio, now president of the Latin American Council on Adult Education, "Popular education cannot be defined only by the modality it assumes as an educational process (out-of-school or not), nor by the didactic methods, techniques and procedures it employs, but rather by its class character" (Osorio, January/March 1988, p. 14).

There is no commonly agreed-upon definition of popular education, but two components seem key: the pedagogic and the sociopolitical dimensions. In the pedagogic arena:

- Popular education proposes a methodology for learning that is participatory and egalitarian, designed to eliminate the power component of the educator's role.
- Popular education strives to develop among targeted social sectors a critical social awareness and understanding of how society functions.

It is often combined with skills training in which two levels of knowledge are valued: (1) the traditions, knowledge, abilities, and experiences of participants; and (2) the transmission of new technical skills and information.

In the sociopolitical arena:

- Popular education programs work with those sectors of the population most marginalized by their socioeconomic status, targeting women, unemployed youth and adults, peasants, and indigenous groups.
- Proponents of popular education strive to facilitate the active involvement of participants in social change processes, as subjects in the historical process rather than passive bystanders.
- Popular education is part of a broader effort aimed at building social movements and transforming society through social and structural change. It is a vehicle for the development of skills necessary to forge this more just society (Fink, 1988, pp. 9-10).

Paulo Freire's Contribution

The roots of the popular education movement predominant in Latin America today can be traced to the work of Paulo Freire (particularly Freire 1970), the Brazilian educator and theoretician. Through literacy training programs with peasants in Recife, Brazil, in the early 1960s, Freire began identifying characteristics of an effective learning methodology. His approach emphasized the symbiotic relationship between awareness and action. Students learned to read and write through the discussion of basic problems and concerns, such as their limited access to land for farming. Freire used the term *concientização*, generally translated as the development of a "critical consciousness," to describe the process of moving from personal experience to reflection and analysis of those experiences, and then to action in the social and political arena. The methods used by Freire led participants to acquire literacy skills while simultaneously understanding and altering their own living conditions.

Freire maintained that education is never politically neutral. Education either serves to reinforce and sustain existing social structures and disparities or challenges them. It can either help liberate people by helping them become critical, creative, and active members of society or oppress them by reinforcing their subservient position in society.

Although Freire was forced into exile following the 1964 military coup in Brazil, his work continued. His new and challenging educational concepts contributed toward a critique of traditional views of Third World development and the development of social change strategies.

Critique of Formal Education

Popular education, then, is not to be viewed as simply an alternative to formal schooling; in fact it cannot and should not fulfill many of the functions of the school system. Rather, popular education posits a critique of the formal educational system as a center for the socialization of students by reinforcing and reproducing the established system of social and class relations.

Popular education offers an alternative model to the top-down hierarchical structures prevalent in traditional school systems. By using democratic practices in the learning process, popular education provides a training ground for alternative, cooperative learning. Those styles of learning and working can be carried over into community organizations, political parties, government institutions, and society as a whole, providing a vehicle for altering traditional social relations. This emphasis is articulated in a training manual that uses a popular education methodology:

> Our means for planning and carrying out our programs are actually our ends in the making, and if they aren't involving, democratic, and interesting, they will never lead us to the participatory future that we envision. Our success with social change depends on our ability to implement our visions within our own organizations even as we work toward them in the outside world (Dale and Mitiguy, 1978, p. 84).

Freire sums this up when he describes education as *práctica de la libertad* (practice of freedom). Pramod Prajuli, a Nepalese popular educator and researcher, maintains that popular education is not simply another form of nonformal education but an educational response to broader questions regarding the strengthening of social movements and national development itself. Popular education, he contends, is a critique both of nonformal education and of "modernization" approaches to Third World development because

> It has practiced a "bottom up" approach instead of "trickle down"; a self-reliant mode instead of a model based on foreign aid; a reactivation of the local and civil sector instead of the state and international agencies; a participatory approach in defining and articulating development goals and strategies instead of accepting decisions from above. . . . It has opted for the transformation of an oppressive social structure instead of merely changing values and attitudes of individuals (Prajuli, 1986, pp. 32–33).

This vision, albeit ideal and not always consistently applied, sets the stage for understanding the opportunities and limitations presented to women by popular education programs. As will be discussed, when not addressing women's needs and skills specifically, many popular education programs and social movements do not adequately incorporate gender issues.

▲ **Popular Education as a Vehicle
for Breaking Women's Isolation**

Low-income women, rural and urban, often lead an isolated social
existence. Single women find themselves bound to their families by
tradition and custom, while married women become locked into traditional household and childrearing obligations. A growing proportion of
women also work outside of their homes, a necessity that has emerged in
response to the economic crisis of the region. Many find employment in
the informal economic sector with small street vending businesses or
doing domestic work. Others have occasional salaried positions in the
service sector. But the subsequent *doble jornada* (double shift)—working
a job while fulfilling full-time household responsibilities—does not lend
itself to extended social relations. The kinds of kinship relationships men
enjoy in the workplace and the public sphere are less accessible to
women.

Nonformal and popular education programs often become a key
meeting place for women, offering a support group and a sense of
community. They provide a means for women to share some of the daily
concerns and problems they face. One outcome of women's isolation
and hardship is a tendency to blame the family's hardships and socioeconomic problems on oneself or one's husband. The chance to break out of
the daily routine, to sit down on a regular basis with other women
and community members with similar burdens, helps women recognize
that they are not alone, that their problems are shared, and, upon
further analysis, that the root causes go beyond individual fault or
responsibility. This relieves women of a tremendous burden and allows
them to move slowly from an individual to a collective perspective. It opens
the prospect of analyzing problems and identifying social causes, a
politicizing process that can eventually lead to broader types of social and
political action.

Building self-confidence and self-esteem (*autovalorización*) is integral to
this process. One Chilean participant described how a health education
program sponsored by the American Friends Service Committee (AFSC)
impacted her personally when she said, "Before, I didn't have much
character—but now I do." Similarly, Honduran popular educators working
with OEF International's Program of Education for Participation found that
when they asked a group of peasant women about their expectations for the
future in an initial session, participants were unable to project beyond two
months or so. But after participating for half a year, one woman expressed
that within a few years she expected to help construct a training center. The
group experience helped women break out of their fatalistic attitudes and
isolation.

Strengthening Cultural and Historical Identity

Popular education also stresses personal identity and culture, recognizing that if participants do not have a strong sense of self and an identification with their cultural and ethnic roots, then the foundation for broader social contribution is not created. Many programs integrate cultural expression—the creation of songs, poems, theater, and art—as a vehicle for self-affirmation and the strengthening of cultural identity. In the Dominican Republic a cultural component is considered essential by popular educator Angela Hernández, a poet and feminist:

> If a woman feels ugly because she is mulatta, because her hair is coarse
> . . . if she doesn't identify with her cultural roots, with her Caribbean
> physiognomy . . . if she feels that her way of speaking is inappropriate,
> that her skin color isn't beautiful, that her traditions and images are
> inferior, well, this mediates all her relations, from the personal to the
> community. It's a huge obstacle. That's why the cultural work of popular
> education is a very energizing factor and provides a benefit to the nation
> as well (October 1989).

Other programs look to history to identify popular expressions of resistance and opposition to power structures that are not documented or publicly known. In Bolivia, the Taller de Historia Oral Andina (THOA) carried out an education and research project to document the role of Aymara and Quechua women in diverse self-defense efforts against *latifundistas* and the Bolivian government in the first half of the twentieth century. Through extensive interviews and testimonies from women who survived that period, the significance of the takeover of communal lands and the challenge to cultural identity were more deeply understood, as well as how pressures surrounding these conflicts led to increasingly active measures of resistance by women who traditionally played a fairly passive role (THOA, 1986).

Methodologies and Activities

Socialized to be passive and dependent, women are often the first to believe the myths of gender differentiation and women's inferiority. It is not uncommon among the early activities of popular education programs to identify what kinds of work women perform, because, with much of it unpaid, it is not conceived of as true labor. For example, in a simple exercise that divides a pie with the range of women's tasks and responsibilities from morning to night, women begin to recognize and legitimize their contributions.

A board game called Mental Health Dominos, designed in Chile by the Educación Popular en Salud (EPES) program of the Lutheran church, links personal and societal problems. It was designed for women from urban

Santiago shantytowns participating in popular education programs in health. The domino graphics represent issues of concern to shantytown residents—unemployment, family health, marital strife, alcoholism, and basic survival. They derive from conflict situations, drawing the players into understanding the roots of the psychological anguish such problems precipitate, enabling them to deal with the problems more constructively in their day-to-day lives. One cartooned domino portrays a woman asking her husband for money. He gets angry—"Leave me alone!" One player responded, "He's mad because he's got no money to give her. He doesn't have a job, but how will she feed the family?" The women who play this game are "monitors," shantytown residents who have participated in a popular education workshop series on health issues and are now preparing to teach other community members. They joined together to confront local health problems, including pregnancy and postnatal health care. These programs tap the skills and experiences of women, young and old, who ventured beyond the confines of their homes to learn, to teach, and to organize, a process of empowerment for those who have previously had minimal opportunities to advance themselves.

The training of "monitors" or "promoters"—community members who are prepared to work on the local level as educators—is a fairly common component of popular education programs in Latin America. It is predicated on the belief that knowledge should not remain the domain of a privileged minority. Rather, the attainment of information and skills is important as marginalized social sectors gain the requisite abilities and understanding to take the future into their own hands.

Participants frequently attest to the value of learning from and with their peers. One 54-year-old Chilean woman participating in a popular education program commented:

> It's very important for people that the teachers speak just like you. You don't have to feel restrained, as if you didn't have the right to speak because your language and vocabulary aren't like other people's. . . . In the schools, only the teacher speaks and no one else. . . . In our meetings we bring the newsprint and we say, "Let's talk about X, we want to know your opinion. What do you think about this, what do you think about that?" We learn from each other. . . . And the fact that they shared their knowledge makes them feel important; they feel like they've been taken into account, that as human beings they've mattered (Fink, 1986, p. 7).

A Response to Immediate Needs

The EPES and AFSC programs previously described, like other programs throughout the region, focus on immediate interests and basic daily concerns. They are initially attractive because they help women attain new skills related to many of their responsibilities—feeding families, responding to children's health problems, and providing clothing. In these cases, the political consciousness of participants is low at the beginning, and the process of change is quite slow. Nonetheless, work with unorganized sectors that in the long term can make a social contribution is of great value. One popular educator explains:

> The fact that one of the program's objectives is to bring out women who are confined to the four walls of the home and who go out probably for the first time due to a felt need creates the conditions for a consciousness that is stronger. The work is slow and must be seen in the long term.

In its early days, popular education focused principally on the development of a "critical consciousness," but that has changed. Nonformal education specialist Suzanne Kindervatter explains: "Today's programs are moving beyond 'conscientizacion' in order to foster the skills needed to solve problems once they have been analyzed" (1988, p. 41). This shift in orientation is in part a response to the severe economic crisis that has shaken Latin America, where living standards have sharply declined and basic survival in the early 1990s is a more formidable task than it was a decade earlier.

The brunt of this economic crisis, precipitated by growing foreign debts, has fallen largely on the shoulders of women, who increasingly are heads of households and in general assume primary responsibilities for attending to children and domestic concerns. Recent studies show that many of the social advances made by women during the 1970s in expanded participation in the labor force and greater access to education were reversed by 1985, as unemployment levels soared and the decline of social and public services put new demands and burdens on women (Ramírez, 1987, p. 36).

With programs that emphasize a strictly educational or consciousness-raising program finding it more difficult to draw in participants, educators have responded with a renewed focus on productive and economic projects. According to Angela Hernández from the Centro de Solidaridad para el Desarrollo de la Mujer (CE-Mujer) of the Dominican Republic, this has created a great challenge for popular educators who do not want to lose the empowerment and consciousness-raising dimension of the work to a focus on immediate needs. It is important to be responsive to women's needs, she maintains, but women must also develop other skills, both analytical and practical, that will give them greater control over their lives.

Particular political environments have also helped shape the evolution of popular education programs. In countries dominated by military dictatorships or military-dominated civilian governments (Chile under Pinochet and contemporary Guatemala), consciousness-raising and community develop-ment activities are considered subversive and to be equated with political organizing. In rural Guatemala, it is not unusual for those carrying large pads of newsprint and markers—common tools of such projects—to be stopped by military patrols and interrogated about their activities. Several participants in popular education projects in Guatemala have disappeared after being taken into custody. In these repressive environments, infrastructural components such as training for running a community store or planting communal gardens are more politically acceptable and help popular education projects survive.

Strategies for Survival

A range of collective responses for basic survival has emerged to compensate for the public and social services not adequately provided by the state. From the *ollas comunes* (collectively run soup kitchens) and *botiquines* (first aid centers) in Chile to the *comedores populares* (people's kitchens) in Peru and the shantytown mobilizations in Brazil, organizing efforts with a strong educational component have become predominant. According to Colombian researcher and educator Socorro Ramírez:

> Women from low-income sectors have increasingly joined together to provide all types of health, training, education, cultural and recreational services, as well as attention for the handicapped and children, building of housing, collecting and recycling of garbage, managing environmental problems, building plumbing systems, etc.
>   These organizations respond to the needs of the community as well as to the individual needs of women as participants in the community. In the majority of cases, the organization's work is voluntary, and not paid. While these activities represent a greater workload for women, paradoxically this situation also provides women with the opportunity to break their isolation and confinement to the home, and to discover their social utility (1987, p. 39).

Despite the impressive accomplishments of many of these organizing efforts, there has been concern about their tendency to reinforce women's socially determined roles in the domestic arena. According to Ramírez, there is a need to continue the search for women's identity in this process, to understand their specific needs and forms of subordination, and to strengthen autonomous women's organizations. She contends:

> Actions which are designed solely to obtain better conditions in which to carry out traditional work help women to survive a crisis, but at the same time reinforce the sexual division of labor. When the crisis passes, women return to their traditional subordinate roles. Their enormous assistance in overcoming the crisis doesn't enable them to attain full social and political citizenship (1987, p. 40).

The dire economic quandary that initially propelled many women into involvement in these projects, however, can serve as a springboard for the development of leadership skills, strengthen local organizations, and build networks among groups, thus having a much broader impact. Both informal learning and more structured popular education efforts within such projects provide a vehicle for women to gain skills related to identifying and articulating their needs and enhancing organization skills, from running a meeting to organizing a community development project.

▲ Popular Education and Social Movements

Throughout Latin America, popular education work has contributed to the emergence of new and diverse social actors on the political scene: youth and shantytown movements, cultural movements, women's organizations, Christian communities, and others. Although some observers have been critical of the popular education movement and its numerous intermediary organizations for their detachment from more direct political processes (i.e., political parties and liberation movements), recognition has been given to their role in the formation and growth of new forces that emerge from these grassroots struggles.

Rocío Rosero, an Ecuadoran feminist and popular educator, notes that popular education programs usually develop in one of two ways: the first, as described previously, in response to immediate community needs; the second, through external influences, such as political parties, social movements, cooperatives, and unions, which prompt participation and organization in a more explicit and conscious manner.

Popular education is viewed increasingly as an important process for the building of social movements in Latin America, transforming educational action into a source of support to social change efforts. Popular education is an experience that has extended "throughout the continent. . . . It's becoming increasingly important to develop an education which contributes not only to the formation of a social consciousness, but also to the organization and construction of a new society" (MUDE, 1988, p. 11).

When combined with political action and mobilization, popular education can help strengthen and develop political and class consciousness, improve the organizing capacity of low-income groups, and make accessible the knowledge, abilities, and skills that will enhance their participation in society. Many social movements and organizations have consciously incorporated the concepts underlying popular education into their daily work. Peasant associations and unions such as the Central Nacional de Trabajadores del Campo (CNTC) in Honduras have developed literacy and health education programs aimed not only at building concrete skills but at helping members better understand the function and structure of their organization and analyze and confront social problems.

Other smaller organizations, like the Committee in Defense of the Hills of Escazu (CODECE), a Costa Rican environmental movement that has mobilized around the erosion of land and the pollution of water resulting from a major tourist development project, have also integrated participatory methodologies into their organizing work. CODECE has used popular educational materials (comic books, guides for organizing, coloring books), cultural activities, and a training program for community leaders as elements of a strategy aimed at mobilizing residents of seven communities to stop the development project and pressure for protective legislation.

Women may be involved as members of mixed organizations (environmental groups, cooperatives, and peasant unions) or through all-women organizations. Many feminists contend, however, that mixed groups pay inadequate attention to sexism and gender subordination in both society at large and within the organizations themselves. Although women have become more actively involved in social movements, Rosero notes:

> This participation has not been exempt from multiple limitations and difficulties derived just as much from contradictions in the domestic sphere as in the popular organizations and institutions where mechanisms which subordinate women to men are still reproduced and, as a result, traditionally assigned male and female roles are maintained (1987, p. 10).

In the case of CODECE, for example, almost all leadership positions are assumed by men, and when women are involved they tend to provide supportive services, such as cooking for fund-raising activities or taking notes at meetings. Overall, in mixed social and political organizations women tend to be underrepresented. Even where they are present in large numbers, they are generally not in positions of authority. This is the case in many organizations involved in political interest aggregation and articulation (e.g., labor unions and peasant federations). The case of the Costa Rican UPAGRA, the Association of Peasants and Small Farmers of the Atlantic Region, is reflective of this situation; no women are represented on the board of directors and very few are in leadership positions. In recent years UPAGRA has initiated efforts to involve women more actively by training them as community educators or "promoters," building their leadership skills, and linking health activities vis-à-vis medicinal plants (an area traditionally of women's domain) to productive work. There have also been efforts to raise the consciousness of men about the obstacles to women's participation on the interpersonal, organizational, and societal levels. Although changing attitudes of machismo ingrained for years is a difficult task, UPAGRA and other groups have shown some disposition toward seeking creative ways to broaden women's involvement and roles.

All-women organizations have stressed the development of leadership skills. Members of the National Confederation of Peasant Women (CONAMUCA) in the Dominican Republic regularly participate in a five-week training program for preparing women to be leaders, sponsored by a local nongovernmental group, the Center for Research for Women's Action (CIPAF). The training incorporates women with a range of formal educational backgrounds, from functional illiteracy to a high school degree, and provides them the opportunity to develop analytic capabilities in such areas as analysis of the role of rural women in Latin American and Caribbean economies and to learn to organize similar educational methods for building democratic participation.

Women-Only Versus Integrated Efforts

Feminists critical of popular education work contend that when such educational efforts are posed within the context of social movements, they generally do not pay sufficient attention to gender-specific oppression, relegating these issues to secondary importance vis-à-vis class issues. Minimization of the gender dimension has led to debates on the relative effectiveness of work in mixed organizations versus a focus on all-women groups. Some people argue that an all-women orientation runs the risk of setting up small isolated women's groups, incapable of impacting more mainstream efforts. Their activities may not be taken seriously and may be considered either too radical or too limited in focus if they are not part of a more integrated effort to incorporate women and, in so doing, influence male perspectives.

Results from social science research indicate that women more effectively develop initial participatory and leadership skills in mutual support environments such as all-women groups. Social expectations, often ingrained during formal education, tend to leave individuals with a perceived low-prestige social status less likely to participate in group discussions and decisions than those having high-prestige status. For women to develop some of the skills traditionally reserved for men, particularly related to leadership and public speaking, women's groups provide a more effective starting point (Stromquist, 1986, p. 15). Discussions with female participants and observations contrasting women in mixed groups and all-female settings support this notion. Nongovernmental institutions, both First and Third World, have become more adept at designing programs that can produce effective results and that prepare women for participation in other settings.

Sally Yudelman carried out an in-depth study of five women's organizations in the Caribbean and Latin America, maintaining they offer women "the opportunity to acquire knowledge and trust in themselves in a favorable environment and dispel general myths about women's function in society. Such organizations facilitate women's access to resources and permit them to assume increasing economic and political responsibilities" (1987/1988, p. 1).

At the same time, there is some agreement that women-only groups should be seen not as direct alternatives to integrated projects but rather as complementary efforts.

> Given the complex situation of poor women and the diversity of the political and cultural contexts in which they live, a combination of both approaches is advocated to ensure that, on the one hand, some critical skills are developed and, on the other hand, that women's needs and problems are not "ghettoized." The challenges ahead are to determine when to promote which type of project and how to make sure that the "integrated" projects do not mean absorption to the point of invisibility for women (Stromquist, 1986, p. 17).

Effects on Male-Female Relationships

The increasing ability of women to articulate their needs and play an effective role in projects tends to draw conflict over traditional sexual roles into the home, as men perceive women's involvement as a threat to the hierarchical social structure of the household. In 90 percent of the educational projects I have been acquainted with in Honduras, Guatemala, Costa Rica, and Chile, at least one woman is prohibited from participating in the group by her spouse and is confronted with the dilemma of having to acquiesce or suffer repercussions from her partner.

In one example in rural Honduras, a jealous husband damaged the door of a peasant farmer's home because he had walked back to the village with the man's wife after one training session. No one expected her ever to return, but the woman was back the next day, an indication that she felt the benefits of participating outweighed her fears. In another case, a woman active in urban organizing efforts in Tegucigalpa became president of the local women's group after several months of participating in a popular education program. Her husband disliked that she was frequently away from home and finally left her—for three months. When he came back he asked her, "Well, are you still involved in all that committee work?" "Yes," she said. "And now we have to show for it the community center which we built." She continued her work and he adapted to the situation and stayed on.

Although an ongoing concern, there is heightened sensitivity within the popular education programs to avoid precipitating tensions within the family. Some efforts have been made to incorporate men into the programs and help them recognize the benefits offered by such programs to both their wives and their families. Several participants maintain that they have actually seen their marital relationships improve in the process. As men see concrete benefits in the household, they gain respect for their wives' new skills. A staff member of Dominican Women in Development (MUDE) observed that when a woman brings home money earned from selling the cow's milk, it opens her husband's mind to continued participation, and when her organization sells the milk in the community at a low price, she gains her neighbors' respect as well.

Linking Local Issues with Policy Change

Two dimensions of popular education work previously mentioned—responding to immediate needs and serving as a tool for building mass movements—highlight its relevance to both individuals and groups. Nonetheless, popular education work around women's issues is probably weakest in linking local-level activities to national policies and practices. The micro, or project-oriented, focus of most programs tends to consume vast amounts of energy. These efforts certainly build individual and group skills, but they often fail to address adequately the broader issues such as laws, policies, and economic structures that inhibit women's full contribution to society and national development.

Various types of work would be of relevance to the process of incorporating the macro dimension into popular education. Two examples are to increase the capability of participants to comprehend the bigger picture and context in which they function, and to prepare people to develop broader strategies and actions that confront obstacles to full participation and equality.

Does popular education work incorporate a macrolevel analysis? A diverse range of experiences exists. There are indications that popular education work in Latin America is often narrowly focused (Torres, 1988; Fink, 1988). Examples can be seen in some of the health education programs studied in Chile, such as a program run by the Vicariate of Solidarity of the Catholic Church. It was often so information- and skill-oriented that it failed to address the structural causes of poverty and inadequate health care. Such approaches treated individual health as if it were a purely personal problem that could be altered through new behaviors and information, overlooking issues like the professionalization of health care, the curative orientation of the health industry, and the failure of governments to treat good health as a right and not a privilege (Fink, 1988).

Nonetheless, several programs can be cited that attempt to demystify the economic and structural causes of the problems people experience on a day-to-day basis. The organization Taller PIRET (Promotion and Exchange of Educational Resources and Technologies) in Chile designs workshops aimed at helping grassroots organizations and trade unions analyze root causes and understand the role of the government's economic model in their daily lives. One of their most well-received training series is entitled "Why Are People Hungry?" Through a participatory process of identifying causes of hunger and unemployment, they are able to move from immediate needs to a more global perspective.

Other efforts, such as the Colombian Workshop on Women's Resources, bring together various women's organizations to better comprehension of the impact of the external debt and economic crisis on women. Through a series of three-day workshops, women share the manner in which the crisis is felt on a day-to-day basis. Analysis moves from the individual to the family and to the community levels, and on to an understanding of the cost to social services and national production that the debt has incurred and the role of the International Monetary Fund in that process.

Although educational efforts to this end are of critical value, the move from education to action is the next step needed, though often the most difficult. The Center for Information and Development of Women (CIDEM) in Bolivia is doing fascinating work in this arena around the role of food aid programs sponsored by the United States and Europe. As those women's groups directly involved as recipients of food donations have become educated, activities have surged and new policies have been proposed to counteract the negative impact of such programs. Through popular education workshops and educational materials, women have begun to question the role of food aid programs that require women to perform unremunerated labor and participate only in groups that fulfill certain criteria in order to obtain food. Women move from an understanding of the personal implications to the national impact, analyzing how such policies promote dependency. Normally, rather than increasing domestic food production and defining their own formulas for receiving aid, the groups and the nation overall become "beneficiaries" of charity efforts that orient them toward the consumption of food products not traditionally their own. CIDEM's educational efforts have been instrumental in facilitating organizing initiatives by women's groups so that they may exert leverage in the decisionmaking processes of intermediary agencies like Catholic Relief Services, CARE, and USAID and in opening up a policy debate about food aid and the macroeconomic structures that propel it.

In her writing on the role of nongovernmental organizations in empowering women, Stromquist identifies the need to move from immediate local concerns to greater audiences and macrolevel impact (1986, p. 19). She uses Maxine Molyneux's distinction between "practical gender interests" and "strategic gender interests," in which the former are "short term and linked to immediate needs arising from women's current responsibilities vis-à-vis the livelihood of their families and children, while the latter address bigger issues such as the institutionalized forms of gender discrimination, the establishment of political equality, freedom of choice over violence and control over women" (Stromquist, 1986, p. 19).

Margaret Schuler's work on women, law, and development addresses "strategic" interests by identifying the legal system as a tool for reinforcing women's subordination because of its potential to serve as an instrument of social transformation. Her analysis of the relationship between the law and socioeconomic development processes that have kept women marginalized opens a new scope of strategies for empowerment: legal rights programs that educate women about their rights, redress grievances, and work to change discriminatory legislation and policies (Schuler, 1986, p. 5).

A number of women's groups throughout Latin America have acted as advocates in this arena, working to eliminate the more institutional roots of women's subordination and using popular education methodologies as a tool in the process. Groups like Perú Mujer, the Center for Women's Action and Promotion (CEPAM) in Ecuador, and the Luisa Amanda Espinoza National Nicaraguan Women's Association (AMNLAE) have educated and mobilized women on such issues as domestic violence, discriminatory labor codes and practices, and inheritance and family law. They have the dual intent of building grassroots efforts and enacting change at the superstructural level. Specifically, the Honduran Federation of Peasant Women (FEHMUC) pressured the government for the passage of agrarian reform legislation, while the Center for Working Women (COMO) in Mexico played an important role in forcing factories to set up health centers and provide on-site nurses to serve their predominantly female employees.

Recent networking efforts among such groups demonstrate a growing recognition of the need to organize with this legal and policy-level perspective. In January 1988, a number of groups coalesced to form a regional organization, the Latin American Committee for the Defense of Women's Rights (CLADEM), with headquarters in Lima, Peru. CLADEM provides a support network, an opportunity for sharing program successes and failures, and an emergency response network for coordinating actions and strategies throughout the region. A June 1989 example of this coordination was a human rights call for CLADEM members to send international telegrams to the minister of defense in El Salvador concerning the death of Cristina Gómez and the disappearance of four women from the National Commission of Salvadoran Women (CONAMUS).

CLADEM's regional efforts bring together academics, lawyers, psychologists, community activists, and low-income women in a joint cross-class and interdisciplinary project. Member organizations focus on helping women deepen their understanding of the legal, cultural, political, and economic underpinnings of their subordination and develop action strategies for change. They aim to demystify the legal system, develop the skills to use it where possible, challenge it or subvert it where necessary, redress injustices, and increase access to economic and political resources (Schuler, 1986, p. 1).

Popular education is an important tool in demystification efforts because the language of legal specialists is translated into terms that can be understood by women with minimal schooling. Using comic book–style booklets and board games, role playing, and theater, women can "learn by doing" about specific laws and policies that affect them. In Peru, women are trained as "legal promoters" who serve as a resource for and advocate on behalf of their neighbors. Through a range of educational activities, women discover their power to act in defense of women's rights, to speak in public without fear of criticism, and to deal with police and judicial authorities (Schuler, 1986, p. 228).

What is striking about these efforts is that they promote change on the policy level (legal, institutional, governmental) and actively involve grassroots women's groups in the process. Such work has stimulated the discussion and development of an alternative conception of the law and the role of professionals, with an eye to building the link to broader social change. The combination of individual change and superstructural change enhances prospects for women's empowerment and the possibility of having a long-term impact.

▲ Impact of Popular Education Efforts

The impact of popular education programs has been discussed on a range of levels. On the individual level, women have the opportunity to escape from the isolation of the household, strengthen their self-confidence and cultural identity, and socialize experiences. Their families benefit from the attainment of new skills and options for family survival as well as from having mothers who are role models assuming a range of new responsibilities.

On the group level, a sense of community and common purpose is forged. Popular education is instrumental in the development of collective survival projects and the improvement of living standards. It provides the building blocks for continued organizing and networking on community and regional levels by helping women develop leadership skills and play a greater role in grassroots organizations.

Creating long-lasting impacts on the national level by working to affect governmental policy and change legislation can also be attained. But achievements in this area are more difficult and, where they have been achieved, less visible. This results in part from the long-term nature of such work and its requirements of better analysis, mobilization capabilities, and networking strategies. The trend toward integrating popular education approaches into social movements and organizing will cause its effect to be less direct, perhaps, but present in broader efforts for change. To ensure that gender issues are incorporated into the demands of social movements will require the constant presence of and pressure from those concerned with challenging women's subordination.

Because popular education often functions with limited economic resources, insufficient attention has been devoted to measuring its impact. There is a need to identify and incorporate into these projects indicators that reflect the extent to which women have changed and made changes as a result of participation in nonformal and popular education. The generation of indicators on individual, family, group, community, and national levels would be a service toward documenting the need for and contribution of these efforts.

▲ Conclusion

Over the past two decades, the growing popular education movement in Latin America has incorporated new groups and sought new methodologies. More egalitarian relations in the learning environment are considered a key tool in preparing individuals for protagonism in society at large, and the building of more democratic organizations is part of the vision of greater social equality. No longer are popular education programs viewed narrowly as pertinent only to the educational domain; rather, they are seen as a vehicle for empowering marginalized social sectors and creating an ideology of challenge to the dominant society—a counterhegemony.

A number of the dilemmas and tensions described in this chapter will be at play in that process: the microlevel versus macrolevel orientation of such efforts; the reinforcement or alteration of traditional gender roles; and the tension between developing critical consciousness and developing technical skills, an issue about method versus content. In brief, these debates are as follows:

Micro versus macro: By definition, grassroots organizing emerges on the community level, but its focus on resolving local problems often precludes the macrolevel dimension of those issues. The tension here is the gap between microlevel self-help initiatives and the macrolevel causes and social factors that propel such problems. How to bridge that gap—respond to needs and also have a long-range effect—is a question about effectiveness that challenges popular educators and organizers.

Reinforcing versus altering women's roles: Collective strategies for survival in which popular and participatory education plays a key role often fall within the domestic domain. Women are the principal actors in such efforts, but they also bind women to traditional skill areas—food, health, child care. These abilities undoubtedly help women survive the crisis, but they also reinforce the sexual division of labor. The challenge, then, is to alleviate women's burdens and also move into new nontraditional economic and political arenas that enhance women's potential for overcoming social marginalization.

Method versus content: This tension is manifested in the struggle over developing critical thinking skills or developing technical or "hard" skills. Neither gender consciousness nor earning power alone will empower women, yet finding the appropriate balance seems to be difficult. Stromquist's work to find a viable and thorough definition of "empowerment" that nonformal education programs can advance cites three types of knowledge and skills necessary: reproductive, productive, and emancipatory. Reproductive skills seek to alleviate the traditional time- and energy-consuming responsibilities of women; productive skills provide women with capacities to enter the economic system under more advantageous conditions; and emancipatory skills and knowledge offer women the analytic ability and critical awareness of their subordination and inequality to work more effectively to change them (Stromquist, 1988, p. 11).

The inclusion of these three components in any given popular education program directed at women would be an unrealistic expectation and responsibility, particularly given the constraints under which such programs generally function. Still, the definition moves us a step closer to identifying a tangible combination of resources that allows women to advance on multiple fronts. The challenge is to develop women's potential fully to contribute, from the local to the broader national levels, addressing women's specific needs and working to overcome social, economic, and political subordination within society at large. To achieve a true incorporation of women, efforts toward such democratization must also be reflected in daily activities and domestic life—from the community to the home—recognizing that social relations in these settings are also of a political nature.

As the economic crisis in Latin America deepens under the weight of foreign debt and ineffective economic models, the need to address pressing survival needs will likely mount. The challenge then becomes one of working to meet those needs without losing sight of, or placing on a secondary plane, the demands of women for greater equality and opportunity and the chance to participate actively in the formulation of alternatives.

▲ References

Arnold, Rick, and Bev Burke. *A Popular Education Handbook*. Ottawa: CUSO, 1983.

Buvinic, Mayra, and Margaret Lycette. "Women, Poverty, and Development in the Third World." In John Lewis (ed.), *Strengthening the Poor: What Have We Learned?* Washington, D.C.: Overseas Development Council, 1988, pp. 149–162.

CIDEM (Center for Information and Development of Women). *La donación de alimentos: Una cuestión de mujeres*. La Paz: CIDEM, 1986.

Dale, Duane, and Nancy Mitiguy. *Planning for a Change*. Amherst: Citizen Involvement Training Project, University of Massachusetts, 1978.

Fink, Marcy. *La evaluación participativa: Aplicada en programas de salud*. Santiago: Centro de Investigación y Desarrollo de la Educación, 1988.

———. "Evaluation: The AFSC Education Program for Pregnant and Nursing Mothers in Santiago, Chile." Unpublished manuscript, 1986.

Freire, Paulo. *Pedagogy of the Oppressed*. New York: Herder and Herder, 1970.

Garcia-Huidobro, Juan Eduardo. *El sentido político de la educación popular*. Santiago: Centro de Investigación y Desarrollo de la Educación, 1988.

Hernandez, Angela. Personal interview, Santo Domingo, Dominican Republic, Otober 19, 1989.

International Council for Adult Education (Women's Program). "The Feminist Challenge to Adult Education." *Voices Rising,* special report; April/May 1988.

Kindervatter, Suzanne. "Whatever Happened to Nonformal Education?" *Grassroots Development,* vol. 12, no. 2, 1988, pp. 41–42.

La Belle, Thomas. *Nonformal Education in Latin America and the Caribbean: Stability, Reform, or Revolution.* New York: Praeger, 1986.

MUDE (Mujeres en Desarrollo Dominicana, Inc.). *Espigas y amapolas en la cosecha: Evaluación del programa de capacitación.* Santo Domingo: MUDE, 1987.

Osorio, Jorge. "Educación popular en América Latina." *El Canelo,* January/March 1988, pp. 14–17.

———. "Polémicas y afirmación de la educación popular en America Latina." *El Canelo,* August/September 1988, pp. 13–18.

Pineda, Magaly. "Feminism and Popular Education: A Critical but Necessary Relationship." In ISIS International (ed.), *Women, Struggles and Strategies: Third World Perspectives.* Rome: ISIS, 1986, pp. 111–113.

Prajuli, Pramod. "Grassroots Movements, Development Discourse, and Popular Education." *Convergence,* vol. 19, no. 2, 1986, pp. 29–39.

Ramírez, Socorro. "Las mujeres resisten la crisis económica y reclaman participación." In ISIS International (ed.), *Mujeres, crisis y movimiento: América Latina y el Caribe.* Rome: ISIS, 1987, pp. 33–41.

Rosero, Rocío (ed.). *Taller latinoamericano sobre feminismo y educación popular.* Montevideo: CEEAL, December 1986.

———. "Feminismo y educación popular." In ISIS International (ed.), *Crecer juntas: Mujeres, feminismo y educación popular.* Rome: ISIS International, 1987, pp. 9–13.

Schuler, Margaret. *Empowerment and the Law: Strategies of Third World Women.* Washington, D.C.: OEF International, 1986.

Social Studies and Publications Center of Peru, Women's Department. "Feminism and the Grassroots Movement of Poor Women." In ISIS International (ed.), *Women, Struggles, and Strategies: Third World Perspectives.* Rome: ISIS, 1986, pp. 99–103.

Stromquist, Nelly. "Empowering Women Through Education: Lessons from International Cooperation." *Convergence,* vol. 19, no. 4, 1986, pp. 1–21.

———. "Women's Education in Development: From Welfare to Empowerment." *Convergence,* vol. 21, no. 4, 1988, pp. 5–15.

Taller de Recursos para la Mujer. *La deuda externa y la crisis económica: Cómo nos afecta a nosotras las mujeres.* Bogota: Taller de Recursos para la Mujer, May 1987.

THOA (Taller de Historia Oral Andina). *Mujer y resistencia comunitaria: Historia y memoria.* La Paz: Hisbol, 1986.

Tinker, Irene. "Feminizing Development: For Growth with Equity." *CARE Briefs on Development Issues,* no. 6, 1987.

Torres, Rosa. "Discurso y práctica en educación popular." Paper presented for Encuentro Latinoamericano sobre Educación Popular. Quito: Centro de Investigación CIUDAD, 1988.

Vicioso, Chiqui. "La educación integral: Un 'oficio' de mujeres." *Ciencia y Sociedad,* vol. 13, no. 1, January/March 1988.

World Education. *Reports: The World According to Women.* Boston: World Education, Fall 1987.

Yudelman, Sally. *Una apertura a la esperanza: Estudio de cinco organizaciones femeninas de desarrollo de América Latina y el Caribe.* Washington, D.C.: Inter-American Foundation, 1987/1988.

▲ 10

Vocational Training and Job Opportunities for Women in Northeast Brazil

Elena Viveros

This qualitative study provides a glimpse of the gender-construction processes operating within nonformal education programs. Through interviews with school personnel and the personal perspectives of four students in a computer programming course, Viveros shows how the program, family messages, and internalized social expectations combine to reaffirm women in their traditional roles as women and future wives.

Of special interest is how a new field, such as computer programming in the context of northeastern Brazil, quickly becomes defined in such a manner that better-rewarded positions go to men. That both men and women receive training in computer science does not prevent employers from offering different jobs to men and women graduates of these programs. Thus men are promptly defined as "programmers" and women as "word-processor technicians." Confronted with stale definitions of women's abilities, the women graduates from this program express disappointment at their limited chances for finding appropriate and well-remunerated employment; at the same time, they also show a willingness to accept the conditions in which they live and to give priority to family and marriage plans.

In the end, a new occupational field that can be equally filled by women and men is recast so that it fits existing perceptions of femininity and masculinity. This suggests that the introduction of technologies is not necessarily accompanied by shifts in gender and social relations.

—*Editor*

▲ During the last decade in Brazil, and especially in the northeast region, substantial changes in the extent to which women are incorporated into the labor force have occurred. There have also been major shifts in the distribution of occupations among the three sectors of the economy (primary, secondary, and service). These changes can be attributed to longer-term processes that affect the Brazilian economy as a whole and the position of the northeast region in the regional distribution of labor.

According to Superintendencia de Desenvolvimento do Nordeste

(SUDENE), the distribution of the labor force in northeastern Brazil in 1980 presented a concentration of workers in basically two sectors of the economy: the primary (agricultural) sector, with 50 percent of the total work force, and service, 35 percent. The secondary (industrial) sector employed only 15 percent of the labor force. Between 1970 and 1980 the number of workers in the primary sector increased only slightly (from 5.2 million to 5.6 million), while the services registered a 75 percent increase in the same period, going from 2.2 million to 3.8 million (Table 10.1).

Analysis of the gender composition of the sectors for 1980 shows that the primary sector can be characterized as "masculine"—84 percent of the workers are men, probably because much of the women's work in this sector belongs to a category that can be classified as the "free family labor force" and is not considered in labor statistics. The service sector, on the contrary, employs more women, who account for 45 percent of the workers in this sector.

An important question to ask is, "Under what conditions are women entering the labor force?" The level of formal education of the workers in the northeast is very low, especially in the primary sector, where 80 percent are reported to have had no instruction or less than four years of primary instruction. In the service sector 40 percent of workers have very low educational levels.

The income level for the region is also low. In the more favored service sector, half of the male workers earn two minimum salaries (double the minimum wage, or about US $120 per month); in the same sector 83 percent of the female workers earn as much. Only a minority of women workers (less than 5 percent) earn over five minimum salaries (US $300 per month), though 7 percent hold a higher education degree. In contrast, 7 percent of the male workers hold university degrees, but 15 percent earn over five minimum salaries (SUDENE, 1983). Thus, in the northeast the same level of education does not always yield the same income for men and women.

There is extensive literature providing explanations for these facts: Inequality between the sexes in the occupational structure is conceived as reflecting the existence of separate spheres of work, resulting in differences in status, wealth, and power. The "masculine" areas of work concentrate most of the wealth and power, whereas the "feminine" areas have few of these attributes. "Much of it derives from the distinction between the value of work in private (or domestic) and public domains" (Kelly and Nihlen, 1982, p. 163).

Since the mid-1970s there has been an increasing interest in the sexual division of labor, and many studies have debated and demonstrated the ways in which an understanding of the pattern of sexual ascription continues to be relevant to understanding social relationships both within the family and in the wider social structure. "Attention was drawn to the ways in which assumptions and expectations which structure family relationships are

Table 10.1. Sector Breakdown of the Labor Force 1970–1980, Northeast Brazil (absolute frequencies and percentages)

Economic Sector	1970			1980		
	Total	Males	Females	Total	Males	Females
Primary	5,224,810	4,632,324	592,486	5,628,796	4,713,314	915,482
%	62.6	68.6	36.8	50.4	57.2	31.3
Secondary	887,945	769,216	118,729	1,711,824	1,436,926	274,898
%	10.6	11.4	7.4	15.3	17.4	9.4
Service	2,240,684	1,340,439	900,248	3,823,844	2,087,445	1,736,399
%	26.8	20.0	55.8	34.3	25.4	59.3
Total	8,353,442	6,748,979	1,611,463	11,164,464	8,237,685	2,926,779

Source: SUDENE (1983), pp. 255–257, 154–156.

reinforced by experiences in the educational system and set the framework for differential patterns of occupational experiences" (Keil and Newton, 1980, p. 98).

According to some authors, the inequitable position of women in the labor market can be attributed to existing cultural traits:

> An important feature of this differential structuring of educational and occupational opportunities by sex is the articulation of assumptions and expectations about women's family relationships with employers' perspectives on the recruitment and selection of the employees. This results in strategies for recruitment, selection, training and promotion which rest upon the conventional wisdom that women have or will have two roles, domestic and occupational, and that they will give priority to the domestic. As a consequence it is "natural" to assume that women are not seriously committed to the labor market and need only to be regarded as temporary or relatively short-term workers who may be seeking part-time rather than full-time work, and who may be relegated to the secondary sector of the labor market with lower pay and poor conditions of service when compared to their male counterparts. In such context it is almost inevitable that opportunities for training with the concomitant overtones of serious commitment and potential for promotion are restricted (Keil and Newton, 1980, p. 98).

Other authors believe psychological factors also play an important role and point to the fact that a considerable number of women graduates have limited career ambitions and do not want to find themselves in highly competitive situations. These factors act as barriers in women's career development (Chisholm and Woodward, 1980, p. 163).

Still others believe that economic factors also are responsible for the sexual division of labor. Clarricoates studied the constructs of "masculinity" and "femininity" in primary schools and how they differed by class and area of origin. She observes that sex-role attributes accorded to males and females varied, and what was considered normal in some schools was abnormal in others. She cites Sharpe, who says the values and attitudes of sex differentiation do not develop in an arbitrary way, but are influenced by the nature of the economic structure of a society and the division of labor that has developed around it (Clarricoates, 1980, pp. 26–27).

A main concern in this study is to understand the role of the school in the reproduction of inequality and, therefore, in reinforcing the sexual division of labor in society. This subject has been extensively studied. Research on the formal school's authority patterns, textbooks, time of exposure to school activities, subject matter segregation, and formal and hidden curricula and the effect of all these factors on the reproduction of the sexual division of labor in the United States and in other countries are reported by Kelly and Nihlen (1982, pp. 162–177) and Finn, Reis, and Dulberg (1982, pp. 107–126).

In the study discussed in this chapter, I attempt to discover how and to what extent these discriminatory mechanisms are present in vocational schools; I assume that the presence of such factors can hinder the chances of women with vocational training in the labor market. But before I present the research and its results, a brief examination must be made of the geographic area where the study was conducted because, as mentioned earlier, the values and attitudes of sex differentiation are influenced by a society's economic structure and division of labor.

Study Region

João Pessoa is the capital city of Paraiba, one of the nine northeastern states. According to the latest census, it had nearly 300,000 inhabitants in 1980. A city of rapid population growth (4.07 percent annually during the period 1970–1980), its population represented at that time over 10 percent of the total population of the state. Paraiba and the rest of the region constitute the poorest section of Brazil. Its population suffers from hunger and lacks minimum conditions of health, education, and other bare necessities. Moreover, the region suffers chronically from both droughts and floods, disruptions that make the situation for its population nearly unbearable.

The main products of the area, sugarcane and cattle, require equipment and are seasonal and thus have resulted in the massive underutilization of labor, which is reflected in the rapid growth of the urban areas. João Pessoa's population in fact more than doubled in the 1960–1980 period (SUDENE, 1983).

The contribution of industry to the total regional output showed a steady decline from 10 percent in 1947 to 6.3 percent in 1968, while the agriculture of the region has continuously increased its participation in the total national output, from 19.9 percent in 1947 to 24.6 percent in 1968. In recent years this trend has become more intense as a result of federal policies of industrialization of agriculture (Oliveira and Reichstul, 1973, p. 136). The most important program, PROALCOOL (alcohol as fuel from sugarcane) was encouraged by the oil crisis in the 1970s. It had a tremendous social cost, causing the expulsion of a large proportion of the peasant population from the land. The results were a great decrease in subsistence agriculture and a massive rural-urban migration.

The recent history of the area shows tremendous social unrest began around the 1960s because of the sharp class inequalities existing in the region. Today, the landed aristocracy appears decadent and unable to give the workers decent salaries and conditions of work; at the same time, it is not willing to give up land to settle the peasant population.

The central government, in an effort to diminish regional inequalities, has promoted the industrialization of the region. The main result of this effort is that since 1962, when the federal credit was put into effect, the industrial structure of the region, which consisted mainly of the production of low-priced commodities for local consumption, collapsed and was replaced by industries of intermediate and capital goods—subsidiaries of southern and/or multinational companies (Oliveira and Reichstul, 1973). In other words, the actual industrial structure of the region today appears completely divorced from the needs and income level of its population and responds exclusively to the needs of capital expansion at the national level. After the military coup of 1964, one solution was to promote the transfer of residents from the northeast to the industrializing south in order to alleviate social tensions. The construction of Brasilia also absorbed a great contingent of northeastern workers. This process of migration affected mainly young males, and only recently does it appear that the migrant population has become more balanced in terms of gender. For example, in the 1970s for every 100 women in the region there were only 87.6 men, and some states like Paraiba showed a more extreme situation, with only 79.6 men for every 100 women.

With respect to the numbers of migrants, in the 1970–1980 period the northeast lost 5.5 million from a total population of 25 million (SUDENE, 1983). With the migrant population concentrated in the 20–39 age span, the northeast can actually be characterized as a population composed of women, children, and the elderly. Although in the 1950s the Brazilian economy entered a period of heavy industrialization with large-scale participation of foreign capital, the northeast lagged behind, and its role seemed to be only to contribute a large reserve army of labor.

What is the role of women in this process? According to several studies, the participation of women in the various branches of the economy underwent a considerable decline after the intensification of the industrial expansion. In 1960 the industrialization of the northeast was insignificant, but of the total labor force employed in the secondary sector, 36.5 percent were women (Saffioti, 1976, p. 242). The 1980 census shows that the women represented only 16 percent of the workers in the secondary sector that year (Table 10.1).

The data for Paraiba present a similar pattern. The 1980 census shows that in the state only 9 percent of the workers in industry are women. Even if allowance is made for some underestimation, as some authors suggest, the situation does not appear encouraging (see Madeira and Singer, 1973). In agriculture 21 percent of the women are reported as economically active, although this low number can be explained by their participation as "free family labor force." It is in the service sector that the participation of women is the greatest. This can be explained by the widespread domestic service, which is cheap and easily available. Teachers and nurses also represent a large proportion of the female workers (25 percent in Paraiba). Public administration accounts for a small proportion of women workers (4 percent), but the opportunities in this sector are much better than in the others and will attract the best trained workers (SUDENE, 1983).

This overview of the recent socioeconomic history of the region and its role in the national distribution of labor gives some hints regarding the role of women in it. As stated earlier, the pattern of sex differentiation is shaped by the economic structure of a society and its ensuing division of labor. The brief information presented here is enough to give an idea as to how difficult it has been to organize the people in the area and how strong the class oppression that keeps the people ignorant, poor, and undernourished is so that they would not constitute a threat to the interests of the powerful.

In this situation, it was women who suffered a double oppression: First, they were the remaining labor power, after the massive migration of young males; second, because of and in spite of women's increased economic role, the predominant values in an agricultural, traditional society relegated women to a secondary position. Women's contributions to productive activities in all sectors of the economy go greatly unrewarded, a clear evidence of which is found in the low level of wages earned by female workers in the service sector, as previously mentioned. These low salaries are true not only in Paraiba but in the entire northeastern region.

The motivation for this study came from an analysis of the data presented. If there is a chance for women to improve their situation in the labor market in the urban areas of the northeast, this chance appears to be in the service sector, whether in public service or in private firms. But in order to get those opportunities, women first need adequate training. Yet does training really ensure women's access to jobs? This is the question addressed in the study done at SENAC.

▲ SENAC

The Serviço Nacional de Aprendizagem Comercial (SENAC), or National Training Service for Commerce (Trade), was created in January 1946 by presidential decree number 8621. It is financed by taxes from the private sector amounting to 1.5 percent of the total salaries paid by these firms.[1] It is a private institution linked to CINTERFOR, an agency of the International Labor Office.

SENAC is operated at the national level by a centralized administration where the National Confederation of Commerce and unions of trade ownerships are represented. Also included are representatives of the Ministries of Education, Work, and Welfare. At the state level the administrative structure is approximately the same.

SENAC was chosen to be studied for several reasons: First, it offers short-term courses for the training of the service-sector labor force. These courses train students for very specific abilities, such as hygiene and beauty, telephone and telex operator programming, and word processing. Second, most SENAC students are women—that is, for women SENAC represents a definite chance of entrance into the productive sphere with specific abilities. Finally, SENAC has a placement service for its graduates and periodically contacts those who were employed through it. Thus, SENAC courses and diplomas can serve as effective means to help women enter the labor force with marketable skills that can guarantee them better positions and better salaries.

According to SENAC's director of professional training, the institution's main function can be summarized as follows: to train a labor force to fill the needs of the commercial firms existing in the area. But SENAC also trains personnel for public administration because, at least in Paraiba, it constitutes one of the most efficient schools of vocational training. The coordinator of the computer department of the Center for Professional Training in João Pessoa reported that a group of about thirty-two professionals (including twenty-three doctors) from several agencies of the Ministry of Welfare were being trained at SENAC at the time of the study.

The link between SENAC and the government is quite close. Aside from the participation of state officials in all SENAC higher councils, there is a direct control by the state of SENAC's resources. According to information from the interviews, all contributions from private firms go first to the state and then pass on to SENAC. It is extremely difficult to find out how much the federal government receives from the firms, especially in a state like Paraiba, where many of them are subsidiaries of large national and multinational firms.

In Brazil, a country with sharp regional differences, Paraiba represents one of the poorest states. This is clearly reflected in the quality and quantity of its commercial activities. Therefore, SENAC-Paraiba could be expected to be a modest institution; on the contrary, SENAC operates with an extensive network of activities in the state. In addition to the centers for vocational training, SENAC supports vocational training within firms, such as hotels, restaurants, gas stations, and beauty salons. There is a program of continuing education for those who have full-time jobs. SENAC also has mobile units providing health facilities and beauty salons.[2] Some of SENAC's hotel schools have become so well known that they now constitute obligatory points for tourists to visit, as is the case of the school in Salvador. In Paraiba SENAC trained 21,000 students in 1987. In a state with an unemployment rate estimated at 26.6 percent, a large majority of the students find in SENAC a possibility for employment. SENAC, however, rarely finds jobs for its graduates in the local firms.

In order to attend to the so-called marginal population—illiterates and those who live in very poor conditions—SENAC has developed courses in crafts using coconut straw, the production of homemade chairs, and the like. But this appears to be just a way to mask the existing unemployment because of the low price this type of handicraft commands in the market; the misery of the artisans will remain unchanged after the training. By helping them to improve their way of working, SENAC is in no way helping to solve the problem of unemployment in the state.[3]

An analysis of the composition of SENAC's student body in the nine northeastern states shows that in 1986 70 percent of the students were in the 14–24 age span. Most of them were single (more than 80 percent) and unemployed (75 percent) (SENAC, 1986, pp. 52–53). The level of education varies according to the type of program they are engaged in.[4] Overall, 2.7 percent had a university diploma, 38.4 percent a high school diploma, and almost 40 percent either complete primary school or incomplete secondary school. Only 20 percent had less than eight years of schooling (SENAC, 1986, pp. 54). Thus, SENAC's students are well above the average level of education of the northeastern labor force. This fact supports the assertion that in the northeast the workers in the service sector are more highly educated than their counterparts in the other sectors of the economy.

SENAC's staff also has a high concentration of women. In João Pessoa's Center for Vocational Training, women hold high administrative positions. For example, the heads of the two divisions directly under the regional director are women (but not the director). Both women have degrees in education complemented by several on-the-job training experiences. The salaries at SENAC are low, but, as with most SENAC employees, the director of professional training continues to work there in spite of the low salary because, as she states, the work is interesting, employees have many opportunities for training, and they often travel.

I asked this director how she manages with her low salary. She responded that her salary is very good for a woman, but she could not live on it alone. Fortunately, she is married to the director of the state agency, who earns a salary sufficient to meet the family's needs. In her opinion, the low salaries explain why most of the personnel at SENAC are female. All of the men who work in the institute have other jobs or economic activity. She stated:

> Women are very much discriminated against in this state. I've never seen a woman manager in a service sector firm. If this were to happen, I'm sure it would be in a family firm, where the owner is the husband. In the secondary sector it is even worse. Women get jobs only as secretaries or workers. There is a tremendous inequality between "jobs for men" and "jobs for women." In the state administration there is only one woman in the highest level, the secretary of welfare.

Later interviews confirmed this pattern. A typing teacher reported earning two minimum salaries (US $120). She would be unable to live on that money, but she lives with her mother who has a fashionable boutique. When asked why she did not get a better-paying job, she answered that she loved her job at SENAC, she was respected, and she had many opportunities for training. She recently finished a course in word processing and is planning to move into that field in the future.

The interview with the coordinator of the computer department further confirmed the low salaries. While he worked part-time at SENAC, he attended his 300-hectare sugarcane plantation. His wife also worked as the financial director of a firm. When asked how SENAC maintains the good quality of teaching in the area of computer programming despite the low salaries, he responded that most of the professors in the department were not full-time teachers. SENAC often hires distinguished professionals in a given field to teach just one course.

SENAC's salaries are low and do not guarantee a decent standard of living for a family. No one would consider them acceptable for a man. If male professional services are needed, they are hired with the deficient wages kept in mind. That is why only part-time or specific services are required from most male professionals.

In the case of women, it is implicitly understood that they are not entitled to better salaries; SENAC offers a "good salary for a woman" (whatever that may mean) and requires full-time dedication to the job. Another assumption is the woman's dependence on another source of income, from either the husband or parents. Work, even full-time, does not mean financial independence for a woman. I inferred that this would also be the dominant ideology among Paraiban employers.

▲ The Study

The study I undertook aims to discover the existence of discriminatory mechanisms that contribute to the reproduction of the sexual division of labor in northeastern Brazil. It attempts to discover how and to what extent these discriminatory mechanisms are present in vocational schools. A main objective is to find out how social and labor expectations of administrators, teachers, and staff act as a barrier to the success of women with vocational training in nontraditional fields. This research was done in the Center for Professional Training in João Pessoa and is based on extensive interviews conducted over a period of five months (November 1987–March 1988) with students and staff at the SENAC vocational school in João Pessoa. During this period I interviewed staff, teachers, and graduates from the computer programming courses. For more information on the methodology, see the appendix at the end of this chapter.

In my first visit I met the regional director, who offered all the necessary information as well as introduced me to the main administrative personnel. He also gave me a tour around the center. The center has functioned since 1974 in a pleasant four-story brick building, located in the commercial center of João Pessoa. On the first floor are two "firms," as the Director called them, and the Data Center. Around the interior garden, full of blooming trees, is a restaurant with several small tables and chairs spread around the patio. It offers hamburgers, hot dogs, and fruit juices at very reasonable prices and is managed and served by SENAC's students. To the left, there is a shop offering regional crafts, also managed by students. Toward the back of the patio is the Department of Computer Science. It basically consists of three rooms: a noisy office, where secretaries attend to the public and where professors and students meet; the computer laboratory, where several boys were working; and an air-conditioned classroom, where I did some of my interviewing. On the second floor are the infirmary, the typing classes, and two large rooms crowded with tables, manual typewriters, and about fifty girls working in each room. I was informed that because of the great demand, there are typing classes at practically any hour of the day.

Also on the second floor is a beauty salon, where several women were getting their hair done, while others were getting manicures. I saw very few men on the second floor. The beauty salon was functioning in temporary facilities because half of the next floor was being remodeled for that purpose. I visited the new salon, and even though it was still unfinished, it seemed to be quite a sophisticated project. I finally visited the upper floor where the administration functions. The offices were small but well equipped.

From the first observation, plus the analysis of SENAC's documents and later interviews, it appears clearly that the separation of areas of specialization brings together a situation of segmentation of knowledge associated with class and gender stratification. Courses like hygiene and beauty, health, restaurant operation, and communication require a minimum of formal education and attract the more modest students. In contrast, areas such as management or computer science have higher educational prerequisites and attract students of higher socioeconomic levels.

I also observed sex segregation among the areas. SENAC's student body is composed overwhelmingly of women, and the men seem to concentrate in two areas: management and administration and computer science. Surprisingly, according to the statistics, the number of men and women is equal in these areas. In 1985 management and administration courses had 1,500 women students and the same number of men. Computer science had 40 men and 45 women. However, the interviews and the observation in the center reveal that it is difficult to find a woman working in computers, and males constituted the majority of students in these courses. Exactly the opposite can be said of areas like hygiene and beauty, where hardly a man can be seen, even though the 1985 enrollment statistics show 1,150 women students and 42 men.

SENAC's pattern of sex segregation by area of specialization can be analyzed from a double perspective, the first of which is fragmentation of knowledge. According to MacDonald, the stratification of knowledge reproduces the hierarchy of male over female, with particular school subjects and disciplines classified as "masculine" or "feminine." This separation contributes to the acceptance by the students of the sexual division within the labor force (MacDonald, 1980, p. 21). The second perspective deals with segregation of subject matter and staff. Research results show that the concentration of female teaching staff in some fields parallels women's participation patterns in the work force. Subjects taught predominantly by women correspond to occupations in which the representation of women is disproportionately high. The gender of a teacher in a subject that tends to be sex-segregated may well implicitly tell the students that the particular subject matter is legitimate knowledge for one sex rather than for both sexes (Kelly and Nihlen, 1982, p. 169).

It is possible, therefore, to understand SENAC's internal organization as preparing the students for different levels within the occupational structure; indeed, given the sharp sex segregation, an initial impression might be that SENAC is contributing to the reproduction of the inequality of the sexes in the labor market (assuming that SENAC's courses act as a screening device to allocate individuals to different positions in the occupational structure).

It is not by chance that "feminine" areas are also the more modest prospects in the labor market and the ones with less job mobility (e.g., health and beauty worker, phone and telex operator). Males, however, show preference for areas such as administration and management or computer science, areas traditionally considered "masculine." The fact that they have, according to SENAC's statistics, equal numbers of men and women as students is interesting—even more so because these fields represent potential avenues for women's occupational improvement. Though it is true that women do have a chance to enter these courses, the fact that they are seldom seen in the computer laboratory raises doubts that once enrolled in the course they are equally encouraged and taken as seriously as the males who are also taking the course. Research results analyzed later suggest that school can discriminate against women in subtle ways.

These facts lead to further exploration of some cases of women who abandon the "appropriate" channels of entrance into the labor market and try to enter traditionally all-male fields. These women have escaped the message of the school in terms of sex roles. As some authors point out, some women "slip through the cracks of socialization." How many and at what cost are still open issues. But they are important questions because they show an attempt by women to resist very real oppression (Kelly and Nihlen, 1982, p. 176). It has also been found that this is not an easy road—these women have to confront many obstacles.

Schools can resist attempts to change through several mechanisms, from open resistance (Keil and Newton, 1980, p. 106) to "hidden" forms. For example, certain knowledge may be denied to women in the classroom in subtle ways, such as teachers not taking female students seriously or their academic performance being systematically devalued (Kelly and Nihlen, 1982,

p. 173). These studies suggest that even if women are in the same classroom with men, there is a manipulation in the distribution of knowledge that will later result in different achievement between male and female students. A study to test these assumptions will require a methodology different from the one employed here, because students will likely be unaware of these manipulations. Interviews will prove an inefficient instrument for this purpose and are suggested for a later stage. This study attempts to determine only who the women in computer science are, what aspirations they have in terms of family and job future, and what kinds of experiences they are encountering in the job market. The area of computer science was selected for study because it is a relatively new field and offers a good future in the job market.

According to the coordinator of computer training, the profession of "programmer" in Brazil is quite new. It was only ten years ago that the use of microcomputers for personal and professional tasks became widespread. In João Pessoa the number of these professionals is barely more than 100, among them a few women, not over 15 percent. The salary prospects are exceptional by João Pessoa's standards: between five and ten minimum salaries (US $300 to $600) plus fringe benefits. (Less than five minimum salaries is considered low, over ten very good.)

Salaries vary depending on the firm. The southern and multinational firms offer the best salaries and working conditions; local firms, with managers who do not even know exactly how the use of the computer can help their firms, tend to pay lower salaries. In some cases these managers buy the best equipment but hire a programmer at a low salary. They think the equipment by itself will solve all the problems. At the same time, they make unrealistic demands. Often they do not value the professionals—that is why they pay very little. In other cases the manager knows the value of the professional, but does not have the resources to pay the person a decent salary. SENAC does not interfere with employers' decisions and leaves space for open negotiation between the firm and the SENAC graduate.

The types of local firms that are adopting the use of computers in João Pessoa are those in the textile, garment, food processing, and construction industries. The coordinator estimates that of the firms that use computers, 40 percent are in commerce, 30 percent in industry, 15 percent in liberal professions, and the rest in rural firms.

I asked the coordinator whether firms request more men than women professionals; he assured me they do not. He could enumerate several times when he recommended women and remembered the case of a multinational firm hiring a woman now being trained in Germany. In spite of these assurances, I discovered that he was having difficulty finding a woman programmer employed that I could interview, though he could easily find unemployed women graduates. He recognized that some of the firms were "machista" in that they preferred male to female professionals.

When I asked about the great number of unemployed women graduates in computer science, he blamed the students for this situation. He mentioned some cases in which women were offered jobs and declined for lack of time because they were attending college. They were said to prefer a degree to a job.

He spoke still of another problem—women who graduate from SENAC's courses are very young (18–20 years old). "It is hard to tell what their future will be," he said. He apparently was referring to the widespread expectation that when women marry, they will give priority to the home and children. He recalled his experience: Of those who graduated with him, the men had good careers; the women married and had children and remained in the position they started. Others went to public service where "you do not have to do much." (This is a rather widespread view of public service in João Pessoa.) Unfortunately, what the coordinator was saying is confirmed by research in other countries. Chisholm and Woodward state that in order to achieve the salaries of even the lowest-paid of their male peers in professional occupations, women should enter teaching or another of the public-service professions (1980, p. 167). Keil and Newton report that employers tend to recruit personnel according to well-established categories of work "which had long been recognized as appropriate for men or women." On the other hand, "open" recruitment is found in the bureaucracies of local and central governments, and the achievement of formal educational qualifications rather than "traditional managerial practice" is used to distinguish among potential recruits (Keil and Newton, 1980, p. 102). Carnoy and Levin show the state's tendency to employ college graduates, especially minority males and women. Government jobs pay blacks and women more than the private sector does for similar jobs. "The state sector, therefore, provides opportunities for minorities and women that the private sector is apparently not willing or able to provide" (Carnoy and Levin, 1985, p. 60). These authors also show the importance of the union movement in determining state policies.

In northeastern Brazil, however, the situation appears quite different. It is true that women have more opportunities in the public sector and are able to find permanent jobs. But the recruitment, especially at the state and the local levels, is made by considering not academic qualifications but rather the candidate's links with influential local politicians. The same can be said about promotions. Therefore, salaries are low and barely correlated to the employee's academic qualifications, which explains why employment in the public sector, except at the federal level, has low prestige.

As for the employers, the coordinator of the computer science department acknowledged that many of them do not want to hire women; reportedly, employers do not want problems associated with pregnancies. However, recruitment for word processors (*digitadoras*) is aimed at women. They are employed mainly in offices of doctors or lawyers and are in contact with the public. Employers make specific demands that the word processor have a good appearance.

This is not the case with programming, a new profession that still has to prove its utility to the private sector. Needed in this field are competent, aggressive professionals, able to show the managers that they are good and necessary for their firms. Employers prefer men as programmers. Coincidentally, programmers earn the best salaries. I concluded that the coordinator was implicitly defining the most prestigious section of the area of computer science as a "masculine" area. Women find opportunities in word processing. After all, they are hired mainly for their looks and not so much for intellectual capacity.

Employers' preference for hiring women for their appearance and attitudes and men for their qualifications has already been reported in the literature (Keil and Newton, 1980, p. 101). Obviously, employers hire according to the common wisdom about what is a proper job for a man or a woman. It is difficult to expect SENAC to struggle for greater democratization of job opportunities because the institution is directly dependent on the employers and shares their ideology.

The coordinator analyzed the case of some of the women who graduated during the term he held this position and concluded that they did not progress as far as the men did. He was reluctant to probe deeper to find the reasons that this happened or to discuss how the situation could be changed. He simply accepted the fact probably because it confirmed his own ideas on the subject.

He had still another important argument: This is the way the employers have defined things. And obviously he is not willing—or is not in the position—to argue about this. He simply did not expect women in computer programming to do very well, nor to be well accepted by future employers.

This idea is also shared by the other teachers, and some effects may be widespread. The effect of teacher expectations and the concomitant behaviors has been extensively studied. It translates into more attention by the teacher, more academic contacts, and more support and encouragement to some students and not to others. In the case of computer science, the men would be "privileged"; women's academic performance would be devalued—women would be less encouraged and not taken seriously. The results are easily predicted, and the literature shows enough evidence to expect significant differences in academic performance, in spite of equality in initial abilities (Finn, Reis, and Dulberg, 1982, pp. 121–125; Kelly and Nihlen, 1982, pp. 173–174).

In the case of SENAC, the academic results are very important because they influence students' attitudes toward occupational roles and the job market. Whether students feel valued or unworthy will greatly determine their level of occupational aspiration, type of job, and wage level they will feel entitled to. Furthermore, given the scarcity of jobs available, a good recommendation by SENAC has undeniable importance in getting a reasonable job, unless the job seeker can get a position in the father's or husband's firm, as many professional women do in this area.

In order to get some insights about who the graduates from the computer science courses are and what their experiences in the job market have been, four students were interviewed in depth. It can hardly be said that conclusions can be generalized from so small and unrepresentative a sample (that was not the objective of this pilot study), but some important insights can be drawn to guide other more representative studies.

The "sample" is composed of three women and one man, all about twenty years old. The man interviewed served as a kind of "control," so that factors characteristic of João Pessoa's labor market are taken into account because they affect male and female workers equally. He was at the time unemployed.

The case of the women is especially important because by choosing computer science, they had abandoned the "appropriate" channels of women's entrance into the labor market and were entering a field defined as "masculine." They had escaped the school's message about sex roles and were trying a new path. Of the three women interviewed, one was unemployed, another would probably be unemployed in the near future, and the third was employed at SENAC as a typing teacher.

Getting into computer science is not easy. Candidates have to confront stiff competition. According to the coordinator, 1,000 candidates compete for 45 places. They have to go through a test to measure logical abilities that leaves only 70 candidates. In the second stage they take a one-week course in programming, and 45 are selected based on the results. For women, the competition is even stiffer. They represent 50 percent of the initial candidates but only 35 percent of the final group. This, then, is enough proof of the abilities of the women interviewed. They were able not only to enter the course but also to finish it successfully.

Case 1: Severina

Severina, a young woman of nineteen, finished the course in April 1987. Since then she has been looking for a job.

Severina comes from a rich, traditional family of landowners. She has four sisters and two brothers. She graduated from a prestigious private high school in João Pessoa and considered herself a reasonably good student in school. Her mother, now sick and retired, was the director of a primary school in the small traditional city where they lived, and where her parents still live. Her mother has always been very active in church and community activities; even now that she is sick, her current project is a retirement home for poor elderly people. Severina identifies very much with her mother, but apparently resents her father, a possessive man. She defies him by smoking and drinking, behavior he will never accept, even more so because he does neither.

Severina lives in João Pessoa with two sisters and a younger brother. The older sister is thirty-two and single, and Severina stated that after her boyfriend died in 1979, her sister never had another. Severina is different. She likes parties, dancing, beaches, and going out with her boyfriend. This behavior is not accepted by the older sister or even the younger sister, who is studying to be a nurse (she warns Severina about AIDS). Severina resents this excessive control, while her brother (age fifteen) can do as he wishes.

Severina wanted to get into business administration but failed. She got a job in a small boutique where she was heavily exploited by the owner and earned less than a minimum salary (US $60). She heard of the computer course from her boss, and because she was tired of her job, she decided to try. She was admitted and now she is a programmer in three languages: COBOL, Dbase, and BASIC. She tried to find a job in the local firms and went from one disappointment to the next: "I tried to find a job. I'm a programmer. But when you get there they offer you a position as word processor (*digitadora*) with one minimum salary or less. I don't know. They should think I'm not able. It's very difficult to find a job here in Paraiba. In one firm they offered me a three-month test. No pay. Only the money for transportation. They want to test my capacity as a *digitadora*. If they like me they will pay a minimum salary. A man is proud, he wouldn't accept. A woman needs it and she will accept."

Was this a common complaint of women graduates in data processing?

"Yes, I have a friend who also graduated and she is having the same difficulties."

What do you think is the main problem?

"It's because of the age [nineteen] and because I'm a woman. And also because in Paraiba you only get a job through the politicians. This week they hired a boy in the Bank of Paraiba and he did not know anything about computer programming. He came to SENAC for training, because he already has the job."

If the course is worth so little, why do you invest so much in your training? Isn't it easier to get a "godfather"?[5]

"I don't like that. Here in Paraiba the party in power gets its members employed. When it goes to the opposition, they all lose their jobs. I want to be good and get a job because I'm qualified."

I ask if she plans to marry and have children and how she will combine that with a job. She answers she wants to have a house and children but not yet. "João Pessoa is good, but it doesn't have places where you can have a good time." She would like to live in a large city, like Rio de Janeiro. She and her boyfriend have been together for only a month, but he is making plans for the future. He imagines their life together: running on the beach early in the morning, going together to work, picking her up for lunch, and then going to work together again in the afternoon. He agrees that she should work and is helping her to find a job.

Should the husband help with the house chores?

"I have an uncle. His wife is so bossy. I don't think a woman should be like that."

How do you define the role of husband and the role of wife?

"I think the wife should work outside the house but should also be a housewife. The husband has the duty to provide enough for the family. I don't think I have the right to be with my friends chatting and laughing while the husband takes care of the house chores. I wouldn't dream of my mother making my father clean the house, change diapers, or wash panties. That's absurd. The man has his position, the woman has hers. My father has ten people to provide for in his house, and he also helps us here [in João Pessoa]. He has too many responsibilities. Why should he do the things that are for the mother, daughters, and maids to do?"

How are the house responsibilities divided?

"We have a maid who is in charge of everything, like a housekeeper. And also a woman who comes to do the laundry every week."

Severina does not want to be confined to the traditional mother/wife role. She wants to have more opportunities and live a little before taking on the heavy responsibilities of a married woman. She had worked hard in her training but had not had any success in her attempts to find a job. She is not taken seriously as a professional programmer and is offered jobs below her actual capacity. After all, when an "unusual" job choice is made, new "rules of the game" have to be discovered. Women in computer programming are a challenge to male dominance in this field and thus confront the ideologies and structures of the traditional division of labor. A similar case is reported by Keil and Newton when women are trained as engineering technicians (1980, pp. 98–112).

Severina sees the situation as unfair, but when asked what the roles of the husband and wife should be, it becomes very clear that she is not intending to be the main supporter in her house or to have financial independence. She defines the role of husband as provider, quite a traditional view, and therefore I assumed she would accept that jobs be denied to her and given to a man with the same qualifications. After all, the man really needs the salary to support the family.

The main supporter of the house where Severina lives in João Pessoa with her siblings is her older sister, a psychiatrist at the University Medical Center. She earns a good salary and supports the house, with some help from the father. Somehow Severina finds it improbable that she will be faced with a similar situation, and she is certain she will find a husband who will provide for her future home. By passing the responsibility to provide for her house to a probable husband, Severina becomes an accomplice of those who deny her the job she deserves. In this position she is unable to do something to change things.

A similar attitude was observed in the director of professional training. She considers her salary "good for a woman," even if by all standards it is low. The same was observed when the typing teacher was interviewed. She earns two minimum salaries, but is happy with the job because she is respected and has good opportunities for further training.

None of these women feels entitled to a salary that can guarantee her economic independence. Even if she has a full-time job, it is understood that she must depend either on the husband or on the parents. After all, it is the man's obligation to provide for the home, not the woman's.

Case 2: Rina

Rina (age twenty), as Severina, is an attractive girl. She looks serious, responsible. Her father works in a large national construction firm. During her childhood, the father was frequently transferred, though only to cities close to João Pessoa. She has two sisters (twenty-one and sixteen). Rina has a happy family—the father works and the mother stays home, looking after the home and the children. Rina complains that her mother is overprotective. Rina and her sisters could not go unaccompanied to school until after age fifteen. The father will not let them go out except with friends or relatives he trusts, and never to sleep over at a friend's house. He also forbids them to dress in what he considers "inappropriate clothes"—shorts, for example. In spite of all that, she considers her father an extremely sweet person. He hugs and kisses them frequently. She receives a lot of encouragement from both parents to excel academically. Some studies show that this is an important factor of success (Fuller, 1980, pp. 60-62). I asked her if the father helps at home. "Yes. He loves cooking. But cleaning he did only before the children were born. Now, with three girls at home, it is their job. And the three divide the tasks with their mother."

Rina finished high school at a prestigious high school in João Pessoa. She went into training for almost a year, taking several courses to be an executive secretary. After that, she looked for a job for about a year without success. Finally, she was hired by SENAC to teach typing temporarily because of a shortage of teachers. Each time, she signs a three-month contract. Now, she is finishing the second renewal and is afraid of becoming unemployed again.

In order to find a job, she was trained in word processing. It looked as if this course would widen her chances for employment. But again, she was not successful. Two of her colleagues did find a job. They were men. "It is the firm that chooses and most of them want men."

Now she wants to go back to school because she cannot find a job. She wants to try law school this year, having applied to business administration last year and failed.

Are you thinking of marriage?
"Not yet. Probably in four, five, six, seven years from now."

Your boyfriend wants to get married?
"Yes, and he has a good job, but I have my plans."

What if you get pregnant, would you marry immediately?
"If that happened, it's because I'm aware of the consequences. I don't want my boyfriend to be responsible. I alone would have to be strong and financially independent, because I would have to face my family. My family wouldn't accept it, especially my mother."

Are you planning to leave your job after marriage?
"I've struggled so much to get a job, I would never give it up."

What about the children? Wouldn't they be a problem?
"No. I think I can manage work, house, and children."

Your boyfriend agrees?
"He encourages me to work and is worried because my contract finishes soon."

If you marry, how would you like your marriage to be?
"The ideal solution is when both work. It is terrible to have to depend on somebody. You see, when I don't work, I have to depend on my father. When both work, there is no problem. Whereas when the husband works, the wife will ask for money. The husband may say he doesn't have it. She won't believe him and they will fight."

Are you planning to share the house chores with your husband?
"Both should help. Some men learn to do everything. I have a cousin who washes dishes, helps with the laundry. He can do anything. But I think it's better if both help. Most men say they don't know how to do things. They are afraid to look bad in front of their friends, to be criticized by society. The man wants to be the one to give orders, not to do things, even less, women's tasks. Let women do them, and if a husband helps, the friends will laugh at him and make him fight with the wife."

Have you tried to find a job through SENAC?
"Yes, but it is very difficult. They have fifteen people for each position and they have recommendations. Another problem is that the employers require experience. How can you get experience if you never get a chance to get that experience?"

This is a frequent complaint among young people looking for their first job. It appeared in the interview with Carlos, the young male. In the literature it appears as a problem frequently faced by young people entering the labor market in other countries as well.

Would you like to find a job paying 10,000 cruzados [US $100 at that time]? [The salary for a programmer in João Pessoa should be between US $300 and US $600.]
"How much? That would be like a dream."

Rina has struggled to find a job and could only get a temporary position at SENAC. She does not seem to resent the fact that her male colleagues are preferred by the firms. She is ready to struggle for a job—a job that can guarantee her financial independence. She is firm about the fact that she is not happy depending on someone, not even her father with whom she has a good relationship. She also does not seem to resent the restricted life she has had with her oppressive parents. Actually, the parents' attitudes are not unusual among the traditional families of the area. But perhaps her desire for financial independence is a form of resistance to the family or her future husband's oppression.

Her salary aspirations do not correspond to her goals, but this can be attributed to lack of experience. She says she does not expect the husband to be her financial support. She seems to have a less traditional view of what the role of wife or husband should be. Her conception of the division of labor in the house and in providing for the family seems democratic, quite the contrary of what she has experienced in her traditional family.

If she does not find a job, she will return to school. Instead of just waiting for the improbable job, she tries to get more training. This can be seen as positive as long as it does not turn into a strategy for survival. Studies, in this case, are not a way to get the training necessary for a job; they become a job in themselves. This is a fact that also caught my attention in other interviews. The lack of jobs leads young people into an unending pursuit of courses and degrees.

Case 3: Maria

Maria is twenty-one and lives with her mother, who is divorced and the owner of a successful atelier for upper-class João Pessoa women. Maria was hired at SENAC as a typing instructor and teaches three classes every day. Her last salary increase brought her pay to two minimum salaries a month (US $120). She likes her job, even if it does not pay enough, because she feels independent and respected and has the chance to work in a prestigious place. She finished a course in computer science with the hope that it might help in her profession. She does not have high ambitions: "I have my job, my house, my family. All Brazilians are like that. When you have something, you are afraid to leave what you have and start for an uncertain life. But I have ambitions, since I'm getting into computer science. I think that it is a better profession than the one I have. But I will not leave SENAC, not unless something much better appears and only if I can do something that I really like. But to go out of SENAC and stay in the same situation—that I will not do."

Are you thinking of college?

"I tried two times to get into business administration, but I did not succeed. I had not studied very much. I was in a *cursinho* [a program preparing for the university entrance exam] and I had to stop because I was teaching every day until 3:00 p.m. Then I had the word processing course until 5:30. I attended the *cursinho* from 6:00 to 10:30. The next day I was tired and I could not teach, so I would sleep in the classroom. I was always in a bad mood, so I decided to stop."

Do you think that computer science is a profession "appropriate" for a woman?

"I do not think there are professions for women and professions for men. What I like in SENAC is that most of the staff is composed by women. I think it is because of the low salaries. But women can live with low salaries. I mean, lower than the men's. The man is the supporter, and if the wife does not work he should have a higher salary. But here [at SENAC] the administrative director is a woman. And she is very respected. She is a very dynamic person, and I like her work very much. And many men are subordinated to her. I mean, they are professionally subordinated to her. I think it is good because she manages everything, and in most firms it is very difficult for them to hire a woman manager and for her to do the job right. It is very difficult."

If you stay at SENAC, do you have a chance to become the administrative director?

"I do not think so. Here at SENAC they do not let you get higher. If you are an instructor, you will be an instructor for the rest of your life. I have been here for eighteen months, and I have not seen anybody being promoted."

But you know the case of Ana, she started as supervisor and now is the director of professional training.

"Yes, but that was a long time ago. She really started as a supervisor, then she went to Human Resources and now she is a director. And I think there are other cases, too. You know, Pedro [the coordinator of the computer science department] is always asking me if I would really leave typing to get into computer science. I always answer that if it is better for me, I would do it. But if I go to computer science, I will still be an instructor."

You talked about your boyfriend, Julio, who is the head of one of the administrative sections at SENAC. Would he mind if you had a more important position than his?

"I really was not prepared for that question. I do not know how he would feel, men are always machista. Perhaps there would not be any problem."

Maria has traditional ideas with respect to male and female roles. The husband is the provider and is, therefore, entitled to better salaries than the woman. Like Severina, Maria shares the views of those who think it is appropriate to pay low salaries to women.

Maria does not show much confidence in women's capabilities to do well in high managerial jobs. As she put it, "Not many firms will hire a woman manager, and it is difficult for her to do the job right." This fact would explain why Maria is not taking her own profession seriously. In spite of her full day, she is not clearly decided as to what course of action would really lead her to professional success. She tried to get into college, but she did not undertake serious preparation for it and so failed twice. Unfortunately, this can seriously undermine her self-confidence. Maybe she is trying to prove to herself and to others her lack of ability. She tried the computer course, but she is afraid that the change of departments at SENAC will not improve her position because she will continue to be an instructor with a low salary. Her only way out of this situation is to find the husband-provider. Until then she seems to be planning to live with her mother. The successful professional women around her, including her own mother, do not seem to influence her ideas.

Case 4: Carlos

Carlos, age twenty-two, was born in Rio de Janeiro, the eldest son of a navy officer who was transferred to João Pessoa a short time ago. At that time Carlos had just finished vocational secondary school. He lives with his parents and two brothers. The mother does not work outside the home.

Carlos entered computer science because he thinks it will be easier to find a job with this diploma. He finished the course a month ago, but he is still unemployed. He offered his services to at least ten firms (public and private), but after filling out a form and talking with people from personnel, he was asked to wait for an opportunity. He was called by a large food industry firm, but was offered only a minimum salary. He did not accept. In a textile firm he was given a test and passed it, but is still waiting for a chance. He thinks the job market in João Pessoa is limited. Employers complain because the applicants do not have experience, but they do not give them the chance to acquire it. Carlos has already discussed the problem with some employers. The answer was that because they are late with their production quotas, they have no time to train anybody; they want somebody to do the job now. Carlos has finished other courses, including mechanical design, bank teller, typing, and accounting. He thinks that an administrative position would be good for him because he has all the training in that area, but if it is necessary, he can take a job in another area. He just wants a job with good prospects for the future. He does not mind starting in a low position as long as it leads to a better one.

Carlos's attitude about a job seems very different from that of Maria. Maria is not concerned about the future or the possibility of getting a promotion. She is happy with her job at SENAC because it is a prestigious place where she is respected. But she acknowledges that there is no future in that job. She says that she has never seen someone promoted during the eighteen months she has worked at SENAC. In my opinion, she is underestimating the possibilities of promotion at SENAC. But the important point is that her future job possibilities make no difference to her. She is not concerned about making a career, and this is decisive for her future possibilities. For Carlos it is exactly the opposite. It does not matter where he starts as long as the job has a future.

Do you talk to your parents about your difficulties in finding a job?
"Oh yes, I talk a lot. They have both tried to help me by talking to their friends, but they were not successful. They say that while I do not find a job, I should improve my résumé, and that's why I should continue to study."

The problem of youngsters getting into one course after another was already discussed. In Carlos's case, the parents encourage this behavior. They consider that while he is studying, and if they can support him, he should not take just any job. Studying becomes a profession.

Carlos also comments that half of his friends are also unemployed. The ones who have jobs are mainly those who studied education and are teaching. Carlos thinks that the problems of the job market result in part from the legal rights of employees. Employers do not want to give employees all those advantages. For example, when an employee has a certain seniority in the firm and wants a better salary, the manager fires the employee and hires somebody at a lower salary. Carlos thinks this is wrong.

Workers' legal rights were greatly extended in the new Brazilian constitution. For example, the three-month paid maternity leave was extended to four months. It was also complemented with an eight-day paternity leave, so that the new father can take care of the wife and newborn baby. The right to strike was extended to more categories of workers, including those in public service. Unemployment compensations were improved and the time of work necessary for retirement was reduced for teachers. All these new requirements and many others have created a strong reaction in employers who do not want to comply with the law and are getting rid of women workers in great numbers.

How many women were in the word processing course where you studied?
"Only three girls. One for every ten men."

You think they have a good chance to find a job?

"I think a man has a better chance to find a job, to earn a better salary, and to be promoted in the job. Besides, I see more men in the area."

Carlos's views about his women peers' chances in the job market show a negative stereotyping with respect to women in computer science. Fuller, in her article on West Indian black girls, reported that during the interviews most of the girls said they thought boys considered themselves superior to girls. Boys wanted to be the bosses and have women do the work; women were perceived as inferior. Fuller reports the girls in the sample were skeptical or amused by this view (Fuller, 1980, p. 60).

With respect to his career aspirations, Carlos would like to find a job, an administrative position, that would pay enough to support a family. When asked how much he estimates he should earn, he says "around 50,000 cruzados" (US $500). That represents a reasonable to high salary for a programmer, but too high for those who graduated in word processing. He is aware of this fact. He thinks that with his level of education it is quite difficult to fulfill his aspirations. He thinks that in order to achieve that level of salary he should have a university diploma, but he failed in the university entrance exam. He also says that he tried to stay in the navy after his military service, but he did not pass in the area he wanted: electronics. He passed for radar operations, but he did not want to stay for this. Now he regrets his decision, because the navy is a good place and jobs there have stability.

In terms of personal life, Carlos likes João Pessoa. It is a nice, quiet city. He thinks he could have better chances in Rio de Janeiro, where he has some relatives, but he likes the life here better. For the time being, he is not planning to look for a job in another place. He has a girlfriend, but he is not planning to marry in the near future. First he wants to have a house and furniture. Living with his parents is no problem for him. He can go out anytime during the day or night. He has no sisters, but if he had one, he would be protective of her.

What about the girls you meet?

"Some have to be home by midnight. Others stay at parties well after I leave."

What do you think about that?

"I do not agree. Women should be more responsible and be home early. I take my girlfriend home early, and sometimes I go out later with my friends."

Carlos has clear ideas of what his responsibilities will be after he marries and is in no hurry to get into that kind of commitment. He also has clear ideas about the job market, workers' rights, and employers' views. He has had chances to get a job, but because he has no urgent need, he is waiting for a better offer. At twenty-two, he still depends on his parents and is counting on their help to get a good job. He is not very ambitious in terms of a career and only desires a job he likes and one that will allow him to have a salary high enough to support his family.

He declared he wants a job with a good future, but his salary aspirations are not very high. He also does not seem to be seriously interested in a college diploma. Even if he is not very motivated to get a job and is less qualified than Severina, he has received better job offers than she. The fact that he is a man probably helps.

Both Carlos and the women in the sample are suffering from the restricted opportunities of the job market in João Pessoa. Yet he seems much less affected by it than the women. He is content depending on his parents, but the women want their financial independence badly, even if they do not believe that a job will guarantee this.

What clearly distinguishes Carlos from the women is that he knows for sure that when the time comes to have family responsibilities, he will have to rely on his job to provide for these. That is why he wants a job with a future, no matter where he starts now. In the meantime, he is happy to live with his parents and not to have such responsibilities.

The women, in contrast, have an ambiguous attitude toward their career. They want a job, they want their money now, but they do not see themselves as taking the complete financial responsibility for a home. They count on the husband-provider. That is why they are not taking their profession as seriously as they could and why they agree to receive salaries under their capacity. At least this is what was observed in two cases out of three. Of course, a much larger sample will be necessary to confirm these detected patterns.

▲ Conclusion

From the interviews, several facts become apparent: First, none of those interviewed is in a position to support himself or herself. They all belong to families with reasonable resources that can support them. They are all satisfied with their families. Only Severina feels controlled and dreams of a more exciting life. This small sample of the computer science graduates shows that they are not poor students in search of a chance to improve their condition. They seem to come from families at the medium to high socioeconomic level.

Second, they are all intelligent and receive strong support from their families to achieve academically. In two cases the mother is a strong model of success (one with and one without a husband); the other two have traditional mothers. But all the families are strongly motivated. Thus, in spite of the community values and school expectations that push women toward traditional feminine roles (strong in this very traditional city), these students come from homes that encourage them to strive for educational achievement.

Third, they are all aware of the problems of the job market in João Pessoa. But they have happy families and good friends, the place is lovely, and they do not have the need (or the drive) to go elsewhere to find a job.

Fourth, they all dream of going to the university. They think a degree can guarantee them a job. They keep looking for a job, but when they do not find one, they continue to apply to the university and take one course after the other.

The study suggests that for such unemployed youth, taking courses is a strategy of survival and not just training for a job. They study, instead of working, because the opportunities in the area are so limited. I have had the same experience with the university students. It is frequent to see bright students taking two programs at the same time: engineering and administration, or medicine and law. Instead of getting engaged in the labor market, even in temporary positions, they continue to expand their training even to unreasonable limits. Their awareness of the lack of job opportunities leads them to make an exhaustive use of the good educational opportunities the area has to offer. It is no wonder Brasilia is full of northeastern intellectuals. Once more, this region's role in the national economy seems to be only to contribute a large reserve army of labor.

Fifth, the women interviewed plan to marry and have children, but not one of them is planning to leave her job after marriage, not even while her children are young. As Rina says: "I've struggled too much to get a job. I would never give it up." They are aware of the subordinate role women have in a traditional region like northeastern Brazil, but at the same time they will not accept this subordination for themselves. Their strategy for survival includes acquiring qualifications (one course after the other) and pursuing a job that they will not easily give up, certainly not for marriage and children. I consider these aspirations unrealistic. Husbands refuse to cooperate with the working wife in most cases and construct all sorts of obstacles to the woman's professional development. The husband will not forbid the woman to go to work—but only because he values her financial contribution.

Sixth, in spite of the strong determination of these women to work, employers still hold traditional attitudes about women. The coordinator of the area remarks: "Women who graduate from computer science are very young, and it is hard to tell what their future will be." It is implicit that they will marry and have children, but they do not expect that to make any difference in their career. There are many examples of this possibility. In SENAC some women in important positions are married and have children, but for these women to accomplish their goal, they have to rely on maids. And this fact creates another dilemma for the working woman. Because she cannot count on the husband's help, the maid—usually an illiterate rural migrant—becomes a key element in the working woman's life. She has to entrust the house and her young children to the maid with all the risks this entails. Nursery schools are expensive, and the woman's salary will not always permit full-time specialized care for her children. Therefore, these women have to rely on the cheapest available labor. Maids are badly exploited, but in turn most of them are unreliable. This makes the situation of the professional woman quite difficult.

Even more difficult to confront is employers' attitudes. Severina complains that her diploma in programming is not taken seriously and she is offered jobs as a *digitadora* at less than a minimum salary. She was offered a three-month test period with no pay and only the money for transportation. Rina complains that employers will not give her a job because she has no experience, but they will hire her male colleagues in the same situation.

The job market is tough for young people in João Pessoa, especially for women who have to confront employers' assumptions and expectations of what their family and occupational future will be. Employers do not want problems with pregnancies; this fact influences them to offer lower pay and poor conditions of work to women, as reported by the women in the sample. Women are not seen as seriously committed to the labor market, and they are regarded by employers as temporary or relatively short-term workers who may be seeking part-time rather than full-time work.

It is difficult to expect that SENAC will struggle for greater democratization of job opportunities because it is an institution directly dependent on the employers and it shares their ideology. The study does not prove a priori that it is the private character of SENAC that makes things worse for women and blacks, given the high unemployment rate existing in the state. In order to have more evidence, it would be necessary to study the situation in a public vocational school.

The director of the professional division says that a slow change is being seen in the labor market in João Pessoa, and she thinks women are getting training in order to be able to compete. Among the factors cited as responsible for this change are these: "Men are getting smarter. They do not want to marry an unemployed woman" (director of professional training). "Women now want to be equal to men" (coordinator of the computer science department). But many problems are confronted by the married working woman in João Pessoa, as the director of the professional division pointed out:

> They don't have any help from the husband. Some women go to sleep late, fixing lunch for the next day, and have to wake up very early to help the children with the homework and still get to work on time. The husband usually arrives from work and goes to rest in the hammock waiting for the woman to prepare dinner. Husbands don't like their wives to travel because they think they go just to meet other men. Frequently a woman wants to study and her husband won't allow her. And

if the husband retires, he will want the wife to quit the job and stay home full-time.

In my opinion, this situation is sustained with the women's implicit approval. Women seem ambiguous about their careers. They want to work and to earn money, but not because they really need it. It is because they want some money of their own. But implicit in their views is that it is the husband-provider who will actually support the family. This perspective makes them accept poor jobs, ones with poor prospects and salaries clearly under their qualifications. Some of them live with women who have to support their homes, either because they are separated or single. But in spite of this obvious reality, they do not see themselves continuing this situation in the future. On the other hand, they complain that they are not taken seriously as workers. The problem is that as long as they do not take their careers seriously, they cannot expect others to do so.

I ask myself what SENAC is really doing in a state like Paraiba, where job opportunities are slim. Nevertheless, SENAC has the credibility of being an organization linked directly to the Chamber of Commerce and to the employers, and that strengthens the illusion of greater job prospects. My conclusion is that what SENAC is really doing is creating a great trained "reserve army of labor" for the commerce and service sectors. Because SENAC's students are mainly women, it is a reserve army composed mainly of women who are unconsciously contributing to maintaining low salary levels and poor working conditions.

▲ Appendix

The data collection was done through the following procedures: (a) observations in the Center for Professional Training in João Pessoa, (b) interviews with teachers and staff and with students of the computer science department, and (c) analysis of relevant documents about SENAC.

The data collection started in November 1987. For six weeks I visited the center using different reasons: interviews with the regional director, collection of documents, and interviews with the director of professional training and the coordinator of the computer science department. I made the observations during the periods of waiting for somebody or for some document and after the interviewing. I spent some time in the coffee shop, sitting at the tables in the patio while I had a snack and made some notes; I stayed usually no more than thirty minutes so that my behavior would be considered normal.

The center closed for fifteen days for the holidays. Around mid-January I started my visits to the center again, in order to set the schedule for the interviews of the students. The contacts were always made through the coordinator of the computer science department, which is how I got to talk extensively with him.

Several times he made contact with students for interviews and they canceled at the last minute. Finally, four students were interviewed. It can hardly be considered a representative sample, but for the purpose of this pilot study it was sufficient. The interviews show consistent patterns regarding the type of students who entered the computer science department, their academic experiences, and their first steps in the search for jobs. Even more, what was observed in Paraiba in some respects is very different from the result of studies done in developed countries, though it is similar in others. All this is reported in the study.

The interviews were recorded, and the recording was checked immediately after the interview. This process continued until March 1988. It was not possible to interview women graduates employed in the private firms. The coordinator had several excuses every time: They worked in the industrial district, could not participate in an interview during working hours, and got home very late; thus, he was unable to set up an interview with them. This is one of the limitations of the study—the coordinator had more control over the interviews than I did. Obviously this is not a correct research procedure and should be improved in a more representative study.

The interviews were guided by a set of general themes and were flexible either in the order the themes were covered or in the time devoted to each. Each interview lasted approximately ninety minutes, plus a period of clarifying obscure points in two cases. In general there were no objections to the recorder.

I transcribed the interviews with the help of a research assistant, then analyzed them. This method is slow, but it allows a more in-depth understanding of the material. The interviews were analyzed by subject according to the objectives of the research.

▲ Notes

1. This information was taken from the official documents of SENAC. In an interview with the regional director, he informed me that the 1.5 percent contribution of the private firms is not of total salaries paid but of wages under twenty minimum salaries (US $1,200). SENAC is closely related to the Serviço Nacional de Aprendizagem Industrial (SENAI), which provides middle-level technological training. For an excellent account of the role of SENAC in the transmission of technological skills and the process of class mobility, see Kempner and de Moura Castro (1988).

2. A possible explanation for this fact is the redistribution system SENAC adopts to channel resources from rich to poor states. The rich regions send some of their surplus to the poor ones.

3. According to the 1980 census data, the unemployment rate of Paraiba, including underemployment, reaches 26.6 percent. The official unemployment

rate is 2.15 percent, the visible underemployment is 24.5 percent which is defined to include the working population employed in a less-than-40-hour job (SUDENE, 1983, pp. 91, 129, and 132).

4. Students in on-the-job training programs present the best level; 40 percent have completed secondary education and 13.4 percent have a university degree. Students in the centers for professional training also present a high level; 42 percent have completed eight years of primary school, 36 percent have secondary school, and 4 percent have a university diploma. In distance education, 43 percent have complete primary, 38.5 percent complete secondary, and 5 percent complete university degree. The lowest educational level is found among the students who attend the mobile units (84 percent have primary school or less) and in the units of vocational training (78 percent have primary school or less) (SENAC, 1986, p. 115, Table 4).

5. The so-called godfather is an important local politician who is entitled to assign friends or relatives to public jobs in the state or local administration, usually in exchange for political favors to the party in power.

▲ References

Ashton, David, and M. Maguire. "Young Women in the Labor Market: Stability and Change." In R. Deem (ed.), *Schooling for Women's Work.* London: Routledge and Kegan Paul, 1980.

Carnoy, Martin, and Henry M. Levin. *Schooling and Work in the Democratic State.* Stanford, Calif.: Stanford University Press, 1985.

Chisholm, Lynne, and Diana Woodward. "The Experiences of Women Graduates in the Labor Market." In R. Deem (ed.), *Schooling for Women's Work.* London: Routledge and Kegan Paul, 1980.

Clarricoates, K. "The Importance of Being Ernest . . . Emma . . . Tom . . . Jane: The Perception and Categorization of Gender Conformity and Gender Deviation in Primary School." In R. Deem (ed.), *Schooling for Women's Work.* London: Routledge and Kegan Paul, 1980.

Finn, J. D., J. Reis, and L. Dulberg. "Sex Differences in Educational Attainment: The Process." In G. Kelly and C. Elliott (eds.), *Women's Education in the Third World.* Albany: State University of New York Press, 1982.

Fuller, Mary. "Black Girls in a London Comprehensive School." In R. Deem (ed.), *Schooling for Women's Work.* London: Routledge and Kegan Paul, 1980.

Keil, T., and P. Newton. "Into Work: Continuity and Change." In R. Deem (ed.), *Schooling for Women's Work.* London: Routledge and Kegan Paul, 1980.

Kelly, G., and A. Nihlen. "Schooling and the Reproduction of Patriarchy." In M. W. Apple (ed.), *Cultural and Economic Reproduction in Education.* London: Routledge and Kegan Paul, 1982.

Kempner, Ken, and Claudio de Moura Castro. "Higher Education for Mid-Level Technology: A Comparative Analysis of Brazil and the United States," *Comparative Education Review*, vol. 32, no. 4 (November 1988), pp. 478–493.

MacDonald, Madeleine. Sociocultural Reproduction and Women's Education." In R. Deem (ed.), *Schooling for Women's Work.* London: Routledge and Kegan Paul, 1980.

Madeira, F. R., and P. Singer. "Estrutura de emprego e trabalho feminino no Brasil 1920–1970." *Cadernos CEBRAP*, no. 13, 1973.

Ministerio da Fazenda. *Sinopse estatística do nordeste*. Rio de Janeiro: IBGE, Ministerio da Fazenda, 1973.

Oliveira, F., and H. P. Reichstul. "Mudanças na divisão interregional do trabalho no Brasil." *Cadernos CEBRAP*, no. 4, 1973.

Saffioti, H. *A mulher na sociedade de classes: Mito e realidade*. Rio de Janeiro: Vozes, 1976.

SENAC (Serviço Nacional de Aprendizagem Comercial). *SENAC legislaçao*. Rio de Janeiro: Departamento Nacional, SENAC, 1976.

——. *Quem e o aluno do SENAC?* Rio de Janeiro: Departamento Nacional, SENAC, 1986.

SUDENE (Superintendencia de Desenvolvimento do Nordeste). *Indicadores Sociais do Nordeste* (1970–1980). Recife: SUDENE, 1983.

PART 4

Making Changes

▲ 11

Altering Sexual Stereotypes Through Teacher Training

Gloria Bonder

Teachers, as an integral part of educational settings, play a key role in the transmission of gender ideologies. Through everyday actions, notions of femininity and masculinity are shaped, strengthened, and transmitted. Teachers have been the targets of many change efforts, usually through short in-service training sessions. Rarely, however, do they go through systematic efforts designed to produce attitudinal change.

In this chapter, Bonder reviews the studies on sexual stereotypes in Argentine textbooks and then gives a detailed account of one carefully conceived intervention that, although time-intensive, was not expensive in terms of the resources required. That this intervention took place in Argentina, a country with a strong belief in its gender progressiveness, makes it all the more interesting because the intervention confronted its participants with evidence of inequality and subordination that contradicted prevailing perceptions of gender equality in that society.

The intervention, in the hands of a skillful psychologist, shows that well-conceived treatments—even though brief in comparison to the whole of experiences and situations that women teachers undergo in their everyday life—can be powerful in creating modified perceptions and attitudes. The in-service training implemented by Bonder also shows that technologies such as audiocassettes can be used effectively to provide stimuli for group discussion and that these group discussions can result in significant and stable changes among the participants.

An additional important contribution made by Bonder lies in the identification of the fears and conflicts that emerged among women teachers as they moved from a traditional to a more progressive, emancipatory view of gender relations. As described in her study, concerns about engaging in "a war between the sexes," creating domestic conflicts, and losing their "power in the domestic sphere" were troubling the teachers as they went on to implement changes in their individual lives. One inference from this is that women cannot readily change; in their everyday practice they will encounter transactions with men and family that make them unhappy and uncertain about the new terrain they are entering. Bonder's study, when juxtaposed with that of Sara-Lafosse, suggests that students in both coeducational schools and single-sex schools may be facing teachers who are themselves very uncertain about altering their own notions of femininity and masculinity.

—Editor

▲   Any time the situation of women in Argentine society is discussed, it can be expected that both men and women will exalt the educational levels that women have attained in recent decades. It is implied, thus, that at least in the educational sphere there is no evidence of discrimination against women, and that these gains reveal an undeniable and even exceptional progress in their social condition.

This argument is based on information that is partly correct, although the same cannot be said of the conclusions drawn from the argument. If one counts women's participation in the formal educational system of Argentina from a strictly quantitative viewpoint, it can be affirmed that compared with women from several other Latin American countries and even from some developed countries, Argentine women have achieved what can be considered an extraordinary educational situation.

Educational legislation (Law 1420) enacted in 1884, more than a century ago, prevented discrimination against women in educational access. Even before the enactment of this law, Argentine women were able to have access to primary school, which they did in large numbers.

During this century and particularly in the last three decades, the great educational expansion in this country benefited women significantly. By 1970 the minuscule differences between male and female enrollment in primary school had been erased, and today women slightly surpass the enrollment of men at the secondary level. By 1980, 24 percent of women ages 40–49 and 48 percent of those ages 20–29 had received or completed secondary schooling. These data indicate that "neither is the access of women to secondary and university levels a recent development, nor is it open to all women" (Gibaja, 1986). At the university level, their participation is practically equivalent to that of men, and in some cases, as in the University of Buenos Aires, it is even greater. With respect to educational performance, the rates of repetition and dropping out indicate that women, in larger measure than men, remain in the primary and secondary cycles and that they finish these studies within the expected ages (Braslavsky, 1985).

It is true that in secondary and tertiary education, the bulk of women continue to select fields of study that are traditionally feminine, but it has also been observed, especially in the last two decades, that women's participation is increasing in "masculine" fields of study: Medicine, law, and architecture are today careers that can be considered "neutral" from the point of view of gender access. Only engineering, agronomic sciences, business administration, and economic sciences at the university level, and technical-industrial education at the high school level, continue to have an under-representation of women. It cannot be ignored that the educational situation of women has evolved substantially and that new social sectors have become integrated into the educational process as the educational system has expanded throughout diverse regions of the country.

This brief historical background suggests that the early incorporation of women into the educational system, their massive presence at all levels of education, the widening of their field-of-study choices, and even their limited participation in technological careers are similar to the educational situation of women in countries that are more industrially developed.

How can this situation be explained? Although governmental policies on education may have played a role during certain periods of Argentine history, their effects have been minimal. I believe other factors have been more important.

First, it is important to underscore the fact that the large European migratory component of Argentine society has been characterized by a strong value attached to education. These immigrants, who arrived in Argentina toward the end of the eighteenth century and the beginning of the nineteenth century, placed on education much of their expectations for integration into the nation and for social and economic mobility. Even though at the family level gender stereotypes were maintained for types of study, length of study, and the significance of schooling on the future lives of their children, it can be affirmed that for Argentine families the education of their daughters had an indisputable value.

Furthermore, the compulsory character of primary education and the free nature of the education offered by the state at all levels of schooling were important stimuli for the use of the educational offerings by both sexes, and this reduced one of the constraints that families frequently face: the economic investment in their children's education.

Last, it should be noted that one of the ideals of Argentine society is to resemble, at least at its cultural level, the European countries and, conse-quently, to distinguish itself from the other Latin American countries. This cultural model has reinforced the tendency of a wide sector of the population (primarily the middle classes) toward participation at the highest levels of education, the accumulation of cultural goods, and the sophistication of these goods. But it can also be observed that among the various masking effects that produce a cultural model of this nature has been the myth derived from interpreting the "cultural" level of the Argentine population as an accurate indicator of the degree of its socioeconomic development.

Women, especially those from the middle classes, have benefited from this cultural model for the promotion of both their educational and cultural aspirations. I nonetheless believe that Argentine women, particularly those most highly educated, have been affected by this fiction that treats as equivalent educational and social development.

The history of women's participation in the formal educational system and the high levels reached by women do not seem to have produced substantial changes in the social recognition of the various discriminatory situations women face, including those forms of discrimination inside the educational system. On the contrary, it would seem that these historical gains have contributed to create in the consciousness of many women—and in the social discourse of wide sectors of society—a mirage effect: that educational equality equals social equality. This illusion has been reinforced by the comparison of Argentine women with other Latin American women.

These fictions of equality and the somewhat exceptional position of Argentine women have not contributed to the development of a consciousness about discrimination of women in society. The scarce diffusion of feminist ideas in Argentina and the rejection of feminism by many educated women can be explained, to some extent, by this mirage effect.

I believe that even though some educated women realize that access to education is not a panacea, many women are fascinated by the educational achievements that have been reached and those that will be reached in the future. These women attribute conditions of social inferiority only to women in less developed countries and subordinate social classes, anticipating that the continuous democratization of Argentine society will bring the inescapable result of full participation of women in all areas of society. This discourse discards the need for "intentional and coordinated actions designed to change the condition of women, [without which] any social efforts will produce social transformations to which women will not directly contribute" (Gibaja, 1986).

It is not possible to determine how widespread this notion is, but I estimate that it is sufficiently disseminated to merit attention when evaluating the effects of education upon the processes of awareness that many women undertake regarding the condition of their gender and the social change linked to it. The strong value given by the family and society to formal education for both sexes has fostered the belief that individual actions prevail in the attainment of education. This belief today leads to the premise that "if one wants it, it can be done," and thus that women can have access to all kinds of education independent of the conditioning factors of gender (Gibaja, 1986).

It is not surprising, therefore, that the attempts to study and transform the educational settings in light of the gender question are recent and scarce in the country. It is not surprising either that this research theme awakens a resistance in several educational sectors and even in the academic community. This resistance stems not so much from fear of the "great changes" that the investigations could unleash as from the fact that the topic of "women and education" is usually considered irrelevant in comparison with other issues of greater significance and urgency linked to the social participation of Argentine women.

Underlying the lag in research on this theme in Argentina are other reasons, such as the regression that social science research suffered during the years of dictatorship and the very limited presence of a feminist movement. As is well known, there is a high correlation between the strength of the feminist movement and the amount of research on gender issues in any particular country. This is true in several Anglo-Saxon countries and some developed Latin countries such as Italy and, more recently, Spain. In Latin America, the production of knowledge about the situation of women from a feminist perspective is recent, though in a state of rapid development. For this reason, and in the specific case of research on gender and education, the studies conducted in Anglo-Saxon settings are necessary points of reference not only for their empirical findings but also for their theoretical development.

Subirats (1988), citing various English authors, notes that the lines of research within the gender-and-education theme have been (1) works on ideology and patriarchy, which seek to determine in theoretical terms the impact of patriarchy on the educational system; (2) works on the transmission of gender differences within schools, with this research following three lines of analysis: teachers' expectations regarding boys and girls, classroom practices, and school rituals; (3) studies focusing on the differentiation of curriculum for boys and girls; and (4) the position and characteristics of women teachers. Subirats notes also that from a theoretical perspective, this theme of research is not cohesive and offers a series of analytical frameworks and heterogeneous explanations that, sometimes, are scarcely related to the central theoretical perspective.

Among the works produced in Anglo-Saxon settings, particularly in England, however, one observes a considerable interest in the formulation of a coherent theoretical framework, which in most cases relies on the thesis of critical reproduction (Barrett, 1980; Wolpe, 1978). Into the classical thesis within this current, the English feminists have incorporated the forgotten dimension: gender. This research, though invaluable, shares the merits and problems that have already been identified in studies based on reproduction theories. As Giroux (1984) notes, "The merit of this approach is to have taken education away from its lack of political consciousness and to have connected it with the social and cultural matrix of capitalist rationality." Giroux further observes that in contradistinction with free-will and subjective currents, which fail to consider structural determinants, reproductivism sees the educational system in direct relation with the state and the capitalist economy; therefore, the function of schooling is to reproduce a labor force stratified by class, race, and sex to provide each social collective with the appropriate knowledge and training to occupy different places in the productive system and to inculcate the dominant ideology.

In applying this thesis to the educational situation of women, authors such as Wolpe (1978) and Barrett (1980) affirm that the educational system contributes to reproducing not only the hierarchies based on class but also those based on gender, using to this effect the images in textbooks, the teachers' expectations, the gender discrimination in formal and informal activities conducted in the school, the gender stratification of the teaching profession, the differing guidance toward profession and occupations, and the conveying as "legitimate" knowledge of primarily that learning based on male parameters and values.

Various authors have questioned the reproductive notions (see, e.g., Vera, 1984), underscoring that these, by overemphasizing the structural determinants, see the school as a black box and fall into the trap of a conspiratorial view of history. By not incorporating social actors as active protagonists of the educational event, they do not allow an understanding of phenomena such as mediation, resistance, and creativity in the educational setting. From a practical viewpoint, these approaches can lead to a posture called "structural pessimism" (i.e., the belief that it is impossible to produce changes in the educational system without first changing the socioeconomic and political structures). Even though some feminist studies could suggest this conclusion, I prefer to agree with Arnot (1985):

> If there is an obvious premise in any feminist analysis, it is the necessity for educational reform as a prior and indispensable condition for the liberation of women. Whatever the political viewpoint regarding how and why women are subordinated to men, the concept of the role of education as the key agent in the transmission of value, knowledge, and preparation for adult life is a constant. Thus, even in those cases in which the educational system is not identified as a key change agent, all social change capable of transforming gender relations will demand important educational reforms.

If we accept these premises, the problem becomes where to begin. And the immediate question is, Which are the most effective strategies for social change?

On past occasions, and even today in some countries, priority has been given to changes through antidiscriminatory legislation affecting education. In more recent years actions have taken place regarding the expansion of the ill-defined "coeducation" (which in fact should be called mixed education), and in the poorest countries the highest priority is access to education for women from the most marginal sectors.

The progress made by legislation in the participation of women in the educational sector and in the refinement of theoretical conceptions that support feminist research on these themes has oriented the analytical focus toward the less obvious forms that educationally sexist practices assume today. It is undeniable that the forms in which sexism finds an expression in the educational system are changing. They are more subtle and hide behind the formal equality with which schools are presented. They are not manifested in the physical segregation of women, nor do they have marked consequences in educational outcomes. "They seem to affect more the construction of the personality of individuals . . . and the internalization of social norms differentiated by gender, which entail diverse types of expectations and possibilities and a hierarchization of individuals" (Gorlier, 1989). The processes for the inculcation of social values in the educational sphere are not so simple and schematic as might be believed. Direct coercion and conscious obedience are not the characteristic forms of transmission and internalization, at least in the majority of educational settings that seek to be egalitarian.

Given the social function it plays, the school needs to appeal to rationality to produce consensus on the truth, goodness, and justice of the values that it transmits because schools—like other social institutions—use a certain strategy to discipline subjects to accept the unequal distribution of the social patrimony. Thus, the school "relies more on the production of reasons to obey than on the repression of possible disobedience. To that end it resorts to a wide range of procedures, from the imposition of a 'legitimate appointment' to the transmission of all-encompassing visions and accounts . . . [thus creating] the multiplication of a series of behavioral models and maxims for social performance that will become part of the 'common sense' of the discriminated" (Gorlier, 1989). In this regard, it can be affirmed that the transmission of sexual values is not limited to explicit messages; also important are the values and content that are "absent"—the practical knowledge that is internalized in an unconscious manner in time and space and that determines, unconsciously, the development of a realization of what is possible and attainable for each gender. The complexity of these processes requires the development and use of complex methodologies, capable of unmasking how gender discrimination operates within educational contexts.

▲ Sexism in the Argentine Primary School

Gender Stereotypes in Textbooks

The most exhaustive study carried out in Argentina on this topic analyzed the masculine and feminine images presented in reading textbooks used in Argentine primary schools during a 100-year period (Wainerman and Raijman, 1984). The authors conclude with a categorical statement: "a case of a century-long immutability." In fact, the books printed during the period covered do not present meaningful modifications on this matter. All of them show a clear and harmonious sexual division of labor, which is justified by the "natural differences among the sexes." These books foster different socialization norms to fit men and women into the social roles they must play, they assign greater prestige to activities carried out by men, and they idealize the functions of women as housewives, but they do not recognize the characteristics of the various occupations, and except in the role of teacher, women are scarcely presented in work activities. Although the results of this study may surprise those who have studied this question in other countries, what is shocking is the contrast between these images and the evident modernization of the pedagogical aspects of the reading textbooks—together with the partial but significant changes that have occurred during the century in the position of Argentine women in family and society.

It goes beyond the scope of this work to attempt a global explanation for this situation; therefore, only several hypotheses are identified. As indicated earlier, the educational attainment of Argentine women seems to have created a mirage in the social discourse, which leads one to interpret these indicators as a reflection of a progressive improvement in the social inequalities between the sexes. But also, and complementing what was noted earlier, the equality and even the greater improvement of women over men in access and retention in schooling tend to confirm the myth that schools are neutral and do not discriminate along gender lines. These factors contribute to a failure to recognize sexism as a social problem and to hide it behind the increasingly large cohorts of "educated" women.

To create a debate on this problem, it is necessary to shift attention from a quantitative approach that focuses on how much education women get to an alternative analysis that attends to what, how, and for what women learn within an educational system that offers representations and cultural values historically insensitive to social conflicts and out of synchronization with the changes in gender roles and shifts in discrimination that women face. Only after having illuminated some of these aspects through exhaustive investigation is it possible, as Alberdi (1985) points out, to mobilize action so that "sexism becomes an object of discussion and controversy, about which there are different analyses and different demands." Ideally, this discussion should bring as a consequence the development and implementation of an official plan of action in which "all those implied in the topic, basically the feminist movements and the representatives of women and the authorities of the Ministry of Education, should participate."

Nothing of this kind has occurred in Argentina thus far. The only official initiative in this respect is a recently approved project by the council of the municipality of Buenos Aires calling for compliance with the norms of the UN Convention on the Elimination of all Forms of Discrimination Against Women, which recommends the elimination of stereotypes and discriminatory models in the representation of feminine and masculine notions in the reading textbooks in primary schools and the need to have these books reflect the current situation of Argentine society. The municipal council recommended the use of information produced by the National Institute of Statistics and Census Data.

This project is doubtlessly important progress, even though it is not sufficient. Experiences from other countries (Spain, for instance; see Instituto de la Mujer, 1987) suggest that changes in the images and content of textbooks should be accompanied by in-service training programs of teachers to help them to examine the attitudes, expectations, and values they use and transmit when teaching boys and girls; to enable them to reflect on the consequences these images and content have upon the social performance of both sexes; and to enable them to use their creativity to implement educational actions that permit these students—free from gender discrimination—to develop their capacities, interests, and aptitudes.

But in order to implement a training program of this kind, it is necessary to overcome the first stumbling block: Gender values and stereotypes are usually internalized in the beliefs, attitudes, and daily behaviors of teachers, who are simply not aware of them and participate in their reproduction, "blind in the face of the obvious" (Heiser, 1981). The consequences of "naturalizing" effects produced by any ideological influence—the habitual and repetitive nature of the process and interactions that occur in the educational milieu, the egalitarian beliefs that derive from legislation, and the passive position, discouragement, and indifference that the functioning of the educational system forces on teachers—are some of the factors supporting this phenomenon of lack of awareness. These conditioning factors produce a significant challenge for any proposal to transform sexism in educational practice and compels researchers toward a design of methodologies and content for teacher training that may be effective in generating a progressive and lasting process of transformative action and consciousness raising.

Attitudinal Change Among Teachers: Project Structure

A study by Bonder (1986) constitutes the first of its kind in Argentina. The key objective of this investigation was to evaluate the effects of an experimental program based on reflexivity and training for primary school teachers regarding the transmission of sexual stereotypes in the teaching-learning process in various areas of the school curriculum.

This experience consisted of eight group meetings, which lasted 1.45 hours per week. Each meeting addressed a specific sexual stereotype; a set of seven audiovisual models (cassettes and brochures) was developed for this purpose and used in each meeting (except in the eighth, which focused on the evaluation of this experience).

The modules deal with the form in which sexual stereotypes are reflected in our society and how they intervene in school practices and the consequences that this phenomenon has upon the education of boys and girls as well as on the future roles they will play in society. The modules also seek to develop educational strategies to modify sexism in the primary school setting.

The cassettes for this study have features similar to those described in the "cassette forum" (Kaplun, 1984) regarding the use of audiovisual means to stimulate group communication. "The cassette delivers information that does not address isolated passive receptors, but rather a group which is stimulated into participation. The targets of the cassette are organized into a group and receive the message under conditions that allow collective analysis and reflection." Each cassette begins with the introduction of the team that coordinates the experience, the themes to be developed, the materials (cassette and brochure), and the form in which these will be used. All the cassettes have the same format to enable them to be used singly.

After listening to the cassette, participants are exposed to different types of stimuli so that they may experience personally the cognitive, affective, and attitudinal processes upon which stereotypes are formed. For instance, one proposal consists of analytical games for the classification of persons, another of making statements regarding the behaviors of boys and girls, and a third, more concretely, of working as a group in the formation of stereotypes through an exercise about opinion creation. For example, in the cassette on the topic of physical education and sports, comments about stereotypes among men and women regarding physical and sports abilities are discussed and teachers are invited to express opinions and to reflect upon these stereotypes. In the cassette on the question of science, participants are asked to conduct a game that consists of distributing eleven scholarships for workshops in science, literature, and math among male and female students.

The first five modules offer a consciousness-raising exercise on the development of stereotypes. Participants express judgments about persons from different social classes, nationalities, professions, genders, religion, and so on—for example, a female airplane pilot, a rabbi, a Korean immigrant. These stimuli facilitate the connection between teachers and the selected topic, and from the start they become active participants in the discussion of the theme. Subsequently, participants get into the concrete task of analyzing the effects of gender stereotypes on each area of the primary school curriculum.

The first module introduces teachers to the problem of sociocultural differences between men and women. It focuses attention on psychological, social, and cultural traits that reflect gender differences. It also proposes various explanatory frameworks for these issues (e.g., theories of social learning, cognitive theory, psychoanalytic theory). The next five modules address the school practice concretely and take into account how gender stereotypes usually manifest themselves in the teaching-learning processes regarding reading and writing, math, science, physical education, and Argentine history. The seventh module concludes the experience by asking for a reflection on the participation of women in the history of Argentine education and on the role of the primary school teacher in the transformation of sexism in the educational milieu. The design of these modules makes possible the use of self-managed groups because the same cassette performs as the group coordinator through the raising of questions, requests for exercises or group plays, partial syntheses of the themes to be debated, and suggestions for bibliography and techniques to modify sexist attitudes within the school practice.

In the creation of modules, the authors took into account the need to stimulate teachers through the development of cognitive tasks that would make it possible to identify the problem, to examine it, to understand it, and to transform it. From the cognitive viewpoint, each module seeks to enable teachers to meet the following objectives:

1. Perceive and analyze school practices in the light of gender values and through detached analysis of their daily experiences in the school.
2. Detect the relationships among gender values transmitted by the school experiences, those that predominate in the social environment, and those that orient their personal experiences.
3. Name the "new reality" built through these processes, build their social rationality, and develop a critical judgment about gender inequalities.
4. Formulate utopias for the role of education in the transmission of gender inequalities.
5. Set priorities for transformational actions and for the identification of short-, medium-, and long-term goals.

It is important to underline that the modules seek to involve teachers actively in these experiences, which implies a personal involvement in the selected topics. To this end, the message on each cassette seeks to have the teachers adopt active positions in the discussion of themes and avoids blaming them for the reproduction of gender inequalities. On the contrary, the cassette seeks to strengthen the teachers' self-esteem through the recognition of the value of their intellectual capacities and through the legitimation and expansion of their social change ideals.

Each cassette contains ample information about the various topics, including the following:

1. Research findings on the differences between sexes in terms of biology, intellect, personality, interests, abilities, and performance.
2. Beliefs, myths, and stereotypes about sexual differences.
3. Explanations about the process of socialization from early childhood up to adolescence; about the family, the school, and the community as socialization agents; and about the incidence of sexual stereotypes throughout the entire socialization process.
4. Cultural differences in definitions about femininity and masculinity.
5. Statistical data on the education and work outcomes of men and women in Argentina.
6. Laws and national and international conventions regarding the

social, economic, and employment participation of men and women.

7. Images and values regarding men and women transmitted by the mass media.
8. Biographical data about distinguished women in various cultural fields in Argentina and in the world (literature, science, politics, education, sports).
9. Information about the history of the participation of women in education, politics, and science in Argentina.
10. Information on the new lines of historical, psychological, anthropological, and social research regarding the condition of women and gender differences.
11. Bibliographical references for the selected themes.

This information seeks to identify the problem of social beliefs and myths regarding gender differences. It does not seek the mechanical substitution of a "scientific truth" for a belief or myth. Rather, it seeks to amplify the perspective of teachers by stimulating their critical judgment, seeking the application of the knowledge thus far acquired.

The proposals for group discussion have several objectives:

1. Facilitate the verbal expression and exchange of impressions and experiences regarding the selected information. For example, after the presentation of information that is highly theoretical in nature, new, or of high impact among teachers, it is suggested that they debate the information beginning with their subjective impressions.
2. Connect the topic being treated to the personal, family, and educational history of the participating teachers. The objective here is to bring the problem of sexism to the subjective level through the recovery of personal and family memories (e.g., occupational preferences, experiences in the domestic sphere).
3. Generate explanations (cultural, historical) about the causes and consequences of gender stereotypes. For example, the participants are asked to reflect on explanations for the limited participation of women in the process of scientific knowledge production and in the top leadership positions in political institutions.
4. Reflect on a frequent teacher stereotype in the educational milieu: the teacher as a second mother. The objective here is to enable teachers to develop a self-image as professionals in education.
5. Increase the awareness and critical examination of gender stereotypes transmitted through the mass media.
6. Insert personal, family, and work problems in the history of women in Argentine society. For example, teachers are invited to remember the histories of their grandmothers in relation to the process of

European immigration to Argentina and the access of women in their family to education. The purpose here is to facilitate the recovery of "forgotten" events regarding the participation of women in the history of Argentina, through the development of a historical memory in each teacher.

7. Propose actions for the transformation of discriminatory stereotypes—for instance, the creation of educational materials, games, and role-playing exercises to foster in students the perception of gender patterns and their change.

The cassette is structured in time periods for the reception of the information and for group work. A question is followed by a bell ring, and this signal marks the passage from reception to active participation by the group.

The Teachers' Experience

One hundred twenty primary school teachers from the capital city and Greater Buenos Aires participated in this study. They were selected from among women who were between the ages of thirty and forty; who were married, widowed, or separated; who had children; and who had a continuous teaching experience of six to twelve years.

Before their participation in the study, the teachers were administered a questionnaire that evaluated their perceptions, attitudes, and values regarding their gender identity and sexual roles. In the questionnaire, it was important to obtain information on two aspects that mediate the shaping of the values and attitudes leading to gender inequality: the degree to which individuals perceive gender patterns in their social milieus and their disposition to accept and value the sociocultural changes that favor equality. These issues were assessed through attitudinal scales. The questionnaire also included a set of stimuli (incomplete phrases, situational tests, and expectations tests on the school performance of boys and girls) so that gender values specifically connected with school practices could be examined.

To evaluate the specific impact of the modules and to dissociate this from other intervening factors in the experience (in particular the gender-consciousness effects derived from the participation and reflection in a women's group), the sample of participating teachers was divided into six groups. Three of them used the modules; the other three addressed the same topics in a discussion setting but did not use the modules.

Five months elapsed between the first and the second administration of the questionnaire. Finally, fifteen in-depth interviews with participating teachers from both groups were held to evaluate exhaustively the effects of this experience on the school practice and on personal, family, and working life. Following are some of the notions teachers had at the beginning of their experience:

1. Most of them perceived that in Argentine society men and women occupy different spheres and perform different roles that, from childhood, and with the help of the family, the mass media, and to a lesser extent the school, tend to promote the development of personality features and behavioral traits that match the differentiated social roles these individuals will perform in the future.

2. They believed that Argentine women had reached important educational and work objectives and had high political participation. In other words, they did not perceive important factors in the discrimination of women in these areas.

3. They did not seek significant changes in the relative positions that men and women occupy in Argentine society, except in those related to the education of girls. On this matter, they thought that girls should receive more incentives in their families and schools to be able to develop diverse interests and capacities, although it must be noted that this aspiration focused especially on early childhood. They did not use the same criterion for boys.

In general terms it can be asserted that the teachers evinced a conformist vision about the situation of women, a finding similar to that reported by Gibaja (1986), who observed that conformist positions were characteristics found not only among "housewives but also among those who are in occupations that do not require substantial commitment, are part-time, or who do not seek to make a career (i.e., are in mid-levels in teaching positions or hold secretarial jobs)." Continuing, Gibaja states:

> Those who have this image do not object to the right of women to work or to perform in different spheres of public life, but they observe that these activities must be subordinated to the performance of the mother and wife roles. . . . They fear that these aspirations by women for a greater independence and progress in their jobs may lead them to overlook their home, their femininity, or their moral values. In this vision of contemporary society, the woman seems to have attained conditions close to the ideal: she can work, she carries weight in family decisions, and she has a greater social participation. . . . Within these parameters society does not force her. . . . Those who think in this manner see no reason for the women's dissatisfaction.

Frequently this vision includes an optimism that is not based on future possibilities for women. One supposes that those women who want a major role in public life will achieve what they seek, because if no social discrimination can be perceived, the merits of these women will be the only determinant.

On the topic of gender values and expectations that mediate school practices, the answers to the situations presented in the questionnaire indicate the following:

1. Among the teachers' expectations, it was "natural" that girls would obtain better grades than boys. However, this situation is not attributed to the intellectual capacity of girls but to their tendency to obey school nonns, to please the teachers, and to compete with other girls. On the other hand, good performance among boys was attributed to their intelligence and to a personal effort to overcome some "appealing" characteristics of masculinity: "Boys loaf around; they are interested in other things."

2. Although the teachers disciplined boys more strongly than girls, the sanctions occurred in cases of serious transgressions, and except in very extreme situations, much of the inappropriate conduct by the boys (from the point of view of school discipline) was tolerated by teachers, who saw them as manifestating their masculinity. For example, the aggressive and competitive behaviors of boys were accepted within certain limits, and their expression through alternative channels was encouraged inasmuch as it promoted success in the future. On the other hand, aggression among girls, in particular its physical manifestation, was practically unacceptable.

3. The passive character of girls presented few conflicts, given the efforts by teachers to work in classrooms with numerous students and their constant concern with discipline. However, the teachers considered the boys' games more interesting, even though they required more attention and mediation.

4. Answers to questions about the motivations needed for the development of interests and abilities revealed a phenomenon observed in previous studies. Gender discrimination in this regard is less marked in the first years of schooling, but increases notably when teachers relate to young people who are reaching puberty and adolescence. In fact, the teachers suggested the same books and activities to boys and girls in the first grades, but after ages eleven or twelve they considered it necessary to make clear distinctions. The reason for this differentiation was to motivate girls who were becoming adolescents toward the shaping of a "feminine image," characterized by the inhibition of ambition and the desire to succeed and by an increased interest in personal appearance and manners suitable to a "young lady." These studies corroborate this norm in other countries and demonstrate the consequences upon school performance of adolescents and the emergence of a symptom characteristic of many young women, which Horner (1974) has termed "fear to succeed."

5. Most of the teachers perceived differences in the personalities and behaviors of girls and boys. They considered that these differences were "objective" and stemmed from justifiable causes (biological or social). They expected different behaviors from boys and girls and treated them according to this expectation. In the teachers' opinions, the dominant characteristics of feminine behavior were affection, expressiveness, and dependency. They also accepted activity, creativity, and even a certain independence as features of the feminine personality, but there was a limit beyond which the behavior of

girls would become something abnormal for teachers. This limit was delineated by the disobedience of school norms. In the case of boys, the dominant characteristics were initiative, independence, and impulsiveness. Also included were expectations that boys would be affectionate and would manifest a certain dependency, but it was unacceptable for them to be docile or be subjugated by girls or by authorities.

It is evident that the positions noted here, although not conscious, guaranteed the existence of a hierarchical order between the genders and reinforced the stereotypical features of both genders. It can also be affirmed that the teachers idealized the masculine stereotype and denigrated the feminine, a situation that matches the conception of the dominant culture. In this sense it is clear that, within certain limits, teachers did not fear so much the masculinization of girls as the feminization of boys.

The participation of teachers in the training experience and in particular in the groups that use the modules produced significant changes not only in their attitudes but also in their behaviors. In the first place, for most of them these experiences represented the first opportunity to observe that sexism is a social and thus educational problem that requires the teachers to reflect collectively on the problem, to adopt critical attitudes against preconceived ideas, and to generate change proposals.

One of the most significant outcomes was that the teachers modified their previous explanations concerning the differences between the sexes. The existential, biological, and functionalist ideas were replaced by conceptions that attributed to social and cultural determinants a fundamental role in the construction and reproduction of gender inequalities. With this change, they incorporated into the examination of "observable" differences a political and historical dimension, which led them to perceive many situations previously seen as mere manifestations of the biological differences between the sexes to be instead manifestations of inequalities that could be transformed through several means, including education.

Other important factors in the changes produced were the examination of each of the curricular areas, the access to ample information about the omitted or silenced aspects of women's conditions in society—in the past as well as in the present—and the implementation and evaluation of innovative practices in the school during and after the development of this experience. Among these concrete activities that teachers conducted were the development of educational materials with nonsexist content, the incorporation of biographies of women in the teaching of history and science, dramatizations and debates with the students designed to promote reflection on the causes and consequences of inequalities of gender, proposals for the educational authorities to modify curricular content, and meetings with colleagues to discuss the problem of sexism in education.

However, it is necessary to note that throughout these meetings it was possible to observe the emergence of fantasies, fears, and conflicts activated in connection with this topic; these reactions produced both progress and retreat in the consciousness-raising process and in some cases produced withdrawal from the program. This situation is not surprising considering that these women had internalized the representation of gender values very early and in good measure unconsciously. Often, these representations and values link and give meaning to a person's fundamental notions about self-identity, the opposite sex, social ideals, body self-image, desires, and the modality of interpersonal ties. It is to be expected, therefore, that a certain degree of anxiety will emerge and that in this situation individuals will link feelings of ambiguity with threatening fantasies characterized by psychosis, bisexuality, impulsivity, impotence, omnipotence, and the like.

In the case of the teachers, there were certain fears and conflicts that were relatively conscious:

1. Fear that the progress of women—understood as greater participation and social and economic prestige in the public sphere—would bring in consequence the "defeat of men." This situation was seen in one view as a threat of solitude for women and in another as the beginning of a new "war between the sexes," in which men would become vengeful toward women in the future.
2. Fear that the changes in the definitions of gender would automatically involve the emergence among new generations of an extended female and male homosexuality.
3. Emotional conflicts regarding an egalitarian participation by men and women in domestic tasks, especially in the rearing of children.

This third possibility was associated with (a) a loss of real or imaginary space or power by women in the domestic sphere that could not be compensated by the attainment of power in other spheres and (b) a loss of social prestige for the teachers, given their age and their aspirations to belong to the middle class, and the increased participation of their husbands in activities that could be considered signs of economic poverty more than of modernity. It must be clarified that the traditional cultural values of the middle class in Argentina suggest that the man must fulfill the "provider" role sufficiently to ensure that his wife can devote herself primarily, if not exclusively, to domestic and childrearing duties. The change of these norms was associated with survival under critical economic situations and therefore was taken as a sign of descent in the social scale.

In the interviews conducted eight months after the experiences, it could be verified that many of the changes were lasting, but so were the conflicts that the teachers were facing in their institutional context, which was blind to this problem and thus very resistant to accepting innovations. For some of the teachers, participation in this experience meant a considerable modification of their attitudes and behaviors in the family and work setting.

Finally, from analysis of the teachers' oral participation throughout the experience, it is possible to extract their "strategic vision" for a change in the gender roles. This vision is expressed consciously and complements the subjective and objective obstacles they continue to face.

At the end of the experience, the teachers considered that women can and should develop their intelligence and creativity to the same extent that men do. They believed that women should learn to recognize their own criteria and opinions and defend them. They should get an education to be able to perform in a wide range of occupational and social situations. In situations of competition with men, women should develop and use their astuteness and in some cases use some feminine "weapons," such as charm, mothering of men, or seeking their protection. They should also have joint projects with their spouses and their families, but should not postpone their occupational plans. They should have intellectual, work, and social ambitions, but should avoid showing them excessively in public. They should try to imitate the successes women have gained, but simultaneously reaffirm certain feminine characteristics that they consider valuable, such as the capacity to have empathy and the ability to express affection. They could compete with men within certain limits—that is, avoid defeating them—but in case of defeating them, learn to hide the satisfaction derived from this situation. They should maintain a feminine appearance in their dress, gestures, and way of expressing themselves.

The teachers accepted that men's intelligence and creativity were not superior to those of women, but they felt men could not be inferior, especially to their fiancés or wives. They felt that men and women should confront each other with their criteria and opinions and that they should accept a dialogue and the joint resolution of problems, but when facing a discrepancy with women, men should not easily accept the viewpoint of women. Men should get training so that they can face work and social situations that are becoming increasingly competitive. This includes training in domestic tasks so that these may be shared with their wives.

The teachers in the experiment thought that men should have a definite heterosexual orientation, even though the men were not expected to have, in the same measure as women, a clear personal project regarding marriage and family. Men should have intellectual, work, and family ambitions and be successful in training for them. They should know how to defend their rights and could in certain cases use force to attain these rights. They should find a way to take care of their children but they should also be astute enough not to enter into competition with mothers in the main role of childrearing. They should accept conditions of competition with women without discrediting themselves. They could be interested in traditionally female roles, but if they adopted them, they should be very successful in them. As can be observed, the teachers identify with great precision some of these strategies as "alarm signals," to which individuals from either sex must adjust in order to avoid profound transformations in the definitions of gender that could make a reality the fears they expressed earlier.

The emphasis on competition and success also reflects social values that are strongly active in Argentine society given the economic crisis that faces the country and the uncertainties that this situation brings to the Argentine middle class, in particular the fears it produces regarding the new generations. It is also clear, however, that men's economic, work, and social successes constitute in the teachers' opinion a reaffirmation of the masculinity necessary to enable men to conduct traditional female activities and functions without reducing their self-esteem and their social recognition. In other words, the teachers felt that it was not the same for a man to conduct domestic tasks, childrearing, or other traditionally female duties out of frustration with his work as for him to perform the same duties while being successful in his work. Women's success and failure is measured with a different yardstick. For the teachers, a woman is successful if she can develop various capabilities and obtain work and economic success, but she should not allow herself to be considered by others as "responsible" for the failure of men—and particularly for the failure of the married couple.

▲ Conclusion

The teacher-training strategies discussed in this chapter could be considered reformist and even speculative, but they constitute a significant advancement over the strongly theoretical conceptions with which the teachers started their experience. Nevertheless, they underline with great clarity the complex and profoundly mixed feelings that changes in gender definitions awaken.

In this respect, and beyond the useful application of the experience in the school setting and in the lives of the teachers participating, the study produced valuable data regarding the process of consciousness development, including the subconscious resistance that modifications in gender definitions create. The study also highlighted the need for future incorporation of content and stimuli to facilitate the consideration of masculine as well as feminine stereotypes. If this is not done, one can still arrive at a conception of what is considered desirable and sufficient to transform gender hierarchies or to attain the advancement of women in social participation within the context of values and ideals of male stereotypes, without subjecting these stereotypes to a detailed questioning. Similarly, it is important to promote a greater debate about the oppressive and repressive elements of the conditioning factors regarding gender among males.

Studies of this nature and, above all, the technical resources such as those used in this experience can facilitate an implementation of interventions in the educational system that do not require serious economic investments or structural reforms. This form of experience could, for instance, take place during the training of future teachers in normal schools, in in-service training programs, and in meetings between teachers and parents.

Nevertheless, to make this type of action concrete, one crucial problem must be resolved. This problem is not academic in the strict sense of the word, but it is a key problem in terms of the objectives of transformation pursued by feminist research. It is the link between feminist research in the educational field with the spheres of policymaking and with the programs of formal education. To make this linkage effective poses a challenge that must be faced if a transformation of gender hierarchies is to be accomplished through education.

▲ References

Alberdi, Ines. "El papel de los enseñantes." In *Mujer y Educación*. Madrid: Instituto de la Mujer, 1985.

Arnot, Madelaine. "La coeducación y la lucha por una educación antisexista en el Reino Unido." In *Mujer y educación: El sexismo en la enseñanza*. Barcelona: Instituto de Ciencias de la Educación de la Universidad Autónoma de Barcelona, 1985.

Barrett, Michele. *Women's Oppression Today: Problems in Marxist Feminist Analysis*. London: Verso and NLG, 1980.

Bonder, Gloria. *Estereotipos sexuales en la educación primaria: Evaluación de una experiencia de cambios de actitudes con maestras primarias*. Buenos Aires: Centro de Estudios de la Mujer, 1986.

Braslavsky, Cecilia. *La discriminación educativa en Argentina*. Buenos Aires: FLACSO, 1985.

Gibaja, Regina. *Fuentes y límites del discurso acerca de la mujer*. Buenos Aires: CICE, 1986.

Giroux, Henry. "Teoría y resistencia en educación: Una pedagogía para la oposición." Reseña de Beatrice Avalos. *Dialogando*, no. 4, March 1984.

Gorlier, Juan Carlos. "Notas sobre producción de consenso." Buenos Aires, mimeo, 1989.

Heiser, Ich. "Blind to the Obvious." In James Henslin (ed.), *Down-to-Earth Sociology*. New York: Free Press, 1981.

Horner, Mattina, and M. Walsh. "Psychological Barriers to Success." In R. B. Kundsin (ed.), *Women and Success*. New York: Morrow and Co., 1974.

Instituto de la Mujer. *Plan para la igualdad de oportunidades de las mujeres, 1988–1990*. Madrid: Instituto de la Mujer, 1987.

Kaplun, Mario. *Comunicación entre grupos: El método del cassette-foro*. Ottawa: International Development Research Center, 1984.

Subirats, Marina. *Rosa y azul: La transmisión de los géneros en la escuela mixta*. Madrid: Instituto de la Mujer, 1988.

Vera, Rodrigo. "Taller de educadores como método de investigación y perfeccionamiento docente, operando a nivel de los condicionamientos culturales de un proceso de democratización escolar." *Dialogando*, no. 5, June 1984.

Wainerman, Catalina, and R. Raijman. *La división sexual del trabajo en los libros de lectura de la escuela primaria argentina: Un caso de inmutabilidad secular.* Buenos Aires: CENEP, 1984.

Wolpe, AnnMarie. *Feminism and Materialism.* London: Routledge and Kegan Paul, 1978.

▲ 12

Women and the Microsocial Democratization of Everyday Life

Beatriz Schmukler

Parents, particularly low-income parents, have little power and ability to negotiate the education of their children. This disadvantage is suffered essentially by women, who as mothers are expected to be the ones to supervise the education of children, or at least to become more involved in it than are their husbands.

In this chapter, Beatriz Schmukler discusses the careful although fragile construction of a space where parents can negotiate and renegotiate educational services and practices with school authorities. Although these parent–school authority transactions occur mostly in the area of democratizing participation, they concern gender issues in two ways. First, the democratization of school practices involves mothers more than fathers because mothers must respond to the social norm that they are responsible for their children. Second, as some parents negotiate new relations with school authorities, such as the creation of student centers that could foster more student discretion, they are opposed by other parents who are concerned with the morality of their daughters and want to keep traditional authoritarian practices in schools. Schmukler describes an experiment that was intended to increase the flexibility of key actors in the educational system: parents, teachers, and school authorities. She discusses the limits of participation— the school challenges the possible contributions of mothers as educators and seeks collaboration only for the purpose of facilitating the school's task. A school's call for participation will fail because teachers differentiate also among parents, the good parents being those whose children have no problems. Thus, those more likely to have legitimate demands upon the school are disqualified from participation. Further, mothers continue to think in narrow, immediate family terms. Schools fragment parental participation, so these women have little opportunity to organize themselves autonomously. Hard-to-break authoritarian patterns of school and the fact that mothers are the main interlocutors make it even more difficult because mothers are expected to support, not question, the socialization of their children. As children move up the educational ladder, the role of mothers becomes further limited because they are seen as resources to avoid school failure. Mothers are doubly subordinated (because of class and gender) by school authorities to act as socialization agents for children, and this presumes that mothers accept the school's messages.

The study by Schmukler shows that it is possible for mothers to participate and to become more aware of their rights regarding the education of their children. Yet this participation is fraught with self-doubt and requires mothers to confront behaviors by school authorities and teachers that circumscribe participation to a few aspects of the educational setting.

—Editor

▲   Private life is the kingdom of inequality, whereas public life assumes, under democratic conditions, the existence of game rules that create possibilities for equal participation (Arendt, 1958; Conti Odorisio, 1979; Elshtain, 1982). To be deprived of the public sphere implies deprivation of reality, inasmuch as human and political reality coincides with a possibility of obtaining and having juridical existence. Life in the private sphere refers to the idea of being deprived of the most human and elevated rights.

This general statement reflects consensual social values in any democratic society. It is a belief that allows people to struggle legitimately for the recognition of personal rights in public life. It is also one of the fundamental ways in which private needs become reality when they take the form of public demands.

In this chapter I examine that gray zone between the public and private worlds, beginning with the relationship between the state and the social actors to whom it supplies services. This area, in modern societies, is a part of what Balvo calls the "culture of need," understood as an area of social relations where needs and the "concept" of happiness are defined (Balvo, 1976).

One of the main reasons for analyzing this area is that these concepts of happiness and need have been negotiated on a daily basis at the local level in the relationship between families and the state since the democratic regime was reestablished in Argentina in 1983. In addition, some aspects of the process of democratization belong to the realm of interpersonal social interaction transcending both private and public spheres and cannot be entirely labeled as political. Their transcendence challenges authoritarian patterns of interaction; thus, they have important impacts on the ways social policies are administered by the state. This area of confluence between individuals and the state can rapidly become an area of confrontation where new modes of interaction are created as the actors are reorganized and new forms of collective action developed.

Social relations in these areas are colored by the affective ties of interpersonal relations, by concerns for individual matters, and by the follow-up of specific cases. They deal with personal relationships that articulate both the private and the public worlds—relations that can both facilitate and obstruct democratization. Even in moments when democratic regimes are being set up, the degree to which personal preoccupations transcend the private sphere and become social demands opens the possibility of an encounter between public policies and collective needs. Private needs and desires can become general goals when the groups involved process them in a creative way—avoiding violations of intimacy, allowing respect for diversity, and, at the same time, satisfying needs recognized by the groups.

Frequently, however, everyday relationships in the private-public borders develop formal and bureaucratic rituals that block true participation of the subjects involved, who are usually individuals marginalized by class, cultural, or gender prejudice.[1] Some of the specific features of these groups are suppressed or are treated as isolated or abnormal. Hence, state agents delegitimize certain realities that represent changes in family life or are simply differences with respect to a middle-class idealized culture.

Changes in women's consciousness and participation during the last decade have produced an impact upon the forms of negotiation that have taken place in this public-private area. Women, as representatives of the families in daily social interaction with state agencies, have developed new forms of organization in order to make their private needs more audible or to replace the inefficiency of the state in the provision of social services.

In Argentina today there is a promising space for the negotiation of services, a process that has typically been resolved by the state. In the case of education, this negotiation is especially pertinent with regard to the middle and popular sectors. Nevertheless, almost at the end of the constitutional transition in which political democracy was reinstalled after years of authoritarianism and state terrorism, there is still a huge gap between the democratic game evinced in the political system and the authoritarianism in daily life.

The focus here is on this public-private border zone—this intersection between schools and families that seems immune both to pressures from above to open up to negotiations and to signals that come from the more private changes the actors of the educational system are experiencing. The purpose is to understand the degree to which the relations between the school and the family allow the latter's proposals to be acted upon. Thus, one question posed is whether negotiations between a collective actor—the "parents," though the mother is the primary actor—and the authorities of each state establishment can be set up to overcome bilateral relations between mothers and the school. The latter type of interaction tends to underestimate the needs of children as they are seen by their mothers and makes it difficult to transform needs into explicit social demands. The aim is to find out to what extent the tie between the school and the family has favored, starting in 1983, more equal relations, thereby creating a better fit between the various elements of the educational community. In this case the hierarchical relations between the school and the family may become a potential arena of negotiations between equals, requiring creation of institutional arrangements in which both actors get appropriate recognition as citizens.

The tie between parents and school authorities was analyzed to permit understanding the behavior of those who act as representatives of each institution. It is particularly important to outline the way in which mothers relate to school authorities because they are more involved with the school than the fathers. For example, in the research discussed here, about seven mothers for every one father were present in school meetings. There was also more participation in the organization of complementary school activities (food tables and amusement activities during school festivals, kiosks for servicing the students during extracurricular activities). Further, mothers develop a more continuous dialogue with the school when the children have behavior or learning problems. They are also intermediaries when the father is required to deal with serious disciplinary problems—those that call for "taking steps."

Also explored here is whether women's participation as mothers encapsulates women in an altruistic and traditional maternal function that makes them appear as mere representatives of the family group or as extensions of the children. Representation is a twofold concept that makes it necessary to establish the difference between the authorities' appeal and the mothers' mode of self-presentation. Face-to-face interaction between the mothers and the educators reinforces the traditional role of mothers because women are asked to help the school to continue their children's supervision, but differences in the mothers' values and educational criteria are ignored. In addition, teachers and authorities assume mothers have ample capability to respond to the children and to school needs—to attend school meetings or help children at home at any time. In response, mothers are unable openly to criticize school disciplinary rules and conceptual orientations that contradict their beliefs and values or clearly expose their personal limits. Women feel more comfortable showing they share an altruistic morality of motherhood, though they recognize their frustration and inability to oppose the school claims frankly.

However, this situation could change under different conditions of relationship. If negotiations with authorities would develop on a more democratic basis, both women and educators might acknowledge the mothers' specific needs and rights to control their children according to the mothers' personal and cultural values. Both sides would also be able to recognize the mothers' contributions to the knowledge of children and their need to be participants in educational decisionmaking. Futhermore, opportunities for coming together around common interests can originate in collective organizations of mothers, thus overcoming the atomization of private life. These organizations can help women to have a sustained interest for specific issues while generating collective demands.

Researchers in participatory projects carried out in secondary schools in the Argentine federal capital and Greater Buenos Aires in the period 1985–1988 tried to find the mechanisms that inhibited the growth of democratic practices in this intersection of the public-private spheres.[2] The investigation was particularly timely because it coincided with efforts by the state to bring the school and community closer together. Also, the changes experienced by women during the past forty years allowed them to increase their social participation in the public sphere.

One of the principal factors preventing further democratization of the educational system lies in the unequal distribution of educational services among the diverse socioeconomic groups of the population. In the state elementary schools, for example, the system does not respond to the needs of the poorer population; these families have a higher average number of children and the parents have a lower level of education. Poorer learning environments are offered in schools in less advantageous areas. The passage to secondary school, on the other hand, favors redistributing pupils in a structure of inequality. The most fortunate enroll in the best schools, reinforcing the relationships among the level reached in school, achievement, and socioeconomic status (Braslavsky, 1985; Tedesco, 1983).

A second factor, no less important, relates to the lack of democracy in the educational system. This is the low level of teacher participation in deciding central school issues, such as curriculum guidelines and disciplinary criteria (Batallan et al., 1988).

Tenti Fanfani (1989) incorporates a third variable in analyzing what slows democratization of the system: the quality of the contribution by those involved in the process of producing the educational service itself. Teachers can work only with the students, and the differing contributions of both induce disparities in the quality of services given and obtained. To this one must add the fragmentation of resources given by the state to the most needy sectors. This is part of the more general phenomenon, extensively discussed in the literature, about the role the educational system plays in reproducing social inequality in Latin America.

The inequality within public schools also has to do with a barrier the system erects against receiving "contributions" from socially disadvantaged parents and children and even from the most active and modern parts of the middle class. This barrier is based on a tie established between teachers and families. The teacher is deemed sacral, while it is assumed that other actors have no right to participate in the school's daily life.

The ideological mechanisms that work within this bond are based on the assumptions that educational services are provided only in a one-way direction, that the provider is omnipotent, and that the power of production operates only in one group of the actors in this relationship. They do not envision, for example, the subordinate position of the teacher vis-à-vis the state, as Batallan does, nor the contribution of the user, noted by Tenti Fanfani. In short, the authoritarian tie that exists between teachers and families not only presupposes the myth that their cooperation is unnecessary but also implies that this cooperation produces a deterioration in educational offerings.

It is interesting to observe how strongly teachers, pupils, and parents endorse these beliefs, thus making the production of changes more difficult. In spite of this fact, the researchers wanted to test whether it was possible to legitimate the parents as productive actors and whether parents, teachers, and pupils could conduct a study of their own needs. The objective was to discover the degree of flexibility needed at the base—at the microsocial level of the educational system—to develop democratic ties.

The hypothesis was that a modification of relations could be possible if parents were represented in an organization that would serve as a collective actor. This organization, however, would have to be based on the principle of wide, nonsexist inclusion—it would have to respect the sociocultural heterogeneity of families and include mothers, the principal intermediaries between school and family, in important positions. An organization with these characteristics would make it possible for parents to win power as a group, as individual negotiations tend to be one of the causes for marginalization of the neediest sectors.

Thus, it was necessary to study (1) how possible it was for parents to create an organization that would involve the needy participants as well as those who question the school the most; (2) the point at which these actors overcome fragmentation and find a voice that would register the marginal sectors' needs, which are rarely taken into account when preventing failure in school; and (3) the point at which the voices of mothers can be included, because they are participants with little credibility in the teachers' eyes, in spite of their being the most involved actors in the children's socialization in the private sphere.

The project proposed, to be conducted jointly with parents and authorities of each school, placed the researchers in the strategic role of being intrusive external agents. The immediate objective was to provoke interest among authorities, teachers, parents, and students in researching their own reality and analyzing relationships among themselves. Research over three years (1985–1987) in one secondary school developed a process for experimenting with all the members of the family and school: school authorities, teachers, members of the school's Directive Commission of the Parents' Cooperative, mothers, fathers, and students. During these years the project began to shape itself as a permanent workshop involving authorities and parents of all the pupils, from the first to the fifth grade. Those who most persistently came to the meetings were mothers of first to third graders—these women were the most interested in preventing their children's failure and in understanding what secondary school was like and, further, still believed in the possibility of adjustment and improvement by the school. Work with the students was through a drama group directed by a specialized teacher; the adolescents' aspirations and illusions were reflected in their plays.

It quickly appeared that the school selected for study was an exceptional organization, whose members wanted to try and who were capable of exposing themselves to the "dangers" of participation, as they themselves called it at some point. For precisely this reason, such participatory research was possible, and the participants worked together even when there were serious conflicts that threatened the project's continuation. When parents began to form groups with the teachers and to demand that steps be taken, the authorities, in spite of their mistrust of the parent workshop methodology, went ahead with the project.

This experience revealed the limits of the educational system. The schools at that time registered the degree of democratization that could be reached during the first years of attempted change, taking into account the authoritarian tradition of secondary school in Argentina and the obscurantist effects of the years of military government.

In 1988, starting with an initiative developed in cooperation with the Ministry of Education, the researchers established parent workshops in other secondary schools in Buenos Aires. This new attempt drew on the previous experiences that allowed the team to set more realistic objectives, which were limited to facilitating the dialogue and communication between parents and the school and including the teachers as new intermediaries.

▲ Methodology for Approaching the Community

In approaching the community, the researchers wanted to explore the thesis that the school tends to exclude its poor clients and those with a better income level but who question the educational system. An objective was to determine the system's elasticity—the potential for transforming ties when external factors that facilitate dialogue are introduced. The research team in this case served as a sounding board for the conflicts that arose between the actors and as a depository for mutual distrust, absorbing criticism coming from both sides and addressing the tensions generated as agreement was attempted. As Brown (1977) observes, this "intrusive" position makes it possible to put aside the habitual norms of interaction between groups, facilitating situations with a better balance of power between them.[3]

The place that the team occupied in the community was an issue discussed at the group level. The researchers tried to be seen neither as representatives of the authorities nor as indifferent to real social interests but as facilitators of cooperation between both groups, without taking either side. The researchers could not avoid being judged adversely, sometimes by the school board or by the teachers, who had been criticized by the parents, and sometimes by the mothers, who were unable to make their opinions prevail.

The team organized workshops with parents, which allowed them to meet among peers without the persecutory look of authorities. The absence of school authorities allowed parents to express more openly their hopes and disappointments with respect to their children's education. They could also elaborate proposals that approached the ideal autonomous organization, independent of the cooperative and the board. In the parent workshops the research team not only acted as an observer of the interaction but also proposed alternative ways of communication, with the objective of facilitating an environment for peers to listen to and understand each other. From this position the team observed the process that was taking place, researching possibilities for resolving the conflicts and the criticisms that seemed central when parents met as a group, in contrast to those brought forth in personal interviews with school authorities.

The team's intervention can be divided into four stages. First was a *probing intervention*, designed to evaluate the possibilities for and obstacles to cooperation between families and schools. This required identifying the possibilities for overcoming the authoritarian ties, varying the objectives according to the group membership (i.e., whether it comprised school authorities or parents). The authorities needed to become conscious of how they limited participation through their style of interaction with parents, such as holding meetings and dialogues sporadically and only in crisis situations (student academic failure, lack of discipline, or antisocial behavior); the parents needed to learn to legitimate their worries and value their opinions. The authoritarian tie had at its center the difficulty of allowing the parents to constitute a group that could succeed in uniting heterogeneous interests. To do this, it was necessary to reconstruct the image that fathers and mothers had of themselves, without their falling into reciprocal blame for the child's failures.

School authorities, upon establishing boundaries of normality in the family and legitimating themselves to judge it on that basis, set up parameters that contribute to the fragmentation of parent groups. The capacity not to cause problems and to have children "without problems" is valued. In this way, the school's conduct is upheld and is awarded the quality of normality. Parents validate, with their criticisms, the unpopularity of those families that the school, using conventional criteria of family organization, sees as abnormal. The most typical things parents said when the workshops first began were "I don't have any problems," "My child doesn't have problems," "I have no problems with the school." Only later did they talk about the multiple oppressive issues regarding their children's education.

Bilateral contacts in emergency situations reinforce the idea of the family and school coming together as a crisis detector. There is no room for parents to meet in peer groups to discuss concepts of familial normality, to think about family models, and to discuss those mechanisms that lead to their children's failure in school. The team's principal objective in this initial stage was to promote regular meetings of the parents of pupils from every grade, without the presence of school authorities, with the goal of counteracting this type of linkage. The agenda in these meetings was to investigate the events that led to the child's failure in school and to detect common problems in the group of parents as a whole.

Throughout the life of the project, parents developed projects that surpassed the team's initial vision by far: They suggested meetings about issues by sectoral theme, meetings to discuss teacher performance, general protest meetings, meetings to organize a club for both relaxation and the treatment of anguishing topics concerning teenagers (such as drug addiction and teenage pregnancies), and meetings to produce a bulletin in which parents would write. They also proposed a discussion committee to deal with specific problems with public authorities and teachers and among children.

The second stage, *implementation intervention*, was characterized by the team's involvement in putting parents' proposals into practice. The team rejected the role of transmitting information between parents and school, making room for direct communication between the two. Conflicts that had before been veiled came out with more clarity, as did the division between the parents and the school authorities over the latter's strong opposition to allowing parents to participate on all levels of school life.

Mothers became fragmented into four groups. The first included those who were allied with and dependent upon the school authorities and who joined and accepted all the steps they took. This sector of mothers did not support other parents; they thought the others "only come to make a mess."

The second group of mothers did not publicly criticize the school for fear of teacher reprisals upon their children, but neither did they openly support it. They were apparently indifferent and did not get involved or express an opinion; this group made up the silent majority.

A third sector represented the most active mothers who led various collective activities. In certain cases they created the parent organizations that became independent from the cooperative. In other cases they held leading positions in the cooperative for a while, trying to change its dependent character. These mothers had a higher level of education and had the possibilities of an egalitarian dialogue with authorities and teachers.

Finally, there was a group of mothers with less income and education who were close to the group of leaders and who continuously participated in activities organized by them. They were very aware of their children's school life and were inspired by the desire that their children continue studying and obtain better jobs than they or their husbands had.

From the school authorities and the cooperative came open resistance to the parents' participation in this stage. This appeared dangerous and anarchic. Faced with a highly conflictive situation, school authorities had strong reactions:

"Parents get together and make vile remarks about the teachers."

"You can't let them meet and express themselves without giving them a guided issue."

"They take advantage right away to make impossible demands."

"Parental participation can happen, but beforehand it must be decided why."

"You can't allow parents to form pressure groups."

"People don't always have good intentions."

"I think the idea in itself is good and can work, but not in a school because the system is too rigid."

As a result of the evaluations conducted after the first and second stages, the team proposed a third stage, *balance-of-power intervention*, in an attempt to even the power relationship between parents and school. In this new stage, three objectives were set. The first was to blur and extend the limits of those groups that already had institutional backing; this meant incorporating into the cooperative new members from the groups of mothers who participate the most in committees and subcommittees of the cooperatives. The second aim was to continue the team role as facilitator of the dialogue among parents and between parents and school authorities, clarifying in the end the expectations of the groups involved, anticipating conflict, and proposing alternative ways of resolution that would impede the habitual marginalization of some sector. The third objective was to propose actions to balance the power equation—to accept and facilitate proposals of independent organizations led by mothers, to show bonds that would encourage nonorganized parents to come together, and to research the criteria for normality/abnormality that bring about fragmentation (Schmukler and Savigliano, 1988; Brown, 1977).

A corollary to the severe conflicts that emerged between authorities and parent representatives was that the team entered a fourth stage in which the negotiations between them started. The group of mothers with the most autonomy organized a club, thereby generating a tie among themselves that did not depend on the vagaries of the authorities. They developed activities of solidarity between families, and they disseminated information on issues regarding the education of children that cause general concern, thus producing a transformation of parents from "object group" to "subject group," according to Barbier's (1985) definition. The most active group of mothers (of whom there were about twelve), with the intermittent participation of three fathers, designed a strategy for consolidation that was tolerated by the authorities. Fragmented sectors were able to join this group and discuss and produce jointly. They proposed a strategy of action that avoided confrontation with the authorities. They tried to fight against marginalization and the school's failure to educate their children, while bringing to light issues such as alcoholism and drug addiction. They also tried to find ways to support their children's projects. They found a place for collective discussion of the particular questions they raised, even though these questions did not interest the school authorities.

The organization of the parents' club served as training and education for those mothers who could then become integrated in a less dependent way into the cooperative committee. The club supported the activities of the student center that was tolerated, though with certain restrictions, by the school authorities. These authorities, possibly using the club as an example, encouraged another organization of mothers, whose children had higher probabilities for failure because they had failed previous subjects.

At the end of the second year of intervention, the team saw the emergence of new social actors—the parents' club, the group of mothers with repeating children—and the strengthening of the student center. These events were accompanied by a splintering of the school authorities, as one faction accepted greater parental participation and another faction rejected it. Finally, a proposal that called for cooperation with parents to work out problems concerning their children's school failure was approved. However, the authorities agreed on the need to control the independent actions of organized parents, who decided to extend part of their activities to private homes, but this approach made the possibility of greater impact more difficult.

▲ Democratization in Everyday Life After 1983

Two major factors could have come together in the democratization of the bond between parents and school, beginning with the constitutional government elected in 1983. First, a declaration by the Ministry of Education and the Board of Middle Education to promote an opening of the educational community included parents expressly. Projects were implemented to deepen integration by young people and their parents into the educational community. At the national level, the creation of advisory committees in each school was promoted. They were proposed by the National Board of Middle Education and painstakingly implemented by school principals. In the province of Buenos Aires, this policy acquired even more defined characteristics with the creation of school advisories, which sought to stimulate democratic participation, community spirit, solidarity, and freedom for the entire educational community (teachers, nonteachers, pupils, parents).

Second, changes in women's social participation allowed a redefinition of power and authority relations between men and women in family groups. The way of practicing motherhood, within and outside the domestic arena, was also affected.

The increase in women's economic participation since the 1940s and of homes with female family heads in the last two decades led to new legislation concerning the family, which tended toward more equality in men's and women's rights.[4] These changes have allowed the beginning of a demystification of the essentialism or naturalism in the complementary functions of maternity and paternity, which take away men's and women's creative energy in either the public or private sphere.

The set of changes observed in this period raises the possibility of a flexible approach to the authoritarian familial system as the dialogue between parents and young people grows and as there emerges a greater understanding of the methods of raising children so that they have more freedom to intervene and give an opinion. The two faces of symbolic violence in the family—(1) arbitrariness in the message transmitted and (2) arbitrariness in the determination of the individuals who appear to be or who define themselves as being in authority roles (Bourdieu, 1977)—are affected. The biological reasons that legitimize authority, such as age and masculinity, start to be questioned. It is important to mention here that during the Alfonsin government a number of important changes regarding family rights were made: changes in the Law of Patria Potestas to favor equal rights of the father and the mother, and the enactment of a law allowing divorce (for the first time in the history of Argentina).

The changes in family legislation reflect, in part, the greater social equality achieved in the relationships between men and women. In Argentina women in the lower and working classes have shown themselves able to adapt to crisis situations, accepting informal jobs, with irregular schedules, at home and away, as happens in other Latin American countries. Between 1960 and 1980 Argentine women increased their degree of participation in the labor force from 22 percent to 27 percent. Kritz (1983) estimates that between 1960 and 1970 the increase in female labor improved families' socioeconomic level. The economic crisis that started in 1980 increased the need of sharing economic responsibilities at home between both parents and the older children, but despite this participation, there has been a decrease in the per capita income.

As a consequence of these juridical and economic changes, domestic roles in families of low-income sectors were redistributed to some extent between the sexes, increasing negotiations and competition for authority. These changes also demanded a redistribution of the job of controlling and supervising the children, which, together with the new juridical rules, created a weakening of male authority. These developments favored the woman's participation in the public sphere, which in turn acted against the family's symbolic violence (Schmukler, 1985).

The research team anticipated that more autonomy for women in the family would be related to more participation outside of the domestic world, starting with a clearer identification of personal and familial interests. A process with these characteristics could lead women to reject arbitrary rules coming from the school and to take advantage of meeting with other parents in a more active way, generating ties of solidarity and cooperation. This linkage would be the result of a process of democratization of each of these two institutions and would be reflected in a greater family involvement in the daily practices of the school and in resistance to the discipline the school tries to exercise over family life. In other words, the team anticipated that the democratic transition would make it possible to develop processes characterized by greater exchanges between the community and the school.

The inquiry, then, was to determine what articulations would allow the changes in the family structure to correlate to women's participation as mothers. A process of democratization could imply an increase in the subjects' participation helped by patrimonial institutions of the state in the elaboration and execution of institutional management.[5] If the social processes in the juridical and political sphere provoked a weakening of feminine subordination within the family, then women, as intermediaries between the family and the school, could collaborate to make these articulations transfer the democratization from the family to the school. This could happen through the organizations of these women in any patrimonial institution: education, health, or social services (Donzelot, 1979).

▲ Social Participation and the Maternal Role

The research methodology made it possible to work with mothers and to identify the possibilities of organizing women through their maternal role. In this case, a study of the desire and potential for uniting around an interest for their children's development was attempted. The team found that these objectives could be defended only when working in pursuit of the school's democratization, because the symmetry of the bond depended on the possibility of knowing and adapting to requirements of the most needy sectors. Bilateral relations, based on the fragmented parent actor, hide the paths that enable the students to have success in school.

In order to make the needs clear, to generate needs, and to propose concrete solutions, a political project within the school facility had to be developed. For mothers, this project offered the possibility of overcoming the atomization of private life while enabling them to understand and recognize private life—in this case, the specificity of the adolescents' life and that of their families. This project sought to create a social actor whose role on the private side would allow the articulation of demands in a public sphere in such a way that individual concerns would be included. This implied overcoming the traditional concept of maternity because it demanded solidarity in pursuit of the creation of a social identity and relied on the women's self-recognition as a group or movement of mothers. As Lobo (1987) suggests, only when the action brings together these conditions, and when allies, interlocutors, and enemies have been identified, can one have a political action.

The process of democratization, therefore, demands a redefinition of motherhood as a public practice. In order to participate as a subject instead of an object when representing the child at school, the woman must resist activity that erases her as a person, abolishing her creativity. The place for mediation between the school and the family, when political action through real participation is not possible, describes the twofold subjection of the woman who carries out this role. Motherhood implies, in these cases, a personal commitment to responsibilities concerning exclusively the protection and care of children. It has as its basis the notion that women engage in altruistic action, forgetting their own needs. The idea, upheld by mothers as well as teachers, is that the mother, as her children's primary socializing agent, should control and supervise their homework, without worrying about her own potential, work schedule, or specific interests and without asking herself how she could contribute to the schools through her own experience as a child raiser and educator in the private sphere.

Statements such as the following, heard in interviews with women, seem to justify the model of an always available mother as the ideal. These ideas are expressed by mothers from diverse socioeconomic and cultural levels, who may or may not work outside the home and who have a varying number of children:

"We mothers go to school because we don't have a set schedule."

"The father is loaded down with the weight of his job."

"It takes away the men's time, they come home tired."

"It is well understood in this society that the child's education is taken care of by women."

"The father passes the buck to the mother" [a rarer comment, one said with a hint of protest but with resignation].

Fathers also consider that the mother's involvement in all of the child's affairs is natural. One father represents the feeling of many others when he says: "Look, I get involved when my wife tells me to. She is the one who is on top of the child. If he is ditching class, has bad grades, then she tells me and I get involved. Otherwise, my wife takes care of everything."

Mothers justify their greater dedication: "I notice when they study and when they don't." Adolescents reinforce this vision. A daughter said to her father in a family interview: "You help if we come ask you to, while mom asks me if I need help every day. When she comes home from work, she helps me."

Even if there is less emphasis on it at the secondary level than in grade school, the mother is still considered an appendage of the school whose role is to perform functions that cannot be carried out in a school environment. The maternal role certainly implies, in part, involvement—understood as representation—but it could encapsulate more personalized methods of involvement. For example, those women who want to could exercise a practice that is closer to educational management or to the development of projects parallel to homework that would permit the school to extend into the community.

The majority of mothers, as opposed to fathers, see their participation as collaboration with the school. What matters is what the school needs—as defined by the school. Mothers express these reasons for becoming involved in the school:

"To help in everything possible."

"To fulfill a duty to the school."

"When they ask me or I see that they need me, I offer to get involved."

"I cooperate with the school."

"If I can give a hand, I'm always willing; there are always ways to get involved."

"I support the school leadership."

"I support the school's work."

This vision emerges because "the school," as an abstract and sacred entity, asks the parents to become more involved when it finds it convenient and necessary. There is no suggestion of joint decisionmaking but rather of "collaboration," which really means assisting school authorities. Mothers are the ones who are given the duty of selling raffle tickets to collect funds, or they get involved when there is an urgent problem that needs resolution: "I have already told them that when they need me, I will get involved."

Interestingly, conflicts with the school always appeared after a series of general expressions and abstract affirmations of a desire to collaborate. The parents seem to be fulfilling a ritual in which, before expressing their disagreement, it is necessary to pay honor to the sacred image of the school. Afterward, the "true" school appears with the pile of complaints against it.

This description of the interaction between mothers and the school reflects society's expectation that women carry out their maternal role as well as a mediating role between the family and patrimonial institutions. The mother should create interinstitutional harmony, confirming her traditional job. This job, in turn, inhibits her participation from a personal perspective that identifies her own needs.

One of the ways of overcoming subordination of women is rooted in the possibility of their participation as subjects and citizens in everyday activities. This implies the right to be heard and to break into institutional management, public or private. Here the possibility of social participation from a maternal stance and microsocial democratization intersect. The fight for women's improved status, prestige, authority, and self-worth happens as much in individual negotiations in the family as in the political action of everyday life.

When this project began, the team assumed there would be several factors that would coalesce to foster collective action by the mothers through the creation of parents' associations in each school. This collective action was expected to create conditions for equal negotiation between schools and families. The collective presence of the "parents" was expected to generate demands that would bring the public institutions closer to the needs of the private groups by taking into account the learning problems of the students as a whole while at the same time respecting the voices of the popular sectors traditionally ignored. Also, other factors would come together, beginning with the restoration of the democratic regime, that would impel mothers to collectivize their actions by means of forming an organization of parents in each school.

The team assumed that the parents' collective presence, although it might provoke resistance from the school, in the long run would allow an equal dialogue. Individual negotiations, on the other hand, generally lead to sanctions against the poorest sectors, strengthening the causes of repetition and failure among the students from popular sectors. In this way, authorities confirm the worst expectations they have concerning poor families, feeling unable to modify the percentage of failure. There is an underlying idea that these families, conditioned by their poverty, are destined to cause their children's failure. A feeling of impotence spreads that stops families from devising methods that could improve their children's fulfillment in school. Moreover, a strategy to prevent this failure from establishing the current differences between males and females does not exist. Among the female pupils, for example, one influence that might become an obstacle for continuing their studies would be the domestic role they carry out in their homes and the low parental expectation regarding daughters' occupational trajectory (Stromquist, 1987). These different issues do not enter the discussions with the families; ideas that put the blame on the parents are elaborated in place of working together to find what causes failure.

▲ The School as Authority:
Authoritarian Interaction in Participation

The team analyzed the possibilities for parents' collective presence subsequent to the democratic opening of 1983, examining how collective organizations of parents could be sustained given the obstacles coming from very different actors of the educational system. The following comments reflect the perspective of the school's management:

"Parents are not interested."

"They come with their demands when it's already too late. They don't take charge. They don't go through the learning process with their children."

"It is because there are many unorganized families, the parents are divorced."

"There are also families where the parents didn't finish high school, and they don't understand, and for that reason can't help."

"There are families that hide what the children do, they lie to us . . . There are also families in which the mother works outside . . . families in poor socioeconomic situation . . . The experience of isolation many families felt during the military dictatorship. . . . The children then fail and leave school."

The school represents an authority facing a wide group of parents. Traditionally, all of them relate to the school bilaterally, not as an associated or corporate group. The various committees of the cooperative do not constitute real organs of representation for the parents. Rather, these institutions are dependent on the management, with the strong presence of those parents with economic possibilities and a higher level of education, tied personally to the authorities, and developing activities at their request.

Given the fact that no one speaks out against its authority, the school has the possibility of not only disciplining and molding the pupils but also of judging the parents and their ability to educate. The school's nominating capacity encourages a breaking and distancing among parents. This brings together all the reasons that inhibit them from becoming part of the educational community. The legitimacy for the participation of parents is affected not only by the prejudices that move from the school to the home but also by the parents' tendency to grant the school the right to decide what makes good and bad parents. They set themselves up—just like the children—to be ordered by the hierarchy in accordance with a healthy or normal model. In this way, they accept the concept of prescribed normality and the educational categories for evaluating success.

The prejudices of the parents themselves are an important obstacle in their becoming a collective actor: "It is better to be few and good," and "If they haven't shown interest before, it is useless to force it." After conflictive meetings among parents in which difficult issues were addressed, one mother commented: "To listen to these vile remarks I [might as well] meet other mothers in the market."

The children's failure seems, for many parents, a personal failure. It is an echo of those educators who accuse mothers of not knowing how to supervise their children's studies and of overprotecting them. Not being able to give their children an adequate cultural base or not knowing how to communicate with them becomes for parents from popular sectors a source of guilt. Some of them see their children's scholastic failure as their own, measuring their parental function according to moral codes set by experts legitimized by the state or the dominant culture (whether they be doctors, psychoanalysts, journalists, or teachers). For others, the responsibility resides in the school and its ability to accept pupils with fewer means. In these cases a climate of reciprocal blame develops, which hinders a dialogue and a combined search for the roots of the pupils' failure. In any case, as Krawczyk (1985) observes, there is an emphasis on individual responsibility—on the teacher, on the child, or on the mother who cannot ensure the continuation of studies at home. But there is a lack of comprehension about the need for a protagonist group made up of pupils, parents, and teachers and about the specific responsibilities that the state should assume (Krawczyk, 1985).

The school authorities' call to participation, in this context, is carried out not as part of recognizing the need for cooperation but rather as an invitation to be present, to listen, and to become responsible with the expectation of being accepted in this place. The school, for example, can accept formal changes in the dynamics of the meetings, but it cannot change the character of the meetings themselves. The goal of these meetings is to inform parents about the mechanisms of evaluation, of the announced changes in rules by the government ministry, or of the particular needs the school has for cooperation or help on the part of the mothers and fathers. To call the parents in to debate is considered dangerous:

"If there is no concrete proposal, these parents, without culture, tend to criticize and make base comments. . . . It is dangerous."

"The agenda shouldn't touch pedagogical aspects. None of this, because it brings problems. It should not address teachers, nor material."

"The meetings are to inform."

Hirshberg (1989) distinguishes five levels of participation: providing information, allowing consultation, offering recommendations and proposals, permitting comanagement, and permitting self-management. Only at the third level can the parents be considered to have some control over the scholastic management. The level of comanagement implies the possibility of sharing decisionmaking with educational authorities, as much on the pedagogic plane as in administrative matters, or in the infrastructural aspects of the school. At the highest level of participation, the group determines its own methods of management and its own objectives. In line with Hirshberg's study of the different methods of participation created in Argentina during the democratic period, participation beyond the level of information and consultation has not moved to a national scale, although there have been attempts in certain provinces to generate forms of greater comanagement. Some ideas regarding an educational community, however, have been developed (Hirshberg, 1989).

The school's call for participation is an egalitarian message, meant for all the parents. Nevertheless, the process of fragmentation between "good" and "bad" parents causes differing receptions of the message. A contradiction between the general and the egalitarian call is created by the style of discourse that separates as much by the contents as by the language used—a language understood only by those with a higher cultural level. To the rest, it gives a foreign sensation. They do not feel sufficiently attracted to it. Not being able to understand the scholastic language, they consider themselves marginal.

The school, including both the authorities and the teachers, holds views such as these:

"Parents never listen, and they don't know. They don't understand the issues because the majority didn't go to secondary school, they're not cultured. They don't ask questions about the program, the materials, nor do they involve themselves in the issue of discipline."

"Parents are a doubled-edged weapon. If they become involved in the pedagogy and don't know . . . , they fall into subjective postures—for example, 'the problems my child has with professor X.'"

"The issue is that parents don't take responsibility. But when the child fails it is our fault and the parents never feel responsible. In short, it is our fault and the child's."

"Illiterate parents cannot participate; even if they form little groups and there is one person who writes and takes the reins, the one who knows how to write will be the most educated."

"There are no expectations regarding the parents who generally have few resources and are ignorant. The school has to offer them everything."

"One notices right away, through the children, which of the parents are involved and take care of their children. The most wordy children, who come well dressed, have books and notebooks as it should be, are also those who study. One sees that they have a well-organized family. . . . The others, however, don't become involved; there are conflicts at home and neglect."

For the school, the "problem families" are those that do not take daily control of their children's studies and responsibility for their failures. They are the ones not present when there is a crisis in children's behavior. They are the families in which good communication between the parents and between the parents and children is lacking; in which there are unequal amounts of love for each person; in which the parents do not offer clear information about old family history—deaths, disappearances, abandonments. They are families in which there is sexual or other forms of violence, or in which the father or a man who fulfills the authoritative role is missing. In general, there is a mixture of cases of extreme violence or early unwanted pregnancies with modes of affective bonding that seem abnormal when judged from a predetermined conception of what the ideal family is.

The ideal family's legitimacy is based on representations taken from psychological orientations that became popular among the urban middle classes in Argentina and were adopted by teachers as their own. From the point of view of teachers, the "problem" families are those with the following characteristics:

Poor communication:
"Those in which the children hide how things are going in school."
"And when the parents find out they ask us why we didn't tell them."
"We inform them an infinite number of times, and they don't come."
"In the end, those responsible are the school and the children; the parents don't take any responsibility."

Poor family relations:
"Marriages that are going bad."
"Very old parents with arteriosclerosis."
"Mothers who conceal, who take charge of their children to protect them."

"Mothers who think: 'They're children and children will have time to suffer.'"

"Violent fathers."

"A mother's love for the male and not the female, and the father's jealousy."

"Unclear deaths of little brothers or sisters."

"Lack of communication between the parents."

"When one of the two parents becomes the accomplice to protect the child."

"Children who ask us not to tell one of their parents when things are going badly."

"Teenage pregnancies."

Little or no motivation:

"Most important is the lack of motivation because if they are from a more accommodated social class, if they fail one school they go to another. But if they have few resources, they just don't return."

In the first meetings with the school, the research team learned the opinions of the directors. The first thing detected was complaints: "Mothers aren't interested in the school." Authorities did not think they could mend the families that were distancing themselves from the school and from other public or social encounters, whether as an expression of hopelessness or as a rejection of the military regime between 1976 and 1983. The democratic opening was unable to call the community together to reestablish ties and to interest people in forms of participation.

Detected in mothers' responses was that their limited participation reflected a withdrawal of support because of certain repressive ways in which teachers dealt with the children. They also held no hope for any assistance that the secondary school could offer for their children's future employment (Braslavsky, 1986).

A break in communication between the school (teachers and authorities) and parents—seen in their complaints about each other—showed that the existing messages were not destined to bring about a meeting but rather to avoid one. The lack of organization on the part of the parents to overcome fragmentation brought back the lack of hope that parents had about being heard.

When parents want to give their opinions about methods of teaching and the usefulness of materials, they find an impassable barrier. Many of them think they have the right to take part only in matters relating to the infrastructure, the maintenance of buildings, the physical aspects of the education framework, and, in the final instance, in economic matters (such as organizing food for parties, fund-raising to buy a computer, improving school buildings, painting, fixing benches). Normally, those who have economic power establish priorities for spending the cooperative's money and become the representatives on the leading committee. But in determining who will be part of the psychopedagogic team, what type of extracurricular activities will be developed, and which students will benefit from scholastic support, only the teachers are involved. These are pedagogic matters in which the parents should not participate.

The authoritarian rituals observed reproduce themselves in two ways. On the one hand, parents, who invest school authorities with a sacral mantle, demand that the authorities themselves retain unlimited control of pedagogic issues. They expect education to be a service—as if this were possible—without intervention or with a passiveness that inhibits offering a service according to needs. On the other hand, as already seen, school authorities develop a discourse that marginalizes poor, less-cultured families. Even when this discourse calls for participation, the ideological mechanisms implicit in the message deepen the fragmentation of fathers and mothers and the distancing of the most disadvantaged social sectors. Thus a paradox is produced: The academic message renders illegitimate those groups that are the most culturally and economically disadvantaged through its labeling as "abnormal" their forms of family organization, childrearing, or education (Hirshberg, 1989).

▲ Conclusion

Some mothers describe the school as an *aguantadero* (a place just for children to be taken care of while parents are busy elsewhere). In these mothers' view, the time when their children are in the school is the time when they are not in the streets or with dangerous gangs that could tempt them to take drugs or enter a criminal life. Other mothers struggle so that their children will study, but they have little hope that their children will develop a willingness and the discipline to do so. Their anguish is centered at one time on the potential to keep their children in the school system and at another time on their own children's efforts. This anguish also expresses the lack of strategies for taking care of the adolescents in a more creative way. These adolescents have no space in the family, which is busy trying to survive in the country's critical economic conditions that permit the family to offer only shelter. The maternal function, which replaced the lack of social institutions that promote and facilitate adolescent growth, is weakened as soon as women increase their participation in the labor force and become the main source of income generation as male unemployment sharpens.

Among parents with more education, there is a strong criticism of the high school, especially about student-teacher relations. Psychological mistreatment by means of unjust and constant discipline—in which prejudice toward certain social groups is present and sometimes explained by a teacher's own frustration—is denounced.

Rigid, hierarchical relations within the educational system in general and within each school in particular do not allow self-management and meetings of actors as a way of exposing demands and proposing modifications in the structure. This framework includes mechanisms of communication that get in the way of understanding or of allowing validation of points made from inferior positions—closed systems that do not make information about decisions known in a way that allows people to find out who made them and in what forms they will affect students or parents. To the issue of communication between the school and families, other factors can be added. These are tied to the definition of those who form part of the system and the power relations between them.

First, parents are not considered an intrinsic part of the school community needed for reaching decisions that concern the infrastructure and pedagogic activities. Therefore, they are not an integral part of the school authority system, they are not subject to disciplinary sanctions, and they do not submit themselves to control. They are therefore not considered part of the school's hierarchy. They are treated as extensions of their children, who are part of that system, and are thus susceptible to indirect sanctions and rewards. Because of the indirect nature of the sanctions, it is more difficult for the mothers to reply or defend themselves. The sanctions act as latent moral recriminations, given in messages in which the canons of quality of life are set by the school.

Second, the fact that parents pertain to an external system—the family—permits them to judge and sanction the teachers and principals. Those with the most potent voices are the ones who criticize the demagogic deviations of the teachers and directors who seek to move away from authoritarian procedures. Thus, parents and the school act in a mutually reinforcing pattern—when one of the two slackens its control over the young people, a conservative demand develops in the other. In high schools serving poor neighborhoods, parents from diverse social extraction and educational background are together; however, only the voices of the most authoritarian parents prevail. In the analyzed schools, groups with participatory and democratic tendencies coexist with others that push the school authorities into a more rigid control of their children, thus preventing the emergence of creative and bonding experiences.

Thus, two mechanisms that block democracy are fused. When the parents want to appropriate a part of the school's space and organize themselves autonomously, the school demands dependent behavior, frustrating the beginning of a participatory process. When the school organizes activities open to the community—such as those showing solidarity with the most needy schools, for instance, or facilitating the development of parent workshops or organizing student centers—a repressive demand is generated by some parents. In the study, the more conservative parents appear to be worried about their daughters' morality, thus watching over events at school that might incite or allow behavior they prohibit at home.

Third, among mothers from the middle class and wage-earning sectors were groups willing to cooperate with the school, pressuring it for more participation in the questions considered pedagogic: student-teacher relationships, weaknesses in their children's learning, and problems related to a teacher's style of teaching. The mothers who developed these activities gradually pulled away from participation because they felt disillusioned by the barriers set up by the school.

Fourth, the difficulties in communication between parents and the school have several causes. One is the distance between the mothers' private logic and the school's public knowledge. Mothers, the principal participants in the dialogue with the school, think in terms of particular and private interests; the school's principal (in this case a male) feels misunderstood in his search for the group's benefits. He thinks in terms of social categories, in terms of the pupils and an average output of the group. He is neither prepared nor does he have the resources to follow each individual student, as is expected by mothers.

Another source of conflict is the preference on the mothers' part and on the part of the principal for informal means of communication, face to face, based on bilateral and confidential relations but with hierarchical relations retained. In this type of relationship the inequalities between the school and the family deepen because the mothers disappear as subjects with a right to their own demands. This informal communication apparently helps the resolution of individual problems, but it prevents the mothers from generating a group dynamic to give structure to global demands. This informal communication establishes the parents as a segmented, dispersed sector, stratified and divided between "good" and "bad" parents, according to the school's judgment. The fragmented communication does not allow the parents to reflect, as a group, about the judgments families receive that agree with the expected level of "normality" and the differentiation between organized and unorganized families. Each mother or father, therefore, must defend herself or himself when faced with pigeonholing and personalized negotiations.

Further, the school's appeal for participation confirms the families' dispersion. The principal summons all the families in the same way, through a broad discourse pronounced at school festivities at the beginning of the academic year and on patriotic anniversaries. But the call for concrete tasks is made only to parents from "organized" families—ones considered appropriate for collaboration. As was seen earlier, the language used in the school's call for specific participation is also pronounced in a cultured style that marginalizes families at the lower socioeconomic level.

The obstacles in the way of the parents' participation also come from diverse sources that have to do with the structure of authority in the high school, which, unlike the elementary school, is alien to many parents and thus leads them to lose their own space and their right to shape curricular and extracurricular activities. Also, parents have not been able to generate a common proposal inasmuch as it is impossible for them to visualize themselves as a group because of the segmentation in which they find themselves. Their inclusion is also rejected by some pupils who fear a more personalized control by their parents. Moreover, economic problems aggravate the parents' distance from school affairs; parents' energy is centered on activities tied to survival, leaving no room for community tasks, solidarity, or collective creation. In these circumstances, parents prefer to delegate to experts.

The parents' difficulties in becoming collective actors manifest themselves in the obstacles mothers find in generating and consolidating an autonomous organization. Dependent organizations, with strong ties to authority, have the ability to survive by not including parents considered conflictive or those with links to "messy" families. They also accept the means of bilateral and informal negotiations that do not put into play parents' limited power over the educational institution. This type of organization does not constitute a threat to the principal, who fears criticism, inspection, or excessive management on the part of the most repressive parents. The principal also fears the anarchy that more autonomous organizations of mothers who do not trust the sacred character of the school's institution could generate. More conservative mothers take a dependent position toward the school that reinforces its authoritarianism.

In short, the reproductive cycles of authoritarianism in family-school ties evince efforts toward transformation that have not yet found stable forms of autonomous organization. Nevertheless, the transforming processes could result in forms of alliance among progressive sectors in the schools, with the participation of democratically inspired mothers and fathers. It does not seem, however, that a movement of demands on the parents' part could count on such support and on possibilities for penetration into the school's institution today.

This chapter has described the behavioral style of women as collective actors in one aspect of their reproductive roles: as educational administrators and supervisors of their children. To the extent that the school takes care of an essential part of children's development from six years of age, it extends the mother's role as a socialization agent, starting at the moment the children enter elementary school. The mother goes from being a principal source of transmission of social representations and values in preschool socialization to becoming an interpreter or evaluator for the children in elementary school, only to have her place, in relation to the school, further limited. Usually, she becomes the child's partner in the effort to avoid school failure.

Although the mother's place is relative according to her level of education and the variety of stimuli that surround the children—originating from the multiplicity and variety of couples or significant adults with whom they interact—the mother's role loses centrality in her child's process of construction of social representations as the child enters secondary school. The maternal voice becomes a background—an acquired tool—used to judge and process new external stimuli.

These changes in the mother's socializing role during the child's growth and development throughout the school cycle also involves transformations in her maternal duty in relation to the state. In the elementary school, motherhood is more aimed at helping the child to integrate socially and to understand and accept the social norms established by the public sphere. In secondary school, in contrast, mothers try to ensure good academic performance in children to guarantee that they successfully face new demands and avoid school failure, which is particularly threatening during the first three years of middle education (Tedesco, 1983).

▲ Notes

I wish to thank IDRC and the Inter-American Foundation for their support during 1985–1988 for this research effort.

1. An approximate idea of the percentage of school failure throughout Argentina can be gleaned from the number of high school dropouts. In the period 1975–1979 this was an average of 40 percent for the whole country. Of young workers ages 20–24 in 1980, those in jobs that pertain to the popular sectors (employees, salespeople, specialized workers, laborers, apprentices, school personnel, office clerks, domestic servants, and other unspecified jobs) represent 93 percent of those who did not finish secondary school, or 280,710 out of a total 299,949 (Instituto Nacional de Estadistica [INDEC], 1985).

2. This research was carried out by Grupo de Estudios Sociales para la Transformación (GEST) with support from the Inter-American Foundation (US) and the International Development Research Center (Canada).

3. This part of the research was coordinated by Marta Savigliano and the analysis from this section comes from the observations in Schmukler and Savigliano (1987). See also Savigliano and Schmukler (1988); Brown (1977).

4. The Law of Patria Potestas, enacted in 1985, established equal rights for the father and mother and for children born in and out of wedlock. If a woman lives with a man, it is assumed that the child is the man's, unless the contrary is proved. The law also gives special privileges to children within the family.

5. Patrimonial institutions include those integrated in the educational judicial system and those that provide social assistance to families. The institutions that form this group tend to dissolve the parents' resistance or misunderstanding when the parents cannot ensure a "correct" socialization of the adolescents and children. The concept of patrimonial institutions implies family protection as much as controlling and protecting supervision of the changes (see Donzelot, 1979, 99ff.).

▲ References

Arendt, Hanna. *The Human Condition*. Chicago: University of Chicago Press, 1958.

Balvo, Laura. *Stato di famiglia*. Milan: Gruppo Editoriale Fabbri, 1976.

Barbier, R. *Pesquisa-açao na instituçao educativa*. Rio de Janeiro: Jorge Zahar Editorial, 1985.

Batallán, Graciela, María Saleme, and José Fernando García. *Talleres de educadores. El mundo dial niño y el aprendizaje escolar*. Informe Final. Buenos Aires: FLACSO, 1986.

Braslavsky, Cecilia. *La discriminación educativa en la Argentina*. Buenos Aires: FLACSO, 1985.

Bourdieu, Pierre. *Outline of a Theory of Practice*. Cambridge: Cambridge University Press, 1977.

Brown, L. D. "Can 'Haves' and 'Have-nots' Cooperate? Two Efforts to Bridge a Social Gap." *Journal of Applied Behavioral Science*, 1977, vol. 13, no. 2, pp. 211–224.

Conti Odorisio, Ginevra. *Donna e societa nel seicento: Lucrezia Marinelli e Arcangela Tarabotti*. Rome: Bulzoni, 1979.

Donzelot, Jacques. *La policía de las familias*. Valencia: Pretextos, 1979.

Elshtain, Jean. *Public Men, Public Women*. Princeton: Princeton University Press, 1982.

Filmus, Daniel, and Cecilia Braslavsky. *Obstáculos a la democratización del sistema educativo*. Buenos Aires: FLACSO, 1986.

Hirshberg, Sonia. "The Educational Community's Participation in Secondary Education." Buenos Aires: FLACSO, mimeo, 1989.

INDEC (Instituto Nacional de Estadística y Censos). *La juventud en la Argentina, estudios 3*. Buenos Aires: INDEC, 1985.

Klein, F., and L. J. Gould. "Boundary Issues and Organizational Dynamics: A Case Study." *Social Psychiatry*, 1973, vol. 8, no. 4, pp. 204–211.

Krawczyk, Nora. *The Way Popular Sectors Perceive the State's Responsibility in the Education of Their Children*. Documentos FLACSO no. 15. Buenos Aires: FLACSO, 1985.

Kritz, Ernesto. *Trabajo femenino, actividad doméstica y crisis económica: El caso de la Argentina*. Proyecto Gobierno Argentino. Buenos Aires: UNDP/ILO, 1983.

Lobo, Elisabeth. "Mulheres, feminismo e novas práticas sociais." *Revista de Ciências Sociais*, special issue ("Mulheres e os novos espaços democráticos na America Latina"), 1987, vol. 1, no. 2.

Schmukler, Beatriz. "Gender and Authority in Lower-Class Working Families in Buenos Aires." Ph.D. dissertation, Yale University, 1985.

Schmukler, Beatriz, and Marta Savigliano. "Authority Relationships between the Family and the Secondary Schools." Final Report. Presented to IDRC and the Inter-American Foundation. (Buenos Aires: GEST, 1987).

———. *Cooperativismo o autoritarismo en el vínculo Familias-Escuela*. Buenos Aires: Ediciones GEST, 1988.

Stromquist, Nelly. "Gender Disparities in Educational Access and Attainment: Mainstream and Feminist Theories." Paper presented at the western regional meeting of the Comparative and International Education Society, Los Angeles, 1987.

Tedesco, Juan Carlos. *El proyecto educativo autoritario*. Buenos Aires: FLACSO, 1983.

Tenti Fanfani, Emilio. *Estado y pobreza: Estrategias típicas de intervención*. Buenos Aires: Biblioteca Política Argentina, Centro Editor de América Latina, 1989.

▲13

The Women's Rural School: An Empowering Educational Experience

Ximena Valdes

This chapter by Ximena Valdes offers a firsthand account of the evolution of an educational intervention with low-income women in Chile. It depicts how what started as brief gender-consciousness sessions gradually became redesigned into a rural women's school to provide its participants the space and time needed for an effective reflection of their situation as women and workers.

This account details the strategic decisions that program designers had to make in order to serve women effectively. Working with women who were so heavily involved in domestic and remunerated work activities made it necessary to take them to a new setting (the rural school) for four-day meetings over a six-month period. Pedagogically, it was felt that the identification of labor demands by the women would be a good starting point for the discussion of their subordination in society. Because the low-income women tended to combine work and family issues in their perception of personal problems, the program designers had to create homogeneous groups along lines of occupational interest.

Valdes shows that this popular education program, in terms of creating a critical understanding and new visions among the participants, was successful. However, two major problems were encountered: first, the tension the women developed between solving immediate economic problems and addressing longer-term social change; second, the tendency among the participants to engage in collective action and to adopt a feminist discourse while attending the rural school, but to encounter difficulties in continuing such practices upon return to their communities. The resolution of these tensions calls for supportive measures in the social and economic arenas of the country as a whole, a condition beyond the program designers' control. Although the popular education program will go on, its developers raise questions about the opportunities that may emerge now that Chile has a democratic regime.

—Editor

▲   Education is a field within which systems of domination are reproduced; popular education has not been an exception. The notion of "people"[1]—a group undifferentiated by gender—upon which popular education as a liberating education has been based does not contribute to attack one of the oldest systems of domination in the history of mankind, that of gender. The "people" are composed of men and women, and both sexes are part of a patriarchal culture that expresses, through diverse means, the domination that men exert over women. The individual in the "people," by the mere fact of being part of the people, is not exempt from being the carrier of behavioral patterns and social practices that hurt the female segment of the popular sector. This individual and counterparts from other social strata are part of a culture in which women are subordinated.

Through social practices in everyday life, through the differential socialization of girls and boys in the family, through formal and informal education, through the workplace and the working life, through state policies, and through religions, female subordination is produced and reproduced in all social sectors, although in varying forms.

Popular education, with its multiple purposes, is addressed to diverse social sectors: peasants, slum dwellers, indigenous groups, women, and so on. Since its inception with Paulo Freire, popular education has tried to create a pedagogy for the oppressed, but it has not delved deeply enough into how to address the problem of women. A popular education that does not recognize women's subordination is not removed from the reproduction of the sex-gender system of domination.[2]

For these reasons, the educational proposals of the institute I have been involved with, the Center for Women's Studies (Centro de Estudios de la Mujer), have been developed with the aim of rendering explicit among rural women the various forms in which female subordination is expressed and creating the conditions under which women can develop demands to satisfy not only social class but also gender needs. This is what I term the attempt to "genderize" popular education.

These ideas and practices have been influenced by the difficult and conflictual path that women in Chile have traveled on their way to the construction of an autonomous social movement. The institute's educational proposal seeks to relate education to social movements, meaning by this the creation of a social movement that allows the existence and expression of a specific sector of society. This process of movement building can produce a major democratization of civil society because the expression of differences— of gender, ethnicity, class—is potentially the precursor of a societal project that can guarantee not only formal democracy but also the democratization of social relations and the daily life among individuals.

Much has been said in Chile about the emergence of the women's movement. Given its characteristics, some have argued that it reflects women in movement rather than a movement of women. Under any interpretation, there is strong evidence that under fifteen years of military rule that continued through the late 1980s, women reached a level of agency greater than that attained during the current democratic period.[3] This can be attributed to multiple reasons and is susceptible to different interpretations. But regardless of the problems of a semantic nature and the use of different interpretive frameworks, the "silent chorus has gleaned the possibilities for rebellion" (Nun, 1984).

The identification of women's demands is a significant phase reached by the women's movement because these demands express the state of the movement or an important step in its development and constitution. For this reason, the field of popular education and the concrete educational interventions that take place within it constitute a privileged space to deepen such demands. The set of documents produced by women's groups and the women's units within labor unions (in both the countryside and the city) between 1983 and 1987 reveal how the emergence of women in public life under an authoritarian regime has been crystallized. Yet a comparison of the two groups shows that they have varying viewpoints about the "woman's question"—the first (women's groups) emphasizes gender problems, and the second (women's units in labor unions) underscores class problems. Under the class emphasis, it is anticipated that a democratic victory would resolve in good measure the multiplicity of problems that afflict women, whereas the gender perspective assumes that the problems of women are not resolved with the victory of democracy and that women must continue to struggle to eradicate all forms of discrimination and oppression, not only within political structures but also within their culture and family. In all, these do not represent a large number of women but rather a limited sector of women in social and political organizations.

Therefore, the educational proposal discussed here is located at the intersection between the women's movement and the need to deepen the gender-consciousness level of women at the grass roots. The educational intervention conducted should be seen as a link between the macrolevel and microlevel. The rural school for women established since 1986 seeks to create conditions for the strengthening of women as social actors.

▲ Rural Women and Women Agricultural Workers

During the last decade the situation of women in the countryside has become enormously complex as a result of the increasing heterogeneity of rural society (Bengoa, 1985; Ortega, 1987; Valdes, 1988). This heterogeneity can be explained to some extent by the change processes that have affected the rural world and their subsequent impact on women. Today there is greater incorporation of women into remunerated labor as a result of the expansion of the fruit export industry. Although this phenomenon occurs only in certain regions, particularly the central part of the country, in general the changes in the composition of the female labor market have affected all areas of agricultural production.

Parallel with the increased size of the remunerated female labor force has come sexual segmentation of the labor force. Women in export agriculture perform tasks different from those of men; they represent more than 40 percent of the seasonal labor force. This rate of participation represents a substantial increase over the past, a change termed the process of feminization of the agricultural labor market. The seasonal agricultural workers (*temporeras*) today are greater in number than the women in industry.

In addition to the *temporeras*, there is a greater number of women who work on small properties and minifarms (*minifundios*). They represent a vast sector of workers that are identified as "unremunerated family helpers." They play an important role in the maintenance of peasant economies; the women are linked to the production of basic staples for the country in addition to the tasks they perform relating to reproductive activities. Many of the peasant women, especially those who live in *minifundios* and depressed peasant economies, perform other types of income-generating activities. Among these activities, handicraft production is important. Its historical persistence is a manifestation of female resistance to the processes of social decomposition and pauperization. Handicraft production is also an expression of the local culture, particularly in regions where ethnic minorities prevail and in some peasant communities in the central part of the country.[4]

During the last decade there have been other types of economic activities promoted, such as the creation of family orchards, rabbit breeding, and beekeeping—essentially all of which are overseen by women. Many of these programs have been promoted both by the government and by nongovernmental organizations (NGOs). The massive entry of women into the agrarian labor market as *temporeras* as well as the revitalization of traditionally feminine activities and the new productive activities in which women participate indicate a restructuring of the segmentation of women into a wide range of productive activities. This is a result of the transformations in the agricultural labor market and of previous economic policies toward the small landowners.[5]

The greater participation of women in remunerated activities or in the production of goods has not led to an improvement in the situation of women. Quite the contrary, women continue to be placed in the worst-remunerated activities and to be strongly discriminated against in salaried work, as they are usually assigned piecework. The literature refers to a greater participation of women in development, meaning an increased participation of women in remunerated activities or income-generating activities. But the evaluation of these measures has revealed that women usually play a fundamental role during situations of economic crisis. Their level of participation in development is increasingly reduced as rural women have to perform more and more hours of work to satisfy their family needs

(Yudelman, 1987a, 1987b). It would seem that the costs of the economic crisis are borne essentially by women, whereas the benefits from the periods of economic expansion tend to be received by men. Examples exist of males benefiting from the agrarian reform that gave men more access to the land but excluded women (Garret, 1982).

▲ Demands of Women in Peasant Organizations

Within socialist organizations there are efforts to incorporate the demands of rural women. The women's units of some of the largest union federations, in response to the protagonism of women in public life during recent years, have recognized gender issues as important. A reflection of this position is the elaboration of the "Demands of Rural Women" in 1986 (Comisión Nacional Campesina, 1986).

It is important to underscore that within a set of class vindications, there are gender demands that express the need for peasant organizations to fight for the abolition of laws that discriminate against women regarding land inheritance and property and the lack of married women's autonomy in economic transactions. The "Demands of Rural Women" identified the need to modify the Civil Code and eliminate various forms of sexual and domestic violence against women. The document also questioned the exclusion of women from and their discrimination in union organizations, where women have demanded the right to assume all types of leadership positions and responsibilities. Also voiced was the need to have literacy programs and skills training programs appropriate for rural women. On the subject of work issues, the document refers to the right to work and to equal working conditions for both sexes and calls for "equal pay for equal work." The "Demands of Rural Women" clearly seeks to promote legislative, educational, and cultural changes by questioning and calling for the modification of various discriminatory conditions against women.

However, the document is limited on the working question. On the issue of equal wages, it does not consider the real subordination women face in the workplace, particularly the *temporeras*, who perform activities different from those of men, except in a limited number of areas relating to agriculture for domestic consumption, where the sexual division of labor is less marked. It is difficult, therefore, to forecast the extent to which a demand such as "equal pay for equal work" could accomplish change in the condition of women in the labor market.

Likewise, the document does not address the working conditions of the overwhelming majority of women who work in rural areas because it does not make a clear pronouncement about handicraft production, thus not acknowledging that women play an important role in the peasant economy. It is also unclear about the new categories that today tend to be presented as "advantageous" for the incorporation of women in the development process. Because of such situations, the working conditions of women are more veiled, and their work is rendered invisible to society. Labor unions are not exempt from this blindness.

Overall, the "Demands of Rural Women" signifies progress. Yet it is still too general and fails to pay attention to the concrete problems that rural women face in the marketplace and in agrarian and artisanal production. It does not address the problem of women who work for wages or in domestic activities. Without doubt, the long working day is one of the greatest obstacles to the participation of women in organizations, in addition to the fact that women are not motivated to participate in these groups because women themselves do not recognize the problems they face.

▲ Educational Interventions for Women

The notion that intervention serves as the link between the microlevel and macrolevel began to acquire meaning at the Center for Women's Studies when the limitations of the process with respect to rural women became evident. In the center's trajectory of work with rural and indigenous women, the following phases can be distinguished:

Recovery of a Collective Memory

This first stage can be identified as the recovery of a silenced history. During the initial phase of the program, there was talk in the country of repairing the torn social fabric—a necessity imposed by the dismantling of the social and political organizations that existed until 1973. It was foreseen that women would be essential actors in this process because there there were numerous organizations working on human rights, welfare, and reflection groups for women that began to cover the uninhabited organizational scenery.

In this phase, using life-history methodologies, the center collected a series of personal accounts from women throughout Chile to learn about various aspects regarding the condition of the rural women and their internal diversity, including how women lived different cultural realities, what their vision of recent history was, and what problems they faced. These life histories raised questions about the "official history," in which—aside from its various ideological messages—women have not been treated as subjects. Through the recovery of their collective memory and experieces, the women have become the carriers of a world vision heretofore unknown.

The work of the center's team of university-trained women (composed of sociologists, anthropologists, psychologists, and geographers) had led to recognition of the androcentric vision of the social sciences. For this reason, the first phase of the work questioned many of the well-known paradigms and began the revision of the center's approaches and knowledge. The book *Testimonial Histories of Women in the Countryside*, published in 1983, gathered part of these life histories and was published with several objectives: to disseminate an unknown reality; to share it with peasant, social, and labor organizations to sensitize them to the problems facing women; and to devolve the histories to their protagonists.

The testimony by one of the remunerated rural workers, heir to the hacienda system, captures the value of the book for its protagonists: "I believe that to know history helps to bring about change. To know the history of women helps to become united. A single woman can do nothing and in the union of women lies the solution of our problems. I think that it helps to know life."

Although the book captured individual lives, many women reflected on the history narrated by others. The women's world vision widened exposure to the experiences and multiple realities that were woven by the women's narrative. This material was of great utility as a pedagogical tool for the educational work in the women's groups that were later formed. It helped enormously in the conception of a shared gender reality, beyond revealing the cultural differences among women in the countryside.[6]

Women's Groups

In the second phase the purpose was to foster the creation of women's groups. They were formed, to a large extent, on the basis of the contact established with the women interviewed for the life histories, a contact later made with other women. This phase sought the formation of local groups to help the center identify some problems around which to work. The participants expressed great interest in creating groups to reflect upon the various themes and to increase their income.

Many of the small groups that first reflected on given themes later became groups seeking to engage in productive activities. This was particularly true of the groups created by indigenous women, who produced most of the handicrafts. In the reflection groups, mostly those located in the central region of the country, themes treated were linked to sexuality, health, work within and outside the family, and working relations.

Although these women often built up their economic resources and acquired substantial new knowledge to handle themselves in different settings, these programs did not involve the majority of the population in a given community, except in a few cases. Participants in these groups were the women who were interested and those who could ask their family and neighborhood networks to participate. Generally, the women who adopted the functions of leaders established relations of domination with others, which tended to exclude forces outside their personal networks of family and neighborhood (*compadrazgo*). Personal growth could be observed among the participants, including the acquisition of new knowledge and tools to improve their family situations or increase their individual income. But these women did not carry out any actions beyond the boundaries of their immediate goals. Despite this, some degree of gender consciousness was generated among the groups. The social fragmentation that Chile was undergoing prevented emergence of action of a vindicatory type, addressed to different interlocutors.

The small groups of women, self-centered in their own activities and facing pressures in trying to satisfy economic needs, became groups of a community-assistance type; thus, they lived circumscribed to the local space and had difficulties linking with social organizations. When women became associated with these other groups, they did so individually; for instance, when they participated in labor unions, they transferred their domestic role from their home to the syndicate.

During this phase, the program assisted women in the women's units of peasant labor federations. The objective was to strengthen the unionized women so that they would have more negotiating skills within their unions. This training was conducted through discussions to raise gender consciousness and through educational activities in which women saw how the domestic subordination of women was carried into the union sphere and how they could claim their own spaces within the unions. Even so, given the relationship between the program and the groups, the women were a captive clientele.

Program Design and Objectives

The program limitations previously mentioned explain the creation of the Rural Women's School in the third phase of the work. Its existence since 1986 has been the result of a process of critical reflection on the preceding phases, which provided evidence that in both the small groups of women and in the various union organizations women often engaged in activities that merely extended their domestic roles or limited them to immediate actions.

Taking into account this experience, its possibilities and limitations, the center created an educational space where women could participate while bringing their children so that it would be possible for them to be away from the home and removed from domestic responsibilities.[7] The Rural Women's School was designed as an educational space that would permit the linking between various types of women and their organizational experiences.

Many groups from the provinces were invited to participate. The school attracted agricultural workers, handicraft workers, farmers, and housewives of varying ages. During its first two years the school operated in Santiago and offered a one-semester program per year, through monthly meetings of four days each. During the third year the school was implemented at the regional level, in three provinces. This three-year experience led the center to run the school with only *temporeras* working in domestic and export agricultural markets.

Among its general objectives the school sought to create a nexus between the women's social movement and the local women's groups, linking in this way the various groups and developing content and methodologies that reinforce the processes of self-identity among women, generate a gender consciousness, and promote appropriate forms to change the women's position through the transformation of private and public practices. A series of factors, discussed in the next few pages, led the center to narrow the selection of social subjects to whom its projects are addressed. The program began with a very wide female universe, for women are subject to diverse cultural realities (e.g., indigenous, nonindigenous), and the early phase centered on women from the central area of the country who at least shared some history. Present plans are to develop the school only for agricultural workers.

It is pertinent to examine the center's current position: Within a framework that links popular education with the social movement, there is a point of permanent tension between educational interventions seeking to reinforce the process of identity formation (gender identity in this case) and those interventions addressed to generating processes of social change. When working with a heterogeneous group of women, one can attain a reinforcement of gender identity through, for instance, the unmasking of sexual discrimination against women, the oppressive mechanisms within the family, or other problems that arise in gender relations. Through this method women can internalize their specific gender conditions, and within this specificity they can become aware of discriminating and oppressive mechanisms that affect their lives. Educational interventions enable women to see the complex reality of accommodation and resistance in their lives.

On this sinuous path, the question of social change appears as complex, with many diverse angles and several questions that can be raised, even though the context makes it difficult to evaluate actions and their effects outside the educational arena. It should be mentioned that although the discourse of women changed toward visualizing women as agents—thanks to the evidence that a woman experiences not only her own personal problems but also those common to other women—the daily practices in the family and in the public sphere tended to be reproduced without alteration.

In the evolution of the Rural Women's School, interventions have been increasingly addressed toward specific subjects, such as subsectors of women potentially united by the same interests. Beyond common elements among women (gender identity), there are specificities that stem from the position of women in society. This element can facilitate the use of methodologies that assure the transformation of feminine practices in the private and public world, because the linking of the class-gender elements allows for a collective search toward transformative practices, albeit mostly in the world of work.

For women, in isolated positions within their homes, the reelaboration of their daily family practices can become an impediment if this action is not united with the actions of other women.

In this regard, the center's hypothesis is that the confrontation between the work and family spheres and the distinct expressions of subordination in both emerge as elements in the process of consciousness acquisition. Linked to the fact that once women are exposed to the working world they are better able to visualize the struggle for the betterment in working conditions, wages, and changes in gender relations, the expressions of subordination in the family and the contradictions between family and work appear as issues to be raised after women have had such collective experiences.

▲ The Rural Women's School

Meaning of Educational Intervention

Popular education is an appropriate context in which to probe the type of problems discussed here. Because of its active and participatory methodologies and its potentially liberating content, it can be most helpful for the transformation of women into social actors and for the constitution of specific demands.

Only in recent years have issues such as sexual discrimination and the oppression of women received attention within popular education. This focus can be attributed to the emergence of women's movements in Latin America. Within the context of the strong development of popular education in the Latin American region, the feminist movement has attempted to move forward, producing methodologies that are useful for consciousness raising and expanding projects to transform the condition of women.

In terms of pedagogical proposals, there are a few propositions and methodologies, but a transferable body of knowledge and methodologies can be attained only in partial terms. Nonetheless, there are efforts to elaborate on pedagogical proposals within the framework of popular education that may facilitate the establishment of more liberating social practices for women.[8]

It is believed that a popular education differentiated by gender in content and methodologies can contribute to the promotion and expansion of a greater consciousness among women regarding their identity and the concomitant need to take women out of their subordinate position. A constant goal sought by the center's professional women has been to develop an appropriate curriculum to promote an *education of the difference* in an effort to render the course content explicit in the historical and daily mechanisms as well as the structural and cultural processes that affect women's condition. This search for an effective curriculum is reflected in the experience with the rural women's school.

Curricular Content

Over a three-year period work proceeded on a curriculum that covers three areas: identity, work, and organization. The identity focus seeks to unmask the forms of socialization of girls and boys within the family setting. This focus has been accompanied by workshops in health, sexuality, and violence; these have varied over the years in the forms in which they have been implemented. The objective here is to see how socialization and the accompanying mechanisms explain why and how women and men grow and are socialized within the family setting.

The purpose in the work area is to render visible the work women perform within their home. The family setting and the reproductive work are linked to the work outside the home so that the concept of work is redefined and also so that women may learn and be able to understand the forms of discrimination related to work outside the home.

Last, the organization focus seeks to rescue the public experience of women, either at the level of peasant organizations or at the level of governmental organizations such as in the mothers' centers. The objective is to identify definite obstacles that women face in public life so that organizational forms congruent with the specificity of women may be developed.

Implementation

The school has been implemented through day-long meetings and workshops by theme. The center conceived nonformal education as a set of tools to promote consciousness raising and to foster the creation of class organizations from which women may contribute to the women's movement. In 1986 and 1987 women attended four days per month during a six-month period in Santiago. The school operated in a place where the women could bring their small children because child-care services were provided. During these four days, women slept, ate, and attended workshops in the same place. Transportation as well as food and child-care expenses were paid by the program. Invited to participate were women from the central region of the country and from the various provinces. Thirty women were then selected to participate in the program. Between 1986 and 1987 there was a follow-up of a third of the women who attended the school. In 1988 the school was implemented in three provinces in three annual sessions; the regional sessions had the participation of thirty women from neighboring provinces.

Several changes in the implementation of the school were considered necessary to improve the outreach mechanisms and correct the errors that diminished the effectiveness of the school.

Methodology

Starting with the hypothesis that the women's world visions and their memories can be explained by the social practices that women experience (which are very different from those experienced by men), the center produced a set of educational materials depicting how women live and what they do: their immediate experiences, their own testimony, and fragments of their life histories. This focus on the production of educational materials was selected to touch upon the experience of these women; the use of these materials was enriched by the contribution of the participating women.

Although the work capitalized on the knowledge of women, there was other information that women did not have or possessed only in fragmentary fashion. In these cases it was necessary to link the life experiences of women with global processes, to create conditions that enable women to see their position within society.

Result of Intervention

Considered here is the extent to which women who went through the school experience became capable of developing gender demands. They produced these demands as women and workers, reflecting upon the entirety of problems and needs they faced in the concrete situations in which they lived. In this sense, the result of the educational intervention appears as an evaluation of the process of learning and a process of consciousness raising around the multitude of problems faced by women in the reproductive and productive spheres. Concretely, this evaluation focuses on the transformation of problems into demands, which offers the advantage of visualizing problems while simultaneously allowing the women to imagine possible changes.

In order to address the theme of demands, women were distributed in nine groups according to occupational position: seasonal agricultural workers (*temporeras*), tile makers, spinners, weavers, beekeepers, rabbit breeders, herb sellers, agricultural workers, and housewives. Among the women who made handicrafts (tile makers, spinners, and weavers) there were different situations regarding their access to land. Generally, the traditional artisans had a *minifundio*. All of them lived on land characterized by poor quality: arid or eroded and of scarce productivity. The beekeepers and rabbit breeders came from areas of small property or areas where there has been a forced relocation because of the reversal of the agrarian reform in those regions. The agricultural workers included women engaged in paid agricultural activities. The seasonal agricultural workers included two types: those who worked with grapes for export and those who worked with vegetables for domestic consumption. It should be noted that the *temporeras* who were heads of households carried out self-generated activities during the winter such as crocheting and overlock sewing. Among the younger women, domestic employment was common. This juxtaposition of productive activities among women is a common feature of their insertion in the labor force; therefore, rural women as a group have been characterized as "multiple workers" (Aranda, 1982). This multiple employment stems from their great responsibility, as family heads, to generate income in the months of unemployment or to complement income derived from agriculture. Last, the group of housewives was composed of women without access to land, who did not have income-generating activities and who engaged only in domestic-reproductive work.

After forming the groups, women worked toward the formulation of demands. The result of this work was the elaboration of a listing of demands by group; these demands were later explained and justified in front of all the participants.

Demands presented by the seasonal agricultural workers:

1. Uniforms to avoid using personal garments; face masks provided by the company to avoid contamination with pesticides.
2. Provision of tools by the company: clippers, hoes, and knives. The women explained that these tools are necessary in order to work with grapes and to harvest other crops.
3. Cafeterias and eating places in the farms because there are numerous workers who at lunch must sit on the ground, underneath the vineyards and close to the presence of pesticides.
4. Two liters of milk per person to counter the toxic effects produced by the breathing of chemical products.
5. Good treatment of women by bosses and foremen; rejection of sexual harassment in the workplace.
6. Equalization of salaries among enterprises and within similar work activities; better salaries.
7. Transportation expenses from place of residence to place of work.
8. Social benefits and work contracts.
9. Family subsidies for women who are heads of households.
10. Child-care centers in the workplace (firms, fruit-packing settings, vineyards) because there are many women in these activities. The pertinent legislation, according to which there should be child-care centers for enterprises with more than twenty women workers, is not respected.
11. Retirement at age fifty for women because they, having a double day of labor, work more than men who have responsibilities only for productive and remunerated tasks.

Demands presented by the tile makers:

1. No fee, as usually charged by municipalities, for rights to have stands in fairs and markets.
2. Right to market tile products in the mothers' centers twice a year; greater quotas for buying and paying cash for products.
3. Permanent places for the sale of tiles close to markets and fairs, subsidized by the municipalities.
4. Family subsidies paid directly to women because they have greater work stability—they work year-round but their husbands work only seasonally.
5. Retirement at age fifty because tile work is heavy and produces eye ailments (from the baking of the products) and bone ailments (from the humidity of the workplace).

Demands presented by the spinners:

1. Credit to obtain raw materials (the fleece) because the peasants have lost their herds and many of the spinners not only have no sheep but no lands.
2. Training in the processing of the raw material (using the spinning wheel) and the dying of the wool.
3. Greater autonomy to negotiate the price of the wool because spinning by hand receives low payment while the price of raw materials is high and rises between the time of shearing (end of springtime) and winter.
4. Creation of organizations to market the product; attention to problems of marketing that women face in peasant organizations, such as the cooperatives and guild unions, which generally are interested only in products derived from agricultural production and not from handicraft production.

Demands presented by the weavers:

1. Better prices for the handmade fabrics.
2. Reductions in the price of wool and other raw materials of industrial origin.
3. Creation of organizations for the marketing of their products.

Demands presented by the beekeepers:

1. Creation of credit for the acquisition of honey.
2. No payment of taxes for the small producers of honey.
3. An easier procedure to obtain health permits.

4. Credits for beekeeping tools, sanitation of beehives, and medicines.
5. Technical assistance.
6. Control of diseases by governmental entities.

Demands presented by the rabbit breeders:

1. Low-interest credit for the acquisition of cages, rabbits, and food.
2. Facilities for the marketing of rabbit skins.
3. No tax payment by the small producers.
4. Technical assistance and training in the spinning of rabbit hair in order to sell finished products and earn more than from selling just the skins.
5. Prenatal service for all (eliminate the lottery system).
6. Retirement of women at age fifty because of the excessive work that women conduct at home and as producers.

Demands presented by the herb sellers:

1. Facilities to disseminate and promote the use of medical herbs.
2. Promotion of the marketing process and improvement of the existing networks.
3. Retirement of women at age fifty because of the excessive workload in their activities.

Demands presented by agricultural workers:

1. Low-interest credit for fertilizers and seeds.
2. Technical assistance.
3. Marketing and establishment of proxy buyers to avoid the low prices paid by intermediaries and by private warehouses.
4. Reduction in installment payments for land lots; forgiveness of debts; reduction in the payments of taxes.

Demands presented by housewives:

1. More jobs for women and men.
2. Higher salary levels.
3. Access to housing for young couples.
4. Valorization of the women's work.
5. Access to education and training for women; creation of training programs for women so that they may escape from their isolation and grow as persons.
6. Protection of single women and mothers.
7. Rejection of sexual harassment against women.

8. Greater responsibility of men in domestic tasks; training of men in child care and cooking.
9. Control of clandestine bars and places where alcohol is sold to combat alcoholism and violence of men against women.
10. Retirement at age fifty. Even though some women may not work outside the home, their work is heavy, unremunerated, and unrecognized.

Analysis of the Demands

A first observation that can be made from this educational experience is that groups develop a consciousness about their condition and about the possibility of changing it. It is evident that each woman experiences firsthand these working problems regardless of the occupation in which she finds herself. It is important to underline that only women carry out activities that tend to be hidden and scarcely acknowledged. Yet women in these concrete situations can generate demands specific to their occupations. They must become aware that there are activities, occupations, and certain tasks that are feminized. To be a tile maker, a spinner, a grape washer, or a packer in a packing house is not generalizable to the masculine population: these occupations are women's work, generally less remunerated than those involving other products (either in terms of wages or market prices), and less recognized by the labor unions. In this respect, existing class demands made by unions seek mainly the improvement of the male segment of society because they address the improvement of wages, occupations, and types of work where men are concentrated.

With this observation, it is important to emphasize that labor demands in the sphere of social production—that is, demands by women as workers— also have a specificity in the sense that although these women compose part of a strata or specific social class, they do not establish the same type of work relations as men because they occupy different positions in the sphere of production.[9] It is possible then to "genderize class demands" (Valdes, 1987) on the basis of the working reality of women. Thus, for instance, when women make explicit the need for employers to furnish them with aprons and face masks, it is because women are in direct contact with grapes during the clearing of the vineyards or during the activities of washing and packing grapes. Women have witnessed in their places of work the frequent fainting and stomachaches, a consequence of the enormous quantity of pesticides in the vineyards. Women must also wear their own garments and return home with "dirty clothes."[10] They want greater protection against toxic fumes and an improvement in their working conditions. It should be underlined that women are concerned only on the basis of empirical knowledge and not on the basis of scientific knowledge of the effects of toxic products, which in fact are much worse than the women imagine.[11]

When the women identified the need to establish a national system of wages for the *temporeras*, they did so only after revealing to each other how much they earned during the season and thus discovering that different enterprises pay different salaries for equal work: washing and packing grapes, packing bags of beans, or harvesting tomatoes. This inequality in wages can be a significant factor in the mobility and rotation of women from enterprise to enterprise, which gives employers an argument to affirm that they cannot rely on women because, for "natural reasons," they are not responsible toward their jobs.

After the women listed their demands regarding specific work, they identified many problems that trouble them in productive tasks. These problems affect women in traditional handicrafts—spinners, weavers, pottery makers—in specific communities (Pomarie, Pilen, Quinchamali, and La Florida for pottery; Quinamavida and Mata Redonda for spinning and weaving) and in other regions in the precarious situation characteristic of the peasant economy in the *minifundios* (Valdes and Matta, 1986).

The demands presented by the women in traditional handicrafts and those in income-generating projects, such as honey production and rabbit hair, touch on problems of marketing and commercialization, of credit and technical assistance, of diversifing and improving production, and of cost and procurement of raw materials. But the problem is not about price or credit policy for producers in general—it concerns activities and occupations that are feminized and about which women may be able to question the state, the municipality, and the farmers' cooperatives. Likewise, women believe that the farmers' cooperatives can respond to their demands and thus interpret the needs of an important segment of their membership, needs that have been weakly attended to, particularly during the period of agrarian reform.

It is remarkable to observe that the greater the feminization of certain occupations, the greater the capacity of articulation and expression of the women's demands. From the list of demands by the women who participate in agricultural activities and who conduct tasks that are only complementary to labor essentially performed by men, it can be seen that their demands do not address women in particular but rather the groups of persons who work in the family type of exploitation, an area generally dominated by men. In these cases, there are no demands specifically appropriate to women, but the demands made by the pottery makers or the spinners reveal a clear gender specificity.

Within the list of women's demands is a subset that can be characterized as gender demands. These demands do not address concrete steps of how to move women into remunerated work or production. Rather, they consider the fact that women, in addition to being workers, are also women. The expression of demands linked to their gender identity in the majority of cases cuts across work activities or occupations. By being women and having to work daily in the domestic sphere—thus having two jobs—the women think they should be able to retire at age fifty. Even though it is difficult to imagine what family stipend self-employed workers, such as the ceramic workers, should earn, it is clear that their work is valued because they are producing the most permanent incomes in their respective households. There is thus a reinforcement of a worker's identity that emerges from a concrete occupation; women see themselves as the main pillar of the family economy given the stability of their income and the intermittent character of the men's income through the sale of agricultural products or other jobs.

Within this set of problems, the seasonal workers demand child-care centers in the workplace. This is mandated by law in places where there are more than twenty women workers (González and Norero, 1986). However, this legislation is not enforced either in the countryside or in export agriculture. This demand, felt by the mothers who work for wages, is also not present in the labor agreements of rural workers. This lack of attention to the problems of women workers on the part of entrepreneurs and labor unions shows how, in an activity in which the participation of women exceeds 40 percent of the hired labor force, concrete problems such as having child-care services are not considered.

In the list of demands presented by the housewives, a major problem had to do with sexual harassment. There are also demands linked to the transformation of cultural social values in society, such as an assignment of greater value to the work of the housewife and protection for single women and unmarried mothers.[12] When women call for greater control of the places clandestinely providing alcohol, they do so because of the domestic violence in which men engage when they become drunk. The demand for training and education of women emanates from their need to grow as persons and to combat the isolation to which housewives are subjected. It is also believed that training for men is important so that they may contribute to reproductive and domestic tasks.

When women talk about generating work for men and women, it is evident that this reflects the unemployment that currently affects both sexes. From the women's perspective, it is necessary to work outside the home because of economic needs, but it also allows them greater independence from their fathers or husbands. In this regard, women have an interesting perspective about their housework: they equate their domestic work to the labor conditions found in the traditional hacienda framework under the system of *inquilinaje* (work in exchange for rent).[13] In the same way the *inquilinos* and their family were once obliged to work on the hacienda in order to have a place to live and to use some of the crops, women feel obliged to perform domestic tasks. In their discourse, the women are aware that the former labor obligations within the hacienda and theirs inside the home constitute relations of domination. The wish to work outside the home to attain economic autonomy can be interpreted as the first questioning by women of male domination.

▲ Evaluation and Follow-up of the Educational Effort

The nonformal educational spaces in previous years tended to become ghettos, basically as a result of the repressive political system in Chile. The search for themes to be treated within nonformal education spaces is based upon the need to change the conditions of women. Thus, the themes move from the development of women's identity to the formulation of class and gender demands.

The earlier reference to the axis of permanent tension between the process of identity construction (one expression of gender differences) and social change alludes to the difficulty of promoting strategies and activities to create a presence of women as social actors interested in change. In fact, the drafting of demands by the women and workers has been an attempt to break the barrier between the educational space and society.

To help define the curriculum of the school, the workshops were organized so that the development of demands by the women would also serve as an indicator to evaluate the learning process. Underlying this strategy was the realization that women tend to be mobilized by concrete and immediate problems and that the work-demands relationship would be congruent with the search for solutions to their problems.

Work—even though genderized—is a place for the constitution of identities, as much as are the family, formal education, and religion. In this regard, the individual is a working woman, not a worker without gender. The labor needs of women, their occupations, and the tasks they conduct in social production reflect the gender of the actor who performs them. In addition, the identity workshop addressed issues related to family socialization, issues that were also discussed in part by the women who saw themselves as housewives.

However, the development of demands by the seasonal workers and the artisan women has not been completed. Who are their interlocutors? To whom do they present their demands? How can they organize their change strategies, in what spaces, and at which junctures?

After the limits of the curricular content became evident, other methodologies were explored to avoid the impasse. A 1987 workshop entitled "Making the Daily Experience Problematic" sought to analyze the use of hours and days in the lives of women so that they would identify the social relations they established with different interlocutors, whether in the family, in the place of work, or in the market. This methodological effort to go beyond the educational space represented an improvement over the 1986 work. However, the questions concerning the impact of the school upon the lives of the women were still not answered.

The program being carried out by the Rural Women's School for over seven years seeks to make its line of work congruent with the needs of the women for whom it is intended. The experience of the previous years has enabled program organizers to identify two lines for educational intervention:

• The first step was redefinition of the women's school to serve a specific social sector: the remunerated women workers in the agricultural area, who, because of the load of their work, the problems they face as working women, and their working conditions (they work in a group at least several months per year), represent an important sector in terms of the possibility for their mobilization.

• The second move was the establishment in 1986 of a farmers' store, as an educational space for the artisans and as a parallel support system for the marketing of handicrafts. As in the school, the themes of identity have been treated in the farmers' store. Another effort has been to set up an organization to enable the artisans to address questions regarding the marketing of their products. This support for the rural artisans is based on their being a feminized sector, which carries a cultural identity capable of resisting the process of incorporation of some of the rural population as agricultural proletarians. Because of their relation with the market, the artisans enjoy an economic independence similar to men's and are experienced in the public world.

After working with the rural housewives and women who assisted in the agricultural production led by their husbands, parents, or brothers, program organizers turned their attention to agricultural workers and seasonal workers and artisans. The confinement of many of these women to the domestic sphere, their absolute dependence on the husbands, and the slight possibility of contact and ties with other women led the organizers to give priority to the women's occupations with the greatest potential for mobilization.

The educational interventions with each type of women were usually accompanied by a constant effort to advance organizers' knowledge about several aspects of the history of rural women, their position in the labor market, and the increasing feminization of the rural artisan sector. To accompany the educational interventions, written and audiovisual materials have been produced, and these have been distributed through labor unions, farmers cooperatives, and groups of women who carry out similar programs. These activities occur in the context of a complex and changing reality and serve as ways to detect errors and successes in the concrete interventions. Disconnected from the existence of the women's movement, however, these activities would lose their raison d'être.

▲ The New Chilean Sociopolitical Context

Limits of Educational Interventions

At the beginning of this chapter, I spoke of the tie between popular education and social movements. This tie must be reexamined today in Chile in light of the emergence of a new sociopolitical context and a critical reading of the school's experience.

The link between the school and the social movement of women should be understood as an attempt to create educational spaces where women, in a process that combines training and consciousness raising, can develop actions centered on the improvement of their condition in society.

However, it has not been evident that this space leads to immediate mobilization or vindicatory actions. Moreover, the school's experience, which takes place four days per month over a semester, with some follow-up in the homes of the participating women, has in itself been a space for participation.[14] This result emerges from the perception women have of the school. They value the horizontal relation with the educators (program staff) and the trust that is generated in the educational space. They also value the friendship and affection they have developed with other participants there. The methodology is valued as a process by which knowledge is not transmitted but built up through the experience of the participants, and in this manner they gain access to a new knowledge and a new code in their discourse.[15]

When the school's facilitators announce on the fifth day that the school experience has come to an end, there is a feeling of emptiness among the participants. The strong emotionalism expressed at departure time is evidence that the participants do not see this process as something that will continue to develop, whether in their own community or in some local organization. This reinforces the notion that the school is perceived by the women as a space for the sake of participation and as an experience that tends to be dissociated from their lives, even though this experience is highly esteemed.

Between 1982 and 1985, before the school was established, program organizers viewed women as captive clients. This generated a change in the way the program recruited participants. The new process eliminates clientelism, but it cannot prevent the encapsulation of the educational experience vis-à-vis the daily lives of women. The dissimilar situations among women make it very difficult for them to disseminate their experiences. Some women are not articulate enough to do so; other women assert that the school has been key to their lives because in that setting the notion of "we, the women" was established. Other women think the school was important for practical reasons, such as learning to speak or overcoming fear of addressing an audience. The nature of the women's evaluations gives only impressionistic evidence about the modifications the school has provoked in the social practices of the women.

Thus, for instance, there is an evaluative moment when women talk about the pedagogical relations, the acquisition of new knowledge, and the relationships created during the workshop days. There is a new discourse in which they talk about the configuration of "we women"—be it in the spoken language, in theatrical plays, or in the women's identification of various problems and themes for discussion in the workshops.

But how can women bring this "we women" concept to their lives at home and in the place of work? What validity do the school curriculum and methodology have when it is so difficult to identify precise forms of evaluation of the results and suitable times for the evaluation? What is hidden behind the women's new discourse? Even though it cannot be expected that educational processes of this kind have some linearity (knowledge acquisition, leading to consciousness raising, leading to mobilization), the empirical and theoretical evidence of this process at the individual level leads to this question: What is the impact of an educational intervention of this type, taking into account the brief nature of the intervention relative to the lives of the women? This question has led program organizers to modify the invitation to participate in the school, to be more precise in the types of women called upon, and to work in a more distant geographic space so that the women may be able to dissociate the school space from their concrete lives. This supposes a tighter follow-up of the objectives pursued: to trigger an educational space with distinct strategies and mechanisms and to create strategies to promote changes in the social practices of the women in the family, social, and work environments.

In this phase, the theme of the demands should be confronted with concrete interlocutors. It also should be seen as a link between the educational space and the real world surrounding the women. The next step is to go beyond the identification of demands (an objective sought in previous years) to identify strategies to implement these demands. This new objective requires a follow-up of the school's impact, an analysis considered as important as the experience of the school itself.

Implementing Educational Actions

In October 1988 the country participated in a plebiscite that broke fifteen years of the military regime. This break has allowed a movement toward gradual democratization, in which political parties are forming again and preexisting social movements are now being overshadowed. The political space tends to be absorbed by the parties, and women tend to occupy their historical place (beside the youth, the aged, and the indigenous people) at the bottom of each political party's program.

Politics then tends to define itself as the task of specialists. It can be foreseen that in this period of democratization women's mobilization may become invisible next to the mobilization of the political parties. Moreover, it might disappear or become mute if the parties are not capable of incorporating women into their change proposals.

If during the fifteen years of military rule the field of popular education was perceived by its beneficiaries as a space for participation, beyond the objectives set by those providing the programs, the new sociopolitical context presents new problems and challenges. The new space for the participation of civil society will be much more open, significantly beyond the spaces created by NGOs, churches, and other institutions that offered resistance during the times of the dictatorship. Thus, in the context of increasing democratization of civil society—when the vindication aims of many programs of popular education have lost their raison d'être—the NGOs see as their challenge the implementation of their proposals. Vindicatory programs, such as the rural women's school, should protect the existence of the differences (of gender in this case) in order to ensure that women, as a specific social sector, are actively maintained as social actors capable of creating relations and vindicating their demands vis-à-vis social organizations such as labor unions, farmers' cooperatives, local state institutions (e.g., the municipalities), and the political parties.

If many of the educational programs from the military era were characterized as giving improved skills training for the better administration of material resources (credits, technical assistance), this occurred because of the radical transformation of the state under the military government. In a new sociopolitical context, this will change. It is possible, therefore, that the state will recover its functions of material and technical support for the low-income sectors.

It seems less evident that the state will respond to cultural transformations and that it will operate through educational and cultural institutions to support the cultural processes already in motion. It is in the fields of culture and education that the programs and work of NGOs must be strengthened. Blindness—to the present changes in the sociopolitical context and to the potential for opening new channels for participation—can be a suicidal strategy for many programs assisting women in the low-income sectors, including the rural women's school.

During the process of democratization that can be foreseen, the women's movement could be seriously weakened if the educational programs do not leave their protected space and act to prevent their isolation. Social and political institutions are seeking to reestablish their roles in Chilean society, but it is not clear that they will be sensitive to gender demands or to the cultural changes that occurred in response to both the dictatorship and a modernization process that affected the entire Chilean society.

▲ Notes

1. For a critique of the notion of "people" within popular education, see Martínez (1987).

2. Latin American women have made significant progress in this sense. Examples of this are the publications produced by Centro de Investigación para la Acción Femenina (CIPAF) (Dominican Republic) and Centro Flora Tristán and Centro Manuela Ramos (Peru).

3. To learn more about the history of women as social and political actors during this century, see Kirkwood (1986); Gaviola (1986); Salinas (1988); Poblete (1987); Serrano (1986); Muñoz (1987).

4. There are men artisans, but rural artisans are predominantly women, thus reflecting the phenomenon that women perform the lowest-paid occupations.

5. In 1975 Robert McNamara, in a speech on behalf of the World Bank made in Nairobi, confirmed the failure to incorporate the poor into the process of development through the green revolution and agrarian reform. He alluded at that time to the transfer of appropriate technologies for small-scale farmers and to development plans in well-delineated geographical areas, in contrast to the national policies implemented in the 1970s. In this context, farmers in specific types of production receive priority, such as those breeding rabbits or those being served through "integrated rural development" approaches. But this tends to make peasants domestic producers for exporting companies.

6. This was accomplished with life histories of indigenous (Aymaran and Mapuche) women, women who had witnessed transformations in agricultural and rural society in central Chile, and peasant women in diverse areas of the country.

7. A nursery was set up; this was run by a man as part of the hidden curriculum of the school.

8. See, for instance, the proposals developed by CIPAF, Centro Flora Tristán, and Centro Manuela Ramos, in CEEAL (1986) and CEEAL/ISIS (1987).

9. There is a strong relation between gender and type of occupation in the tasks rural women perform; their activities are related to manual tasks requiring dexterity, learned at home from childhood.

10. Most women aspire to have "clean jobs."

11. This topic was covered in the school. Information on the effects of pesticides was presented in written and audiovisual form.

12. During the 1988 school, the women received a "Chart of Women for Democracy" developed by women's groups throughout the country. This is the first representative and legitimate document produced in Chile toward the process of democratization. In the dissemination of this document, the role of educational programs run by social organizations was seen as a key mode of transmission.

13. The *inquilinaje* system was abolished only with the agrarian reform of 1964–1973.

14. See Martinic (1988). In this article, Martinic examines, from the perspective of program participants, the various experiences of popular education. Participants see in these programs a space for the distribution of material resources (e.g., credits, seeds) and symbolic resources (new cultural codes, knowledge, language). This enables participants to move to other social levels (state, other NGOs, city governments) and to engage in a process of social promotion.

15. Language, ideas, and concepts that amplify the cultural capital of women.

▲ References

Aranda, Ximena. *Partipación de la mujer en la agricultura y la sociedad rural en áreas de pequeña propiedad*. Santiago: FLACSO, 1982.
Bengoa, José. *El campesinado 10 años después de la reforma agraria*. Santiago: SUR, 1985.
CEAAL (Consejo de Educación de Adultos de América Latina). *Taller latinoamericano sobre feminismo y educación popular*. Montevideo: CEAAL, 1986.
CEAAL/ISIS (International Women's Information and Communication Service). *Crecer juntas: Mujeres, feminismo y educación popular*. Santiago: CEAAL, 1987.
CNC (Comision Nacional Campesina). "Demanda de la Mujer Rural," *Boletín Tierra*. Santiago: CNC, October 1986.
———. "Boletín informativo." *Tierra*, no. 34, August 1986.
Garret, P. "La reforma agraria: Organización popular y participación de la mujer en Chile 1964–1973." In M. Leon (ed.), *Debate sobre la mujer en Latinoamérica y el Caribe*. Bogota: ACEP, 1982.
Gaviola, Edda. *Queremos votar en las próximas elecciones*. Santiago: ILET/ISIS Fempress, 1986.
González, S., and M. Norero. *Los derechos de las mujeres en las leyes chilenas: Guía práctica*. Santiago: Ediciones Quercum, 1986.
Kirkwood, Julieta. *Ser politica en Chile: Las feministas y los partidos*. Santiago: FLACSO, 1986.
Martinez, Javier. "La educación para la libertad: Algunas cuestiones conceptuales." *Proposiciones*, no. 15. Educación Popular y Movimientos Sociales, 1987, pp. 42–56.
Martinic, Sergio. "Elementos metodológicos para la sistematización de proyectos de educación y acción social." In S. Martinic and H. Walker (eds.), *Profesionales en la acción. Una mirada crítica a la educación popular*. Santiago: CIDE, 1988.
Muñoz, Adriana. *Fuerza feminista y democracia: Utopía a realizar*. Santiago: VECTOR, 1987.
Nun, Jose. "La rebelión del coro." *Nexos*, 1984, pp. 18–21.
Ortega, Emiliano. *Transformaciones agrarias y campesinado: De la participación a la exclusión*. Santiago: CIEPLAN, 1987.
Poblete, Olga. *Día internacional de la mujer en Chile: Otro capítulo de una historia invisible*. Santiago: Ed. MEMCH, March 1987.
Salinas, Cecilia. *La mujer proletaria: Una historia por contar*. Santiago: LAR, 1988.
Serrano, Claudia. "Chile, mujers en movimiento." In M. A. Mesa (ed.), *La otra mitad de Chile*. Santiago: CESOC, 1986.
Valdes, Ximena. "Hacia la generización de las demandas de las trabajadoras del agro." *Agricultura y Sociedad*, no. 5, 1987, pp. 27–40.
———. "La feminización del mercado de trabajo agrícola en Chile central." In *Mundo de mujer: Continuidad y cambio*. Santiago: CEM, 1988.
Valdes, Ximena, and Paulina Matta. *Oficios y trabajos de las mujeres de Pomaire*. Santiago: Ed. CEM/PEHUEN, 1986.

Yudelman, S. *Hopeful Openings: A Study of Five Women Development Organizations in Latin America and the Caribbean.* Washington, D.C.: Inter-American Foundation 1987a.

———. "The Integration of Women into Development Projects: Observations on the NGO Experience in General and in Latin America in Particular." *Development Alternatives: The Challenge for NGOs, World Development,* vol. 15, 1987b, pp. 179–187.

▲
Contributors

Nelly P. Stromquist is associate professor of international development education at the University of Southern California. She specializes in gender and education, research methodologies, and evaluation. Her most recent publication is *Daring to Be Different: The Choice of Nonconventional Fields of Study by International Women Students* (1991).

Gloria Bonder is an Argentinian psychologist. She cofounded and directs the Center for Women's Studies in Argentina and has authored numerous articles on gender issues, ranging from marital violence to sex education in schools. She coordinates the Network of Women's Studies in Latin America and the Caribbean.

Cecilia Braslavsky is an Argentinian educator. She has conducted numerous consultancies for UNESCO and is currently the director of the M.A. program on education and society at the Latin American and Caribbean Faculty for the Social Sciences (FLACSO). She has written several books, including *La Discriminacion Educativa en Argentina* (1985) and *Respuestas a la Crisis Educativa* (1988).

Lisa Catanzarite is a sociologist currently working as a postdoctoral fellow at the University of California, Los Angeles. She has conducted several studies on the nature of women's work, income, and labor conditions.

Regina Cortina is assistant professor at Brown University and assistant director of its Center for Latin American Studies. She specializes in international development education and women's issues.

Marcy Fink has conducted many development projects dealing with income generation and nonformal education for women in Central and South America and currently works closely with Neighborhood Reassessment Corporation, a nonprofit organization in Washington, D.C. She also works as an adjunct professor in international education at American University (Washington, D.C.).

Haydée M. Mendiola is associate professor at the University of Costa Rica. She specializes in international educational development and has conducted quantitative investigations on the effects of higher education on income and occupational status.

Fulvia Rosemberg is senior researcher at the Carlos Chagas Foundation in Sao Paulo, Brazil, one of the foremost educational research and gender issues organizations in Latin America. She has conducted numerous investigations on the condition of women in the educational system of Brazil, particularly in the intersection gender/race field. She has written two books: *A educação da mulher no Brasil* (1982) and, with Regina Pinto, *A educação da mulher* (1985).

Violeta Sara-Lafosse is senior professor in the Faculty of the Social Sciences at the Catholic University of Peru. She has been one of the pioneers of research on gender in that country and has examined a broad range of issues, including attitudes toward gender roles and women's political participation.

Beatriz Schmukler is a sociologist and former Tinker-Lampadia fellow at the University of Massachusetts. She has been actively involved in programs to bring communities and their schools closer together. She currently works as a full-time consultant on women and development issues at the Inter-America Development Bank.

Ximena Valdes is a geographer. She is cofounder of the Center for Women's Studies in Chile and an experienced educator of peasant and marginal women. She recently cofounded the Center for Studies on Women's Development, which provides technical assistance to peasant and urban marginalized women. She has written several articles and coauthored two books on women in agriculture and popular education.

Elena Viveros is professor at the University of Paraiba, Brazil, where she has played a leadership role in the M.A. program on adult education. She conducts research on various aspects of adult education, particularly as they concern women. More recently she has been working in higher education.

▲

Index

305

▲
About the Book

Despite their extremely high rate of participation in the education system, women in Latin America evince higher levels of illiteracy than men, experience differential treatment within the system, and concentrate in only a few academic fields. This book explores the role of education—broadly defined—in reproducing inequality and sexual divisions of labor and finds the causes of women's inferior situation to be both ideological and material.

The authors focus on four themes: the relation of education to the state and the economy, women's experience within the formal education system, their participation in emancipatory forms of "popular education," and educational efforts aimed at changing the status quo. Central to the book— and relevant to the emerging process of redemocratization—is the point that knowledge can be used to contest and transform meaning and thus to question existing authority and create new power.